BRITISH BOTANICAL AND
HORTICULTURAL LITERATURE
BEFORE 1800

Gerard: *The Herball*, 1597. Portrait of John Gerard engraved by William Rogers and signed with his monogram on the lower margin, towards left (p. [xviii]). 7·0 × 5·6″. The reproduction is from the hand-coloured copy of the *Herball* given to Sir Thomas Bodley by the printer John Norton.

British Botanical and Horticultural Literature before 1800

COMPRISING A HISTORY AND BIBLIOGRAPHY OF
BOTANICAL AND HORTICULTURAL BOOKS
PRINTED IN ENGLAND, SCOTLAND, AND IRELAND
FROM THE EARLIEST TIMES UNTIL 1800

BLANCHE HENREY

I

The Sixteenth and Seventeenth Centuries
History and Bibliography

LONDON
OXFORD UNIVERSITY PRESS
NEW YORK   TORONTO
1975

Oxford University Press, Ely House, London W. 1

GLASGOW NEW YORK TORONTO MELBOURNE WELLINGTON
CAPE TOWN IBADAN NAIROBI DAR ES SALAAM LUSAKA ADDIS ABABA
DELHI BOMBAY CALCUTTA MADRAS KARACHI LAHORE DACCA
KUALA LUMPUR SINGAPORE HONG KONG TOKYO

ISBN 0 19 211548 0

© *Blanche Henrey 1975*

*Printed in Great Britain
at the University Press, Oxford
by Vivian Ridler
Printer to the University*

*This work is dedicated to
the Principal Keeper and Staff of the Department of
Printed Books in the British Museum (Bloomsbury)
and to
the Keeper and Staff of the Department of Botany
in the British Museum (Natural History)
with gratitude and appreciation*

CONTENTS

VOLUME I

CONTENTS

VOLUME II

THE EIGHTEENTH CENTURY—HISTORY

CONTENTS   ix

VOLUME III

BIBLIOGRAPHY FOR THE EIGHTEENTH CENTURY

PREFACE

THE present work on botanical and horticultural literature published up to 1800 in England, Scotland, and Ireland is in two complementary parts: a *History*, in which the books are divided into centuries and information is given concerning the works and their authors under broad subject headings, and a *Bibliography*, alphabetically arranged with title-entries under the names of authors. The books of the sixteenth and seventeenth centuries are placed together and those of the eighteenth century are dealt with separately. The aim of the *Bibliography* has been to provide a comprehensive collection of English books and pamphlets on the various branches of botany, gardening, horticulture, and silviculture, published from the earliest times until the nineteenth century, together with the names of libraries in Britain and Ireland where copies may be seen. In this *Bibliography* it is believed that a large proportion of the possible total of works has been recorded. Moreover, many books and pamphlets are included that are not known by the writer to have been collated previously by any bibliographer. It is impossible, however, for a work of this nature to be complete and the writer asks to be told of the locations of omitted works if these are in Britain or Ireland.[1] Furthermore, she would plead with any private owner of an omitted book who is considering its sale to offer it first to the British Museum, or to one of the other national libraries, in order to ensure that copies of rare books are available for study in these islands.

A considerable amount of material has been gathered together on eighteenth-century British nurserymen and their publications and also on botanical drawing-books, thereby providing historical and bibliographical details on two subjects that have, so far, received but little attention.[2]

The terms 'book' and 'pamphlet' have been used, so far as the present undertaking is concerned, to include any work issued as a separate publication with a title-page and independent pagination. In the case of a few works, however, with no title-page but with the title at the head of the first page, this rule has been relaxed. Such works include *Directions for the raising of flax* [1744]—an early pamphlet on the subject issued by the Commissioners and Trustees for Improving Fisheries and Manufactures in Scotland—and the rare plant *Catalogue* distributed by the eighteenth-century nurseryman Peter Lauder.

With some classes of material the writer has been selective. Works principally devoted to garden ornaments and buildings, and plant pests and diseases,

[1] In national or institutional libraries.
[2] Since going to press works on the first of these subjects have been published by John Harvey.

have been omitted. So have books on husbandry with sections on planting and gardening which occupy less than a half of the whole work. Books and pamphlets on the use of plants in the cure of diseases are also not generally included if their interest is primarily medical.

The first step in preparing this work was to compile a card index with the names of all recorded books on botany and horticulture published during the period concerned. This was done by systematically going through entries in various library catalogues, including those entitled: *Catalogue of the library of the British museum (Natural history)*, 8 vols. (1903–40); *Catalogue of the library of the Royal botanic gardens, Kew* (1899), *Supplement* (1919); *Catalogue of the Lindley library (R.H.S.)* (1927); *Catalogue of the library of the Linnean society of London* (1925); *Catalogue of the Rothamsted experimental station, Harpenden* (1940), *Supplement* (1949); *Catalogue of the library of the Chelsea physic garden* (1956); *Chronological list of early agricultural works in the library of the Ministry of agriculture and fisheries* (1930); *Catalogue of the library of the Arnold arboretum of Harvard university*, 3 vols. (1914–33) and the *Catalogue of the library of the Massachusetts horticultural society* (1918). Also Jonas Dryander's *Catalogus bibliothecæ historico-naturalis J. Banks*, 5 vols. (1796–1800) and the *Catalogue* of the Hunt Botanical Library, Pittsburgh, Pennsylvania, 2 vols. (1958–61).

Among other works used were: Keynes (G. L.), *John Ray. A bibliography* (1951); Jackson (B. D.), *Guide to the literature of botany* (1881); Johnson (G. W.), *History of English gardening* (1829); Nissen (C.), *Die botanische Buchillustration, ihre Geschichte und Bibliographie* (1951); Payne (C. H.), *Florist's bibliography* and *Supplements* (1913–24); Pritzel (G. A.), *Thesaurus literaturae botanicae* 1872[–7]; Pulteney (R.), *Historical and biographical sketches of the progress of botany in England*, 2 vols. (1790); Séguier (J. F.), *Bibliotheca botanica* (1740); and the Royal Dublin Society's *Bibliography* of their publications from 1731 to 1951.

In addition, the card index was compiled with the aid of the bibliographies and catalogues published in: Amherst (Hon. Alicia) afterwards Cecil (Hon. Mrs. Evelyn),[1] *A history of gardening in England*, ed. 3 (1910); Arber (A.), *Herbals their origin and evolution* (1938); Dunthorne (G.), *Flower and fruit prints of the 18th and early 19th centuries* (1938); Keynes (G. L.), *John Evelyn a study in bibliophily & a bibliography of his writings* (1937), ed. 2 (1968); Loudon (J. C.), *An encyclopædia of gardening* (1824); McDonald (D.), *Agricultural writers* (1908); Thomas Martyn's edition (1807) of *The gardener's and botanist's dictionary . . . by . . . Philip Miller*, Vol. 1, Pt. 1; Rohde (E. S.), *The old English herbals* (1922), *The old English gardening books* (1924), and *The story of the garden* (1932); and Weston (R.), *Tracts on experimental gardening and agriculture . . . The third edition* [n.d.].

[1] Later Baroness Rockley.

Besides the books in the above list many bibliographies on general subjects were consulted in preparing the card index, including: Arber (E.), *The term catalogues, 1668–1709*, 3 vols. (1903–6); Pollard (A. W.) and Redgrave (G. R.), *A short-title catalogue of English books 1475–1640* (1926); Wing (D. G.), *A short-title catalogue of English books 1641–1700*, 3 vols. (1945–51); and Watt (R.), *Bibliotheca britannica*, 4 vols. (1824).

It was originally planned that the period covered by the present undertaking should be from the earliest times until 1850. The final date, however, was changed to 1800 when it was found that more than twice as many works were published during the first fifty years of the nineteenth century as during the years previous to 1800.

Botanical and horticultural writers who published works in both the eighteenth and the nineteenth centuries have generally had all their publications included in the *Bibliography* although the nineteenth-century works are not necessarily noticed in the *History*. Among authors responsible for books published in both centuries are: Adrian Hardy Haworth, Thomas Andrew Knight, Richard Anthony Salisbury, Sir James Edward Smith, and John Sibthorp. Sibthorp published his *Flora oxoniensis* in 1794 and was working before his death, in 1796, on the *Flora græca*. This was completed and published in the nineteenth century.

Normally, nineteenth-century editions of works first published previous to 1800 have been included in the *Bibliography*, and in many cases this has enabled all known editions of a book to be recorded. The writer has, however, been selective with regard to these later editions and in general only those that appeared up to the middle of the nineteenth century have been given. The numerous editions of Culpeper's *English physitian* published after the eighteenth century have been omitted.

Some authors who published no complete work in the eighteenth century began to issue serial publications prior to 1800 which were completed after this date. Such publications are not included in this work. Among these authors is Henry C. Andrews who published in parts *Coloured engravings of heaths* [1794–]1802–1805[–1830] and *The Botanical Repository* 1797[–1815].

Besides the card index with works under the names of authors arranged alphabetically, a loose-leaf book was prepared with an author index and the works arranged chronologically by years of publication. A study of this drew the writer's attention to the fact that it was not unusual for compilers of catalogues, especially those of the early nineteenth century, to copy in turn from each other's book lists, without first verifying the accuracy of the various entries. A number of errors were thus perpetuated over a long period of time. The loose-leaf book was made light in weight, and easily portable, and was used when visiting libraries in the search for the various works needed. For the same purpose it was taken by the writer when visiting antiquarian bookshops. Furthermore it assisted when looking through current issues of catalogues of book sales for the items required. After making a search which has lasted for a number of years it has been possible to locate copies of the majority of the items gathered in the card index when it was first compiled, together with many other works not originally known to the writer.

With the exception of a few rare editions, all works included in the *Bibliography* have been seen and collated by the writer herself. Among items not examined personally are some first editions of which, unfortunately, no copies appear to be extant in this country. They include *A short instruction veric* [sic] *profitable and necessarie for all those that delight in gardening* (1591); *Profitable instructions for the manuring, sowing, and planting of kitchin gardens* (1599) by Richard Gardiner, and the first edition of *An account of the culture and use of the mangel wurzel . . . Translated from the French of the Abbé de Commerell [Edited by J. C. Lettsom]* (1787).[1]

In transcribing titles the opening words have always been kept, omissions have been made of unessential words and phrases in the rest of the title, but always with the conventional ellipsis sign or 'etc.' to indicate the fact. Imprints are given in an abbreviated form and dates in arabic numerals. As too many capital letters on a page are sometimes found distracting, capitals have been used as sparingly as possible. Unless an exact transcription is made when full capitals, small capitals with or without initial full capitals, and lower case are faithfully reproduced, there seems to be no logical reason why the title cannot be transcribed in lower case with capitals inserted only when they are regarded as necessary. In transcribing quotations the printer's capitalization has also not been followed precisely. The current usage of the printers of early books with regard to U and V has been observed in the *Bibliography* but not in the *History*. Accents are omitted from French quotations when not given in the original works.

When obtained by means of subtraction the year of an author's birth has been given with an interrogation mark:

e.g. Lancelot Brown (1716?–1783) who died on 6 February 1783 aged sixty-seven years;

Colin Milne (1744?–1815) who died 2 October 1815 in his seventy-second year.

In the search for information concerning the books and their authors material has been obtained from the works themselves, from biographies, diaries, publications on specialized subjects, magazines, the daily press, journals of learned societies, manuscript material including letters, and many other sources. In the quest for particulars regarding nursery gardeners and their publications many hours have been spent in looking through church

---

[1] This translation was issued three times in 1787.

records, rate books, and local directories. Notes and citations of sources for statements of fact or opinion, or for quoted matter, are given as footnotes printed on the same page to which they refer. Footnotes are thus readily accessible and easy to find and for those who wish to read the text together with full references this method is more convenient and less time-consuming than the practice of citing references in an abbreviated form (e.g. Smith, 1960), coupled with a bibliography at the end of the chapter or of the whole work where references are given in full.

The title of a work given in the *History*, the *Bibliography*, and in the captions to the illustrations, has been transcribed from a woodcut or engraved title only if there is no letterpress title-page. This accounts for the occasional discrepancy between the title shown in an illustration and that given in the caption, e.g. see Vol. 1, p. 91.

Abbreviations by the use of superior letters have been transcribed as given in the original manuscript or printed book. As the point marking the abbreviation is found variously placed before, under, or after the superior letter or letters, the present writer in order to be consistent has placed it under the first of these characters (e.g. improv!, Doct.rs), and left it out altogether if not found in the original.

The ligatures æ, œ are used in the present work when a transcription is made from a title, or any part of a book in which they appear, and in the case of the names of some authors. But the separate letters ae, oe are used for the modern generic and specific names of plants, according to usage in the *International code of botanical nomenclature* (1972).

The writer concludes in the words used by William Beeston Coyte in his *Hortus botanicus gippovicensis* of 1796:

> Benevole lector,
>   Hoc opus accipe—amicè accipe—mente serena lege—benignè corrige. Vale.
>
>   W. B. Coyte
>
> Multum adhùc restat operis, multumque restabit.
>
>   Seneca

> Kind reader,
>   Accept this work, accept it in a friendly fashion, read it with a calm mind and correct it amiably. Farewell.
>
>   W. B. Coyte
>
> Much work still remains to do, and much will always so remain.
>
>   Seneca

NOTE

Vol. I, p. 96; vol. II, pp. 208 and 209 (illustration). The gateway to the Oxford botanic garden is now known to have been designed and built by Nicholas Stone 1632–3.

ACKNOWLEDGEMENTS

THE present publication owes its inception to Mr. Charles H. Gibbs-Smith, Keeper Emeritus in the Victoria and Albert Museum, who in 1945, as Director of Photograph Division of the Ministry of Information, became interested in my researches in the field of botanical and horticultural literature and gave me an introduction to Mr. Geoffrey Cumberlege, Publisher to the Oxford University Press. The task has been long and arduous but now there remains only the pleasing duty of acknowledging the generous and ungrudging aid of those who have assisted in its completion.

First of all I should like to record the debt that I owe to the late Mr. A. C. Townsend, Librarian of the British Museum (Natural History) for his encouragement and critical interest and for his reading of my text until the time of his death in December 1964. Secondly, I owe a special debt of gratitude to Sir George Taylor, formerly Director of the Royal Botanic Gardens, Kew, for his helpfulness and encouragement and for his permission to collate certain copies of books in his private library. Thirdly, had it not been for the interest shown by my sister Miss Katherine Helen Henrey in the project I might well have lost heart. She has my thanks for reading and discussing the manuscript and on many occasions has urged me to press ahead with the work when I felt I had undertaken too great a task.

I have been privileged to read in many national and private libraries and I wish to record my thanks to those members of the staffs of the British Museum (Bloomsbury), the British Museum (Natural History), and the Bodleian Library, who over a very long period have so courteously supplied me with many hundreds of volumes.

Without the vast resources of the Department of Printed Books of the British Museum (Bloomsbury)[1] my work would have been very incomplete. Here I have been able to study and collate the works on English botanical literature collected by Sir Hans Sloane and the many books on botany and horticulture collected by Sir Joseph Banks. Books on these subjects have also been available to me in the Museum's other special collections, such as those included in the Thomason tracts, the Cracherode library, the King's library, and the Grenville library. Furthermore, there are many botanical and horticultural works not in the special collections and these also have been at my disposal.

I must express my gratitude to Mr. K. B. Gardner, until recently Principal Keeper of the Department of Printed Books of the British Museum (Bloomsbury) and to the late Dr. C. B. Oldman, Mr. R. A. Wilson, and

---

[1] Since 3 June 1973 referred to as the British Library Reference Division.

Mr. A. H. Chaplin, the three successive previous holders of this office, who in turn gave me every facility during the years I worked in the department. My thanks are also due to various other members of the department including Mr. Howard M. Nixon, who during the course of my work was kind enough to answer many queries, give me much valued advice, and generously presented me with a botanical work of reference from his private library; Mr. George D. Painter who gave me assistance with a number of problems, especially with respect to early printed books; Mr. Edward J. Miller who helped me with matters relating to State papers, and Mr. David F. Foxon, now University Reader in Textual Criticism at Oxford, who on various occasions gave me advice concerning bibliographical matters and drew my attention to several works of value and interest to the present concern. To Mr. J. L. Wood, Keeper in the Department of Printed Books, and to Mr. J. T. Norton, a former member of the staff, I must record my gratitude for the trouble they took in making a room available in the department in which the photographer to the University Press, Oxford, was able to carry out his work. Among other members of the staff, past and present, who at various times have given me assistance, I owe thanks to Miss Audrey C. Brodhurst, Mr. A. F. Allison, Miss Anna E. C. Simoni, Mr. and Mrs. G. J. R. Arnold, Dr. D. E. Rhodes, Mr. I. R. Willison, Mr. R. J. Roberts, Mrs. S. D. Brown, and of the Map Room, Mr. T. A. Corfe. It is also a pleasure to record my gratitude for help received from Mr. J. P. Hudson of the Department of Manuscripts and to Professor T. J. Brown, a former member of the Department, now Professor of Palaeography at the University of London.

In the Department of Prints and Drawings I am grateful to Mr. Edward F. Croft-Murray, formerly Keeper, for permitting me to collate his private copy of a rare eighteenth-century work entitled *Flora or a concise collection of . . . beautiful flowers*. I also owe a particular debt to Mr. John A. G. Gere, the present Keeper, to Mr. Paul H. Hulton, Assistant Keeper, and to Mr. A. W. Aspital, a former member of the Department, for valuable help and advice in the reproduction of illustrations.

For giving me every facility to carry on my work in the Department of Botany of the British Museum (Natural History) I am deeply grateful to Dr. J. Ramsbottom, Sir George Taylor, Mr. J. E. Dandy, and Mr. R. Ross, all four in turn holding the office of Keeper of Botany. My especial thanks are due to the present Keeper, Mr. R. Ross, for reading parts of my manuscript, and for allowing me to draw repeatedly on his botanical knowledge. I must also thank Dr. W. T. Stearn for giving me much valuable assistance, particularly with regard to matters concerning Linnaeus, and to Dr. E. Launert for kindly obtaining information regarding Sir William Curtius from Dr. Andernacht, Archivdirektor, Frankfurt am Main. In addition I express my gratitude to the following past and present members of the Department who assisted me with the captions for the illustrations of plants by providing the currently accepted botanical names of the various species depicted: Mrs. F. L. Balfour-Browne, Mr. J. F. M. Cannon, Mr. J. A. Crabbe, Mr. J. E. Dandy, Miss M. B. Gerrans, Mrs. L. M. Irvine, Mr. P. W. James, Mr. A. C. Jermy, Mr. J. Lewis, Mr. J. B. Marshall, Mr. G. A. Matthews, Dr. A. Melderis, Mr. J. H. Price, Dr. N. K. B. Robson, Mr. R. Ross, and Dr. W. T. Stearn.

I thank the Librarian of the Department of Botany, Miss P. J. Edwards, for the much appreciated kindness she has always shown me during the years that I have worked in the library under her care.

My best thanks are due to Mr. M. J. Rowlands, Librarian of the British Museum (Natural History) for his interest and encouragement, and for the assistance he and his staff, particularly Mr. M. R. Halliday, have given me in finding copies of several rare editions that I might not otherwise have been able to locate.

Among other persons who have offered me facilities for examining books and manuscripts under their care, and at times given me aid in bibliographical matters, the following should have special mention: the staff of the Département des Imprimés in the Bibliothèque Nationale, Paris; the late Mr. L. W. Hanson, Keeper of Printed Books, and Mr. I. G. Philip, his successor and now Deputy Librarian, Mr. D. H. Boalch, Keeper of Scientific Books and Mr. D. G. Neill, Assistant Librarian, all of the Bodleian Library; Mr. A. Hall, formerly Librarian of the Guildhall Library, London; Mr. E. A. P. Hart, formerly Librarian of the Inner Temple; Miss R. J. Ensing, Reference Librarian at the Kensington Public Library; Dr. A. N. L. Munby, Librarian of King's College, Cambridge; Mr. G. D. R. Bridson, Librarian and Archivist, and Mr. T. O'Grady, Executive Secretary of the Linnean Society; Dr. G. L. Harriss, Librarian of Magdalen College, Oxford; Major H. R. Mitchell, Registrar and Librarian of the Medical Society of London; Madame Duprat, formerly Bibliothécaire en Chef and Mademoiselle Madier, formerly Bibliothécaire of the Muséum National d'Histoire Naturelle, Paris; Mr. R. J. Hayes, the former Director, and Mr. P. Henchy, the present Director, of the National Library of Ireland; Miss A. Lothian, formerly Librarian of the Pharmaceutical Society of Great Britain; Lieutenant-Commander Godfrey, formerly of the Public Record Office; Mr. T. Cawley, Librarian of the Rothamsted Experimental Station; the Librarian of the Royal Academy of Arts, London; Miss R. E. Watson, formerly Librarian of the Royal Agricultural Society of England; Mr. H. S. Marshall and his successor Mr. R. G. C. Desmond, two former librarians of the Royal Botanic Gardens, Kew; Mr. L. M. Payne, Librarian of the Royal College of Physicians, London; Mr. W. R. LeFanu, formerly Librarian of the Royal College of Surgeons of England; Mr. D. J. Clarke, Librarian of the Royal

Dublin Society; Mr. P. F. Stageman, Librarian of the Lindley Library, the Royal Horticultural Society, London; Mr. I. Kaye, formerly Librarian, and Mr. C. P. Townsend, Archivist, of the Royal Society, London; Mr. D. G. C. Allan, Curator-Librarian of the Royal Society of Arts; Mr. P. Wade, Librarian of the Royal Society of Medicine, Mr. E. H. Milligan, Librarian of the Society of Friends, London; Mr. J. S. L. Gilmour, formerly Director of the University Botanic Garden, Cambridge; the late Mr. E. Ansell, and Mr. A. J. Illes, Under-Librarians in the University Library, Cambridge; the Librarian of the University of Cambridge, Botany School Library; Miss M. B. C. Canney of the University of London Library, the Goldsmith's library of Economic Literature; Mrs. H. J. McArdle, Librarian in the University of Oxford, Botany School Library; Mr. C. S. L. Davies, Keeper of the Archives of Wadham College, Oxford; and Dr. F. N. L. Poynter, formerly Director, and Mr. E. Gaskell, formerly Librarian, of the Wellcome Historical Medical Library, London.

In my search for references and details concerning authors and their publications I have corresponded with the staffs of the following libraries, institutions, and universities: the Bath and West and Southern Counties Society; Edinburgh University Library; the Hancock Museum, Newcastle upon Tyne; Marischal College, Aberdeen; the National Library of Scotland; the Nottingham Subscription Library; the Royal Botanic Garden, Edinburgh; the Royal College of Physicians of Edinburgh; the Royal College of Physicians and Surgeons of Glasgow; the Royal College of Physicians of Ireland; the Royal Irish Academy; the University of Glasgow Library and the University of St. Andrews Library. Acknowledgement is also due to the staffs of the county libraries of Cork, East Suffolk, Gloucestershire, Nottinghamshire, Staffordshire, and Wiltshire, the public libraries of Aberdeen, Bath, Birmingham, Bristol, Edinburgh, Gloucester, Hereford, Leeds, Leicester, Lincoln, Manchester, Newcastle upon Tyne, Nottingham, Shrewsbury, and York, and the public libraries of Brentford in Greater London, and Chelsea, Chiswick, Hackney, Holborn, Kensington, Lambeth, Lewisham, Poplar, Shoreditch, Southwark, and Wandsworth in London.

Acknowledgement is due to many other friends and correspondents, all of whom have helped me in various ways. Mr. John H. Alexander of Moffat, Dumfries, Managing Director for fifty years of the Edinburgh firm of Dicksons and Co., gave me details of the early history of that Scottish nursery and seed business; the Librarian of the Arnold Arboretum, Harvard University, sent for my examination a copy of William Burchell's plant catalogue of 1764; Mademoiselle Colette Avignon of the University of Tours drew my attention to several letters in the Evelyn collection at Christ Church, Oxford, in which reference is made to John Evelyn's *Sylva*; Dr. Terry Belanger, Assistant Professor, Columbia University School of Library Service, New

York, permitted me to take advantage of his studies in eighteenth-century booksellers' copyright auction sales and also gave me information concerning the publishing family of Rivington; the late Dr. F. S. Furguson allowed me to take advantage of his considerable knowledge in the specialized field of early English printed books; Mr. John Harvey supplied me with a number of details concerning eighteenth-century nurserymen; Miss Peggie Kerswell assisted me with the preparation of a chronological list of botanical publications up to 1800; Mrs. Ada Leask of Dublin gave me information with regard to the life and work of the eighteenth-century botanical artist William Kilburn; Mr. Albert E. Lownes of Providence, Rhode Island, supplied me with bibliographical details concerning his copy of *A short instruction . . . for all those that delight in gardening* (1591), Lady Mary Lyon sent information relating to Strickland Freeman and his sisters-in-law the botanical artists Charlotte and Juliana Sabina Strickland; R. G. Medley gave me valuable assistance in interpreting legal documents drawn up between Mrs. Blackwell and her husband and the publishers of *A curious herbal*; Mrs. Needham, the wife of the Revd. Canon George Needham, formerly Dean of Kendal, searched through local records for the date and birth of the botanist William Hudson; Miss Katherine F. Pantzer, editor of the forthcoming new edition of the *Short title catalogue*, sent me bibliographical details and locations of copies of certain rare English works published before 1640; Mr. Graham Stuart Thomas provided me with the modern botanical names of two old-fashioned roses illustrated respectively in Curtis's *Botanical Magazine* and in Mary Lawrence's work entitled *A collection of roses*; and Mr. J. B. Trapp of the Warburg Institute gave me assistance on a number of occasions in describing and interpreting figures depicted in allegorical title-pages. I am indebted to Messrs. Bernard Quaritch, Messrs. Wheldon and Wesley, and other antiquarian booksellers for their co-operation in allowing me to examine books of bibliographical interest in their possession, and I am especially grateful to Mr. C. Kirke Swann of Messrs. Wheldon and Wesley who on a number of occasions drew my attention to details of bibliographical interest that I might well have overlooked.

For aid in bibliographical matters concerning certain botanical books not available in this country I am obliged to the staffs of the following libraries in America and Canada: the Henry E. Huntington Library, San Marino, California; McGill University, Osler Library, Montreal; the Massachusetts Horticultural Society Library, Boston; Wisconsin University Library, Madison, Wisconsin; and Yale University Library, New Haven, Connecticut.

For information, research, and other assistance I wish to express my gratitude to Mr. Colin Clair, Mrs. M. Corbett, Mr. John Machell Cox, the late Mr. Warren R. Dawson, Mr. H. E. Edlin, Publications Officer of the

Forestry Commission, Dr. Sylvia England, the late Mr. Julian Franklyn, Mr. Godsman of Aberdeen, Mr. Robert Henrey, Dr. André Jacquinet, Professeur de Clinique Medicale at the University of Rheims, Sir Geoffrey Keynes, Dr. W. F. H. Nicolaisen of the School of Scottish Studies in the University of Edinburgh, Dr. S. J. van Oostroom of the Rijksherbarium, Leyden, Mr. Brian E. Reade, formerly Deputy Keeper in the Department of Prints and Drawings of the Victoria and Albert Museum, Mr. H. S. Torrens of the Department of Geology, Keele University, the Librarian and Curator of the United Grand Lodge of England, Dr. H. D. L. Vervliet of the Museum Plantin–Moretus, Antwerp, and Mr. R. P. Graham-Vivian, former Windsor Herald-of-Arms and subsequently Norroy and Ulster King-of-Arms.

I should like to thank the Trustees of the Evelyn collection at Christ Church, Oxford, for allowing me to use extracts from three letters addressed to Sir Richard Browne by Sir William Curtius, and the editor of *The Friends' Quarterly* for letting me give a transcription (from vol. 51, p. 268 (1917)) of the expenses incurred in publishing Stephen Robson's *British flora* of 1777. I am grateful to the late Robert R. Jeffers for permission to quote from his book *The friends of John Gerard*, and its *Biographical appendix* (1967, 1969), and to the late Mr. Arthur de Carle Sowerby of Washington, U.S.A., for permission to quote as much as I wished from his work entitled *The Sowerby saga* (1952). I am indebted to Count G. Lewenhaupt of the Royal Ministry of Foreign Affairs in Stockholm for sending a photographic copy of the original draft of a letter to John Hill, and to Messrs. Longman Green and Co. Ltd., for the use of their collection of booksellers' copyright auction sale catalogues of 1718 to 1768.

I am indebted to the Trustees of the British Museum (Bloomsbury), to the Trustees of the British Museum (Natural History), and to the Curators of the Bodleian Library, Oxford, for permission to reproduce illustrations from books in the collections under their charge. The coloured illustration from Furber's Twelve plates with figures of fruit, and the two illustrations from *The practical husbandman and planter* edited by Stephen Switzer, are reproduced by courtesy of the Victoria and Albert Museum Library and the Rothamsted Experimental Station Library, respectively.

The Index for the present undertaking was compiled by Miss Sandra Raphael to whom I would offer special thanks for its careful preparation. I am deeply indebted to the Printer to the University Press, Oxford, and his staff, for the trouble which they have taken in the printing of the text and illustrations. Finally, my thanks are due to the Publisher to the University Press, London, and his staff, especially Mr. John Bell, Miss Audrey Bayley, and Mr. Nicolas Barker for unfailing courtesy and efficiency during the various stages in the publishing of this work.

NOTE ON ILLUSTRATIONS

THE illustrations in this publication are very diverse as they have been selected from works on all the various branches of botany and gardening covered by the present undertaking. They are representative of some of the most interesting and attractive woodcuts and engravings to appear in these books during the period 1525–1800 and they include frontispieces, portraits, title-pages, figures of plants, garden plans, head- and tail-pieces, proposals for printing, as well as examples of good typography. Many of the illustrations are drawn and engraved by well-known book illustrators and engravers of the day.

The captions for the illustrations of plants include the modern generic and specific names. The authorities for the plant names have been given in full except in the case of Linnæus and A. P. de Candolle, when the abbreviations 'L' and 'DC' have been used.

Many prints executed in the eighteenth century incorporate the techniques of engraving and etching, sometimes with stipple or aquatint, and for convenience these have been alluded to simply as engravings.

Measurements of actual size of the originals of the illustrations are given in inches to the nearest tenth of an inch. These measurements show the maximum vertical and horizontal distances of the printed area, including textual matter, captions, artists' names, plate-numbers, and the like. Tinted back-grounds are also included. Plate-marks, however, are excluded. The writer has followed the late Dr. Allan Stevenson, the compiler of the second volume of the *Catalogue of botanical books in the collection of Rachel McMasters Miller Hunt*, published at Pittsburgh, Pennsylvania, in 1961, in using a scale divided into inches and tenths. Conversion into centimetres is easy: one inch equals 2.540 centimetres and for a reasonably safe approximation inch measurements may be multiplied by 2.5. Below is given a scale of five inches divided into tenths along-side the equivalent number of centimetres divided into millimetres.

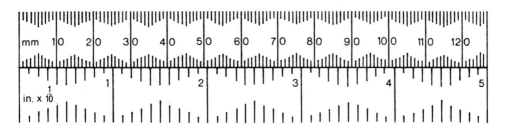

The symbol at the end of each entry in the list of illustrations indicates the library owning the work from which the reproduction was made. These symbols are the same as those used to represent the libraries whose works are included in the *Bibliography*.

LIST OF ILLUSTRATIONS TO VOLUME I

PLATE IN COLOUR

ILLUSTRATIONS IN BLACK AND WHITE

THE SIXTEENTH CENTURY

INTRODUCTION

MANY years of the sixteenth century went by before a book was published in England on a botanical or horticultural subject. Then, about 1520, during the reign of Henry VIII, appeared the anonymous treatise on grafting and planting, from the press of Wynkyn de Worde. Subsequently, until 1550 there followed in succession: Banckes's herbal, *The grete herball*, and two small books by William Turner. In the second half of the century the production of books on these subjects increased, the greatest number appearing between 1590 and 1600, during the reign of Queen Elizabeth I (1558–1603). No botanical or horticultural book, known to the present writer, was published during the sixteenth century in either Scotland or Ireland. Of the nineteen or so such books published in England during the period 1500–1600, about eleven are concerned with herbs and about eight with horticulture.[1] Therefore, in considering the history of these works it will be convenient to divide and discuss them under the two headings: 'Herbals' and 'Gardening books'.

[1] The figures do not include any of the editions of the various works, which in some cases, such as Banckes's herbal, are very considerable.

I

HERBALS

A HERBAL has been defined[1] as a 'book containing the names and descriptions of herbs, or of plants in general, with their properties and virtues', and during the flourishing period of the herbal such a treatise on plants was necessary not only to the herbalist or botanist but also to the physician and apothecary for whom a knowledge of the plants used in medicine was essential. The herbal was also invaluable to the housewife, as in the sixteenth century only the rich could afford adequate medical attendance,[2] and most people used the herbal in the home for looking up remedies for various ailments. It also supplied information about the herbs needed in the kitchen and stillroom, and provided remedies for such varied troubles as evil dreams, sleeplessness, melancholy, and clothes moths. Furthermore the lady of the house went to its pages for knowledge upon how to have 'a fayre face', stains for the nails, and dyes for the hair.

As, however, it is not possible to write about English herbals without constantly referring to those published abroad, with regard to both the text and the illustrations, a short account must first be given of the chief foreign herbals with which our own are connected, beginning with two such works printed in Germany at the end of the fifteenth century.

FOREIGN HERBALS

Many incunabula and early-sixteenth-century books had no title-page in the modern sense of the word, and are described under various names. Such a work, printed at Mainz in 1485, came from the press of Peter Schöffer and is referred to as the *German Herbarius*. It is also called the *Herbarius zu Teutsch*, the *Gart der Gesundheit*, the *German Ortus sanitatis*, the *Smaller Ortus*, or *Cube's herbal*.[3] This herbal is of great importance, not only because it was the foundation for later herbals but also on account of its illustrations which show a great advance on previous work. Many of the woodcuts are evidently derived from direct studies of the plants; they were later copied

---

[1] *The Oxford English dictionary*, 5 (1933), Oxford.

[2] Trevelyan (G. M.), *English social history. A survey of six centuries Chaucer to Queen Victoria*, 119 (1944).

[3] For details of the *German Herbarius*, and its French and English translations, see Payne (J. F.), The 'Herbarius' and 'Hortus sanitatis', *Trans. bibl. Soc.* 6, 89–105 (1903).

and recopied from book to book, and held a supreme place for nearly half a century until 1530 when Schott of Straßburg published the first part of Brunfels's *Herbarum vivæ eicones*.

It appears from the preface to the *German Herbarius* that the originator of the work was a wealthy man who had travelled to the East, and that the text was compiled under his direction by a physician, probably Johann von Cube, town physician of Frankfurt am Main at the end of the fifteenth century.

In 1491 the *Hortus* or *Ortus sanitatis* was printed at Mainz by Jacob Meydenbach. This incunabulum, printed in Latin, embraced a much wider field than the *German Herbarius*, as it deals not only with herbs but also with other subjects, including animals, birds, and fish. It is in part a translation of the *German Herbarius*, this latter work also supplying a certain number of the figures of herbs. Although these figures show a distinct advance in the art of the woodcutter, they show a marked deterioration botanically; they are reduced in size and the subject is often misunderstood. Some of the figures of herbs are new.

'Liber de simplici medicina', known as 'Circa instans' from its initial sentence 'Circa instans negotium de simplicibus medicinis', etc., is a Latin alphabetical dictionary of herbs, produced in the School of Salerno early in the twelfth century and of uncertain authorship, although sometimes doubt-fully attributed to Johannes or Matthaeus Platearius.[1] It was frequently copied in manuscript from the twelfth to the fifteenth century. The Latin text first appeared in print in an edition of Serapion, *Practica medicinae*, Venice, 1497 (the existence of a Ferrara edition of 1488, recorded by Hain[2] relying on Maittaire,[3] does not seem to have been substantiated in modern times). A French version was printed still earlier, at Besançon *c.* 1487, under the title *Arbolayre*, and reprinted as *Le grant herbier en françoys* at Paris *c.* 1498. This was published in numerous editions and it is of especial interest to the present undertaking since it was translated into English and published in 1526 as *The grete herball*.[4]

As already stated, 1530 saw the appearance of the first volume of the *Herbarum vivæ eicones*, generally known as Brunfels's herbal. The second volume was published in 1531, and the third in 1536.

Otto Brunfels (Otho Brunfelsius), the author of this work, was born in 1488 at Mainz. When he grew up he entered a Carthusian monastery, but afterwards renounced monastic life and became a Lutheran and later a school-

[1] Barlow's notion (Old English herbals, 1525–1640, *Proc. Roy. Soc. Med.* **6**, 126–7 (1913) (Section of the history of medicine) that 'Circa instans' was written in 1458 (some three centuries later than its true date) is due to his misinterpreting a French scribal colophon of that year as an author's colophon.

[2] Hain (L.), *Repertorium bibliographicum*, etc. (1826, 38), no. 14694.
[3] Maittaire (M.), *Annales typographici*, tome I, pt. I, nova editio (1733), p. 781.
[4] The present writer is grateful to Mr. George D. Painter for advice on the matters discussed in the above paragraph.

teacher. He also wrote a number of theological works. Finally, he turned his attention to medicine and shortly before his death in 1534, he was appointed town physician at Berne.

Brunfels's herbal marks a new epoch in the study of plants, not because of the text, which is chiefly a compilation from previous writers, but because of the woodcuts. Brunfels wished his work to contain 'new and lifelike illustrations',[1] and in this he succeeded. Hans Weiditz (Johannes Guidictius) was employed as draughtsman and engraver, probably with a staff of assistants.[2] This artist, instead of following the traditional plan of copying the drawings of his predecessors, drew from the plants themselves; and with these realistic illustrations, from which it is possible to identify a large number of the species of plants shown, Brunfels's herbal is considered to have opened the botanical renaissance.

The interest with which the *Herbarum vivæ eicones* was received must have been considerable, and its success doubtless inspired another German, Leonhard Fuchs (Leonhardus Fuchsius), to produce his large and impressive folio *De historia stirpium* (1542).

Fuchs was born in 1501 at Wemding, in Bavaria. He studied at the University of Ingolstadt, and by the age of twenty-three he had graduated as Master of Arts and had received the degree of Doctor of Medicine. While at the University he read the works of Luther and afterwards became a follower of the new faith. Fuchs attained great eminence as a physician and won an outstanding reputation for his work during the epidemic of the plague which swept over Germany in 1529. From 1535 until his death in 1566 he occupied a Chair of Medicine at Tübingen.

Fuchs's famous herbal *De historia stirpium* of 1542 came from the press of Isingrin of Basle. Although the text is notably more scholarly than that of Brunfels's herbal, here again, as with the earlier work, it is not original, being based mainly upon Dioscorides. The woodcuts, however, reach a new level of attainment. They are most outstanding, viewed from either a botanical or a decorative standpoint. The portraits of the three men who were responsible for the figures are given at the end of the herbal. They are Albrecht Meyer, the artist, Heinrich Füllmaurer, who copied the drawings on to the wood, and Veit Rudolf Speckle, the woodcutter. In 1545 an octavo edition of the herbal was published containing only the figures.[3] The work of the three above-mentioned craftsmen influenced botanical illustration for many years and a number of books, published in the sixteenth, seventeenth, and even the eighteenth century, contain illustrations copied from Fuchs or even

---

[1] See Introduction to *Herbarum vivæ eicones*: A2[b] (1530).
[2] Sprague (T. A.), The herbal of Otto Brunfels, *Journ. Linn. Soc. (London) Botany*, 48, 84 (1928).
[3] These figures are smaller versions of those in the original work.

printed from his actual blocks.[1] A German edition of *De historia stirpium* was published in 1543, entitled *New Kreüterbůch*.

A passing reference must be made to Jerome Bock (Hieronymus Tragus) (1498–1554) and Pierandrea Mattioli (Petrus Andreas Matthiolus) (1500–77). The first of these men, Jerome Bock, was a Lutheran pastor who also practised medicine and pharmacy. As an author this German botanist preferred to disguise his name Bock, meaning 'he-goat', under its Graeco-Latin equivalent, Tragus. His great work, the *New Kreütter Bůch*, appeared at Straßburg in 1539. It contains no illustrations and is outstanding for its 'admirable descriptions, written in the plain, racy German of the people'.[2] To an edition of 1546, and later editions, woodcuts were added executed by the Straßburg engraver, David Kandel. Some of these are original, others are adapted from figures in the works of Brunfels and Fuchs.[3] Pierandrea Mattioli was an eminent Italian physician and botanist. His famous *Commentarii* on Dioscorides first appeared at Venice in 1544 in Italian and without illustrations. In 1554 this work was published in Latin and illustrated with a large number of woodcuts, many illustrated editions being subsequently issued.[4] Some versions, published at Prague and Venice, are noted for their fine large-scale figures.

At the end of the sixteenth century the writings of Rembert Dodoens (Rembertus Dodonæus), a physician and botanist in the Low Countries, exercised considerable influence in England. This author was born at Malines in 1517 and died at Leyden in 1585. We are told by Meerbeck[5] that Dodoens studied medicine at Louvain, and afterwards visited the universities and medical schools of France, Italy, and Germany. He finally returned to his native city, and in 1548 was nominated town physician. Dodoens became renowned as a doctor not only in his native land but also in other countries, and in 1574 he accepted an invitation from the Emperor Maximilian II to be court physician at Vienna. On the death of Maximilian he remained for a time with the new Emperor, Rudolf II. He received a Chair of Medicine at Leyden University in 1582.

Dodoens wrote several botanical works, and was the author of a *Crǔÿde-boeck*, a herbal in Flemish. It was published in 1554 by Jan van der Loe of Antwerp, and was illustrated by 715 woodcuts of plants,[6] many of which were copies from those in the octavo edition of Fuchs's herbal. A second Flemish edition appeared in 1563. Charles de l'Escluse (more commonly known as

[1] See Arber (A.), *Herbals their origin and evolution—A new edition*, 70 and 219 (1938), Cambridge.

[2] Ibid. 59 (1938).

[3] See Arber (A.), op. cit., 59 and 221 (1938), and Blunt (W.), *The art of botanical illustration*, 54 (1950).

[4] See Nissen (C.), *Die botanische Buchillu-stration*, etc., 2, 119–20 (1951), Stuttgart.

[5] Meerbeck (P. J. van), *Recherches historiques et critiques sur la vie et les ouvrages de Rembert Dodoens* (1841), Malines.

[6] *Bibliotheca Belgica. Bibliographie générale des Pays-Bas*. Première série, tome 9, folio 107₈ (1880–90), Gand, La Haye.

Charles de l'Écluse, or Carolus Clausius), another celebrated botanist from the Low Countries, translated the *Crüÿdeboeck* into French. This translation, which appeared in 1557 under the title of *Histoire des plantes*, also came from the press of van der Loe of Antwerp. Many of the same woodcuts were used that had appeared in the *Crüÿdeboeck*, with the addition of some new figures which were probably drawn by the artist Pierre van der Borcht,[1] to whom further reference will be made. De l'Écluse was born in 1526 at Arras.[2] After studying at several universities, including Montpellier, where he lived in the house of the eminent naturalist Guillaume Rondelet, de l'Écluse devoted his life to the study and the teaching of botany. He travelled widely and possessed a great gift for languages. In 1593 de l'Écluse was made a Professor at the University of Leyden. He died in 1609.

In 1583 Christophe Plantin published *Stirpium historiæ pemptades sex*, a herbal in Latin consisting of the collected botanical works of Dodoens. In 1581 Plantin had purchased from the widow of Jan van der Loe all the wood-blocks that had been used for the two Flemish editions and the French translation of the *Crüÿdeboeck*. These figures together with others employed in the earlier works of Dodoens, de l'Écluse, and de l'Obel were used to illustrate the *Pemptades*.[3]

During the sixteenth century the Low Countries produced three botanists of world-wide repute. Two of these men, Rembert Dodoens and Charles de l'Écluse, have already been mentioned. The third, Matthias de l'Obel[4] (de Lobel, de L'Obel, or Lobelius), spent many years in England and published his chief work in this country. This botanist and his writings, therefore, will be referred to when we discuss English herbals and their authors.

The last foreign botanist to whom reference need be made is Jacob Dietrich (Jacobus Theodorus), known as Tabernæmontanus, because he was a native of Bergzabern. Born about 1520 he died at Heidelberg in 1590. He was a physician and, like many of the early herbalists, a follower of Luther. He is said to have spent thirty-six years on the preparation of his *Neuw Kreuter-buch*. It appeared in 1588–91, and came from the press of Nicolaus Bassaeus of Frankfurt am Main. According to Arber[5] the figures illustrating this work 'are for the most part not original, but are reproduced from Bock, Fuchs,

---

[1] Ibid., Première série, tome 9, folio 109₇ (1880–90).

[2] For a life of de l'Écluse see Morren (C. J. E.), *Charles de l'Escluse, sa vie et ses œuvres, 1526–1609*, Extrait du *Bull. de la Féd. des Soc. d'Hort. de Belgique*, année 1874 (1875), Liége.

[3] Rooses (M.), *Christophe Plantin imprimeur anversois*, 330 (1882), Anvers.

[4] In a device in this botanist's *Plantarum seu stirpium historia* and *Kruydtboeck*, published in

Antwerp in 1576 and 1581 respectively, are figured two abele-trees (*Populus alba*). This device is said by Morren (C. J. E.), *Mathias de l'Obel, sa vie et ses œuvres, 1538–1616*, pp. 3–4 (1875), Liége, to be the author's canting arms, i.e. heraldic bearings allusive of the name of the bearer. The old Walloon name for white poplars is Obel (see *Historia*, p. 609; *Kruydtboeck*, **2**, 224), thus punning de l'Obel's family name.

[5] Arber (A.), *Herbals their origin and evolution . . . A new edition*, 76 (1938).

Mattioli, Dodoens, de l'Écluse and de l'Obel'. In 1590, the same publisher issued the woodcuts without any text, under the title of *Eicones Plantarum*.

Finally, it will be well to consider a few points of interest with regard to the great Antwerp printer Christophe Plantin (*c.* 1520–89),[1] mention of whom is made a number of times throughout our text on herbals.

Christophe Plantin was probably born in France in Touraine. When he was about fifteen years old he went to Caen and worked as an apprentice to the printer Macé II. While he was at Caen Plantin married and about 1545 he and his wife went to live in Paris. Less than three years later they left France for good to settle in the wealthy and flourishing city of Antwerp where Plantin worked at first as a bookbinder, as he had done in Paris. Later he gave up this trade and set up as a printer instead. He had several daughters, one of whom married Jan Moerentorf or Moretus who was in charge of the shop and who also looked after the firm's accounts. Moretus was a good businessman, an excellent scholar, and an outstanding linguist, and after Plantin's death in 1589 he became his father-in-law's successor. From Moretus this famous press descended through succeeding generations of printers to Édouard Moretus who was the last of the firm and who sold the Maison Plantin to the city of Antwerp. It is now preserved as the Museum Plantin–Moretus. It is unique in the history of typography that a printing-house of the sixteenth century may still be seen essentially unchanged since the days of its founder. The study of book illustration during this period is greatly facilitated by the fact that many of the original drawings made for Plantin by his artists may still be seen in this Museum, as well as the wood-blocks and copper plates. Records have been preserved giving information about the various artists who were employed, the work they did, and the salaries they received.[2]

Plantin published the writings of many of the great scholars of the day, including works by the three renowned botanists from the Low Countries, Rembert Dodoens, Charles de l'Écluse, and Matthias de l'Obel.

Among Plantin's artists and engravers his two most outstanding botanical illustrators were Pierre van der Borcht and Arnold Nicolai. Van der Borcht (*c.* 1540–1608) was a native of Malines.[3] From about 1564, when he started to work for Plantin, he made all the illustrations for the botanical books that came from this printer's press.[4] He was also the artist responsible for drawings made to illustrate many of Plantin's other publications,[5] and his output of work was prodigious in quantity and varied in subject.[6]

[1] For further details see Rooses (M.), *Christophe Plantin imprimeur anversois*, (1882), Sabbe (M.), *Plantin. The Moretus and their work*, (1926), Brussels, and Clair (C.), *Christopher Plantin* (1960).
[2] Delen (A. J. J.), *Histoire de la gravure dans les anciens Pays-Bas et dans les provinces belges ... Deuxième partie. Le XVIᵉ siècle. Les graveurs-illustrateurs*, 79 (1934), Paris.
[3] Ibid. 79.   [4] Ibid. 81, 83.   [5] Ibid. 81–98.
[6] Before 1564 this artist and engraver worked for the Antwerp printer Jan van der Loe, and

Arnold Nicolai was one of the leading wood-engravers of the sixteenth century,[1] and he executed many of the woodcuts that were made from van der Borcht's drawings, including some of his figures of plants.[2] The dates of Nicolai's birth and death are not known and few details concerning his life are recorded, although according to Dr. Vervliet, formerly Deputy Curator of the Museum Plantin–Moretus,[3] documents relating to him have been found in the Antwerp and Plantin archives for the years 1550 to 1589.

Plantin treated his large collection of botanical wood-blocks more or less as a common pool, the same block being used for works by different authors. The Museum Plantin–Moretus still has 3,874 of these original blocks.[4]

The House of Plantin at Antwerp may be compared to the great printing family of the Estiennes at Paris, on account of the important part they played in the history of learning during the sixteenth century. But 'while the Estiennes concerned themselves mainly with the classics of antiquity, Plantin's chief work was the printing of the science of his own day'.[5]

ENGLISH HERBALS

Compared with many other countries, England was late in practising the new art of printing. The earliest piece of printing which can be dated with certainty is an indulgence printed in 1454 at Mainz whence, soon after the middle of the sixteenth century, the new art spread to other towns throughout Europe. By 1476, when Caxton set up his press at Westminster,[6] there were many craftsmen at work in Germany, Italy, France, Switzerland, and the Low Countries. Even by the time of Caxton's death in 1491 it is fairly evident, writes Duff,[7] that 'the book-trade in England was not important and the demand for books was not large', and indeed for many years the art of printing made its way slowly in this country. It is not surprising, therefore, to find that by the time the first herbal appeared in England several such works had already come from continental presses. The latter include the first printed edition of the *Herbarium* of Pseudo-Apuleius, printed at Rome

126 of the botanical drawings that appeared in Dodoens's *Crüÿdeboeck* are by this artist. (Delen (A. J. J.), op. cit. 80–1). For details of a large collection of water-colour drawings by van der Borcht, executed under the direction of de l'Écluse, and at the time of the Second World War preserved in the Preußische Staatsbibliothek, Berlin, see Wegener (H.), Das große Bilderwerk des Carolus Clusius in der Preußischen Staatsbibliothek, *Forschungen und Fortschritte*, Jahrg. 12, No. 29, pp. 374–6 (1936), Berlin; and Blunt (W.), *The art of botanical illustration*, 65–7 (1950).
[1] Delen (A. J. J.), *Histoire de la gravure dans les anciens Pays-Bas et dans les provinces belges ... Deuxième partie. Le XVIᵉ siècle. Les graveurs-illustrateurs*, 98, etc. (1934).
[2] Ibid. 108.
[3] In epist. 27. xi. 50.
[4] Vervliet, op. cit.
[5] McKerrow (R. B.), *An introduction to bibliography for literary students*, 280 (1928).
[6] The first known piece of printing executed by Caxton after he came to England was an indulgence issued at Westminster in 1476. See Pollard (A. W.), The new Caxton indulgence, *The Library*, Series IV, vol. 9, 86–9 (1929) (*Trans. bibl. Soc.*, Series II, vol. 9).
[7] Duff (E. G.), *A century of the English book trade . . . 1457 to . . . 1557*, p. xiv (1905).

about 1484 by Johannes Philippus de Lignamine,[1] and the *Latin Herbarius* printed at Mainz in 1484 by Peter Schöffer.[2] These herbals were followed by two other incunabula printed at Mainz, to which reference has already been made. They are the *German Herbarius* (1485) and the *Hortus* or *Ortus sanitatis* (1491).

About 1495, a few years after he had taken over Caxton's business at Westminster, Wynkyn de Worde published *De proprietatibus rerum*.[3] This English version of a work originally written in the middle of the thirteenth century, consists of a storehouse of information on a variety of subjects including natural history. The author, Bartholomaeus Anglicus (*fl.* 1230–50), was a Franciscan friar and theological professor at the University of Paris who is sometimes mistakenly identified with Bartholomew de Glanville. *De proprietatibus rerum* is divided into nineteen sections or books, and the seventeenth, dealing with trees, shrubs, and herbs, is of interest to us as containing the earliest information printed in England on plants and their uses.

The first book devoted entirely to herbs to be printed in England is a small quarto volume published anonymously, in 1525, by the London printer Richard Banckes. It is in black letter, contains no illustrations, and is often referred to as 'Banckes's herbal'.[4] The origin of the work is unknown, but it is probably derived from an unknown medieval manuscript.[5] The title-page reads: 'Here begynnyth a newe mater, the whiche sheweth and treateth of ye vertues z proprytes of herbes, the whiche is called an herball.' In 1526 Banckes printed the work again, and during the next thirty-five years a large number of editions of this small book came from the presses of more than ten London printers. They were issued under various titles, some appearing under the names of Macer, and Ascham, or the initials W. C. They have been discussed at length by H. M. Barlow,[6] Francis R. Johnson,[7] and other writers.[8]

---

[1] This little Latin treatise is an illustrated medical recipe book. It is believed that it was first written in Greek, probably in the fourth or fifth century. Nothing is known of the original compiler, who must not be confused with Lucius Apuleius, author of *The Golden Ass*. He is sometimes called Apuleius Barbarus.

[2] The *Latin Herbarius* is also called *Herbarius in Latino, Aggregator de simplicibus, Herbarius Moguntinus, Herbarius Patavinus*. This illustrated herbal is anonymous. It is a compilation from medieval writers, and from some classical and Arabic authors. The figures were evidently not made from nature, and it is possible that both they and the text were copied from some now unknown manuscript.

[3] Caxton died some time in 1491, and he was succeeded at Westminster by his chief assistant, Wynkyn de Worde.

[4] For a facsimile reprint and modernized version see *An herbal* [1525] *edited and transcribed into modern English with an introduction by Sanford V. Larkey . . . and Thomas Pyles* (1941), New York.

[5] See Bennett (H. S.), *English books and readers 1475 to 1557*, etc. 99 (1952), Cambridge.

[6] Barlow (H. M.), Old English herbals, 1525–1640, *Proc. Roy. Soc. Med.* **6**, 108–23 (1913) (Section of the history of medicine).

[7] Johnson (F. R.), A newe herball of Macer and Banckes's herbal, *Bull. Hist. Med.* **15**, 246–60 (1944), Baltimore, U.S.A.

[8] For a list of some of these writers see Johnson (F. R.), op. cit. **15**, 246, footnote 1 (1944).

A number of the various editions of Banckes's herbal, including those printed by Robert Redman, Thomas Petyt, William Middleton, William Copland, and John King, differ little from the original work of 1525. Of greater variation, however, are the editions that came from the press of Robert Wyer. These herbals, although drawing most of their material from the original work, have numerous modifications, additions, and omissions. The title-page of one of Wyer's editions[1] reads *A newe herball of Macer, translated out of Laten in to Englysshe*. There was a medieval poem of wide repute on medicinal herbs called the Macer Floridus that was attributed to the classical poet Aemilius Macer (died 16 B.C.), but which was actually written by Odo Magdunensis, a French physician.[2] It was first printed in Naples in 1477 under the title *De viribus herbarum*, and several subsequent editions had appeared before Wyer printed his work called *A newe herball of Macer*. This bears little resemblance to *De viribus herbarum* and there seems no justification for the use of Macer's name on the title-page. Nor is there any justification for Wyer's title reading *Macers herbal. Practysyd by Doctor Lynacro*,[3] 'Doctor Lynacro' being presumably a reference to the noted English physician and classical scholar, Thomas Linacre, who died in 1524.

Robert Wyer was a printer who exploited the rapidly growing market of his day for small cheap books dealing with subjects of a popular nature.[4] Johnson has put forward reasons for believing that Wyer, realizing the commercial value of Banckes's herbal, used it 'as the basis for an inferior compilation of his own'.[5] Thus, in order to impress prospective buyers, Wyer added the name of a well-known authority on the title-page. Furthermore, in order to produce a new book to compete with the successful editions of Banckes's herbal put out by other presses, such as Redman, Petyt, Middleton, and Copland, he made various differences in the text.[6]

A feature of Wyer's work is his use of woodcut initial letters of which he had a large and striking assortment.[7] A number of interesting examples are to be found in his editions of the herbal, the capitals being there adorned with grotesque faces, little figures, and flowers, and greatly resembling some used by Wynkyn de Worde.

On account of the wording of the title, two editions of Banckes's herbal have

[1] Published [1535?].
[2] See Rose (H. J.), *A handbook of Latin literature from the earliest times to the death of St. Augustine . . . with a supplementary bibliography by E. Courtney*, 340–1 (1966). Also Schanz (M.), *Geschichte der römischen Literatur . . . Zweiter Teil*, etc. [*Handbuch der klassischen Altertumswissenschaft*. Abt. 8.] 164–5 (1935), München.
[3] Published [after 1542].
[4] Plomer (H. R.), *Robert Wyer, printer and bookseller*, 11 (1897).
[5] Johnson (F. R.), A newe herball of Macer and Banckes's herbal, *Bull. Hist. Med.* 15, 260 (1944).
[6] For an analysis of the differences between Banckes's and Wyer's books see Johnson (F. R.), op. cit. 15, 249–58 (1944).
[7] Plomer (H. R.), *Robert Wyer, printer and bookseller*, 9 (1897).

1. Some initial letters used by the printer Robert Wyer in his edition of Banckes's herbal, entitled: *Hereafter foloweth the knowledge, properties, and the vertues of herbes* [1540?], natural size.

sometimes been attributed to the astrologer Anthony Ascham.[1] The first of these editions, printed in 1550 in octavo by William Powell, has a title-page that reads: *A lytel herball of the properties of herbes newely amended and corrected, with certayne addicions at the ende of the boke, declaryng what herbes hath influence of certaine sterres and constellations, wherby may be chosen the beast and most luckye tymes and dayes of their ministracion, accordynge to the moone being in the signes of heaven, the which is dayly appoynted in the Alma-nacke, made and gathered in . . . M.D.L. the xii day of February by Anthonye*

[1] Anthony Ascham studied at Cambridge. In 1540 he became M.B., and in 1553 was pre-sented with the vicarage of Burneston, in York-shire.

Askham phisycyon. Some care was taken in the revision of this edition and Anthony Ascham may have been associated with the work as editor, but it seems more likely that the revision was done by the printer, William Powell. It appears that the statement on the title-page 'by Anthonye Askham' refers to the 'Almanacke' from which the 'addicions at the ende of the boke' were intended to be taken, not to the main work. This seems a reasonable supposition when it is remembered that Anthony Ascham was the author of a series of octavo almanacs and prognostications that were printed by William Powell.[1] No copy appears to be known of the herbal in which the 'addicions' are present. It is also possible, as suggested by Johnson,[2] that William Powell intended to bind with his herbal another work he printed in octavo in 1550 by Anthony Ascham. This deals with astrological botany and from the title would fulfil the description of the 'addicions'. It is: *A litell treatyse of astronomy, very necessary for physyke and surgerye, declarynge what herbes, and all kynde of medecynes are appropryate and under the influence of the planetes.*[3]

Errors have sometimes been made regarding the authorship of certain editions of Banckes's herbal that bear the initials W. C. on the title-page. One of the first of these editions was printed about 1552 by William Copland. It is entitled: *A boke of the propreties of herbes called an herball . . . Also a generall rule of all manner of herbes drawen out of an auncyent booke of phisyck by W. C.* As this book is only a later edition of that by Richard Banckes, the initials W. C. on the title-page cannot, as has been accepted by some bibliographers, stand for Walter Cary, the author of *The hammer for the stone* (1580), who in 1552 would have been a child.[4] It appears likely that the initials W. C. stand for William Copland, the printer of the herbal, who seems to have edited this edition and added the last three chapters 'drawn out of an auncyent booke of phisyck'.

The first illustrated book on plants to be published in England is *The grete herball* of 1526, which came from the press of Peter Treveris. It is a much costlier production than Banckes's herbal, it is better known, and more copies appear to exist, but it lacks much of the simple charm of the earlier work.

The grete herball does not claim to be original. At the end of the index there is a note that it 'is translated out yᵉ Frensshe in to Englysshe', and it is in the main a translation of the French *Le grant herbier*. The introduction and

[1] Bosanquet (E. F.), *English printed almanacks and prognostications. A bibliographical history to . . . 1600*, p. 29 (1917).

[2] Johnson (F. R.), A new herball of Macer and Banckes's herball, *Bull. Hist. Med.* 15, 259 (1944).

[3] A copy of this treatise is in the Hunterian museum in the University of Glasgow. See

Johnson (F. R.), op. cit. 15, 259 (1944).

[4] In 1561 Walter Cary, the author of *The hammer for the stone*, was a demy at Magdalen College, Oxford, and was, therefore, too young to have been associated with *A boke of the propreties of herbes* [1552?]. See Humphreys (A. L.), Walter Cary, *Notes and Queries*, Series XI, vol. 7, 253–5 (1913).

The grete herball

whiche geueth parfyt knowlege and vnder

ſtandyng of all maner of herbes & there gracyous vertues whiche god hath
ozdeyned foz our profperous welfare and helth/foz they hele & cure all maner
of dyſeaſes and ſekeneſſes that fall oz myſfoztune to all maner of creatoures
of god created/pzactyſed by many expert and wyſe mayſters/as Auicenna &
other. &c. Alſo it geueth full parfyte vnderſtandynge of the booke lately pzex
tyd by me(Peter treueris)named the noble experiens of the vertuous hand
warke of furgery.

2. *The grete herball*, 1526. Title-page. 8·5 × 6·5″.

conclusion seem to be derived from the *German Herbarius* and the *Ortus sanitatis*.[1] The use of English at that date instead of Latin is of interest. It appears that between 1500 and 1640 a higher proportion of scientific works were printed in the vernacular in England than in any other country except Italy. In regard to a herbal which was aimed mostly at an unlearned public, the use of English was almost obligatory.[2]

De Fragraria. Strawberyes.

3. 'Fragraria, Strawberyes'. Woodcut from from *The grete herball*, sign. Lii[a] (part). 1526. 3·3 × 2·4″.

4. 'Rosa', Rose. Woodcut from *The grete herball*, sign. Vii[a] (part), 1526. 2·5 × 2·4″.

Besides a large woodcut on the title-page of a man picking grapes and another filling a basket with herbs, *The grete herball* contains nearly 500 small illustrations. These are mostly of plants, although figures of animals, minerals, and some other subjects are also included. The majority of the woodcuts are reduced and degenerate copies of those in the *German Herbarius*, and the *Ortus sanitatis*, and have little importance in the history of botanical illustration.[3] In a variety of instances the same figure is prefixed to different plants.

[1] Barlow (H. M.), Old English herbals, 1525–1640, *Proc. Roy. Soc. Med.* **6**, 127 (1913) (Section of the history of medicine).

[2] Arber (A.), From medieval herbalism to the birth of modern botany, 318 (1953), Oxford. (Reprinted from *Science, medicine and history.*

Essays on the evolution of scientific thought and medical practice written in honour of Charles Singer.)

[3] Ibid. **6**, 127. See also Arber (A.), *Herbals their origin and evolution . . . A new edition*, 201 (1938).

Many of the woodcuts occur again in *The vertuose boke of distyllacyon of the waters of all maner of herbes*. This is an English version, with a colophon dated 1527, of the *Liber de arte distillandi de simplicibus* of Hieronymus Braunschweig.[1] The translator, Laurence Andrewe, had business relations with Peter Treveris;[2] and his device and colophon are found in three successive editions of *The vertuose boke of distyllacyon*, though the type is that of Treveris.[3] The whole-page representation of the human skeleton on leaf ✠ 6 of *The grete herball* is boldly drawn and cut, and had been used by Treveris in the previous year for *The noble experyence of the vertuous handywarke of surgeri* (1525). This is a translation of another work by Hieronymus Braunschweig, printed by Treveris and remarkable for its woodcuts.

The last leaf of *The grete herball* contains the interesting whole-page device of Peter Treveris. This consists of a wild man and woman holding up a shield. On the shield are the printer's initials and mark, and beneath the figures is a ribbon with his name. The whole alludes to his address 'in the syne of the Wodows' in Southwark. 'Wodows' or 'woodwoses' (the earliest known use of the word denoting a savage, or wild man of the woods, was in the beginning of the twelfth century) are not uncommon as heraldic supporters, and devices very similar to that of Treveris were used by the Paris printer Philippe Pigouchet (working 1483–1515), and by a number of other printers both here and abroad. The device of Pigouchet was apparently the first of this particular pattern.[4]

Some years ago a proof-sheet of *The grete herball* of 1526 was found in the binding of an indenture dated 31 July 1526 among the muniments of Queen's College, Oxford. This fragment is of interest as being one of the few existing examples giving us evidence of actual proof correction made during the early days of printing.[5]

Peter Treveris printed another edition of *The grete herball* in 1529. Two further editions appeared in 1539 and 1561 respectively. The first of these was printed by Thomas Gibson, whilst the second came from the press of John King.

We now come to William Turner who has been called the 'Father of British botany'. His two little books, the *Libellus de re herbaria novus* (1538) and *The names of herbes in Greke, Latin, Englishe Duche ʒ Frenche* (1548), together

---

[1] Hieronymus Braunschweig, apothecary, surgeon, and author, came from the family of Saulern of Straßburg. He lived at the end of the fifteenth and beginning of the sixteenth centuries. See Hirsch (A.), *Biographisches Lexikon der hervorragenden Ärzte aller Zeiten und Völker*, **1**, 685 (1929), Berlin, Wien.

[2] Isaac (F.), *English and Scottish printing types 1501–35, 1508–41* (1930) (see under Peter Treveris).

[3] Hodnett (E.), *English woodcuts 1480–1535*, p. 63 (1935 for 1934).

[4] Davies (H. W.), *Devices of the early printers 1457–1560*, etc. 344 (1935).

[5] For details concerning this proof-sheet and a facsimile see Gibson (S.), Fragments from bindings at the Queen's College, Oxford, *The Library*, Series IV, vol. **12**, 430–1 and plate (1932) (*Trans. bibl. Soc.* Series II, vol. **12**).

5. *The grete herball*, sign. Ee 6ᵇ, 1526. The device of Peter Treveris, printer in London, whose address was 'in the sygne of the Wodows' over the bridge in Southwark'. 7·6 × 5·2″.

with his most important contribution to botany, *A new herball* (published in three parts, 1551, 1562, and 1568), mark the beginning of modern botany in England. The causes that led up to this development were first felt on the Continent, and can be summarized as follows.

Books had become both cheaper and more numerous as the result of the

❧ The greate Herball. which geueth parfyte knowledge & vn-

DERSTANDINGE OF AL MANER OF HER
bes, and theyr gracious vertues, whiche GOD hath ordeyned for
our prosperous welfare and health : for they heale and cure all maner of diseases and sekenesses , that fall or mysfortune too all
maner of creatures of GOD created, practysed by many
experte and wyse maysters, as Auicenna, Pandecta,
and more other .&c. ❡ Newlye corrected and diligently ouersene. In the yeare of our Lord
God.   M.   CCCCC.   LXI.

6. *The greate herball*, 1561. Title-page. 8·6 × 5·2″.

invention of printing by movable metal types, and the works of the ancients became available to scholars who, previously, had been limited to rare manuscripts which might or might not have been accessible. The end of the fifteenth century was an age of ever-broadening horizons: Columbus discovered America, the Portuguese opened up a new route to the East round the Cape of Good Hope, from newly discovered lands plants were brought home that needed to be described and classified. The knowledge of medicine was improving, and drugs, hitherto unknown, were introduced. This improvement in medical science demanded an increased knowledge of plants on which that science was based. The great artists Albrecht Dürer (1471–1528) and Leonardo da Vinci (1452–1519) were exerting a profound influence on botanical illustration with their exquisitely faithful representations of plants.

The first outcome of this botanical renaissance as far as herbals are concerned was, as we have seen, the publication in Germany of Brunfels's *Herbarum vivæ eicones* in 1530. England, however, lagged behind, for in 1529 and 1539 editions were still being published of *The grete herball*, displaying botanical knowledge at a very low ebb, and characterized by a mixture of superstitions, ignorance, and Galenic doctrine. The only botanical illustrations were those in the 1526 and 1529 editions of *The grete herball*, which were completely out of touch with nature, and which inherited the 'manuscript' tradition of slavish copying from a previous work. With the publication of William Turner's herbal, however, we enter a new epoch in botanical literature in England. Now at last there was available to the physician and apothecary, and also to the student of botany, an English work written on a scientific basis. In the words of Gilmour:[1] 'Turner was the first in Britain to light his torch at the flame of the pioneer herbalists on the Continent, and, breaking away from authority and superstition, to describe British plants from his own observation and experience.'

William Turner, Dean of Wells, Protestant controversialist, physician, and naturalist, was born at Morpeth, Northumberland, 'presumably in or about 1508'.[2] In 1526 he became a student of Pembroke Hall, Cambridge, and in 1531 was elected a Fellow of his college.[3] As a young man he came in contact with two men later to be burned at the stake, Nicholas Ridley (1500?–55), who gave him his early instruction in Greek, and Hugh Latimer (1485?–1555), who influenced him by his preaching. Turner became a most ardent supporter of the Reformation, and twice suffered exile from this country. He was the author of works on religion and natural history. He died in London in 1568.

[1] Gilmour (J.) and Walters (M.), *Wild flowers*, etc. 7 (1954).

[2] Raven (C. E.), *English naturalists from Neckam to Ray*, etc. 49 (1947), Cambridge.

[3] For a life of Turner see *Libellus de re herbaria novus, by William Turner ... reprinted in facsimile, with notes, modern names, and a life of the author, by B. D. Jackson* (1877), privately printed.

Even as a child Turner was interested in birds and plants,[1] but as a young man was frustrated by the lack of instruction available for his botanical studies. Regarding this, he wrote in the preface to the 1568 edition of his herbal,[2]

above thyrtye yeares ago . . . beyng yet felow of Penbroke hall in Cambridge, wher as I could learne never one Greke, nether Latin, nor English name, even amongest the phisiciones of anye herbe or tre, suche was the ignorance in simples at that tyme, and as yet there was no Englishe herbal but one, al full of unlearned cacographees and falselye naminge of herbes, and as then had nether Fuchsius, nether Matthiolus, nether Tragus written of herbes in Latin.

It may be presumed that the English work referred to in this passage is *The grete herball*.[3]

Turner's first botanical work is the *Libellus de re herbaria novus*, a little book written in Latin and containing more than 140 plants with synonyms in Greek and English. The colophon is dated 1538 and it is one of the few non-theological works printed by John Byddell.

In 1540,[4] Turner went abroad until the death of Henry VIII. There is no doubt that his herbal is the richer for his sojourn on the Continent. Unable to take an active part in religion, Turner occupied himself with medicine and botany and took the degree of Doctor of Medicine at either Ferrara or Bologna. During his travels through various countries, including Italy, Switzerland, Germany, and Holland, he recorded and collected the European flora. He also met eminent continental naturalists of the day. In this period were published several of Turner's small religious books, and, on 8 July 1546, we find his name included among those of ten other Reformers in a Proclamation by Henry VIII forbidding any persons to 'receive, have, take, or kepe . . . any maner of booke printed or written' by one or more of these eleven men.[5] It is, therefore, not surprising that the *Libellus* of 1538 is a rare work.[6] Turner's works were again prohibited on 13 June 1555, by a Proclamation set out by Philip and Mary.[7]

On the accession of Edward VI, Turner returned to England and there appeared soon afterwards his work, *The names of herbes in Greke, Latin, Englishe Duche z Frenche wyth the commune names that herbaries and apotecaries use*. The dedication, dated 15 March 1548, is addressed to the Lord Protector, Edward Seymour, Duke of Somerset (1506?–52), in whose house-

---

[1] Raven (C. E.), op. cit. 49 (1947).

[2] See *ii*[b].

[3] The only other English herbal at this time was Banckes's herbal, and it is unlikely that Turner would have referred to this small popular work in preference to *The grete herball*.

[4] See Raven (C. E.), op. cit. 75 (1947).

[5] Ames (J.), *Typographical antiquities . . . augmented . . . by W. Herbert*, **1**, 450 (1758).

[6] For a facsimile of this work see *Libellus de re herbaria novus, by William Turner . . . reprinted in facsimile, with notes, modern names, and a life of the author, by B. D. Jackson* (1877), privately printed.

[7] *The Acts and Monuments of John Foxe, Fourth Edition: revised . . . by J. Pratt*, etc. **7**, 127–8 [1877].

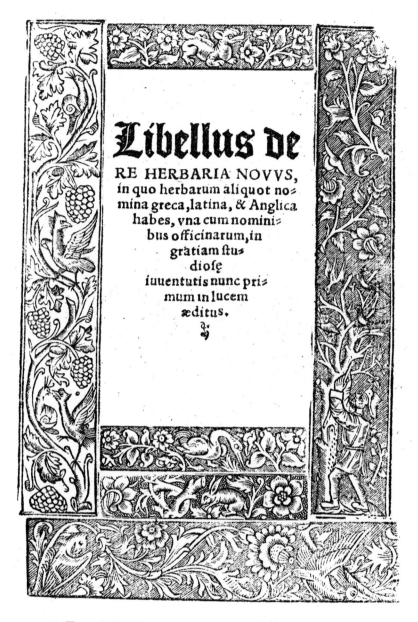

7. Turner's *Libellus de re herbaria*, 1538. Title-page. 6·0 × 4·1″.

hold Turner had been appointed physician on his return from the Continent. It contains 'the earliest recognizable record of at least 105 of our plants, over and above those already identified from his *Libellus*'.[1] Both these books are of botanical interest as including the localities of some of the species

[1] Raven (C. E.), op. cit. 98 (1947). For a reprint of this work see *The names of herbes . . . Edited (with an introduction, an index of English* *names, and an identification of the plants enumerated by Turner) by* J. *Britten* (title-page dated 1881, author's preface 1882), The English

mentioned, and are the first of such local records to be printed in England. Turner declared his work of 1548 to be 'a litle boke, which is no morebut a table or regestre of suche bokes as I intende by the grace of God to set furth here after'.[1] It was, in fact, a forerunner of his *magnum opus*, his celebrated herbal.

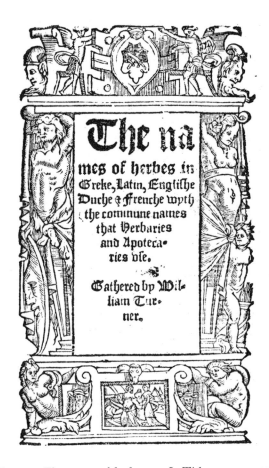

8. Turner: *The names of herbes*, 1548. Title-page. 4·4 × 2·5".

Turner's herbal appeared in three parts. The first part, published in 1551, was printed in London by Steven Mierdman, under the title of *A new herball, wherin are conteyned the names of herbes . . . with the properties degrees and*

Dialect Society. See also the Ray Society's publication (No. 145) of 1965 in one volume of B. D. Jackson's life of Turner together with his 1877 facsimile of the *Libellus* and J. Britten's 1882 reprint by the English Dialect Society of Turner's *Names of herbes*. The lists provided by Jackson and Britten of modern scientific equivalents for the names used by Turner are also reprinted in the above volume of 1965, but with numerous emendations of nomenclature by J. E. Dandy and W. T. Stearn.

[1] Turner (W.), *The names of herbes*, etc. (1548) (Dedication).

9. Turner: *A new herball*, 1551. Title-page ▷ with compartment with the Royal arms at head, and at sides tablets with the letters ER, the initials signifying Edwardus Rex. 11·6 × 6·4".

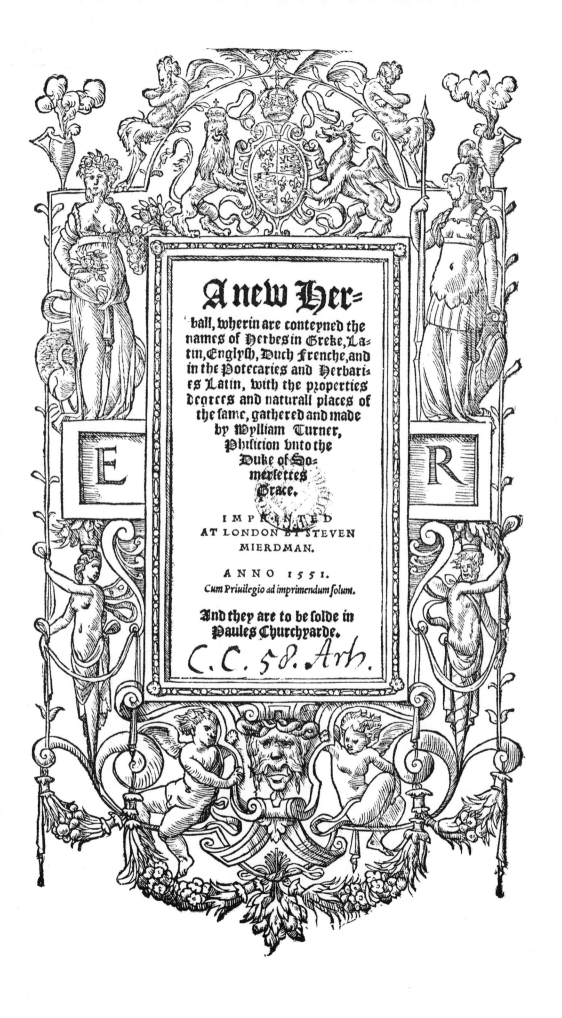

A new Her=

ball, wherin are conteyned the
names of Herbes in Greke, La=
tin, Englysh, Duch Frenche, and
in the Potecaries and Herbari=
es Latin, with the properties
degrees and naturall places of
the same, gathered and made
by Wylliam Turner,
Phisicion vnto the
Duke of So=
merlettes
Grace.

IMPRINTED
AT LONDON BY STEVEN
MIERDMAN.

ANNO 1551.
Cum Priuilegio ad imprimendum solum.

And they are to be solde in
Paules Churchyarde.

E   R

naturall places of the same. The dedication was once again addressed to the
Duke of Somerset. The printer, Mierdman, was born in the Netherlands in
the little village of Hooge Mierde. From 1543 until between 1546 and 1549
he printed in Antwerp. He came to England to escape proceedings against
him by the Conseil de Brabant for having printed heretical books, and in
1549 he was living in the parish of Saint Mary-at-Hill, Billingsgate Ward.
On the accession of Mary Tudor in 1553 Mierdman was forced to leave this
country. He returned to the Continent and finally settled at Emden.[1]

During the reign of Mary, Turner was again in exile abroad, and the second
part of his herbal did not appear until 1562, when it was printed at Cologne
by Arnold Birckman. The final part was printed in 1568, together with a new
edition of the first part and a reissue of the second. This complete edition,
which is dedicated to Elizabeth I, was also issued by Birckman. The figures
with which the three parts of the herbal are illustrated are woodcuts, mostly
copies from those in the octavo edition, first published at Basle in 1545, of
Fuchs's *De historia stirpium*.

So that his herbal could be used by all members of the medical profession
in this country Turner wrote it in English rather than in Latin. 'How many
surgianes and apothecaries are there in England', he asks, 'which can under-
stande Plini in Latin or Galene and Dioscorides, where as they wryte ether
in Greke or translated into Latin.'[2] This epoch-making work in the history
of botany did not receive the notice it deserved in later botanical writings,
published either here or abroad. Canon Raven,[3] in giving details of the extent
and limitation of Turner's influence on the Continent and at home, has shown
that this author's work might have had a greater influence if it had been
written in Latin, and thus made available to all scholars. The same authority
also points out that the final herbal was published in Germany and this 'no
doubt told against its circulation in England'.[4]

After Turner's herbal the next important botanical book to be published
in England is Pena and de l'Obel's *Stirpium adversaria nova*, a folio volume
with the title-page dated 1570 and the colophon 1571. Neither of the authors,
who were both physicians, was a native of this country. Pierre Pena was born
at Jouques, in the arrondissement of Aix, in Provence,[5] and Matthias de
l'Obel (1538–1616) was a native of Lille.[6] The dates of Pena's birth and death
are not known. Although Pena was at first destined to be a soldier he gave up

---

[1] For a paper giving further details concerning Steven Mierdman, entitled 'On the printing
of certain Reformation books' *see* Clair (C.) *The
Library*, Series V, vol. **18**, 275–87, plates 1
and 2 (1963) (*Trans. bibl. Soc.* Series III, vol. **18**).

[2] *A new herball*, etc., Aiii^b (1551) ('The pro-
loge').

[3] Raven (C. E.), *English naturalists from
Neckam to Ray*, etc. 134–7 (1947).

[4] Ibid. 137.

[5] The details in the life of Pena have been
obtained from Legré (L.), *La botanique en
Provence au XVIe siècle. Pierre Pena et Mathias
de Lobel* (1899), Marseille.

[6] Morren (C. J. E.), Mathias de l'Obel, sa
vie et ses œuvres, 1538–1616, *extrait du Bull.
de la Féd. des Soc. d'Hort. de Belgique* (1875),
Liége.

Of cockoupynt.

Cockoupynt.

the roote is whyte as dragones is, the whyche, beynge soden, is eatē because it is not so bytynge, as it was before.

The vertues.

The roote, sede, and leues of aron, haue the same properties that dragon hath. The roote is layd vnto ÿ gowtye membres, with cowdunge: and it is laid vp & kept as dragones rootes are: and because the rootes are gentler, they are desyred of many to be eaten in those countreis, wheras the rootes of coccowpynt are not so bytynge hote, as they are in England and in Germany. Dioscorides semeth by hys wryting, to shew, that where as he was borne, Arō, was not so sharpe, as it is with vs. Galene also wryteth, that aron is hote in the fyrst degre, & drye in ÿ same. But it that groweth with vs is hote in ÿ thyrd degre at the leste.

Wherfore some peraduenture wyll say, that thys our aron is not it, that Dioscorides & Galene wrote of. But Galene in these wordes folowyng: which are wryttē in ÿ second boke, *de elementorum facultatibus:* wytnesseth, ÿ ther are. 2. sortes of arō: one gētle, & another, biting. *In quibusdam regionibus acrior, quo dammodo prouenit, ut prope ad dracontij radicem accerat.&c.* In certayne regyons after a maner, it groweth more bytyng, and sharpe: in so much, that it is allmost as hote, as dragon is: and that the fyrst water must be casten out, and the roote soden agayne in the second. Thys herbe growynge in Cyrene, is dyfferyng frō it, of our countre. for it that is wyth vs in Asia for a great parte, is sharper then it, that groworth in Cyrene.

Of Mugwurt.

Mugwurt is called both of the Grecians, and latines, artemisia: of the duche, byfus, or bifoit. The true artemisia, is as lytle knowen nowe adayes, as is ÿ true pontyke worm wode: & lesse, as I thynke. for this great mugwurt is suche an artemisia, as our wormwood is absinthiū ponticum: that is bastard, and not the true herbe. Dioscorides wryteth: ÿ artemisia, for the most parte

E.i.   gro-

10. 'Cockoupynt'. Woodcut from Turner: *A new herball*, sign. Ei[a]. 1551. 10·1 × 5·3". *Arum maculatum* L., Cuckoo-pint.

his military career to study medicine at Paris. He later travelled widely in Europe, visiting, among other places, northern France, Flanders, Germany, Switzerland, Italy, Spain, and Portugal. In 1558 Pena was at Antwerp. He visited Padua in the same year and again in 1562. In 1563 he made an excursion to Verona and one year later was with Conrad Gesner at Zürich. Finally, in April 1565, Pena arrived at the University of Montpellier where the next month he was followed by Matthias de l'Obel who had been travelling in Germany and Italy. Here at Montpellier these two men were pupils of the physician and naturalist Guillaume Rondelet (1507–66) and, united by a common interest in botany, they became great friends and went on botanical expeditions together.

In July 1566 Rondelet died, having bequeathed to de l'Obel, his favourite pupil, his botanical manuscripts.[1] By the following autumn Pena and de l'Obel had left Montpellier, for we find them at La Rochelle on their way to England. It may have been at this time that the two friends conceived the idea of a joint botanical work. Possibly it was already partly completed, and they now decided to have it published in England which was then prospering under the rule of Elizabeth I. Whatever were the reasons that influenced the two men to come to this country, they arrived in London in December 1569 bringing with them their botanical collections.

During the next few years Pena and de l'Obel botanized throughout the British Isles, and this enabled them to publish in the *Stirpium adversaria nova* a number of plants unknown to William Turner. This book, dedicated to Queen Elizabeth I, is in Latin. Pena and de l'Obel appear on the title-page as joint authors of the work; the part each botanist played towards the combined practical research and theoretical ideas incorporated in the volume, however, cannot be definitely established.[2] The chief importance of this herbal lies in its system of classification which is better than that used by any contemporary botanist. The arrangement is based mainly on difference of leaf character, the monocotyledons being placed together at the beginning of the work, thereby foreshadowing their separation from the dicotyledons. The title-page consists of the Royal arms, with a representation of the solar system above the title, and a map of the western hemisphere below. Hind considers[3] that this anonymous title-plate was 'probably' engraved by Remigius Hogenberg, a native of Malines, who worked in England as an engraver from about 1572 until 1587. During his stay in this country Hogenberg executed several portraits, and some maps for Christopher Saxton's *Atlas of England and Wales* of 1579.

[1] Morren (C. J. E.), op. cit. 5 (1875).
[2] For suggestions as to the share borne by Pierre Pena in the work, see Legré (L.), op. cit., and Morren (C. J. E.), op. cit.

[3] Hind (A. M.), *Engraving in England in the sixteenth and seventeenth centuries*, etc., Pt. 1, p. 66 (1952), Cambridge.

11. Pena and de l'Obel: *Stirpium adversaria* ▷ *nova*, 1570 (–71). Title-page engraved by Remigius Hogenberg? 9·4 × 5·6".

The *Stirpium adversaria nova* came from the press of Thomas Purfoot in London. According to Rooses,[1] the printer Christophe Plantin of Antwerp bought 800 copies of the work for 1,200 'florins'. In 1576 Plantin published *Plantarum seu stirpium historia . . . Cui annexum est Adversariorum volumen.* This work is in two parts, the first part comprises de l'Obel's 'Stirpium observationes' with 'De succedaneis, imitatione Rondeletii'. The second part,

Nicotiana inferta infundibulo ex quo hauriunt fumū Indi & nauclri.

12. 'Nicotiana'. Pena and de l'Obel: *Stirpium adversaria nova*, 1570 (–71). Woodcut on pasted-in slip on p. 252. 4·4 × 3·7″. *Nicotiana tabacum* L., Tobacco.

or 'Adversariorum volumen', contains the 'Adversaria' of 1570–1 with the addition of an appendix by de l'Obel. In this part, pages 1–455, with one additional page, are the original sheets of the 'Adversaria' purchased by Plantin from Purfoot. To these the Antwerp printer prefixed a new title-

[1] Rooses (M.), *Christophe Plantin imprimeur anversois*, 333 (1882), Anvers.

page bearing his own imprint, reading: 'Antverpiæ, apud Christophorum Plantinum . . . M.D.LXXVI'. Purfoot used the remaining unsold sheets of Pena and de l'Obel's work as the second part of a volume which he published in 1605, the first part of which was entitled *Matthiæ de l'Obel . . . in G. Rondelletii . . . methodicam pharmaceuticam officinam animadversiones*. Plantin also purchased from Purfoot, for a further 120 'florins', 250 of the 272 wood-blocks used for the figures of plants in the *Stirpium adversaria nova*. These arrived at Antwerp on 4 May 1580, and they went to swell the large collection of wood-blocks that provided so many of the illustrations for the botanical books published by the house of Plantin during the sixteenth and seventeenth centuries.

After the publication of the *Stirpium adversaria nova*, Pena returned to the Continent where he apparently gave up his interest in botany to devote himself to medicine. He became a prosperous and successful physician and died a rich man. How long de l'Obel remained in England is not known, but in 1574 he was in Antwerp working on his *Plantarum seu stirpium historia* published by Plantin in 1576. A Flemish translation of the work under the title of *Kruydtbœck* came from the same press in 1581. De l'Obel remained in Antwerp until 1581 and during the years he was in this city he practised medicine. Subsequently he became physician to the Stadholder of the Low Countries, William the Silent, and was with him until his assassination in 1584. Not long afterwards de l'Obel returned to England where he settled for the rest of his life. When Edward Lord Zouche (1556–1625) was sent as Ambassador to Denmark in 1598 de l'Obel accompanied him.[1] He became Superintendent of the physic garden on Lord Zouche's estate at Hackney and through his influence received the appointment in 1607 of Botanicus Regius to James I. In 1598 his treatise entitled *Balsami, opobalsami, carpobalsami & xylobalsami, cum suo cortice explanatio* came from the press of John Norton.

When de l'Obel died in 1616 he left an incomplete botanical work from which selections were later made and published in 1655 as a quarto volume, edited by William How, a young London doctor, under the title of *Matthiæ de l'Obel . . . stirpium illustrationes*. The original manuscript from which the book of 1655 was printed and the remainder of de l'Obel's unpublished work passed into the hands of the Hampshire botanist John Goodyer (1592–1664). Since Goodyer's death this material has been in the library of

[1] Edward (la Zouche), eleventh Lord Zouche, or la Zouche (of Haryngworth) (1556–1625), a commissioner for the trial of Mary, Queen of Scots, at Fotheringhay 1586; lived and travelled abroad 1587–93; Ambassador to Scotland 1594, and to Denmark 1598; Deputy Governor of Guernsey 1600–1; Lord President of the Council of Wales 1602–7; Councillor for the Virginia Company 1609, and for New England 1620; Lord Warden of the Cinque Ports and Constable of Dover Castle 1615–24. He was a keen collector of shrubs and trees, and his garden at Hackney contained many plants obtained during his travels (*The complete peerage . . . by G. E. C. revised . . . by G. H. White . . . with the assistance of R. S. Lea*, **12**, Pt. 2, 949–54 (1959)).

Magdalen College, Oxford, with other papers and books also bequeathed by
Goodyer to the College.[1]

In 1578 there appeared Henry Lyte's English translation of de l'Écluse's
French version of Dodoens's *Crŭÿdeboeck* of 1554. It is entitled *A nievve
herball* and is dedicated to Queen Elizabeth I. It was printed by van der Loe
of Antwerp, and sold by Garrat Dewes who practised as a printer and bookseller in London from 1560 to 1591, in St. Paul's Churchyard at the sign of the
Swan.[2] This folio volume is mostly printed in black letter and is illustrated
with many woodcuts of plants.

The fine woodcut compartment surrounding the title is the same as that
of the second Flemish edition (1563), which differs from that of the *Crŭÿdeboeck* of 1554 in that a vase of flowers takes the place of the Spanish coat of
arms. Both states are signed with the initials P. B. and the monogram *A*, the
former standing for Pierre van der Borcht,[3] the artist who illustrated so many
books published by the Antwerp printer, Christophe Plantin, and the latter
for Arnold Nicolai, who became one of Plantin's chief engravers.[4] On the
verso of the title-page is a large woodcut of the translator's coat of arms and
a crest, 'a swan volant silver uppon [*sic*] a trumpet gold', which was not
actually granted him by Clarenceux King of Arms until 'the 24 of June, anno
Domini 1579', the year after the publication of the herbal.[5]

The figures of plants illustrating the English translation are the same as
those used for the Flemish editions and the French version of the *Crŭÿdeboeck*, but the wood-blocks now show signs of wear.[6] A number of the figures
are new and these were probably made from drawings by Pierre van der
Borcht.[7]

The extremely pleasing portrait of the author with the inscription 'Remberti
Dodonæi æta. XXXV' had already appeared in the *Crŭÿdeboeck* of 1554,
and the same block had been used earlier in *Remberti Dodonæi . . . trium
priorum de stirpium historia commentariorum imagines* (1553, Antverpiæ).
The portrait is signed *A*, and it has been suggested that the artist was probably
Pierre van der Borcht, and the engraver Arnold Nicolai.[8] The original wood-

[1] For details see Gunther (R. W. T.), *Early
British botanists and their gardens*, etc. 245–53
(1922), Oxford.

[2] McKerrow (R. B.), *A dictionary of printers
and booksellers in England, Scotland and Ireland,
and of foreign printers of English books 1557–
1640*, p. 90 (1910).

[3] Delen (A. J. J.), *Histoire de la gravure dans
les anciens Pays-Bas et dans les provinces belges
. . . Deuxième partie. Le XVIᵉ siècle . . . Les
graveurs-illustrateurs*, 79 (1934).

[4] Ibid. 98. On account of his monogram
appearing to be composed of the initials A.S.
Arnold Nicolai has sometimes been confused

with Antonius Sylvius (or Bos), Anton Steelsius, and others. See Delen (A. J. J.), op. cit. 98
(1934).

[5] Lyte (H. C. M.), The Lytes of Lytescary,
Proc. Somerset archaeol. nat. Hist. Soc. **38**,
Pt. 2, 46 (1892).

[6] *Bibliotheca Belgica. Bibliographie générale
des Pays-Bas. Première série*, tome **9**, folio 110₅
(1880–90), Gand, La Haye.

[7] Ibid., tome **9**, folio 110₅.

[8] Delen (A. J. J.), *Histoire de la gravure dans
les anciens Pays-Bas et dans les provinces belges
. . . Deuxième partie. Le XVIᵉ siècle. Les graveurs-
illustrateurs*, 80–1 (1934).

13. *A nievve herball*, 1578. Henry Lyle's English translation ▷
of de l'Écluse's French version of Dodoens's *Crŭÿdeboeck*
of 1554. Title-page with woodcut compartment engraved
by Arnold Nicolai after a design by Pierre van der Borcht.
10·1 × 6·5″.

APOLLO.

ÆSCVLAPIVS.

GENTIVS

ARTHEMISIA

METHRI DATES

LYSIMACHVS

A NIEVVE HERBALL,
OR HISTORIE OF PLANTES:

wherin is contayned

the vvhole difcourfe and perfect defcription of all fortes of Herbes
and Plantes: their diuers & fundry kindes:
their ftraunge Figures, Fafhions, and Shapes:
their Names / Natures / Operations / and Uer-
tues: and that not onely of thofe whiche are
here growyng in this our Countrie of
Englande / but of all others alfo of
forrayne Realmes / commonly
vfed in Phyficke.

Firft fet foorth in the Doutche or Almaigne
tongue, by that learned D. Rembert Dodoens, Phyfition to the Emperour:
And nowe firft tranflated out of
French into Englifh, by Henry Lyte Efquyer.

AT LONDON

by me Gerard Dewes, dwelling in
Pawles Churchyarde at the figne
of the Swanne.
1578.

HESPERIDVM HORTI

block is still preserved in the Museum Plantin–Moretus. It is of some interest to record that the present writer has been informed by Dr. Vervliet, formerly Deputy Curator of the Museum Plantin–Moretus,[1] that the blocks used for the title and the botanical figures in the *Crüÿdeboeck* and its editions, purchased in 1581 by Plantin from the widow of van der Loe, are also still in the Plantin collection at Antwerp.

Trichomanes.

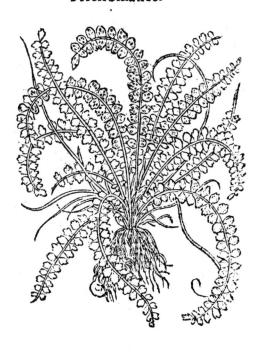

14. 'Trichomanes'. Woodcut on p. 410 (part) of *A nievve herball*,
1578. Henry Lyte's English translation of de l'Écluse's French
version of Dodoens's *Crüÿdeboeck* of 1554. 3·5 × 2·5″. *Asplenium
trichomanes* L., Maidenhair Spleenwort.

Henry Lyte, who made the above English translation, was descended from an old family of his name living at Lytescary in Somerset. He was born about 1529. He became a student at Oxford, but it is doubtful if he took a degree. After leaving the University Lyte travelled on the Continent. Later, he returned 'to his patrimony where, by the advantage of a good foundation of literature made in the University and abroad, he became a most excellent scholar in several sorts of learning'.[2] Lyte was not able to devote himself entirely to scholarly pursuits. From 1559 he had to manage his father's

---

[1] In epist. 27.xi.50.·
[2] Wood (A. à), *Athenæ oxonienses . . . A new edition . . . By Philip Bliss*, **2**, col. 22 (1815).

15. *A nievve herball*, 1578. Henry Lyte's English translation of de l'Écluse's French version of Dodoens's *Crüÿdeboeck* of 1554. Portrait of Rembert Dodoens signed '𝒜' (i.e. the monogram of the engraver Arnold Nicolai), p. [xii]. 5·0 × 3·4".

property in Somerset,[1] and after the latter's death in 1566 he succeeded to this estate.[2] He died in 1607.[3]

Lyte prepared *A nievve herball* with care. He compared 'the last Douch copy' of the *Crüÿdeboeck* with the French version,[4] and in places made corrections and additions.[5] Moreover, it appears that after Lyte had finished his work, Rembert Dodoens sent fresh material, which the English translator

[1] Lyte (H. C. M.), The Lytes of Lytescary, *Proc. Somerset. archaeol nat. Hist. Soc.* **38**, Pt. 2, 53 (1892).

[2] Ibid. 42–3.

[3] Ibid. 59.

[4] See *A nievve herball* (1578). Note at foot of p. 345.

[5] See *A nievve herball* (1578) where we read on p. 311: 'The ende of the seconde part. Twise corrected and augmented by the aucthor'.

incorporated in *A nievve herball*.[1] Lyte's own copy of de l'Écluse's version is now preserved in the British Museum (Bloomsbury).[2] It contains numerous notes in French and English, written in red and black ink, and in a neat, clear hand. References to Turner and de l'Obel are inserted, and the book is carefully annotated and corrected.

Not unnaturally the authors of most herbals were members of the medical profession. Lyte, however, had no professional need for the knowledge of plants; he belonged to that group of people who, by their interest and love of natural history, have done so much to further the subject by studying and writing about it at their leisure. He was in fact, as pointed out by Gilmour,[3] 'the first of a long line of British amateur botanists'.

Among the commendatory verses at the beginning of Lyte's herbal is a Latin poem by Thomas Newton, the author of *An herbal for the Bible*, published in 1587. This work, dedicated to Robert Devereux, Earl of Essex (1566–1601), is based on a treatise by Levinus Lemnius, the *Herbarum atque arborum quæ in Bibliis passim obviæ sunt . . . dilucida explicatio*, which appeared at Antwerp in 1566. Newton points out in his dedication that his work is not a word-for-word translation and, on occasion where the original lacked clarity or when it was not sufficiently succinct, he has made various additions or omissions. Levinus Lemnius (1505–68), a physician and philosopher of Zeeland, is considered to be the first author to describe the plants of the Holy Scriptures.[4] His herbal ran into many editions and, besides the English version, there is also a French translation.

Thomas Newton (1542?–1607) was a native of Cheshire,[5] and he signed the end of his translation of 1587: 'Thomas Newtonus, Cestreshyrius'.[6] He was educated at Trinity College, Oxford, and Queens' College, Cambridge, and about 1583 became Rector of Little Ilford in Essex. He was the author of various publications on historical, medical, and theological subjects, and the translator of several Latin works. He was renowned as a writer of Latin verse.

One of the best-known botanical books ever to have been published in this country is *The herball or generall historie of plantes by John Gerard*.

John Gerard (1545–1612), whose name is considered to be more correctly spelt without the final *e* it assumes on the title-page of his *Herball*, was born in Cheshire. After attending school at 'a village called Wisterson . . . two miles

---

[1] See *A nievve herball* (1578), verses at the beginning of the herbal, headed: 'To the reader, in commendation of this worke'.

[2] Pressmark 442.h.9.

[3] Gilmour (J.), *British botanists*, 10 (1944).

[4] Hoefer (J. C. F.), *Nouvelle biographie générale*, etc. **30**, col. 614 (1859), Paris.

[5] Wood (A. à), *Athenæ oxonienses . . . A new*

edition . . . *By Philip Bliss*, **2**, cols. 5–6 (1815).

[6] This author was apparently very proud of his association with Cheshire. He also appeared as 'Thomas Newtonus, Cestreshyrius' in the superscription over his commendatory verses in Latin in Lyte's herbal of 1578 and again in the superscription above his Latin poem to John Gerard in the latter's *Herball* of 1597.

Of Gillofers. Chap.vij.

❋ The Kyndes.

Vnder the name of Gillofers (at this time) diuerse sortes of floures are contayned. Wherof they call the first the Cloue gillofer whiche in deede is of diuerse sortes & variable colours: the other is the small or single Gillofer & his kinde. The third is that, which we cal in Englsh sweete williams, & Colminiers: wherevnto we may well ioyne the wilde Gillofer or Cockow floure, which is not much vnlike the smaller sort of garden Gillofers.

Vetonica altilis.

Carnations, and the double-cloaue Gillofers.

Vetonica altilis minor.

The single Gillofers, Soppes in wine, and Pinkes, &c.

❋ The Description.

1 THe Cloue gillofer hath long small blades, almost like Leeke blades. The stalke is round, and of a foote and halfe long, full of ioyntes and knops, & it beareth

16. 'Gillofers', Carnations and Pinks. Woodcut from Lyte: *A nievve herball*, p. 154 (part), 1578.
7·9 × 5·7".

from . . . Nantwitch in Cheshire',[1] he decided on the career of a surgeon and was apprenticed, in 1562, to Alexander Mason, a barber-surgeon in London. In 1569 he completed his apprenticeship and was admitted to the freedom of the Company. He attained eminence in his profession and in 1607 was elected Master of the Company. Gerard was married and settled in Holborn where he died in February 1612.[2]

Gerard, at least on one occasion, travelled abroad, as in his *Herball* he speaks of 'Livonia, Polonia, Norvegia, and Russia . . . the iland called Holand within the sownde, beyond Denmarke' and of a journey he made 'from Narva unto Moscovia'.[3] He also writes:[4] 'Denmarke, Swevia, Poland, Livonia, or Russia, or in any of those colde countries where I have travelled'. He may have travelled on a merchant ship belonging to the Company of Merchant Adventurers in London going through the Baltic to Narva. From Narva the journey would have been overland to Moscow.[5] The reason Gerard made this journey is not known, but in his *Herball* he records observations he made concerning some of the plants he saw.[6] Gerard was a keen botanist and he searched for plants in London and its environs,[7] as well as in the Home Counties, especially Kent, Surrey, and Essex. He also studied the plants growing further afield, including Cheshire, Staffordshire, and Lancashire and 'about Excester in the west parts of Englande'.[8] In recording plant localities Gerard was not always accurate in his evidence. Salaman describes how Gerard made certain statements as to the original home of the potato which misled historians for nearly three hundred years.[9] Raven also has complained of inaccuracies with regard to some of Gerard's plant localities.[10] But Gerard acknowledged that his work contained errors and inaccuracies when he told his readers:[11] 'Faults I confesse have escaped, some by the printers oversight, some through defects in my selfe to performe so great a worke, and some by meanes of the greatnesse of the labour.'

At one time Gerard had charge of several gardens in and near London. William Cecil, first Baron Burghley (1521–98),[12] who spent vast sums of money on the buildings and gardens of his various properties, made Gerard

[1] Gerard (J.), *The herball*, etc. 1091 (1597).
[2] The details of Gerard's will, preserved in the Guildhall Library in the Records of the Archdeaconry of London, are given and used to provide the material for an article on Gerard's life and descendants by Mary Edmond, published in *The Genealogist's Magazine*, **14**, No. 5, 137–45 (1963).
[3] Gerard (J.), op. cit. 1177.
[4] Ibid. 1223.
[5] See Jeffers (R. H.), *The friends of John Gerard (1545–1612) surgeon and botanist*, 18 (1967), published by the Herb Grower Press, Falls Village, Connecticut, U.S.A.
[6] e.g. see pp. 1177, 1181, 1223.

[7] For a list of some of the plants found in London localities see Raven (C. E.), *English naturalists from Neckam to Ray*, etc. 209–10 (1947).
[8] Gerard (J.), op. cit. 1138.
[9] Salaman (R. N.), *The history and social influence of the potato*, 81–4 (1949), Cambridge.
[10] Raven (C. E.), op. cit. 210–11.
[11] Gerard (J.), op. cit. (1597) (preface).
[12] William Cecil born 13 Sept. 1521, died 4 Aug. 1598; knighted 11 Oct. 1551; Secretary of State 1550–3 and again 1558–72; created Baron Burghley, county Northamptonshire, 25 Feb. 1570 [i.e. 1571], Lord High Treasurer 15 Sept. 1572 till his death.

the superintendent of his gardens at his residence in the Strand and at Theobalds, his property in Hertfordshire.[1] Lord Burghley was a keen collector of rare plants and his gardens were famous for their great variety of trees and plants. Gerard was in charge of these gardens as early as 1577, as he recounts in the dedication of his *Herball* that he had then been in Lord Burghley's service 'by the space of twenty yeeres'. In 1586 when the College of Physicians decided to establish a physic garden Gerard was appointed Curator.[2] In addition Gerard managed for many years a well-stocked garden of his own near his home on the south side of Holborn, between Chancery Lane and Fetter Lane.[3] In this garden Gerard grew 'all the rare simples which by any meanes he could attaine unto' and here you could see 'all manner of strange trees, herbes, rootes, plants, flowers, and other such rare things, that it would make a man woonder, how one of his degree, not having the purse of a number, could ever accomplish the same'.[4]

In 1596 Gerard issued a catalogue of plants in his Holborn garden and he dedicated this—his first printed work—to Lord Burghley. The title reads: *Catalogus arborum, fruticum ac plantarum tum indigenarum, quam exoticarum, in horto Johannis Gerardi . . . nascentium.* At the end of this list is an attestation by de l'Obel, dated 1 June 1596, stating that the writer had seen Gerard's garden and that he had grown all the plants named. It is considered by Jackson to be 'the first professedly complete catalogue of any one garden, either public or private, ever published'.[5] This small quarto volume, printed by Robert Robinson, with a business in Holborn, consists of more than one thousand species, including the first recorded mention of the potato in print that we know of.[6] It seems possible that only a few copies of the work were printed for private distribution by the author to friends. This would account for its rarity. Jonas Dryander, librarian to Sir Joseph Banks, knew of the existence of one printed copy only.[7] This copy, in the British Museum (Bloomsbury), was formerly in the possession of Sir Hans Sloane. Nearly two hundred years later this catalogue was one of the works used by William Aiton in preparing his *Hortus Kewensis* of 1789. From it Aiton obtained the earliest printed record of the cultivation in British gardens of many exotic plants. Gerard issued a second catalogue of the plants in his garden in 1599

[1] Queen Elizabeth I was a frequent visitor at Theobalds. In 1607 Robert Cecil, first Earl of Salisbury, Lord Burghley's second surviving son, exchanged his estate of Theobalds with James I for the Royal residence at Hatfield.

[2] Jeffers (R. H.), *The friends of John Gerard,* etc. 30 (1967). This garden seems to have been attached to the College buildings then situated in Knightrider Street.

[3] Regarding the site occupied by Gerard's garden in Holborn see Edmond (M.), *The*

Genealogist's Magazine, **14,** No. 5, 142–3 (1963).

[4] Gerard (J.), *The herball,* etc. (1597) (Commendatory letter by George Baker).

[5] Jackson (B. D.), *A catalogue of plants . . . in the garden of John Gerard . . . Edited with notes by B. D. Jackson,* p. xiii (1876).

[6] Salaman (R. N.), *The history and social influence of the potato,* 77 (1949).

[7] Dryander (J.), *Catalogus bibliothecæ historico-naturalis Josephi Banks,* **3,** 97, (1797).

which he dedicated to Sir Walter Raleigh. At the end of the list is the same
signed confirmation by de l'Obel, now dated 1 July 1599, stating that he had
seen all of the plants recorded growing in Gerard's garden. A copy of this
edition in the British Museum (Natural History) originally belonged to de
l'Obel whose manuscript notes it contains. De l'Obel's printed attestation
has been struck through save the word 'attestor' before which is written in
de l'Obel's hand: 'hæc esse falsissima'. After 'attestor' is the botanist's
signature 'Matthias de Lobel'. This edition was printed in folio by Arnold
Hatfield. Hatfield was one of the men forming the Eliot's court printing-
house in the Old Bailey.[1] This syndicate was composed of several printers
who seem to have had an arrangement by which all their names never appeared
together in the imprint in any one book. Typographically Gerard's second
catalogue is better than the first and, although rare, several copies are
known to be preserved in private and institutional libraries.

Gerard's next publication is his *Herball*. It is a large folio volume, printed
in English in clear roman type by Edmund Bollifant, another member of
the Eliot's court printing-house, for the London bookseller John Norton.
The engraved title-page, dated 1597, is followed by the dedication to Lord
Burghley. In this dedication Gerard refers to his success in enriching the
gardens under his care with new plants. He writes:

> To the large and singular furniture of this noble iland, I have added from forren
> places all the varietie of herbes and flowers that I might any way obtaine, I have laboured
> with the soile to make it fit for the plants, and with the plants to make them to delight
> in the soile, that so they might live and prosper under our climate, as in their native and
> proper countrie: what my successe hath beene, and what my furniture is, I leave to the
> report of them that have seene your Lordships gardens, and the little plot of my speciall
> care and husbandrie.

Gerard had many good friends and acquaintances, and twelve of these wrote
commendatory letters or verses in praise of the *Herball* and its author.[2]
Among the writers of these letters and verses were Lancelot Browne (d.
1605), physician to Queen Elizabeth; Matthias de l'Obel, physician and
botanist, and joint author with Pierre Pena of the *Stirpium adversaria nova*
(1570-1); the Revd. Thomas Newton, author of *An herbal for the Bible*
(1587); Stephen Bredwell, who after leaving London practised as a physician
at Chippenham, Wiltshire; and George Baker (1540-1612), surgeon to Queen
Elizabeth, and afterwards to James I. In 1597 Baker was Master of the
Company of Barber-surgeons in London. Following the twelve commenda-

---

[1] Plomer (H. R.), The Eliot's Court printing-
house, 1584-1674, *The Library*, Series IV, vol.
2, 175-84 (1922) (*Trans. bibl. Soc.*, Series II,
vol. **2**).

[2] For biographical details concerning the

twelve authors of these letters and verses, and
also of Gerard's many other friends, see
Jeffers (R. H.), *The friends of John Gerard
(1545-1612) surgeon and botanist* (1967) (*Index*
and *Biographical appendix* published in 1969).

tions is Gerard's preface to the reader, and on the last leaf of the preliminary matter, is a half-length portrait of the author. The herbalist is shown turned slightly left, with right hand on a book, and the left holding a spray of potato foliage with flower and berry. This line engraving is by William Rogers who worked as an engraver from about 1589 to 1604. This engraving is found (1) before signature and (2) signed with the monogram WR on the lower margin towards the left. The first state is rarely found.[1] This portrait, dated 1598, was made when Gerard was aged fifty-three. Regarding this date it may be noted that the title-page and colophon of the *Herball* are dated 1597, and two of the commendatory letters and the author's address to the reader are dated 1 December 1597. Moreover, Johnson, in his edition (1633) of Gerard's work, writes of it being 'printed at the charges of Mr. Norton, an. 1597'. In Hind's opinion there is no doubt that the portrait belongs to the book,[2] a fact suggesting that the work was not published until 1598. So far the present writer has been unable to find definite proof of this.

The title-page of the *Herball* is one of the most attractive that appeared during the sixteenth century. It was executed by William Rogers, who was considered by Colvin to be 'the most interesting and skilful of the English engravers . . . until we come to William Faithorne'.[3] Unfortunately this title-plate is seldom found in good impression. It is interesting to note that it is the woodcut title-border that is particularly characteristic of the sixteenth century; engraved titles did not become usual until after 1600. There are only nineteen recorded English engraved title-pages published during the century, including those in Pena and de l'Obel's *Stirpium adversaria nova* and Gerard's *Herball*.[4] The illustrations of plants in Gerard's work are woodcuts. The majority were printed from wood-blocks obtained by Norton from Frankfurt am Main that had been used in 1590 for the *Eicones plantarum* of Tabernæmontanus. Apart from the Frankfurt figures a number of other illustrations were used, including some from de l'Obel and about sixteen which were original.[5]

The Bodleian Library, Oxford, has a copy of Gerard's *Herball* of 1597, present pressmark L1. 5. Med. with the woodcuts and engraved title-page and portrait of the author most carefully coloured by hand. This copy with its original pressmark G2. 9. Med. is recorded in the catalogue of books in

[1] A copy of the *Herball* containing the first state is in Cambridge University Library (pressmark SSS.1.5).

[2] Hind (A. M.), *Engraving in England in the sixteenth and seventeenth centuries . . . Part I. The Tudor period*, 268 (1952), Cambridge.

[3] Colvin (S.), *Early engraving and engravers in England 1545–1695*, etc. 49 (1905).

[4] Johnson (A. F.), *A catalogue of engraved and etched English title-pages down to the death*

of William Faithorne, 1691, p. viii (1934 for 1933).

[5] See Bauhin (G.), *Pinax theatri botanici* (1623) (Nomina authorum) where we read: 'Jo. Gerardi historia plantarum anglica cum figuris ipsius Tabernæmontani: nonnullis etiam Lobelii: & insuper 16. novis additis. Londini 1597. folio.' See also Gerard (J.), *The herball . . . enlarged . . . by T. Johnson* (1633) (Johnson's preface).

THE
HERBALL
OR GENERALL
Historie of
Plantes

Gathered by John Gerarde
of London Master in
CHIRVRGERIE.

Imprinted at London by
Iohn Norton.
1597

1 *Vitis vinifera.*
The manured Vine.

2 *Vitis vinifera Hispanica.*
The Spanish manured Vine.

18. Gerard: *The herball*, 1597. Two woodcuts of *Vitis vinifera* p. 725 (part). 5·2 × 6·2″. The herbal illustrator was often obsessed by the regularity of the wood-block on which he was working and he tended to accommodate his design to the shape of the block. Although this did not lead to botanical accuracy the result was sometimes very decorative.

the Library of Sir Thomas Bodley, published in 1605. In the Benefactors' Register for 1601 (Vol. **1**, p. 36) the last entry is: 'Donum Ioan. Norton, Gerards Herbal coloured. fo. London. 1597'. Bodley made considerable use of the printer John Norton in obtaining books for the library.

It is told in the *Stirpium illustrationes*, published by William How in 1655, that the publisher John Norton was warned by James Garret[1] that Gerard's work was full of blunders and that many of the figures were incorrectly placed. De l'Obel was therefore asked to amend the work. According to his own account he corrected more than a thousand mistakes until further

[1] James Garret (d. 1610) was an apothecary in Lime Street, in the parish of St. Dionis Backchurch, London. He had a garden near London Wall, Aldgate, where he grew tulips and roses. He was a friend of Charles de l'Écluse and of John Gerard.

◁ 17. Gerard: *The herball or generall historie of plantes*, 1597. Title-page designed and engraved by William Rogers. 12·3 × 7·5″.

revision was stopped by Gerard who became irritated and made insulting remarks about de l'Obel's ignorance of the English language. In the same work de l'Obel accused Gerard of using material from the 'Adversaria' without acknowledgement.[1] The *Stirpium illustrationes* consists of extracts, edited by How, from a work de l'Obel was compiling during the last years of his life.

Some time before Gerard's *Herball* was published, Norton had commissioned a certain Dr. Priest to translate the *Stirpium historiæ pemptades sex* (1583) of Rembert Dodoens from Latin into English.[2] Dr. Priest, apparently the London physician Robert Priest,[3] never completed his task. It is not known when it was begun, how much was ever completed, or what became of the manuscript, only that it is said to have been used by Gerard when preparing his *Herball*. However, as will be seen later, it appears from Gerard's preface that he had never seen Priest's work. One person who knew of the translation was the physician Stephen Bredwell. In his commendatory letter he mentioned Priest and his translation in the following passage:

The first gatherers out of the ancients, and augmentors by their owne paines, have alreadie spread the odour of their good names, through all the lands of learned habitations. D. Priest, for his translation of so much as Dodonæus, hath hereby left a tombe for his honorable sepulture. Master Gerard coming last, but not the least, hath many waies accommodated the whole worke unto our English nation: for this historie of plants, as it is richly replenished by those five mens labours laid together, so yet could it full ill have wanted that new accession he made unto it.

A marginal annotation against this passage lists the names of five botanists: William Turner, Rembert Dodoens, Pierre Pena, Matthias de l'Obel, and Tabernæmontanus.

Bredwell's words indicate that the publications of these five men were the chief sources used in the preparation of the *Herball*. An examination of the book confirms that they were the works of Turner, the *Stirpium historiæ pemptades sex* of Dodoens, the *Stirpium adversaria nova* of Pena and de l'Obel, and the *Kreuterbuch* of Tabernæmontanus.[4] To this list may be added the works of other authors, including *A nievve herball* by Henry Lyte and the early works of de l'Écluse. To the material obtained from the above sources Gerard added the English localities of plants, notes made as the result of his own experience and observations, and information supplied to him by his several friends and correspondents. In the early pages of the

[1] *M. de l'Obel . . . stirpium illustrationes . . . Accurante Guil. How*, 2–3 (1655).

[2] See *Matthiæ de l'Obel . . . in G. Rondelletii . . .* methodicam *pharmaceuticam officinam animadversiones*, etc. 59 (1605) and Gerard (J.), *The herball . . . enlarged . . . by T. Johnson* (1633) (Johnson's preface).

[3] See Jeffers (R. H.), *The friends of John Gerard*, etc. (1967) (*Biographical appendix*, published in 1969).

[4] Jeffers (R. H.), *The friends of John Gerard (1545–1612) surgeon and botanist*, 46–7, 70–1 (1967).

Herball Gerard makes frequent reference to de l'Obel. This botanist corresponded with Gerard, sent him an illustration of the ginger plant,[1] and on at
least one occasion plant-hunted with him.[2] He addressed Gerard in very
complimentary terms in his commendatory letter of 1597, and in the previous
year Gerard's garden catalogue had contained his signed attestation. De l'Obel
arrived in London with Pierre Pena in 1569 and he may have first made the
acquaintance of Gerard some time after this date and before 1574 when he
was back in his native country. Much of the *Herball* is recognizable as having
been translated from the *Stirpium historiæ pemptades sex* of Dodoens. The
arrangement of the work, however, is based on the classification of de l'Obel.

Something of the preparation of the *Herball* is told by Gerard himself in
his preface where he writes:

I have heere . . . set downe not onely the names of sundrie plants, but also their
natures, their proportions and properties . . . their distinct varieties and severall qualities,
as well of those which our owne countrie yeeldeth, as of others which I have fetched
further, or drawn out by perusing divers herbals, set foorth in other languages, wherein
none of our countrie men hath to my knowledge taken any paines, since that excellent
worke of Master Doctor Turner: after which time Master Lyte . . . translated Dodonæus
out of French into English;[3] and since that Doctor Priest, one of our London Colledge,
hath (as I heard) translated the last edition of Dodonæus, which meant to publish the
same; but being prevented by death, his translation likewise perished: lastly, my selfe
one of the least among many, have presumed to set foorth unto the view of the world,
the first fruits of these mine owne labours, which if they be such as may content the
reader, I shall thinke my selfe well rewarded, otherwise there is no man to be blamed
but my selfe . . .

A great deal has been written concerning the *Herball* as an example of
plagiarism, an accusation which seems to be chiefly based on certain remarks
to be found in Stephen Bredwell's commendatory letter in the *Herball*,
Gerard's preface in the same work and Thomas Johnson's preface in the
edition of 1633. Bredwell in the passage quoted earlier from his commendatory letter has been understood to mean that Gerard used Priest's translation as a basis for his own book. And he has been accused of dishonesty in
claiming that his *Herball* was 'the first fruits' of his own labours. But if
Gerard was guilty of plagiarism would he not have suppressed Bredwell's
letter rather than accorded it a place in his *Herball*?

In his preface Johnson states that he was informed 'by the relation of one
who knew Dr. Priest and Mr. Gerard' that Dodoens's 'Pemptades' of 1583
were translated into English by Dr. Priest 'who died either immediately
before or after the finding of this translation'. Johnson accuses Gerard of
using the work and of subsequently concealing the fact. As evidence he cites

[1] Gerard (J.), *The herball*, etc. 55 (1597).   [3] i.e. *A nievve herball*, etc. (1578).
[2] Ibid. 301.

the passage quoted earlier in Bredwell's commendatory letter. Moreover, as further proof Johnson refers to a remark made by de l'Obel in his notes on Rondelet's *Pharmacopoeia* of 1605 in which he found fault with Dodoens for his use of the word *seta* instead of *sericum* that gave occasion for a very absurd error on the part of Priest in his translation, as he was misled into translating it as bristle instead of silk[1]—an error, Johnson points out, also to be found in the *Herball*.[2] Johnson made yet another stricture against Gerard when after referring to Priest's translation and the *Herball* of 1597, he declared: 'Now this translation became the ground-worke whereupon Mr. Gerard built up this worke: but that it might not appeare a translation, he changes the generall method of Dodonæus, into that of Lobel.'

Johnson's accusations against Gerard proved lasting and damaging, but are they entirely reliable or justified? His details concerning Priest were not given from first-hand information but from 'the relation of one who knew Dr. Priest and Mr. Gerard'. Why was this informant not named? Can anyone be sure that his interpretation of the passage in Bredwell's letter was correct? De l'Obel drew attention to the use of bristle instead of silk by Priest. He did not mention Gerard. De l'Obel quotes, and the words are identical with Gerard's, not only the natural mistranslation of *seta*, but a not entirely natural translation of the context in which it appears. Thus, did de l'Obel, with the avoidance of Gerard's name, intend to make an indirect accusation of plagiarism against Gerard?[3] There was ill feeling between de l'Obel and Gerard which had begun at the time of the former's revision of the *Herball*. Did de l'Obel in fact have Priest's translation before him or was it perhaps the *Herball*? Can we rely on de l'Obel's evidence at all? Johnson gave no authority for his statement that Gerard had used Priest's translation and then in an endeavour to hide the fact changed 'the generall method of Dodonæus, into that of Lobel'. He based his evidence, therefore, either on hearsay or on an opinion held by himself. It was easy for Johnson to make his accusation; Gerard had been dead twenty-one years and it is doubtful if any of his friends were still alive to defend him. There is no proof in the work of 1605 that de l'Obel had seen Priest's translation, and Johnson in his preface of 1633 makes no claim to having seen it.

Jeffers in his work entitled *The friends of John Gerard (1545–1612) surgeon and botanist* has attempted to suggest a possible time at which Gerard began to write the *Herball* and he has also tried to describe the circumstances attending its assembly, as well as to indicate the principal sources from which it was derived. In the opinion of this authority[4] the use by Gerard of Dodoens's

[1] *Matthiæ de l'Obel . . . G. Rondelletii . . . methodicam pharmaceuticam officinam animadversiones*, etc. 59 (1605)..

[2] *The herball*, etc. 1160 (1597).

[3] This possibility has been suggested to the present writer by Mrs. G. J. R. Arnold, formerly of the Department of Printed Books of the British Museum (Bloomsbury).

[4] In epist. 4.xii.69.

work was not taken from Dr. Priest's manuscript but directly from the 'Pemptades' as well as from Dodoens's various writings published previous to 1583. There is also evidence in the *Herball* that Gerard and Dodoens corresponded.[1] There are indications that in the preparation of Book I— there are three books in all—Gerard was associated with Matthias de l'Obel, and this fact together with the small size of Book I compared with Book II suggest that it may have been begun between 1569 and 1574, a period during which de l'Obel was in England.[2] Regarding the use by Gerard of de l'Obel's method of classification, Jeffers, in an effort to explain why Gerard did not follow the classification of Dodoens, has put forward the following possible reasons.[3]

A comparison of the *Herball* and the 'Pemptades' shows that:

Dodoens closely adhered to a scheme of classification, essentially pharmacological in character, and the plants described were almost entirely those then held to possess medicinal properties. Gerard, on the other hand, was writing for a very different audience, and a wider one, beside which he aimed to include medicinal, culinary and economic plants, as well as indigenous and exotic plants that did not fall within any of those categories. Hence Dodoens' classification would not have answered his purpose fully. Moreover he had already started to base his work on the classification of L'Obel before Dodoens' last book appeared in 1583.

Gerard made no claim to scholarship but, in his own words, he perused 'divers herbals, set foorth in other languages'. He was fully aware of the magnitude of his task.[4] Moreover, he was conscious that for a variety of reasons it would contain mistakes.[5] In 1633 the *Herball* was published again 'enlarged and amended' by Thomas Johnson and subsequently for several hundred years it continued to be a valued and much used book. Gerard contributed greatly towards the advancement of the knowledge of plants in England, and in his *Herball* he described and illustrated several hundreds of our native flowering plants, including about 182 which were additional to those recorded in earlier works.[6] Together with his diligence in procuring new exotics and rare and indigenous plants, this herbalist had a great love and appreciation of the subject upon which he wrote. To realize this it is unnecessary to go beyond the opening lines of his dedication, in which he remarked that nothing had

provoked mens studies more, or satisfied their desires so much, as plants have done, and that upon iust and woorthie causes: for if delight may provoke mens labour, what greater

[1] *The herball*, etc. 107 (1597).
[2] Jeffers (R. H.), op. cit. 17–18, 20, 25–6, 65 (1967).
[3] Ibid. 49.
[4] 'being a worke, I confesse, for greater clerks to undertake, yet may my blunt attempt serve as a whetstone to set an edge upon some sharper wits, by whome I wish this my course discourse might be both fined and refined . . .' *The herball* (1597) (Gerard's preface).
[5] See above, p. 38.
[6] i.e. in the works of William Turner and Matthias de l'Obel. See Clarke (W. A.), *First records of British flowering plants . . . Second edition*, etc. 188 (1900).

delight is there than to behold the earth apparelled with plants, as with a robe of im-broidered worke, set with orient pearles, and garnished with great diversitie of rare and costly jewels?

Gerard wrote about plants largely for their medicinal qualities, but he also drew attention to their decorative value. He pointed out that *Lychnis chalcedonica* was noteworthy for its 'grace and beautie which it hath in gardens and garlands',[1] and that fritillaries were 'greatly esteemed for the beautifieng of our gardens, and the bosomes of the beautifull'.[2] He paid attention to plants as a source of food, and gave a method of making a conserve of roses 'as well for the vertues and goodness in taste, as also for the beautifull colour'.[3] Above all this herbalist knew how to write, and while much has been written of his faults as a botanist, of the charm of his writings there can be little dispute.

Thomas Johnson's edition of Gerard's *Herball*, sometimes referred to as 'Gerard emaculatus' or 'Johnson's Gerard', appeared with the imprint 'London printed by Adam Islip Joice Norton and Richard Whitakers . . . 1633'. John Norton, the publisher of the original work, had died in November 1612, but after his death the rights were preserved and, on 26 August 1632, they were assigned by Norton's cousin, the printer and bookseller Bonham Norton, and the executor of John Bill, to Mistress Joyce Norton and Richard Whitaker,[4] who on 13 July 1634 assigned to Adam Islip one full third share.[5] The exact date when Johnson was asked to undertake his task is not known, but it must have been roughly twelve months before the work was published, as he complains at the end of the *Herball* that he 'was forced to performe this task within the compasse of a yeare'.[6] The reason for this haste seems obvious. There had been an interval of thirty-six years since the original edition was issued and during this time no other herbal had appeared in England. It was time, therefore, for a more up-to-date work to be published. Possibly on account of its continued popularity and its association with the name of Gerard it was decided to publish an enlarged and amended edition of the *Herball* of 1597. Thomas Johnson, a London apothecary, was asked to under-take the task. He had already shown ability as a botanist and writer when he published a work containing descriptions of a herborizing excursion made by himself and some friends in July 1629 into Kent, and of a similar excursion made to Hampstead Heath the following August.[7] In 1632 Johnson pub-

---

[1] Gerard (J.), *The herball*, etc. 380–1 (1597).

[2] Ibid. 123.   [3] Ibid. 1084.

[4] *A transcript of the registers of the Company of Stationers of London; 1554–1640 . . . Edited by E. Arber*, **4**, 283 (1877). John Bill was a printer and bookseller who at the end of Norton's life managed his printing business. Joyce (also spelt Joice) Norton may have been John Norton's widow and was in partnership during 1632–7 with Richard Whitaker.

[5] *A transcript*, etc. **4**, 323 (1877).

[6] Gerard (J.), *The herbal . . . enlarged and amended by Thomas Johnson*, 1591 (1633).

[7] *Iter plantarum investigationis ergo susceptum a decem sociis, in agrum cantianum. Anno Dom. 1629. Julii 13. Ericetum hamstedianum sive plantarum ibi crescentium observatio habita, anno eodem 1. Augusti*, etc. [1629].

Battata Virginiana siue Virginianorum, & Pappus.
Potatoes of Virginia.

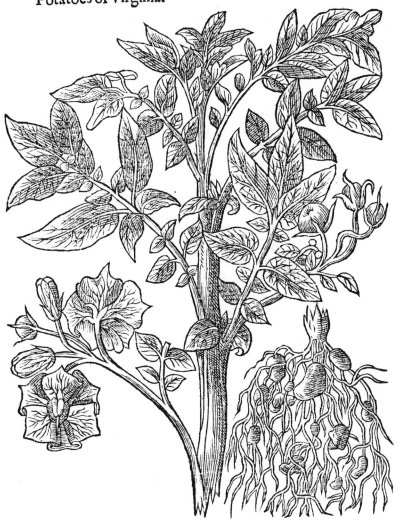

19. 'Battata Virginiana'. Woodcut from Gerard: *The herball*, p. 781 (part), 1597. 6·2 × 4·1". *Solanum tuberosum* L. Potato.

lished an account of a further excursion into Kent and to this record, as to the previous account of 1629, he added an enumeration of Hampstead plants.[1] Thus, by the time the new edition of the *Herball* was published Johnson was already a botanical writer of some note. But while Johnson was employed on the *Herball* John Parkinson, another apothecary and the author in 1629

[1] *Descriptio itineris plantarum investigationis ergo suscepti, in agrum cantianum anno Dom. 1632. Et enumeratio plantatum in Ericeto hampstediano locisque vicinis crescentium, etc. 1632.*

of a famous book for the gardener and florist entitled *Paradisi in sole Paradisus terrestris*, was known to be busy on a new project 'the which', wrote Johnson in the address to the reader in his work of 1633, 'I thinke by this time is fit for the presse'. And indeed his surmise was correct, as on 3 March 1634 [i.e. 1635] the printer Richard Cotes entered in the Register of the Company of Stationers of London a book by John Parkinson 'called Theatrum botanicum or an herball of a large extent'.[1] This then must have been the chief reason for the hurry to get the new edition of Gerard's work published, and it is not difficult to imagine Parkinson's disappointment when this new edition of Gerard's popular *Herball* was issued. It was now of little use to produce a second similar publication and it was 1640 before the *Theatrum botanicum* finally made its appearance.

Notwithstanding the short time at his disposal Johnson produced an edition that was noteworthy for its many corrections, improvements, and additions.[2] In the main it consists of the original work with Johnson's alterations and improvements, if of considerable extent, marked with an obelisk, and with additions and rewritten passages marked with a double obelisk: an arrangement as pointed out by Trimen and Dyer of great convenience to the user of the book.[3] As in the case of the *Herball* of 1597 most of the wood-blocks for the illustrations were obtained 'from beyond the seas'.[4] They had been used previously at Antwerp by Plantin for the works of de l'Obel, Dodoens, and de l'Écluse.[5] A number of illustrations were drawn by Johnson himself,[6] including the stalk and fruit of the plantain or banana tree (*Musa* var.) which he had received from Dr. Argent. Of this Johnson wrote: 'I have given you the figure of the whole branch, with the fruit thereon, which I drew as soone as I received it.'[7] The figures of 'Water purslane' (*Peplis portula*) and 'Creeping water chickweed' (apparently a *Callitriche*)[8] had appeared earlier in Johnson's description of his Kentish excursion of 1632.[9] Another figure, that of 'the saxifrage of the ancients', was drawn by the botanist John Goodyer from an old manuscript.[10]

The *Herball* of 1633 has a title-page by John Payne (d. about 1640), an engraver chiefly of portraits and frontispieces. This line engraving consists of a façade divided horizontally into three. In these divisions are depicted Ceres

[1] *A transcript etc.* **4**, 333 (1877).

[2] In his preface to the reader Johnson apologized for 'any defects' in his work, ascribed in part to his 'haste and many businesses'. For examples of some of these see Raven (C. E.), *English naturalists from Neckam to Ray*, etc. 284–5 (1947).

[3] Trimen (H.) and Dyer (W. T. T.), *Flora of Middlesex*, etc. 371 (1869).

[4] *The herball*, etc. 1630 (1633).

[5] Ibid. See Johnson's preface.

[6] For details of some of Johnson's figures see

Kew (H. W.) and Powell (H. E.), *Thomas Johnson botanist and royalist*, 57–61 (1932).

[7] *The herball*, etc. 1515 (1633).

[8] Hanbury (F. J.) and Marshall (E. S.), *Flora of Kent*, etc. 152, 153 (1899).

[9] See *The herball*, p. 614, figs. 11 and 12 and the work of 1632, figs. 4 and 5. See also figs. 9 and 10 on p. 1570 of *The herball*. These were printed from the blocks used originally for figs. 1/2, and 3 in the work of 1632.

[10] *The herball*, etc. 604 (1633).

and Pomona, Theophrastus and Dioscorides, and in the lower division a portrait of Gerard holding a spray of potato foliage with flower and berry. On either side of this portrait is a vase containing flowers. In the centre of the flowers in the vase on the left is a bunch of bananas. On 10 April 1633 Johnson's friend Dr. Argent, then President of the College of Physicians of London, gave him the stalk and fruit from a banana plant which he had received from the Bermudas. Johnson hung up this stalk with the fruit still green in his shop where the fruit 'became ripe about the beginning of May,

Musæ fructus exactior Icon.
An exacter figure of the Plantaine fruit.

20. Thomas Johnson's edition, 1633, of Gerard's *Herball.* Woodcut made from a drawing by Johnson of the bunch of bananas which he hung up in his shop, p. 1516 (part). 5·7 × 4·6″.

Ceres

Pomona

Ecce dedi vobis omnes herbas sementantes semen, quæ sunt Gen. 1. 29.

Excideret ne tibi diuini muneris Author,
Præsentem monstrat quælibet herba Deum.

THE
HERBALL
OR GENERALL
Historie of
Plantes.

Gathered by John Gerarde
of London Master in
CHIRVRGERIE

Very much
Enlarged and Amended by
Thomas Johnson
Citizen and Apothecarye
of
LONDON

THEOPHRASTVS

DIOSCORIDES

London Printed by
Adam Islip Ioice Norton
and Richard Whitakers
Anno 1633.

Io: Payne sculps:

and lasted until June'.[1] Payne commemorated the gift by including a bunch of bananas in his engraving.

Johnson's dedication addressed to the Society of Apothecaries, but particularly to Richard Edwards, the Master, and Edward Cooke and Leonard Stone, the Wardens, is followed by the preliminary matter printed in the work of 1597.[2] Next comes Johnson's preface, dated 'From my house on Snow-hill, Octob. 22. 1633', with a history of botany from Solomon to Parkinson, a scholarly work which has the distinction of being the first survey on the subject to be published in England, Johnson's account of Gerard's work of 1597, some details of which have been noted earlier, a description of what Johnson performed in his own edition, and finally an acknowledgement of the help that he had received from his friends. The most important of these helpers was John Goodyer, whose reputation as a first-class botanist has been established in recent years by the late R. W. T. Gunther.[3] From Goodyer Johnson received 'many accurate descriptions, and some other observations concerning plants'. Goodyer's descriptions are easily distinguished from the rest as they are inserted as signed paragraphs.[4]

Gerard's *Herball*, especially the edition emended by Johnson, remained popular for many years. Even during the second half of the eighteenth century it was still used by students of botany. Among the latter who went to its pages for assistance was the noted London physician John Coakley Lettsom[5] and the great patron of natural science Sir Joseph Banks.[6] The popularity of this herbal extended into the nineteenth century and, in 1806, Richard Weston, the agricultural and horticultural writer, referred to Johnson's edition of the *Herball* as follows:[7] 'At this day the book is held in high esteem, particularly by those who are fond of searching into the medicinal virtues of plants. Its usual price is three guineas, being very scarce;[8] the other two.'[9] A study of booksellers' catalogues offering books for sale, as well as catalogues of books sold at public auctions, reveals that copies of Gerard's *Herball* of 1597, and the edition 'enlarged and amended' by Thomas Johnson, became more and more expensive as the years went by. Moreover, on account of its greater rarity the first edition became proportionately dearer than Johnson's edition. For example on 17 November 1902 a copy

---

[1] *The herball*, etc. 1515-16 (1633).

[2] Except for two lots of commendatory verses which have been omitted.

[3] Gunther (R. W. T.), *Early British botanists and their gardens*, etc. 1-232 (1922), Oxford.

[4] e.g. p. 871, see under 'Bryonia nigra florens non fructum ferens' (Black bryony, *Tamus communis* L.).

[5] See Abraham (J. J.), *Lettsom his life, times, friends and descendants*, 23 (1933).

[6] See Cameron (H. C.), *Sir Joseph Banks*, etc. 2, 298 (1952).

[7] Weston (R.), A review of the principal authors on horticulture and botany, from 1480 to 1750, etc., *Gent. Mag.* **76**, Pt. 2, p. 998 (1806).

[8] Copies of Johnson's edition (1633) of Gerard's *Herball* cost originally 42s. 6d. unbound, and 48s. bound. See Johnson (F. R.), Notes on English retail book-prices, 1550-1640, *The Library*, Series V, vol. **5**, p. 102 (1950) (*Trans. bibl. Soc.*, Series III, vol. 5).

[9] 'The other' refers presumably to *The herball* of 1597.

◁ 21. Thomas Johnson's edition, 1633, of Gerard's *Herball*. Title-page engraved by John Payne. 12·7 × 7·9".

of Johnson's work of 1633 was sold at Messrs. Sotheby for £15 and on 19 April 1904 the same firm sold a copy of the 1597 edition for £48. On 22 April 1970 a copy of the 1597 *Herball* was sold at Messrs. Christie, Manson and Woods for £480.

Helianthemum album Germanicum. The white dwarfe Ciſtus of Germanie.

22. 'Helianthemum album Germanicum'. Woodcut on p. 1283 (part) of Thomas Johnson's edition, 1633, of Gerard's *Herball*. 3·3 × 5·2″. *Helianthemum apenninum* (L.) Miller, Apennine Sunrose.

II

GARDENING BOOKS

DURING the Middle Ages the garden attached to a house was chiefly used for the cultivation of vegetables, including herbs for culinary purposes, fruit, and medicinal plants. Flowers were grown for their practical use rather than for their beauty, and it was not until the increasing security and wealth of the reign of Elizabeth I that separate gardens were planned 'solely for beauty and pleasure'.[1]

The cultivation of fruit trees was an important part of the horticulture of the fifteenth and sixteenth centuries, and a knowledge of grafting was essential to a good gardener. Fitzherbert wrote in 1523:[2] 'It is necessarie, profitable, and also a pleasure to a husbande to have peeres, wardens, and apples of dyvers sortes. And also cheres, fylberdes, bullas, dampsons, plummes, walnuttes, and suche other. And therfore it is convenyent to lerne howe thou shalt graffe.' The first work printed in England of purely gardening interest, known to the present writer, is on grafting. This is an anonymous treatise in the British Museum (Bloomsbury), entitled *The crafte of graffynge ז plantynge of trees*. Unfortunately this copy is incomplete, lacking all after leaf A4. It contains neither imprint nor date. It came from the press of Wynkyn de Worde and is considered to have been published about 1520.[3] The woodcut on the title-page depicts two men with axes, one in the process of cutting down a tree growing in a little plantation. About 1563 and 1565 respectively, two later editions of the work appeared from the press of William Copland. This printer's predecessor, Robert Copland (died *c.* 1548), had been for many years an assistant to Wynkyn de Worde. When this treatise is compared with a manuscript in the British Museum (Bloomsbury), 'Tractatus Godfridi super Palladium',[4] it appears that Wynkyn de Worde's publication is derived from part of a work by Palladius, that is Rutilius Taurus Aemilianus Palladius who lived some time in the fourth century,[5] and wrote a treatise *De re rustica* in fourteen books, the last being a poem in

---

[1] Crisp (Sir Frank), *Mediaeval gardens . . . Edited by . . . C. C. Paterson*, etc. 1, 45 (1924).

[2] [*Book of husbandry*] Here begynneth a newe tracte or treatyse moost profytable for all husbande men, etc. (The boke of husbandrie) [Formerly attributed to Sir Anthony, but really by John Fitzherbert], h1 ᵃ⁻ᵇ [1523].

[3] See below, Bibliography, under Craft [1563?] 4°, footnote.

[4] Sloane MS. 686, ff. 19–39ᵇ.

[5] Smith (Sir W.), *A classical dictionary of Greek and Roman biography . . . Revised . . . by G. E. Marindin*, 644 (1904).

23. *The crafte of graffynge ₁ plantynge of trees* [1520?], printed by Wynkyn de Worde. Title-page. 5·6 × 4·3″.

eighty-five elegiac couplets upon the art of grafting. Amherst considered Palladius' treatise to be the foundation of nearly all English writings on husbandry for several centuries, and that most of these writings were only translations or adaptations of the original work.[1]

Wynkyn de Worde liked issuing 'small popular books of a kind to attract the general public',[2] and his *Crafte of graffynge ₁ plantynge of trees*, with its

[1] Amherst afterwards Cecil (A. M. T.), *A history of gardening in England . . . Third . . . edition*, 59 (1910).

[2] Duff (E. G.), *The printers, stationers and bookbinders of Westminster and London from 1476 to 1535*, p. 24 (1906), Cambridge.

GARDENING BOOKS

57

ignorant medieval gardening beliefs, was printed in at least three editions. As already stated, the only copy of Wynkyn de Worde's edition (*c.* 1520) known to the present writer lacks all after leaf A4. At the end of the two William Copland editions (1563? and 1565?) comes 'a lyttle treatyse of the .iiii. seasons of the yeare, and also of the .iiii. elementes', followed by a section headed 'The fourme and the measure to mete land by'. The contents of this book as printed by Copland had already appeared in 'Arnold's chronicle',[1] a folio volume first printed at Antwerp about 1503, and again by Peter Treveris in Southwark in 1521.

The earliest English book on general gardening is a small treatise by Thomas Hill, a citizen of London and the author of many popular works on science. According to a list of his printed and projected works appended to his treatise *The proffitable arte of gardening* (1568),[2] he wrote on such diverse subjects as physiognomy, gardening, dreams, astronomy, astrology, bee-keeping, and palmistry. His information was chiefly derived from other men's works; he contributed few original ideas of his own. However, as remarked by Wright,[3] he 'managed to pack into his treatises both curious learning and practical help, and thereby insured the widest popularity for his books'.

Hill's first work on gardening appeared under the title of *A most briefe and pleasaunte treatise, teachyng how to dresse, sowe, and set a garden*. It is undated, but it was probably published sometime between 1557 and 1559, the most likely year being 1558.[4] This little book, published by Hill himself and printed by John Day, consists of advice on gardening matters gathered by Hill from works written by 'Palladius, Columella, Varro, Ruellius, Dyophanes, learned Cato, and others manye moe'. In his address to 'Master Thomas Counstable esquyre', Hill writes of having been moved 'to put in printe this my second enterprise'. His first publication, which is a translation from a treatise by Bartholomaeus Cocles, appeared in 1556 under the title of *A brief and most pleasaūt epitomye of the whole art of phisiognomie*.

The title-page of Hill's treatise on gardening contains a woodcut of a small formal garden of the period. This figure was copied and used not only in later gardening books, but also as a tailpiece to the tract entitled *The coppie of a letter sent into England by a gentleman, from . . . Saint Denis in France* (1590). To the Elizabethan, the flower garden was of great importance and it was designed as a setting to the house. The most usual shape was square, because, as Parkinson said,[5] the 'four square forme . . . doth best agree to

---

[1] 'Arnold's chronicle' is the title commonly given to a compilation by Richard Arnold (d. 1521?), a citizen of London. It consists of a wide variety of topics which the compiler evidently recorded in a commonplace book.

[2] See dd4–dd7.

[3] Wright (L. B.), *Middle-class culture in Eliza-*bethan England, 568 (1935), University of North Carolina Press: Chapel Hill.

[4] See Henrey (B.), The earliest English gardening book, *J. Soc. Bibl. nat. Hist.* 2, 386 (1952).

[5] Parkinson (J.), *Paradisi in sole*, etc. 3 (1629).

A MOST BRIEFE
and pleasaunt treatyse, teachynge
howe to dresse, sowe, and set a Garden,
and what propertyes also these fewe her
bes heare spoken of, haue to our commo-
dytie: With the remedyes that may be
vsed against such beasts, wormes, flies
and such lyke, that commonly noy
gardes, gathered out of the prin
cipallest Authors in this art
by Thomas Hyll
Londyner.

24. Thomas Hill: *A most briefe and pleasaunt treatyse*, 1563.
Title-page of second edition. 4·6 × 2·8″.

any mans dwelling'. There was generally a terrace along the front of the house from which the garden, which was laid out with the utmost formality, could be surveyed. The latter was surrounded by a high wall or hedge or, as is shown in Hill's little cut, a paling. Within such an enclosure were wide walks ('forthrights'), narrow paths, mounts from which 'to look abroad',[1] arbours in which to sit, mazes 'to sporte . . . in at tymes',[2] and knots or flower-beds laid out in curious and complicated designs. Hill's work contains illustrations of two designs for mazes.[3] In a plan of the great parterre of the Château de Gaillon in France, designed by the French architect Jacques Androuet du Cerceau (d. 1592),[4] two similar mazes are depicted; it is pos-

[1] Bacon (Sir F.), essay 'Of gardens'.
[2] Hill (T.), *The proffitable arte of gardening*, etc., fol. 11ᵃ (1568).
[3] The work is illustrated with three woodcuts of mazes, two of which, however, are the same.

[4] Androuet du Cerceau (J.), *Le premier volume des plus excellents bastiments de France*, etc. (1576), Paris. See first plan in section on 'Gaillon'.

sible, as suggested by Rohde,[1] that both Hill and du Cerceau obtained inspiration from the same source.

A copy of Hill's gardening book is in the University Library, Glasgow,[2]
and a later edition, also entitled *A most briefe and pleasaunt treatyse*, is in the
British Museum (Bloomsbury).[3] In the dedication, 'once againe' addressed
to Thomas Counstable, Hill refers to this edition as 'my seconde enterprise
newly encreased'. This edition contains various alterations and additions and
a conclusion that is dated 'Anno. 1563. Mense Martii'.[4] It came from the
press of Thomas Marshe, and is not so well produced as the earlier work.
It has been referred to by many bibliographers and modern authors, and a
description together with a copy of the title-page will be found in *The old
English gardening books* by Eleanour Sinclair Rohde.[5]

The work was further enlarged in 1568 when the title was changed to *The
proffitable arte of gardening, now the third tyme set fourth.* The illustrations

25. Thomas Hill: *The proffitable arte of gardening*, 1568.
Portrait of Hill on the verso of the title-page to the appended
treatise entitled 'A pleasant instruction of the parfit orderinge
of bees. 2·7 × 2·2".

[1] Rohde (E. S.), *The old English gardening
books*, 14 (1924).

[2] Pressmark Af–e.58.

[3] Pressmark C.54.a.24. (This copy lacks leaf
B4.)

[4] The title-page and colophon are undated.
In the list headed 'The bookes and treatises, all
readie printed' in Hill's *The proffitable arte of*
gardening (1568) this edition appeared as follows
under item 4: 'A briefe treatyse of gardeninge
teaching the apt dressing, sowinge, and setting
of a garden . . . encreased by me yᵉ seconde
tyme, ı imprinted by Thomas Marsh. Anno.
1563'.

[5] pp. 10–14 (1924) and plate 1.

include a portrait of the author at the age of twenty-eight,[1] which appears in no other edition of this treatise known to the present writer.

Editions of Hill's popular treatise continued to be published until the beginning of the seventeenth century, and it may be noted that a section headed 'The booke of the art or craft of planting and graffing' in the edition of 1572, and in later editions, is only a version with alterations and omissions of the work already mentioned on trees, published about 1520 by Wynkyn de Worde.[2]

In 1577 appeared *The gardeners labyrinth*, Hill's second gardening book. This was published under the pseudonym of Didymus Mountain.[3] Hill had probably been occupied in writing this treatise at the time of his death, which appears to have taken place some time between 1572 and 1575.[4] At his request it was completed after his death by his friend Henry Dethick.[5] This was Henry Dethick, B.D., LL.B. (d. 1613?), Chancellor of the diocese of Carlisle, and the third son of Sir Gilbert Dethick, Garter King-of-Arms. In the dedication, addressed by Dethick to Lord Burghley, Lord High Treasurer of England, the editor appears to have been somewhat embarrassed with his commitment 'to performe the perfecting of this Englishe treatise' with its 'vulgare stile'. However, he evidently considered the work had value, for he adds: 'worthy were I to be deemed undutyfull, and altogether ungratefull, if that I shoulde omit any oportunitie, whereby I myght encrease so rare a commoditye to my country.'

The gardeners labyrinth came from the press of Henry Bynneman, one of the most outstanding printers of the Elizabethan period whose work was commended by that great bibliophile Matthew Parker (1504–75), Archbishop of Canterbury, who did so much to encourage the printers of his day to produce fine well-printed books.[6]

Hill's posthumous treatise is the better of his two works on gardening. As in the earlier publication, it is chiefly a compilation being gathered 'out of the best approved writers of gardening, husbandrie, and physicke'. It gives the reader an excellent idea of the management and contents of a small garden in the days of Queen Elizabeth I. The illustrations depicting Tudor gardens and their occupants busily at work, dressed in the costumes of the day, are delightful. Especially charming is the woodcut on the title-page of

[1] See verso of the title-page to the annexed treatise: *A pleasaunt instruction of the parfit orderinge of bees*, etc.

[2] See above, p. 55.

[3] Didymus, i.e. Thomas, cf. St. John 11: 16: 'Thomas, which is called Didymus'. Regarding the real name of the author see below, Bibliography, under Mountain (Didymus) pseud. [i.e. Thomas Hill], 1577, 4°.

[4] Johnson (F. R.), Thomas Hill: an Eliza-

bethan Huxley, *Huntington Library Quarterly*, No. 4, p. 332 (Aug. 1944), San Marino, California.

[5] Mountain (Didymus), *The gardeners labyrinth*, etc. (1577) (Dedication).

[6] See Plomer (H. R.), Great Britain and Ireland, in *Printing, a short history of the art . . . edited by R. A. Peddie*, 185, etc. (1927), and Plomer (H. R.), *A short history of English printing 1476–1900*, pp. 67–8 (1915).

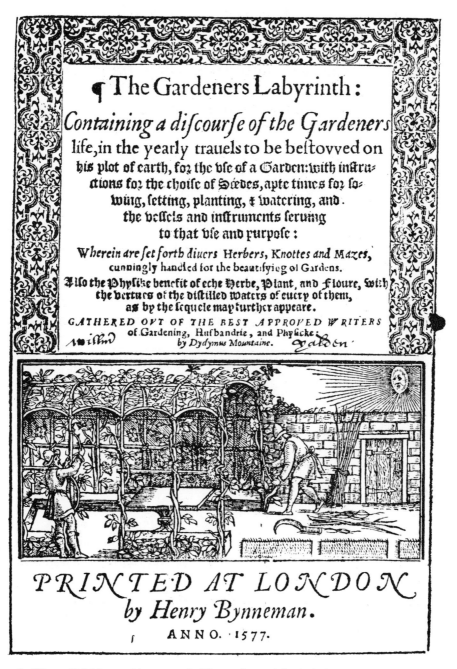

The Gardeners Labyrinth:

Containing a discourse of the Gardeners life, in the yearly trauels to be beſtowed on his plot of earth, foɀ the vſe of a Garden: with inſtruactions foɀ the choiſe of Seedes, apte times foɀ ſowüng, ſetting, planting, ⁊ watering, and the veſſels and inſtruments ſeruing to that vſe and purpoſe:

Wherein are ſet forth diuers *Herbers, Knottes and* Maɀes, cunningly handled foɀ the beautifyiog of Gardens.

Alſo the Phyſike benefit of eche Herbe, Plant, and floure, with the vertues of the diſtilled waters of euery of them, aɀ by the ſequele may further appeare.

GATHERED OVT OF THE BEST APPROVED WRITERS of Gardening, Huſbandrie, and Phyſicke: by *Dydymus Mountaine.*

PRINTED AT LONDON by Henry Bynneman. ANNO · 1577·

26. The well-laid-out title-page of *The gardeners labyrinth*, by Didymus Mountain [i.e. Thomas Hill], 1577, printed by Henry Bynneman. 6·6 × 4·5″.

'The second part of The gardeners labyrinth',[1] showing three people sitting on seats round a table in a garden, with a fence in the background covered

[1] This woodcut appears only in *The gardeners labyrinth* of 1577 and 1578.

The second part of the Gardeners Labyrinth, vttering suche skilfull experiences and worthy secretes, about the particular sowing and remouyng of the most Kitchin Hearbes, with the wittie ozdering of other dayntie Hearbes, delectable floures, pleasant fruites, and fyne rootes, as the like hath not heeretofoze bin vttered of any. Besides the Phisicke benefites of each Herbe annexed, with the commoditie of waters diftilled out of them, ryghte neceffarye to be knowen.

27. 'The second part of The gardeners labyrinth', 1577. Title-page. 6·5 × 4·4″.

by a profusely blooming plant. This cut is signed with the monogram *A*. The artist may have been foreign, and he appears to have obtained inspiration from an illustration in a work published by Jan Steelsius of Antwerp in 1553,[1] illustrated with woodcuts by Arnold Nicolai.[2] This is a translation

[1] *El cavallero determinado traduzido de lengua francesa en Castellana por Don Hernando de Acuña*, etc. (1553), Anvers. See woodcut on recto of folio 21 (i.e. F1ª).

[2] Delen (A. J. J.), *Histoire de la gravure dans les anciens Pays-Bas et dans les provinces belges . . . Deuxième partie. Le XVIᵉ siècle. Les graveurs-illustrateurs*, 93 (1934).

of the French *Le chevalier délibéré* by Olivier de la Marche. Although the monogram on the cut in the English work resembles that of Nicolai, neither Monsieur A. J. J. Delen, nor Dr. Vervliet, formerly Deputy Curator of the Museum Plantin-Moretus, considers that Nicolai was responsible for the English woodcut.[1] Arnold Nicolai who had a workshop in the Lombaarden-veste at Antwerp, was active as an engraver during much of the second half of the sixteenth century. He worked not only for Plantin, but for the majority of the Antwerp printers of the period. Moreover he was responsible for woodcuts in several books printed in England during the reign of Queen Elizabeth I.[2] The popularity of his woodcuts led to their being frequently copied by other artists.

The other illustrations in *The gardeners labyrinth* include a copy of the woodcut of the small formal garden, and the two designs for mazes, found in Hill's *Most briefe and pleasaunte treatise*, also a design for a knot which appeared in *The proffitable arte of gardening*. The intricacy of the latter figure gives rise to the question as to whether it could have been worked out in a garden. It resembles rather a design suitable for use in embroidery. The custom of making use of the same figure for more than one production, or even using it again in the same book, was a common practice among printers of the period.[3] Woodcuts increased the cost of a publication very substantially and Johnson found, during his study of the retail prices of books, that the average illustrated book published in England between 1550 and 1640 'was priced 75 to 100 per cent higher than other books of the same number of sheets'.[4]

A small quarto printed by Henry Bynneman for John Wight appeared about 1569 under the title of *A booke of the art and maner, howe to plante and graffe all sortes of trees, how to set stones, and sow pepynes to make wylde trees to graffe on . . . With diverse other newe practises, by one of the abbey of S. Vincent in Fraunce. With an addition . . . of certayne Dutche practises, sette forth and Englished, by Leonarde Mascal*. The greater part of the book is a translation of Davy Brossard's *L'Art & maniere de semer, ʒ faire pepinieres des sauvageaux*, a work published in France in a number of editions during the sixteenth and seventeenth centuries.[5] Brossard, a Benedictine monk at the

[1] In epist. 16.i.50.

[2] See Clair (C.), The myth of 'Anton Sylvius'. *Gutenberg-Jahrbuch*, pp. 122–7 (1963).

[3] McKerrow (R. B.), Booksellers, printers, and the stationers' trade, in *Shakespeare's England*, etc. 2, 232 (1916), Oxford.

[4] Johnson (F. R.), Notes on English retail book-prices, 1550–1640, *The Library*, Series V, vol. 5, 90 (1950) (*Trans. bibl. Soc.*, Series III, vol. 5).

[5] The earliest edition of Brossard's work, known to the present writer, is in the library of the Bureau of Plant Industry, U.S.A. Dept. of Agriculture. The colophon of this copy is dated: 'Lyon le xxviij. de. Mars. Mil. ccccc. xliij'. See Warner (M. F.), Early horticultural literature, etc., U.S.A. Dept. of Agriculture, Bureau of Plant Industry (1939) (a typescript copy of this unpublished work is in the Lindley Library, Royal Horticultural Society).

abbey of Saint-Vincent near Le Mans, who lived during the second half of
the sixteenth century, was a skilful horticulturist, and in describing this
author's treatise Gibault writes:[1] 'Chose étonnante pour l'époque, le bref
traité de Brossard est exempt des préjugés sur les lunaisons; l'auteur s'est
encore contenté de donner au public les résultats de son expérience person-
nelle au lieu de ressasser les méthodes de culture des anciens.' The English
translation proved extremely popular and it appeared in many editions.
Comparatively little is known of the translator, Leonard Mascall (d. 1589),
who was the owner of a mansion called Plumpton Place, a few miles north-
west of Lewes, in Sussex.[2] He became clerk of the kitchen in the household
of Matthew Parker, Archbishop of Canterbury. It is said that in 1525
Mascall introduced pippin apples into England and established an orchard
at his home in Sussex.[3] An earlier introduction of pippins, however, was made
about 1500, when 'Robert [sic] Harris, fruiterer to King Henry VIII, "fetched
out of France a great store of grafts, especially pippins, before which there
were no pippins in England"'.[4] Apart from the above treatise on fruit trees,
Mascall was the author of works on fishing, poultry, cattle, and various other
subjects.

An entirely original work and the first to be written expressly on the culture
of hops in England is *A perfite platforme of a hoppe garden*, published in
1574. The author, Reginald (or Reynolde) Scot (1538?–99), was the second
son of Sir John Scot of Scots Hall in Smeeth, Kent. He went to Oxford when
he was about seventeen and studied at Hart Hall,[5] but he appears to have
left the University without a degree. He married in 1568 and afterwards
seems to have spent the rest of his life in Kent, where he inherited property
around Smeeth and Brabourne. Ten years after his treatise on hops, Scot
published a work entitled *The discoverie of witchcraft*. This also showed him
to be an author of great enlightenment, and the views contained in it attracted
widespread attention.

Scot wrote his treatise of 1574, 'concerning the making and mayntenance of
an hoppe garden',[6] from his own practical experience[7] and, according to a
twentieth-century authority,[8] in many respects 'the information is as useful
today as it was nearly three-and-a-half centuries ago when it was published'.
A year earlier particulars regarding the growing of this plant in England were
given by Thomas Tusser (1524?–80) in his well-known *Five hundred pointes*

[1] Gibault (G.), Étude sur la bibliographie et la littérature horticoles anciennes: *Journ. de la Soc. natn. d'Hort. de France, Série IV, tome, 6,* 726 (1905), Paris.
[2] Horsfield (T. W.), *The history, antiquities, and topography of the county of Sussex,* 1, 230 (1835).
[3] See Horsfield (T. W.), op. cit. 1, 231 (1835).
[4] Taylor (H. V.), *The apples of England,* 32 (1936). See also F. (N.), *The fruiterers secrets,* etc. (1604) (Epistle to the reader).
[5] Now Hertford College.
[6] Scot (R.), *A perfite platforme of a hoppe garden,* etc. 53 (1574).
[7] Ibid. 53.
[8] Clinch (G.), *English hops, a history of cultivation and preparation for the market from the earliest times,* 70 (1919).

If you laye softe græne Rushes abroade in the dewe and the Sunne, within twoo oz thræ dayes, they will be lythie, tough, and handsome foz this purpose of tying, which may not be foze=

slowed, foz it is most certaine that the Hoppe that lyeth long vpon the grounde befoze he be tyed to the Poale, pzospereth nothing so wel as it, which sooner attayneth therevnto.

(a)

It shall not be amisse nowe and then to passe thzough your Garden, hauing in eche hande a fozked wande, directing aright such Hoppes as

declyne from the Poales, but some in steade of the sayde fozked wandes, vse to stande vppon a stoole, and doe it with their handes.

(b)

Then you may with the fozked ende, thzust vp, oz shoue off, all such stalkes as remayne vpon eche Hoppe Poale, and carie them to the floze pzepared foz that purpose.

The best and readyest way to take the Hoppes from the Poales.

Foz the better dooing hereof, it is very necessa= rie that your Poales be streyght without scrags oz knobbes.

28. Scot: *A perfite platforme of a hoppe garden*, 1574. (a) Tying hops. 3·4 × 3·3″, p. 23 (part). (b) Training hops. 3·5 × 3·3″, p. 27 (part). (c) Stripping hops from the poles. 3·7 × 4·1″, p. 30 (part).

(c)

of good husbandrie (1573). At the time of these two writers interest in the growing of this plant in England was still comparatively new, as hops were not cultivated in this country until 1524 when they were introduced from Flanders.[1] Scot condemned the importation of hops from abroad by pointing out that they could be had 'at home with more ease and lesse charge'.[2] A few years later John Houghton also complained of the importation of hops and recorded that 'in the year 1694,5' London alone received 510 hundred-weight from Flanders and Holland, at a total cost of about £3,570.[3]

Scot's *Perfite platforme of a hoppe garden* is illustrated with clear cuts showing the various stages necessary in the cultivation of this plant. It came from the press of Henry Denham who worked in London from 1560 to 1589. This printer was noted for the excellency of his work, and as pointed out by Plomer,[4] he printed 'with his usual care' the three known editions of Scot's treatise.

After the dedication and preface is a printer's notice from which the following passage is quoted. It is of interest as giving us evidence of the not unusual custom in Elizabethan times for an author to attend in person at the printing-house in order to revise proofs:[5]

Forasmuch, as M. Scot could not be present at the printing of this his booke, whereby I might have used his advise in the correction of the same, and especiallye of the figures and portratures contayned therein, whereof he delivered unto me such notes as I being unskilfull in the matter, could not so throughly conceyve, nor so perfectly expresse, as the expectation of him being the author, or of you being the reader, might be in all poyntes satisfied.

In 1591 was published *A short instruction veric* [sic] *profitable and necessarie for all those that delight in gardening, to know the time and season when it is good to sow and replant all maner of seedes . . . Translated out of French into English*. The imprint on the title-page reads: 'London printed by John Wolfe, and are to bee sold at his shop over against the great south dore of Saint Paule'. The work was printed again by John Wolfe, in 1592.[6] Unfortunately, no copy of the earlier book appears to exist in this country. It consists of thirty-five brief instructions on when to sow seeds, and a number of pages of woodcuts. These woodcuts include illustrations of Elizabethan gardens, men grafting, and designs for knots and mazes. Several of these figures are found

[1] Houghton (J.), *A collection for the improvement of husbandry and trade . . . revised . . . by Richard Bradley*, **2**, 457 (1727).

[2] Scot (R.), op. cit. 54 (1574).

[3] Houghton (J.), op. cit. **2**, 458.

[4] Plomer (H. R.), Henry Denham, printer, *The Library*, new series, vol. **10**, 248 (1909).

[5] See McKerrow (R. B.), *An introduction to bibliography*, 205–8 (1928).

[6] A copy of the work of 1592 is in the Brit. Mus. (Bloomsbury), pressmark C.122.d.7. It was acquired by the Museum in 1950 and was previously in the possession of the Marquess of Crewe. In 1924 Eleanour Sinclair Rohde referred to it as the 'only known copy'. See Rohde (E. S.), *The old English gardening books*, 118 (1924).

A

Short inftruction very profitable and

necceffary, for al thofe that delight in gardening,
to know the time and feafon when it is
good to fow and replant all manner of Seedes.

Whereunto is annexed diuers plots both for planting and grafting, for the better eafe of
the Gardener.

Tranflated out of french into English.

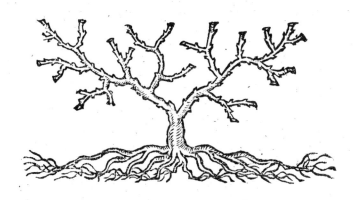

LONDON
Printed by Iohn Wolfe, and are to be fold at his fhop
ouer againft the great South doore of
Paules.   1 5 9 2.

29. *A short instruction . . . in gardening*, 1592. Title-page.
5·9 × 3·5″.

in earlier publications, notably Thomas Hill's *Most briefe and pleasaunte treatise, The proffitable arte of gardening*, and *The gardeners labyrinth*.

On looking back over the various herbals and gardening books so far considered, we cannot fail to be impressed by the lack of originality of many of the illustrations. The same woodcuts often did service for several different publications. And, moreover, they were frequently copied from books published abroad, or made from wood-blocks borrowed from foreign presses.

This reprinting from old cuts and the copying and borrowing of foreign work was practised by printers throughout Europe. Examples of the most interesting illustrations in these sixteenth-century English works include the title-page of *The grete herball* (1526), the engraved title-plates of Pena and de l'Obel's *Stirpium adversaria nova* (1570–1), and of Gerard's *Herball* (1597). The last of these books contains the fine engraved portrait of the author, John Gerard. Some of the woodcuts in Thomas Hill's *Gardeners labyrinth* (1577) are outstanding, and so are the excellent cuts in Scot's *Perfite platforme of a hoppe garden* (1574).

John Wolfe's treatise of 1591 was followed in 1594 by *The orchard, and the garden: containing certaine necessarie, secret, and ordinarie knowledges in grafting and gardening*. This book, from the press of Adam Islip, is again only a translation, being 'Gathered from the Dutch and French'.[1] It includes 'A short instruction verie profitable and necessarie for all those that delight in gardening', which is another edition of the treatise mentioned above printed by John Wolfe. Apart from a number of designs for knots, the illustrations are all found previously in the works by Thomas Hill, and in the *Short instruction . . . for all those that delight in gardening* of 1591 and 1592.

In 1599 appeared *Profitable instructions for the manuring, sowing, and planting of kitchin gardens*, a small quarto volume printed by Edward Allde for Edward White. The work was published again in 1603. The author of this useful little treatise, Richard Gardiner (or Gardner),[2] was a burgess of Shrewsbury, Shropshire. By trade he was a dyer, but he was also free of the Company of Drapers, and he appears to have been a man of some position. The dates of his birth and death are not known. Calvert conjectured[3] that Gardiner was born towards the middle of the first half of the sixteenth century, before parish registers were established by law, and that by the time of the appearance of his *Profitable instructions* of 1603, he was probably not far short of seventy.

Gardiner's *Profitable instructions* has the distinction of being the first gardening book devoted entirely to vegetable growing to be published in England. He writes from his own 'practise and experience', and he includes details in his work concerning carrots, cabbages, parsnips, turnips, lettuces, beans, onions, cucumbers, artichokes, and leeks. Gardiner devotes considerable space to carrots, and rebukes the people of this country for not growing more of this vegetable. He points out:[4] 'It is not unknowne to the Citty of

---

[1] *The orchard, and the garden*, etc. (1594) (title-page).

[2] Spelt 'Gardner' on the title-page of the *Profitable instructions* of 1599, and Gardiner on the title-page of the 1603 edition of the work. Sir Hugh Platt in his *Floraes paradise*, 57 (1608) refers to 'Gardiners kitchen-garden, printed 1599'.

[3] Richard Gardiner's 'Profitable instructions', 1603. Edited by Dr. Calvert. *Trans. Shropshire archaeol. nat. Hist. Soc.*, Series II, vol. **4**, 241–2 (1892). A pedigree of the Gardiner family is preserved in the Borough Library, Shrewsbury.

[4] Gardiner (R.), *Profitable instructions*, etc., D2ᵇ–D3ᵃ (1603).

London, and many other townes and cities on the sea coast, what great aboundance of carrets are brought by forraine nations to this lād, whereby they have received yeerely great summes of mony and commodities out of this land.' Potatoes are not mentioned in this tract. This is not surprising, for although earlier in our *History* we mentioned that the potato was included in Gerard's catalogue of 1596 as one of the plants growing in his garden at Holborn,[1] the potato was a rarity and a costly dish for the table until long after the age of Elizabeth I; in fact, as pointed out by Salaman,[2] it still remained a luxury food until after the middle of the seventeenth century.

Gardiner tells his readers that he has for sale 'garden fruits, rootes and seeds . . . at a reasonable price, and perfect good without deceipt'[3] and gives a list of some of his vegetable and seed prices. He is severe in his condemnation of dishonest seedsmen who deceive customers by selling them 'olde and dead seedes for their gardens' and refers to such people with scorn as 'those catterpillers'.[4] At this time not only were frauds practised by gardeners in the author's own county of Shropshire, but the selling of 'dead and corrupt plants, seeds, stockes and trees' was carried out in other parts of the country.[5] To prevent these abuses, King James I, on the petition of the gardeners in the City of London 'and within 6 miles compass thereof', incorporated them by letters patent on 18 September 1605 as 'The Master, Wardens, Assistants, and Commonalty of the Company of Gardeners'.[6] However, deceits and disorders continued to exist and the Company applied to the Crown for further authority. Additional powers were accordingly obtained from James I by letters patent, issued 9 November 1616.[7]

---

[1] See above, p. 39.
[2] Salaman (R. N.), *The history and social influence of the potato*, 445 (1949).
[3] Gardiner (R.), *Profitable instructions*, etc., D3ᵇ–D4ᵃ (1603).
[4] Ibid. B3ᵃ.

[5] Welch (C.), *The history of the Worshipful Company of gardeners*, 22 (1900).
[6] Crosweller (W. T.), *The Gardeners' Company. A short chronological history 1605–1907*, p. 9 (1908).
[7] Ibid. 10.

CONCLUSION

WE have now completed our survey of sixteenth-century English herbals and gardening books. During the first half of this century, comparatively little was published on these two subjects, although, taking into consideration the books printed and their editions, some twenty works at least appeared by 1550. This is quite a high figure when it is remembered that the whole output of the native press during these years was not great, and that the subjects covered were very diverse. According to the headings in Bennett's *English books and readers 1475 to 1557*,[1] those subjects included religion, law, education, medicine, arithmetic, astronomy, popular science, geography, history, and literature. We should note, however, that in spite of this diversity the largest number of works were of a religious nature, the reason suggested being that this subject, apparently in great demand, provided a steady sale on which printers could rely for their main income.[2] With greater literacy, wider interests, and therefore a growing demand for books on the part of the public, printers during the Elizabethan era were encouraged to increase their production of secular reading matter. It was during this period that we noticed a rise in the number of publications which are the concern of this present work.[3] We will now consider some of the ways in which interest in botany and gardening was expressed in England.

During the century large private gardens were laid out, and among the most famous were those at Nonsuch, near Epsom, in Surrey, the Royal retreat built by 'Henry VIII for his pleasure and retirement',[4] and completed after his death by Henry FitzAlan, Earl of Arundel (1512?–80); the gardens at Hampton Court, first planned for Cardinal Wolsey and later improved and enlarged by Henry VIII; and the celebrated garden of William Cecil, Baron Burghley, at Theobalds in Hertfordshire.[5] These are only three outstanding examples; there were other gardens less famous, and as the century wore on gardens increased in importance. In the words of Banister Fletcher,[6] 'Elizabethan mansions were set in a framework of formal gardens in which forecourts, terraces, lakes, fountains, and yew hedges of topiary work

---

[1] See pp. 65–151 (1952).

[2] Bennett (H. S.), op. cit. 65 (1952).

[3] See above, p. 3.

[4] *Paul Hentzner's travels in England, during the reign of Queen Elizabeth, translated by Horace, late Earl of Oxford*, etc. 58–9 (1797). For brief details concerning the history of Nonsuch, from the time of Henry VIII until about 1772, see below, 2, 504 and 510–11.

[5] For further details see Nichols (R. S.), *English pleasure gardens*, Chapters IV and V (1902), New York and London; and Amherst afterwards Cecil (A. M. T.), *A history of gardening in England . . . Third . . . edition*, Chapters V and VI (1910).

[6] Fletcher (Sir B.), *A history of architecture . . . Twelfth edition*, 778 (1945).

combined to make the house and its surroundings one complete and harmonious scheme.'

During this period there were several interesting gardens devoted to the study and cultivation of medicinal herbs, and to plants of botanical value. Edward, Duke of Somerset, had a botanical garden at Sion, or Syon, at Isleworth, in Middlesex,[1] which is mentioned a number of times by William Turner in his work of 1548[2] and also in his herbal of 1568.[3] William Turner, himself, had a garden at Kew,[4] and afterwards a garden at Wells,[5] when he was Dean of the Cathedral. John Gerard, as already noted, published a catalogue of the plants growing in his Holborn garden;[6] and Lord Zouche had a physic garden at Hackney which was under the superintendence of the botanist Matthias de l'Obel. Such private gardens for the cultivation of plants with a view to the furtherance of botanical knowledge set the example for the establishment, in later years, of the well-known botanic gardens at Oxford, Chelsea, and Edinburgh.

The reign of Queen Elizabeth I was the age of navigators and explorers, and many new plants were brought into the country from abroad. Harrison, writing during this period, says:[7]

It is a world also to see how manie strange hearbs, plants, and annuall fruits, are dailie brought unto us from the Indies, Americans, Tabrobane, Canarie iles, and all parts of the world . . . There is not almost one noble man, gentleman, or merchant, that hath not great store of these floures.

A new interest was taken in herbs for industrial purposes. Richard Hakluyt, giving directions to Morgan Hubblethorne, a dyer sent to Persia in 1579, to find new dyes, tells him that he would find anile in Persia,[8] and further suggested to him:[9] 'if you can procure the herbe that it is made of, either by

[1] In 1415 Henry V founded a convent of Bridgetines at Isleworth, giving it the name of Syon. In 1539 this religious house was suppressed by Henry VIII, and the conventual buildings were retained in the possession of the Crown. In the first year of the reign of Edward VI the monastery of Syon was granted to Edward, Duke of Somerset, the Lord Protector, who had already rented some premises at Isleworth under the convent. On or near the site of the monastery the Duke built a fine mansion. He also laid out the grounds and cultivated a botanic garden. On the attainder of the Duke of Somerset for high treason Syon reverted to the Crown. For the last 200 years and earlier, Syon has been the property of the Dukes of Northumberland. For further details concerning the history of Syon House see Aungier (G. J.), *The history and antiquities of Syon monastery, the parish of Isleworth, and the chapelry of Hounslow*, etc. (1840).

[2] Turner (W.), *The names of herbes in Greke, Latin, Englishe Duche z Frenche*, etc., A5ᵃ, E6ᵃ (1548).

[3] Pt. 1, pp. 39, 66, 83, 145.

[4] *Libellus de re herbaria novus, by William Turner . . . reprinted in facsimile with notes . . . and a life of the author, by Benjamin Daydon Jackson*, p. iii (1877).

[5] Pulteney (R.), *Historical and biographical sketches of the progress of botany in England*, etc. 1, 55 (1790).

[6] See above, p. 39.

[7] *Harrison's [W.] description of England in Shakspere's youth . . . Edited . . . by Frederick J. Furnivall*, Part 1. The second book, 325–6 (1877).

[8] Hakluyt (R.), *The principal navigations voyages traffiques and discoveries of the English nation made . . . within the compass of these 1600 years*, etc. 2, 201–3 (1927), London, J. M. Dent.

[9] Ibid. 2, 202–3.

seed or by plant, to cary into England, you may do well to endevour to enrich your country with the same.'

Together with the increased interest in botany and gardening there developed a new desire for knowledge in the kindred art of husbandry. The term husbandry covered such subjects as tillage, or the cultivation of the soil; the care of gardens, orchards, and woods; and the rearing and care of livestock, poultry, bees, and silkworms. Two early works on husbandry, both written from the practical experiences of the authors concerned, attracted a great deal of attention. These are *The boke of husbandry* [1523], formerly attributed to Sir Anthony Fitzherbert, but now considered to be by his elder brother, John;[1] and Thomas Tusser's *A hundreth good pointes of husbandrie* (1557).[2] Both these works ran into many editions, and they both contain useful information for the gardener.

Edmund Spenser and William Shakespeare made many allusions in their works to flowers. Arber considered that the plant names in the poem assigned to 'Aprill', in *The shepheardes calender* (1577), were obtained by Spenser from Lyte's herbal (1578).[3] Shakespeare with his great love of flowers may also have studied its pages, as well as those of Gerard's *Herball* of 1597.

The Tudors took delight, not only in seeing flowers in the garden, but also in using them for domestic purposes. Levinus Lemnius of Zeeland visited England in 1560,[4] and was enchanted by our use of herbs and flowers in the home. He wrote[5]

their chambers ι parlours strawed over with sweete herbes, refreshed mee, their nose-gayes finelye entermingled wyth sondry sortes of fragaunte floures in their bedchābers and privie roomes, with comfortable smell cheered mee up and entierlye delighted all my sences.[6]

---

[1] Clarke (Sir E.), Early books on agriculture, *Trans. bibl. Soc.* 3, 160–2 (1896).

[2] In 1573, and later, editions of this work were entitled *Five hundreth points of good husbandry*, etc.

[3] Arber (A.), Edmund Spenser and Lyte's 'Nievve herball', *Notes and Queries*, 160, 346–7 (1931).

[4] See Rye (W. B.), *England as seen by foreigners in the days of Elizabeth and James the first*, etc. 77 (1865).

[5] Lemnius (L.), *The touchstone of complexions ... now englished by Thomas Newton*, F8ᵃ (1576).

[6] A transcription of this passage is also given by Rye (W. B.), op. cit. 78–9 (1865).

30. *A short instruction . . . in gardening,* 1592. Tail-piece. 2·5 × 2·5″, p. 8 (part).

THE SEVENTEENTH CENTURY

INTRODUCTION

IN the seventeenth century there were roughly five times as many books published in England on botany and horticulture as during the period from Caxton until 1600, and there were at least two treatises on these subjects printed in Scotland, namely: James Sutherland's *Hortus medicus edinburgensis* (1683) and John Reid's *The Scots gard'ner* (1683). Of the total of one hundred or so books published during the whole century,[1] only about eighteen appeared during the reigns of James I (1603–25) and Charles I (1625–49): the years 1640–9, a period that included the Civil War, producing only about three books. From the beginning of the Commonwealth and continuing during the Restoration, the number of books printed rapidly increased.

The botanical and horticultural books published from 1600 to 1700 covered a much wider field than those that appeared in the previous century, and in considering these works it will be convenient to divide and discuss them under the three headings: Herbals; Early scientific and floristic works; Gardening books and works on cultivation.

[1] These figures do not include any of the editions of the various works.

I

HERBALS

THE last of the English herbal writers belonging to the period of the botanical renaissance was John Parkinson (1567–1650), an apothecary of Ludgate Hill,[1] who received the distinction of being appointed apothecary to James I,[2] and to whom Charles I afterwards gave the title of 'Botanicus Regius Primarius'.[3] Like Gerard, Parkinson also owned a famous garden. It was in Long Acre, and both Thomas Johnson and the Hampshire botanist, John Goodyer, gathered seeds from this garden in 1616.[4] The place of Parkinson's birth is not known, but he was buried on 6 August 1650 at St. Martin-in-the-Fields.

Parkinson's name is especially connected with his popular folio volume *Paradisi in sole, paradisus terrestris* of 1629. It is the earliest important treatise on horticulture to be published in this country, and will be discussed later with other gardening books of the seventeenth century. In the present chapter we shall note a few points of interest with regard to this author's herbal, a large folio volume which was referred to in the nineteenth century by the eminent botanist, Sir James Edward Smith, as follows:[5] 'This work and the herbal of Gerarde were the two main pillars of botany in England till the time of Ray, who indeed gave them fresh importance by his continual reference to their contents.'

Parkinson spent 'many yeares' in the preparation of his herbal.[6] We first learn of his intention to undertake such a project in his *Paradisus terrestris*.[7] The *Paradisus* is divided into three parts, namely, the flower garden, the kitchen garden, and the orchard respectively, and the author informs his readers that he hopes to bring out a fourth part to be entitled 'A garden of simples'. In the 1633 edition of Gerard's *Herball* Thomas Johnson refers to Parkinson's statement as follows:[8] 'Mr. John Parkinson an apothecarie of this

[1] In a collection of medical receipts in the Brit. Mus. (Bloomsbury), apparently for the year 1634, we read: 'On yᵉ first of Septemb . . . Mr Parkinson apothecarye on Ludgate hill', etc. (Sloane MS. 660, f. 72).

[2] Pulteney (R.), *Historical and biographical sketches of the progress of botany in England*, etc. 1, 139 (1790).

[3] See Sir Theodore Mayerne's commendatory letter prefixed to Parkinson's *Theatrum botanicum* (1640).

[4] See Gerard (J.), *The herball or generall historie of plantes . . . amended by Thomas Johnson*, 1628 (1633), and Gunther (R. W. T.), *Early British botanists and their gardens*, etc. 16, 140, 141 (1922), Oxford.

[5] Rees (A.), *The cyclopædia*, etc. **26** (1819) (John Parkinson [by Sir J. E. Smith]).

[6] Parkinson (J.), *Theatrum botanicum*, etc. (1640) (Letterpress title-page).

[7] Epistle to the reader.

[8] Johnson's epistle to the reader.

city . . . in the yeare 1629 set forth a worke by the name of "Paradisus terre-stris" . . . He also there promised another worke, the which I thinke by this time is fit for the presse.' Parkinson's herbal was entered by the printer, Richard Cotes, in the Stationers Register on 3 March 1634 (i.e. 1635).[1] How-ever, Johnson's edition (1633) of Gerard's *Herball* was proving so popular that it was published again in 1636, and it seems doubtful if a market could have been found for another expensive folio on the same subject. Parkinson's book finally appeared in 1640, as a much bigger work than had originally been planned, and with a revised title reading *Theatrum botanicum: the theater of plants. Or, an herball of a large extent.* In the opening lines of the epistle to the reader the author makes the following excuse for the delay in publication: 'The disastrous times, but much more wretched and perverse men have so farre prevailed against my intended purpose, and promise, in exhibiting this worke to the publicke view of all; that their extreame covetousnesse had well nigh deprived my country of the fruition.' As suggested by Kew and Powell,[2] it seems likely that the wretched, perverse, and extremely covetous persons alluded to in this passage were the publishers of Gerard's *Herball* and its editions, the Nortons, and their successors.

Parkinson dedicated his herbal—'this manlike worke of herbes and plants'[3] —to Charles I, as he had previously presented the *Paradisus terrestris*—'a feminine of flowers'—to the King's consort, Queen Henrietta Maria. The engraved title-page is executed by William Marshall, who was active as an engraver from about 1617 until 1649. Marshall did much work for the book-sellers of the day and, regarding his output of work, Colvin records:[4] 'In the years of his chief activity we find him often turning out as many as ten or a dozen title-pages and portrait frontispieces in the course of the year.' In the lower half of the title-page of the *Theatrum botanicum* is a half-length portrait of the author within an oval. He is wearing a cap, and holding a flower in his hand. The figures of plants with which the work is illustrated are mostly inferior copies of the woodcuts that appeared in Johnson's edition of Gerard's *Herball*.

The *Theatrum botanicum* is chiefly a compilation from various botanical writings including the unpublished material left by de l'Obel at the time of his death.[5] This had been purchased by Parkinson.[6] Afterwards it came into the hands of William How who published selections from it under the title of

[1] Arber (E.), *A transcript of the registers of the Company of Stationers of London; 1554–1640,* **4,** 333 (1877).

[2] Kew (H. W.) and Powell (H. E.), *Thomas Johnson,* etc. 32, 103 (1932).

[3] Parkinson (J.), *Theatrum botanicum,* etc. (1640) (Dedication).

[4] Colvin (S.), *Early engraving and engravers in England (1545–1695),* etc. 121 (1905).

[5] For a description of the sources of the *Theatrum,* see letter written by John Ray to John Aubrey, dated 8 May 1678, in *Further correspondence of John Ray. Edited by Robert W. T. Gunther,* 162–3 (1928).

[6] Parkinson (J.), *Theatrum botanicum,* etc. 1060 (1640).

31. Parkinson: *Theatrum botanicum: the theater* ▷ *of plants,* 1640. Title-page engraved by William Marshall. 12·4 × 7·7″.

THEATRUM
BOTANICUM,
THE THEATER
OF PLANTES.
OR
An Universall and Compleate
HERBALL.

Composed by John Parkinson
Apothecarye of London, and the
Kings Herbarist.

LONDON.
Printed by Tho: Cotes,
1640.

ADAM.   SOLOMON.

W. Marshall sculpsit

Matthiæ de l'Obel . . . stirpium illustrationes, a work we have already noted.[1] In this book How made a bitter attack on Parkinson, whom he accused of plagiarizing de l'Obel's work. But it has been shown by Raven that the accusation by How had little justification.[2] The *Theatrum botanicum* contains the names of twenty-eight species not previously recorded in Britain,[3] 'including two famous plants—the strawberry tree (*Arbutus unedo*) from "the West part of Ireland", and the lady's slipper orchid (*Cypripedium calceolus*) from Lancashire'.

Up to the time of Parkinson, many of the herbalists were also the leading physicians and apothecaries of the day who were seeking for a wider knowledge of plants for the advancement of medicine. Gradually, however, botany, from 'being one of the handmaids to physick',[4] assumed an independent position, and became a scientific study in its own right, with writings by authors who were botanists in the modern sense rather than herbalists; indeed, the second half of the seventeenth century saw the establishment of botany as a science. At the same time, whilst science in its various branches was progressing, old superstitions still flourished, and a number of works were published in England dealing with the two contemporary pseudo-scientific philosophies, i.e. astrological botany and the doctrine of signatures.[5]

The leading seventeenth-century exponent of astrological botany was the famous Nicholas Culpeper (1616–54), the posthumous son of a clergyman of the same name and a kinsman of the Culpepers of Wakehurst in Sussex.[6] A biography of this 'student in physick and astrologie',[7] published a few years after his death, is found in *Culpeper's school of physick* of 1659. Another biography entitled 'Nicholas Culpeper and his books' by Dr. F. N. L. Poynter, Director of the Wellcome Historical Medical Museum and Library, who has made a special study of Culpeper, was printed in 1962 in the *Journal of the History of Medicine and Allied Sciences*.[8]

Nicholas Culpeper, after being educated at a free school in Sussex, went at the age of eighteen to Cambridge 'where', we are told,[9] 'he continued some years, profited in all manner of learning, and gained the applause of the University whilst he remained there'. During the time he was at Cambridge Culpeper planned a runaway marriage to a beautiful girl whose father 'was reported to be one of the noblest and wealthiest in Sussex'. The marriage,

[1] See above, p. 31.

[2] Raven (C. E.), *English naturalists from Neckam to Ray*, etc. 267–8 (1947), Cambridge.

[3] Gilmour (J.) and Walters (M.), *Wild flowers. Botanising in Britain*, 10 (1954).

[4] Coles (W.), *The art of simpling*, etc. A3ᵇ (1656).

[5] For details of some of the most famous sixteenth- and seventeenth-century writers who published works dealing with the doctrine of signatures and astrological botany, see Arber (A.), *Herbals their origin and evolution . . . A new edition*, 247–63 (1938). See also pp. 82–92 below.

[6] See Loder (G. W. E.), *Wakehurst place, Sussex, an account of the manor and its owners*, 32, 225, and the pedigree of the Culpepers of Wakehurst, facing p. 24 (1907).

[7] Culpeper is referred to thus on the title-pages of his various books.

[8] Vol. 17, 152–67.

[9] *Culpeper's school of physick*, etc. (1659) (The life of Nicholas Culpeper).

however, was not to be, for while travelling to a place 'near to Lewis in Sussex' where the marriage was to take place, Culpeper's fiancée was struck by lightning and killed. As a result of the tragedy Culpeper was so shocked and stricken with grief that he decided to leave the University. Subsequently he came to London, where he was apprenticed to Daniel White, an apothecary near Temple Bar. About eighteen months later White went bankrupt and Culpeper was then placed 'with Mr. Drake an apothecary in Thredneedle-street, where being himself excellent in the Latine, he taught Mr. Drake that tongue in less then [sic] a year and a half'. It appears that not long after this Drake died, and afterwards Culpeper 'took his masters shop within Bishops-gate, where for some space of time he studied physick'.

In 1640 Culpeper married.[1] During the Civil War he was on the Puritan-Parliamentary side[2] and in 1643 he joined the rebel army 'and was wounded by a small shot over the forepart of the body, which he never recovered of till his dying day'.[3] During the last years of his life Culpeper also suffered from tuberculosis and he eventually died of this illness in his house 'next door to the Red lion', in Spitalfields, on 10 January 1654.[4]

Culpeper became such a popular astrologer-physician that he is said to have attended to as many as forty patients in one morning.[4] His writings show that he had a genuine and passionate concern for the sick poor,[5] and a few years after his death his biographer wrote of him:[6] 'To the poor he prescribed cheap, but wholesome medicines; not removing, as many in our times do, the consumption out of their bodies into their purses; not sending them to the East-Indies for drugs, when they may fetch better out of their own gardens . . .'

Culpeper was a prolific writer and translator of medical works and during the last few years of his life devoted much time to his literary activities. In this work he was assisted by William Ryves who was employed as his amanuensis.[7] The large number of manuscripts left by Culpeper to his wife when he died, referred to by this lady as 'seventy nine books of his own making or translating',[8] indicates Culpeper's vast output as an author and translator. Few of Culpeper's publications appeared before his death. The first, his unauthorized English translation of the *Pharmacopœia londinensis* of

---

[1] Ibid. Although the year of Culpeper's marriage is not given, it is stated that when he died in 1654, he had been married fourteen years.

[2] See Cowen (D. L.), The Boston editions of Nicholas Culpeper, *J. Hist. Med.* 11, 159–61 (1956).

[3] *Culpeper's school of physick*, etc. (1659) (The nativity of Nicholas Culpeper . . . calculated by John Gadbury).

[4] *Culpeper's school of physick*, etc. (1659) (Life).

[5] See Poynter (F. N. L.), *J. Hist. Med.* 17, 156–7 (1962).

[6] *Culpeper's school of physick*, etc. (1659) (Life).

[7] Ibid. Culpeper 'had for some time together a most ingenious manuensis, one Mr. William Ryves'.

[8] See 'Mrs. Culpepers information, vindication, and testimony, concerning her husbands books to be published after his death' in *The English physitian*, ed. 1656, etc.

1618, was issued in 1649 under the title of *A physicall directory or a transla-tion of the London dispensatory made by the Colledge of physicians in London*. Cowen in the *Journal of the History of Medicine* (**11**, 156–65 (1956)) has given details concerning Culpeper's *Physicall directory* and some of its editions. He has also referred to the criticism levelled by Culpeper in this work against the physicians: made for 'reasons that were both professional and political'. At the same time he has drawn attention to the abuse of Culpeper and his work which was published in September 1649 in the Royalist periodical *Mercurius Pragmaticus*. In spite of the great indignation aroused among orthodox medical practitioners *A physicall directory* proved extremely popular, and a third edition was published in 1651. In 1653 Culpeper published a new edition of his work under the title of *Pharmacopœia londinensis: or the London dispensatory*. This consists of a translation, with additions, of the second revised edition of the *Pharmacopœia*, issued by the College of Physicians in 1650. It was pirated in 1654 and reprinted fourteen times before 1718.[1] In 1720 an edition appeared in North America, printed at Boston.

Only one of Culpeper's many publications concerns the present under-taking. This first appeared in 1652 as a folio volume printed by Peter Cole and entitled *The English physitian: or an astrologo-physical discourse of the vulgar herbs of this nation. Being a compleat method of physick, whereby a man may preserve his body in health.* This book, commonly known as Culpeper's 'herbal', proved immensely popular, and not only did many editions appear during the seventeenth, eighteenth, and nineteenth centuries, but it con-tinued to be published during the twentieth century. It has been recorded that since 1652 more than a hundred editions have been printed,[2] and cer-tainly no other botanical book included in the present *History and bibliography* was published so often. Pulteney, in 1790, wrote of Culpeper and the above work:[3] 'But, of the astrological herbalists, Nicholas Culpepper stands eminently forward. His "Herball", first printed in 1652, which continued for more than a century, to be the manual of good ladies in the country, is well known; and, to do the author justice, his descriptions of common plants were drawn up with a clearness and distinction that would not have disgraced a better pen.' The popularity of Culpeper's 'herbal' during the seventeenth cen-tury is not surprising when it is remembered that at this time the English housewife was expected to know how to administer to her family 'many wholsome receits or medicines for the good of their healthes, as well as to prevent the first occasion of sicknesse, as to take away the effects and evill of the same when it hath made seazure on the body'.[4] But it is remarkable that

[1] See Poynter (F. N. L.), *J. Hist. Med.* **17**, 162 (1962).

[2] Ibid. **17**, 162.

[3] Pulteney (R.), *Historical and biographical sketches of the progress of botany in England*, etc.

1, 180–1 (1790).

[4] Markham (G.), *Countrey contentments, in two bookes*, etc. 4 (1615) (The second [book] intituled, The English huswife).

Culpeper's herbal remedies have been used even during the present century. In 1947 the late Mrs. C. F. Leyel, Founder and Chairman of the Society of Herbalists and the Culpeper shops, opened the preface to her edition of Culpeper's 'herbal' with the following passage:[1]

Most of the herbs described by Nicholas Culpeper in his *English physician and complete herbal*[2] are used by herbalists to-day for the same purposes. Distillations have been superseded by extracts and tinctures, not because they are better but because they are cheaper, quicker, and less trouble to make. Infusions, decoctions, ointments and poultices are made in the same way, used in the same way, and for the same disorders.

The frontispiece of the first edition of Culpeper's *English physitian* is the same, but re-engraved, as the frontispiece of Culpeper's *Physicall directory* (1649). It consists of a half-length portrait of the author wearing a plain collar, and a cloak which is wrapped round him with only his left hand showing. In the top left-hand corner is a shield of arms: between two crescents a bend charged with a lion passant gardant. At the bottom of the portrait is engraved 'In effigiem Nicholai Culpeper equitis', beneath which are four lines of verse. The engraving is signed in the bottom right-hand corner 'Cross sculpsit'. This is Thomas Cross, an English engraver who worked chiefly for the booksellers. The likeness greatly resembles the description of the author published in *Culpeper's school of physick* of 1659, where we read:[3] 'Mr. Culpeper was in his deportment gentle, pleasing and courteous. His complection darkish, and swarthy. His visage rather long then round. Of a presence not so beautiful as amiable. His hair black and somewhat curling. His eyes piercing . . . Of a spare lean constitution. In his apparel not exceeding the moderation of one of his degree.'

In the preparation of medical recipes Culpeper advocated the use of plants growing in England, rather than abroad, and the title of his *English physitian* states that the work is 'an astrologo-physical discourse of the vulgar herbs of this nation'. His reasons for stressing the advantage to be gained in the use of English plants over those from abroad are given in the epistle to the reader:

All that have written of herbs either in the English or not in the English tongue, have no waies answered my intents in this book, for they have intermixed many, nay very many outlandish herbs, and very many which are hard, nay not at all to be gotten, and what harm this may do I am very sensible of. Once a student in physick in Sussex sent up to London to me, to buy for him such and such medicines, and send them down, which when I viewed, they were medicines quoted by authors living in another nation, and not to be had in London for love nor money, so the poor man had spent much pains

[1] *Culpeper's English physician and complete herbal arranged for use . . . by Mrs. C. F. Leyel*, 7 (1947).
[2] *Culpeper's English physician; and complete herbal* is the title of the editions of this author's work enlarged by Ebenezer Sibly, and first published in 1789.
[3] *Culpeper's school of physick*, etc. (1659) (The character of Nicholas Culpeper).

In Effigiem Nicholai Culpeper Equitis.

The shaddow of that Body heer you find
Which serves but as a case to hold his mind,
His Intellectuall part be pleas'd to looke
In lively lines described in the Booke.

Cross sculpsit

32. Culpeper: *The English physitian*, 1652. Frontispiece portrait of
Nicholas Culpeper engraved by Thomas Cross. 6·5 × 4·3″.

and brains in studying medicines for a disease that were not to be had; so a man reading
Gerards or Parkinsons herbal for the cure of a disease, he may as like as not, light on
an herb that is not here to be had, or not without great difficulty, if possible; but in mine,
all grow neer him.

Culpeper arranged his herbal alphabetically according to the English names of the plants, with the diseases each herb was supposed to heal listed in the margin. He believed that every disease was caused by a planet and that in order to effect a cure a herb belonging to an opposing planet must be used. For example, diseases caused by Jupiter could be cured by herbs of Mercury, and vice versa. He also held the view that cures could sometimes be made 'by sympathy', that is by the use of herbs under the dominion of the planet responsible for the disease: 'every planet cures his own diseases', he wrote, 'as the sun and moon by their herbs cure the eyes, Saturn the spleen, Jupiter the liver, Mars the gall and diseases of choller . . .'[1]

Culpeper's *English physitian* was a success from the start. As already stated it was first published in 1652, as a folio volume, printed by Peter Cole. In the same year two further editions were printed in duodecimo, one with the imprint 'London, printed by William Bentley' and the other 'London, printed for the benefit of the commonwealth of England': Bentley being, apparently, the printer of both editions. In 1653 Culpeper changed the format of his work. It now appeared as an octavo volume, with a new title reading: *The English physitian enlarged: with three hundred, sixty, and nine medicines made of English herbs that were not in any impression until this.* In the epistle to the reader Culpeper makes it clear that copies of the two editions, mentioned above, not printed by Peter Cole, were piracies. He gives clear directions how these copies, which he calls 'counterfet' copies, could be recognized. For example, they differed from his own books in format, type, and the running headline at the top of each page. The 'counterfet' copies were also 'very falsly printed; there being usually twenty or thirty gross mistakes in every sheet'. Throughout the present *History and bibliography* we shall find that a number of authors on botany and horticulture, including Philip Miller, the celebrated gardener at the Apothecaries garden at Chelsea, had their works pirated.[2] Culpeper, however, was outstanding not only for listing so fully and well the differences between the true and false copies of a work, but he also has the distinction of being one of the earliest botanical writers to provide readers with such information.

As stated earlier, although this work is generally referred to as Culpeper's 'herbal', it was not until towards the end of the eighteenth century that the word 'herbal' actually appeared on the title-page. Then in 1789, the astrologer Ebenezer Sibly (1751–c. 1800)[3] edited an enlarged illustrated edition printed in quarto, with a title reading *Culpeper's English physician; and complete herbal.* This publication, composed of two parts, the first 'containing the

[1] Culpeper (N.), *The English physitian*, etc. (1652) (To the reader).

[2] e.g. Miller complained of the publication of 'a spurious edition' of his *Dictionary*. See below, Bibliography, under Miller (P.), The gardeners dictionary, etc. (1732) folio edn.

[3] Dr. Ebenezer Sibly was born on 30 Jan. 1751. The exact date of his death is unknown, some sources giving merely the year 1799 and others 1800.

herbal' and the second 'containing the medical part', continued to be published for many years.

Four years after the first appearance of *The English physitian* Culpeper was strongly condemned for his astrological beliefs by the herbalist William Coles. The latter wrote:[1]

> Master Culpeper (a man now dead, and therefore I shall speak of him as modestly as I can, for were he alive, I should be more plain with him) . . . he, forsooth, judgeth all men unfit to be physitians, who are not artists in astrology, as if he and some other figure-flingers his companions, had been the onely physitians in England, whereas for ought I can gather, either by his books, or learne from the report of others, he was a man very ignorant in the forme of simples.

Although William Coles was so merciless in his condemnation of Culpeper and the astrologers, he himself was not beyond criticism, inasmuch as he was the author of two botanical works in which he showed himself to be a strong supporter of the doctrine of signatures. According to this doctrine, many plants by their colour, shape, and other characteristics are supposed to indicate the particular use to which they may be put. A passage from Coles's description of the quince tree may be quoted as an example:[2] 'The down of quinces doth in some sort resemble the hair of the head, the decoction whereof is very effectual for the restoring of hair that is fallen off by the French pox, and being made up with wax, and laid on as a plaster, it bringeth hair to them that are bald, and keepeth it from falling, if it be ready to shed.'

William Coles[3] (1626–62) was born at Adderbury, Oxfordshire. He entered New College, Oxford, in 1642, and graduated Bachelor of Arts, 18 February 1650 (i.e. 1651).[4] He afterwards lived at Putney where, according to Wood, he became noted as a simpler and botanist.[5] Coles wrote two works on botany: *The art of simpling*, a small treatise first published in 1656, and *Adam in Eden: or, natures paradise*, a folio volume that appeared the following year. Only brief mention need here be made of the interesting bibliographical details concerning the first of these works, as the subject has been dealt with by A. E. Lownes in his article entitled: 'The strange case of Coles vs. Culpeper'.[6] When *The art of simpling* was first published it contained no dedication. Another edition, however, appeared in the same year with an inscription addressed to the celebrated antiquary Elias Ashmole (1617–92), who a few

[1] Coles (W.), *The art of simpling*, etc. 76–7 (1656).

[2] Coles (W.), *Adam in Eden*, etc. 29 (1657).

[3] His name appears as Cole in a number of works of reference, but as Coles on the title-pages and commendatory letters and verses in his books. His name is also spelt Coles by R. Turner, a contemporary botanist and the author of *The Brittish physician* (1664).

[4] Foster (J.), *Alumni oxonienses*, etc., vol. **1**, early series, 302 (1891).

[5] Wood writes that Coles lived several years at Putney, 'where he became the most famous simpler or herbalist of his time' (*Athenæ oxonienses . . . A new edition . . . by P. Bliss*, **3**, col. 621 (1817)).

[6] See *Journ. New York bot. Garden*, **41**, 158–66 (1940).

years previously had taken up the study of plants.[1] Coles was not personally acquainted with Ashmole,[2] and it is curious that he selected him as his patron, for although the latter was interested in botany, he was also a Royalist and a leading astrologer of the day. In spite of this we find Coles in his dedication going out of his way to point out that he himself was 'a good Commonwealths-man'. Coles also includes in his work some scathing attacks on Culpeper and botanical astrology,[3] an example being the quotation cited earlier. In a later edition of 1656 several pages containing these attacks are rewritten[4] so as to cast no disparagement on astrological beliefs. Was this done at the request of Ashmole? The first two pages of the dedication are also rewritten, apparently for stylistic reasons, but the next few leaves of the inscription, which contain a passage outstanding for its depreciatory remarks concerning Culpeper, remain unchanged. Here the author, in referring to simpling and the study of plants, remarks:

I goe not about to deceive them [my countrymen] with a few empty notions, as Mr. Culpeper hath lately done, telling them many nonsensicall stories of I know not what; when as is evident to those that knew him, or are able to judge of his writings, that he understood not those plants he trod upon. And that which addes to his fallacious assertions, is, that he hath obtruded these things upon the country people, perswading them that they would be much for their be[ne]fit . . .

In 1657 *The art of simpling* was published again with only the date on the title-page changed. In a copy of this issue in the Yale University Library the dedication, with the above attack on Culpeper, has been omitted. This may have been, as suggested by Lownes,[5] because Elias Ashmole withdrew his patronage, or perhaps Coles found that his attacks on Culpeper and botanical astrology made his book unpopular. It is certainly clear that Coles's criticism did little to diminish the sales of Culpeper's 'herbal' which continued to be published during the next three hundred years. Of *The art of simpling* few copies appear to be now extant.

Adam in Eden appears to contain no depreciatory remarks on astrology. There is still evidence, however, of Coles's dislike and disapproval of Culpeper, although now on a much more restrained note.[6] Prefixed to *Adam in Eden* are several commendatory letters and verses. One of these is by the

---

[1] In *Memoirs of the life of that learned antiquary, Elias Ashmole, esq; drawn up by himself by way of diary . . . Publish'd by Charles Burman, esq.*, 19 (1717), the entry under 6 June 1648 reads: 'Having entred upon the study of plants, this day, about three of the clock, was the first time I went a simpling', and on p. 28 under 23 Sept. 1652 Ashmole records: 'I took a journey into the Peak, in search of plants, and other curiosities.'

[2] 'Though I am a stranger to your person',

wrote Coles in the opening paragraph of his dedication to Ashmole, in *The art of simpling* (1656).

[3] See dedication, pp. 2, 76, etc.

[4] i.e. pp. 1–2, 76–80.

[5] *Journ. New York bot. Garden*, 41, 164 (1940).

[6] *Adam in Eden* contains many references to Culpeper and his work. See p. 27 (E2[a]), p. 79 (L4[a]), p. 89 (N1[a]), p. 158 (Dd4[b]), p. 314 (Ddd3[b]), p. 374 (Mmm2[b]), etc.

botanist William How, the author of *Phytologia britannica* (1650). Another
of these pieces is signed by Edward Morgan, superintendent or 'Herbarist
to the physick garden of Westminster' of which How was apparently the
founder or proprietor.[1]

Coles's two works were followed in 1664 by the *Botanologia* of Robert
Turner. Turner was born at Reading on 30 July 1626,[2] and at the age of
sixteen was admitted pensioner at Christ's College, Cambridge.[3] He graduated
Bachelor of Arts in 1639. In 1637 he was admitted at the Middle Temple,
and in 1639 at Lincoln's Inn. This botanist not only professes his belief in
the 'astral influence' assigned to many plants by the astrologers,[4] but he also
avers that 'God hath imprinted upon the plants, herbs, and flowers, as it
were in hieroglyphicks, the very signature of their vertues'. His herbal is
based on Culpeper's *The expert doctors dispensatory* (an English translation of
Methodus præscribendi formulas remediorum by Petrus Morellus) and on
Culpeper's *The English physitian*. Turner, however, was careful to point out
his disagreements with Culpeper on astrological matters. He also referred his
readers to the two works by Coles already mentioned.

The upper half of the frontispiece of the *Botanologia* consists of a bust of
a man, probably the author, wearing long hair and broad falling bands over
a black garment buttoned at the front; the lower half shows a figure digging
among various plants. In a streamer at the head of this line engraving is the
title 'The Brittish or English physitian', and lettered in the margin below is
'Sold by Nathaniel Brooke at the Angel in Cornhill 1664'. No artist's name
is given and the engraver is anonymous.[5]

Among other writers in whose works astrological botany plays a part are:
Robert Lovell (1630?–90), Joseph Blagrave (1610–82), and William Westmacott. Lovell, a native of Lapworth in Warwickshire, was educated at Christ
Church, Oxford, where he graduated Master of Arts in 1653.[6] Later he
practised medicine at Coventry.[7] He was the author of παμβοτανολογια. *Sive
enchiridion botanicum*, a fat duodecimo volume published at Oxford in 1659.
This herbal, which includes a vast amount of material gathered together
from other men's works, shows great industry on the part of the compiler.
The plants are arranged in alphabetical order according to their English

[1] See Raven (C. E.), *English naturalists from Neckam to Ray*, 304 (1947), Cambridge.

[2] Britten (J.) and Boulger (G. S.), *A biographical index of deceased British and Irish botanists . . . Second Edition revised . . . by A. B. Rendle*, 307 (1931).

[3] Venn (J.) and Venn (J. A.), *Alumni cantabrigienses . . . Part I . . . to 1751*, 4, 276 (1927).

[4] Turner (R.), *Botanologia. The Brittish physician*, etc. (1664) (To the reader).

[5] The same plate, with the title blocked out and name and address of the bookseller and the date 1664 removed, was used as a frontispiece in *Blagrave's supplement; or, enlargement to Mr. Nich. Culpeper's English physician . . . By Joseph Blagrave . . . The second impression* (1677).

[6] Foster (J.), *Alumni oxonienses*, etc., vol. 3, early series, 941 (1892).

[7] There is no record that Lovell took a degree in medicine. According to Wood (A. à), *Athenæ oxonienses . . . A new edition . . . by Philip Bliss*, 4, col. 296 (1820), after Lovell settled in Coventry he 'profess'd physic, and had some practice therein'.

THE BRITTISH or ENGLISH PHYSITIAN.

Sold by Nathaniel Brooke, at the Angel in Cornhill,   1664.

33. Robert Turner: *Botanologia. The Brittish physician*, 1664. Engraved
frontispiece, 6·4 × 3·8″. The same plate with the title, imprint, and date
erased was used as the frontispiece of *Blagrave's supplement . . . to
Mr. Nich. Culpeppers English physitian* of 1677.

names. Among details given are the place of growth and time of flowering of
each plant, and the name of the species in Greek and Latin together with its
qualities and uses. In the introduction are named those herbs which were

endowed with signatures capable of curing various ailments, and the names of those plants connected with the planets and the twelve constellations and used in the preparation and application of herbal remedies.[1]

Joseph Blagrave was a native of Reading and a 'student in physick and astrology'.[2] He wrote a *Supplement or enlargement, to Mr. Nich. Culpeppers English physitian* (1674).

Finally, William Westmacott, a physician of Newcastle under Lyme, in Staffordshire,[3] was the author of *Theolobotonologia* [sic] (1694), a small volume containing details of the plants mentioned in the Bible.

Before leaving seventeenth-century herbals, a passing reference must be made to John Pechey's *Compleat herbal of physical plants*, first published in 1694. John Pechey (1654–1717)[4] was educated at New Inn Hall, Oxford. He graduated Bachelor of Arts in 1675 and became Master of Arts in 1678. In 1684 he was admitted a Licentiate of the College of Physicians, and practised in the City and London. He was the author of several medical books, but his herbal has little botanical merit. Regarding its lack of originality Pechey himself writes:[5] 'In compiling this English herbal of physical plants, I have chiefly follow'd Mr. Ray . . . What I have contributed to this work, I confess, is the least part: some virtues, indeed, I have added, and many good medicines; but those I borrow'd too. So that, upon a review, I find little or nothing belongs to me, save only the collection, and translation.'

[1] See *10–12 and **1–6.

[2] *Blagrave's supplement or enlargement, to Mr. Nich. Culpeppers English physitian*, etc. (1674) (title-page).

[3] Westmacott (W.), *Theolobotonologia* [sic], etc. (1694) (title-page). On the title-page of the second edition (1695) the author is stated to be 'Med. Prof. London'.

[4] Born Dec. 1654; died June 1717. See Britten (J.) and Boulger (G. S.), *A biographical index of deceased British and Irish botanists . . . Second Edition . . . revised . . . by A. B. Rendle*, 240 (1931).

[5] Pechey (J.), *The compleat herbal of physical plants*, etc. (1694) (Preface).

II

EARLY SCIENTIFIC AND FLORISTIC WORKS

UNTIL the time of Thomas Johnson (1595/7–1644)[1] information concerning the flora of this country had to be sought for in herbals; the knowledge of botany, as we have already noted, being considered necessary only in so far as it contributed to medicine.[2] Johnson, however, developed a new interest, that of the systematic search for, and the study of, the native flora for its own sake. This eminent London apothecary, with a business in Snow Hill, Holborn, at the sign of the Red Lion,[3] whose name became famous to posterity through his edition of Gerard's *Herball*—referred to by Ray as 'Gerardus emaculatus', 1633 and 1636[4]—'attained', according to his contemporary Thomas Fuller,[5] 'to be the best herbalist of his age in England'. For the purpose of studying the native flora he undertook a series of plant-hunting expeditions into various parts of the country. Descriptions of these tours with lists of the plants found were printed in several small tracts.[6] The first of these is a thin undated quarto consisting of a description of a herborizing expedition into Kent in 1629, from 13 to 17 July, together with an account of a similar excursion to Hampstead Heath and its neighbourhood made the following 1 August. On both occasions the author was accompanied by nine friends. Both accounts are interspersed with lists of the plants observed. This book has the distinction of containing the earliest printed narrations of such undertakings made in England.

In 1632 Thomas Hicks, Upper Warden of the Society of Apothecaries,[7] encouraged Johnson and his friends to make a further herborizing expedition

[1] Johnson was born near Selby in Yorkshire. As a youth he was apprenticed as an apothecary in London and in 1618 was made a freeman of the Worshipful Society of Apothecaries of London. The required period of apprenticeship was seven years, and if Johnson began his apprenticeship, as was usual, between fourteen and sixteen years of age, he was born not earlier than 1595 and not later than 1597, the latter year being the more likely date. See Jeffers (R. H.), *The friends of John Gerard*, etc. 87–8 (1967).

[2] See above, p. 82.

[3] Johnson's epistle to the reader in his edition of Gerard's *Herball* is dated 'From my house on Snow-hill, Octob. 22. 1633'. In 1628 Thomas Crosfield (d. 1663) wrote: 'descending

Grayes in lane [now called Gray's Inn Road]—on ye left hand Mr Johnson at ye Read lyon Snowhill'. See *The diary of Thomas Crosfield . . . edited . . . by Frederick S. Boas*, 20 (1935).

[4] [Ray (J.)], *Catalogus plantarum circa Cantabrigiam*, etc., **6[a] (1660), Cantabrigiæ.

[5] Fuller (T.), *The history of the worthies of England . . . A new edition . . . by John Nichols*, etc. **2**, 510 (1811).

[6] For full details concerning these tracts see Kew (H. W.) and Powell (H. E.), *Thomas Johnson*, etc. (1932).

[7] Hicks was made Upper Warden on 24 Aug. 1631. See Barrett (C. R. B.), *The history of the Society of apothecaries of London*, 38 (1905).

into Kent. The tour was arranged, and Hicks took part and also assisted in defraying the expenses.[1] A small duodecimo volume was published in 1632 containing a description of this second Kentish journey interspersed, as in the earlier work of 1629, with lists of plants. At the end of this account is an enumeration of the plants of Hampstead Heath and its neighbouring localities. This book with a dedication addressed by the whole party ('Socij itinerantes') to the Master, Wardens, and Assistants of the Society of Apothecaries, has a preface by Thomas Johnson, and two pages with figures of plants.[2]

With the books bequeathed by the botanist John Goodyer to Magdalen College, Oxford, is a copy of Johnson's work of 1632,[3] and according to Gunther[4] it 'appears to have been the author's own copy with his MS. index, afterwards extended by How and used in the preparation of his *Phytologia* (1650).'

The eminence of Johnson as a botanist, and the interest he aroused in herborizing, or 'simpling' as it was called, is evident from the names of the distinguished Apothecaries[5] who accompanied him from 14 to 26 July 1634 on his botanical tour from London to Reading, Marlborough, Bath, Bristol, Salisbury, Southampton, the Isle of Wight, Portsmouth, Chichester, Godalming, Guildford, and back to London. A description of this tour was printed in the same year in the *Mercurius botanicus*, with a dedication to four prominent physicians, Sir Theodore de Mayerne (1573–1655), Dr. (later Sir) Matthew Lister (1571?–1656), Dr. Othowell Meverall (1585–1648), and Dr. Laurence Wright (1590–1657). A second part of the work, describing a tour in Wales made during July and August 1639, appeared in 1641 in Johnson's *Mercurii botanici pars altera*. Both parts include a long list of plants, and it is evident that Johnson intended these two catalogues together to be an enumeration of all the British plants then known, nearly 900 in all.[6] The plants in these catalogues, unlike those given in the works of 1629 and 1632 which were not arranged in any sort of order, are listed alphabetically with the English name of each plant following the Latin. Authorities are cited and some synonyms added. Localities are specified in black letter in English for the rarer species e.g. 'In the wood betweene Highgate and Hamstead', but in roman type in general terms in Latin for common plants e.g. 'in muris & tectis'. Kew and Powell, in their biography of Thomas Johnson (1632),

---

[1] Johnson (T.), *Descriptio itineris plantarum*, etc. 1–2 (1632).

[2] These two works were published in Latin, and for a translation see *Thomas Johnson botanical journeys in Kent & Hampstead a facsimile reprint with introduction and translation of his Iter plantarum 1629 Descriptio itineris plantarum 1632 edited by J. S. L. Gilmour* (1972), published by the Hunt Botanical Library, Pittsburgh, Pennsylvania.

[3] Pressmark Arch. B.II.1–18.

[4] Gunther (R. W. T.), *Early British botanists and their gardens*, etc. 215, 232, 275 (1922), Oxford.

[5] For the names of these men see the *Mercurius botanicus*, 6 (1634).

[6] Kew (H. W.) and Powell (H. E.), *Thomas Johnson*, etc. 106 (1932).

point out that the *Mercurius* (1634–41) should be considered 'the first British flora'.[1] Previous to this claim a number of authors had assigned this historical position to William How's *Phytologia* (1650).

In the second part of the *Mercurius*,[2] Johnson expressed his intention to publish, with the help of his friend John Goodyer, a descriptive and illustrated flora of British plants. Unfortunately Johnson's early death prevented this plan from being carried out. He fought for the Royalists during the Civil War and was shot in the shoulder on 14 September 1644, dying from the effects of the wound a fortnight later. He was described in a pamphlet published in 1644 as 'being no lesse eminent in the garrison for his valour and conduct, as a souldier, then famous through the kingdom for his excellency as an herbarist, and physician'.[3]

Johnson's small tracts were reprinted in one volume in 1847, edited by T. S. Ralph, with a covering title reading *Opuscula omnia botanica Thomæ Johnsoni*.[4] Copies of the original works are rare, especially those of 1629 and 1632.

In 1648 the anonymous *Catalogus plantarum Horti medici oxoniensis* came from the press of Henry Hall, printer to the University of Oxford. Before referring further to this work, however, let us mention a few points of interest with regard to the early history of this Oxford garden.[5]

The Oxford physic garden, later known as the Oxford botanic garden, was founded in 1621,[6] through the munificence of Henry Danvers, Baron Danvers of Dantsey (1573–1643 [i.e. 1644]), afterwards Earl of Danby.[7] According to Wood[8] ''twas primarily founded for a nursery of simples, and that a Professor of botanicey should read there, and shew the use and virtue of them to his auditors'. Although the Oxford garden was the first institution of its kind to be started in England, botanic gardens on the Continent had long been established, that at Pisa being founded as early as 1543.[9] Such institutions which contained large collections of plants grown for their botanical and medical interest, and which also formed centres for study and research, played an important part in botanical progress. William Coles thus acknowledged his debt to his early training at the Oxford garden:[10] 'the best hours of my life being spent in the fields and in physick gardens, more especially in that famous one at Oxford, where I made it a great part of my

[1] Op. cit. 136 (1932).
[2] pp. 1–2 (1641).
[3] *A description of the siege of Basing castle*, etc. 16 (1644), Oxford.
[4] Published by W. Pamplin.
[5] For further details see Vines (S. H.) and Druce (G. C.), *An account of the Morisonian herbarium*, etc. (1914), (Introduction) Oxford.
[6] Ibid., pp. x–xii.
[7] Created Earl of Danby 1626.
[8] Wood (A. à), *The history and antiquities of the University of Oxford... published... by John Gutch*, 2, Pt. 2, 896 (1796), Oxford.
[9] The three earliest botanic gardens to be founded on the Continent were at Pisa (1543), Padua (1545), and Florence (1545). See Gilmour (J. S. L.), The University botanic garden, Cambridge, *J. R. hort. Soc.* (London), 80, 206 (1955).
[10] Coles (W.), *Adam in Eden*, etc. (1657) (To the reader).

study to be experienced in this laudable art of simpling'. Robert Lovell also was a student there, and he was careful to note with an asterisk the plants in his herbal of 1659, 'not in the physick garden in Oxford'.[1]

The site selected for the Oxford physic garden was outside the east gate of the city, near the river Cherwell. A surrounding stone wall was built and the magnificent gateway, which still stands, was designed by Inigo Jones. The building of the walls and gates was completed in 1632.[2] For various reasons, the intention of the Earl of Danby to provide the University with a Professor of Botany was long delayed. Finally, in 1669, Robert Morison, the King's physician and Professor of Botany, was appointed to the office.[3] Meanwhile, the first holder of the post of gardener of whom there is any record was Jacob Bobart (1600?–80), and although the exact date of his appointment is not known, it appears to have been about 1641.[4] Bobart was a native of Brunswick in Germany,[5] and under his care the garden flourished and gained a great reputation. When he died in 1680[6] he was succeeded by his son, Jacob Bobart the Younger (1641–1719). Thomas Baskerville, in his 'Account of Oxford c. 1670–1700',[7] wrote of the garden:

After the walls & gates of this famous garden were built, old Jacob Bobert father to this present Jacob may be said to be yᵉ man yᵗ first gave life & beauty to this famous place, who by his care & industry replenish'd the walls, wᵗʰ all manner of good fruits our clime would ripen, & bedeck the earth wᵗʰ great variety of trees plants & exotick flowers, dayly augmented by the botanists, who bring them hither from yᵉ remote quarters of yᵉ world.

The above-mentioned catalogue of 1648 enumerates 1,600 plants that were cultivated in the Oxford garden,[8] most of which were European species. There were also many plants from 'Virginy', and some, such as tobacco (Tabacco of Peru) and maize (Indian wheat) from more distant lands. Bobart is said to be the author of the work.[9] An improved edition was published in 1658 with a title reading: *Catalogus Horti botanici oxoniensis . . . Curâ & operâ sociâ Philippi Stephani M.D. et Gulielmi Brounei A.M. Adhibitis etiam in consilium D. Boberto patre . . . ejusque filio*, etc. Philip Stephens (1620?[10]–79) was a physician and the Principal of Hart Hall, Oxford,[11] and earlier he had

---

[1] Title-page.

[2] Vines (S. H.) and Druce (G. C.), *An account of the Morisonian herbarium*, etc., p. xiv (1914).

[3] Ibid., p. xxvi.

[4] Ibid., p. xvi.

[5] Thomas Baskerville's account of Oxford c. 1670–1700. Edited by Humphrey Baskerville in *Collectanea. Fourth series*, 190 (1905) (Oxford Hist. Soc., vol. 47).

[6] According to the inscription on Bobart's tombstone in the churchyard of St. Peter-in-the-East, Oxford, he died 4 Feb. 1679 [i.e.

1680] in his eighty-first year.

[7] *Collectanea. Fourth series*, 187 (1905) (Oxford Hist. Soc., vol. 47).

[8] See A2ᵇ (1648).

[9] See below, Bibliography, under Oxford.—University.—*Botanic garden.* Catologus [sic] plantarum, etc. (1648), 8°.

[10] Stephens matriculated 24 Mar. 1636 [i.e. 1637] aged seventeen (Foster (J.), *Alumni oxonienses . . . 1500–1714*, etc. 4, 1419 (1892)).

[11] Now Hertford College.

been one of the 'very eminent botanicks' acknowledged by William Coles for having helped him with his *Adam in Eden* (1657).[1] It is possible that this edition of the Oxford catalogue was mostly compiled by William Browne (1629?–78),[2] divine and Fellow of Magdalen College, Oxford. For not only does Christopher Merret refer to him in his *Pinax* of 1666 as the 'author eruditissimus',[3] but Anthony à Wood records that he had 'the chief hand' in its composition.[4] The latter authority also states that Browne 'was one of the best botanists of his time'.

The Oxford catalogue appears to be the first British printed botanical book in which references are included giving the pagination of the works cited; and for fear some readers should think this 'an needlesse worke' the authors explain that they have taken 'that excellent herball the Hortus eistetensis' for an example.[5]

Nine years after the appearance of Thomas Johnson's completed *Mercurius* (1634, 1641) the London bookseller Octavian Pulleyn published William How's English flora, the *Phytologia britannica*.

William How was born in London in 1620. He attended Merchant Taylors' School and afterwards, in 1637, went to St. John's College, Oxford. He graduated Bachelor of Arts in 1641, and took his Master's degree on 21 March 1643 [i.e. 1644]. He then studied medicine. He joined the forces of Charles I and was promoted to Captain of a troop of horse, but on the decline of the Royal cause returned to his medical career and practised in London. How died in 1656 while still a comparatively young man.

How was interested in botany but, unlike Johnson, he does not appear to have done much plant hunting. He evidently prepared his flora by first arranging the two catalogues of the *Mercurius* into one alphabetical list as, in the words of Clarke,[6] the '*Phytologia britannica* (1650) is in the main a verbatim reprint of Johnson's *Mercurius botanicus*'. How augmented this list with a number of other records of plants, some with no name appended, a few from 'Dr. Johnsons MS.', and many furnished by his friends, Walter Stonehouse, George Bowle or Bowles, Richard Heaton,[7] and others. The flora has been described as 'a very hasty and defective piece of work',[8] but a number of the records supplied are held to be of interest and value. In 1659 How's own interleaved copy of the *Phytologia*, containing 'many

[1] Coles (W.), *Adam in Eden*, etc. (1657) (To the reader).

[2] Browne died 25 Mar. 1678, aged forty-nine. Foster (J.), *Alumni oxonienses*, etc., vol. 1, early series, 198 (1891).

[3] A4[b].

[4] Wood (A. à), *Athenæ oxonienses . . . To which are added the Fasti . . . A new edition . . . by Philip Bliss*, 4 (1820) (see *Fasti*, Pt. 2, col. 282).

[5] *Catalogus Horti botanici oxoniensis*, etc.

(1658) (Preface to Pt. 2). *The Hortus eystettensis* was published at Eichstadt in 1613.

[6] Clarke (W. A.), *First records of British flowering plants . . . Second edition*, 188–9 (1900).

[7] For details of these three botanists see Raven (C. E.), *English Naturalists from Neckham to Ray*, etc., pp. 294, etc., 300, etc., 302, etc. (1947).

[8] Raven (C.), op. cit. 299 (1947).

corrections, notes, and MS. lists of plants by the author' came into the possession of John Goodyer, who bequeathed it in 1664 with his collection of books 'de plantis' to Magdalen College, Oxford.[1] These additional notes, made between 1650 and 1656, have been printed in full by Gunther in his *Early British botanists and their gardens* (1922).[2] There is little doubt that they were intended for a revised edition but that the author's early death prevented the accomplishment of such a project.

The *Phytologia* had evidently proved popular, for when the edition was almost exhausted, the bookseller begged his friend Christopher Merret to undertake a new work to replace it.[3] The result of this request was the publication in 1666 of Merret's *Pinax rerum naturalium britannicarum*, a catalogue of British flora, fauna, and fossils, the section on flora occupying more than two-thirds of the work.

Christopher Merret or Merrett (1614–95) was a physician and one of the original Fellows of the Royal Society.[4] After receiving his medical training at Oxford, he graduated Bachelor of Medicine from Gloucester Hall in 1636, and proceeded Doctor of Medicine in January 1642 [i.e. 1643]. He settled in London, and in 1651 was elected a Fellow of the Royal College of Physicians.[5] In 1654 he was elected the first Keeper of the library that had been given to this institution by the celebrated Dr. William Harvey (1578–1657). Twelve years later the College and its library were destroyed by the Great Fire, after which Merret's services were dispensed with.

Merret was to have received the co-operation of Dr. Dale in the preparation of the new work.[6] This was doubtless John Goodyer's friend, Dr. John Dale who died in 1662,[7] but how far this botanist gave any assistance is not known. Merret acknowledges the help of Thomas Willisel, an old soldier who was an excellent field botanist and who was engaged by the former for five successive summers as a collector.[8] Merret's son, Christopher, also made excursions for the same purpose, and Goodyer's nephew and heir, the Revd. Edmund Yalden, lent manuscripts that had belonged to his uncle. Merret was certainly industrious in the preparation of the *Pinax*, but when it was published it proved a disappointment for, although it contains a number of new records,[9] it is chiefly a compilation from previous writers. The author

[1] Gunther (R. W. T.), *Early British botanists and their gardens*, etc. 231 (1922).
[2] See pp. 279–93.
[3] Merret (C.), *Pinax*, etc., A2b (1666). The *Phytologia* was published by the bookseller Octavian Pulleyn, whose address from 1636 to 1666 was the Rose in St. Paul's Churchyard. The *Pinax* was published by Cave Pulleyn at the same address. It is not clear who begged Merret to undertake the new work.
[4] Elected 20 May 1663.
[5] On 30 Sept. 1681 Dr. Merret was expelled from his Fellowship. For reasons see Munk (W.), *The roll of the Royal college of physicians of London*, etc. 1, 262–3 (1878).
[6] Merret (C.), *Pinax*, etc. (1666) (Preface).
[7] See Gunther (R. W. T.), *Early British botanists and their gardens*, etc. 294–8 (1922).
[8] Merret (C.), *Pinax*, etc. (1666) (Preface).
[9] Clarke (W. A.), *First records of British flowering plants . . . Second edition*, 189 (1900).

was also a relatively inexperienced naturalist, and the work was not edited with sufficient care or knowledge.[1]

Merret states that for the purpose of his work he purchased 800 figures of plants which had belonged to Thomas Johnson.[2] These, however, he never used, and it may be assumed that they are the same as those bound in a book now preserved in the British Museum (Bloomsbury).[3] This consists of ninety-seven sheets with woodcut figures of plants, with manuscript notes. A manuscript note signed 'Robert Gray, M.D.', found on a blank leaf preceding the figures, reads:

> This book did belong to Dr Merret author of the Pinax, &c. The wrytinng in it is his hand. Mr Bateman the bookseller who sold it to me (14 Septr 1695) said that these cutts or figures were made by Dr Johnsons command (qui emaculavit Gerardum) in order to serve a new herbal which he designed to set forth. Mr Bateman had this from Dr Merrets executors who sold him this with all the doctors . . . library.

Kew and Powell, Johnson's biographers, give their opinion regarding these figures in the following passage:[4]

> It is observable that Merrett did not state from whom he obtained these figures, or the source of his information concerning their earlier history. But an examination of them, while affording no conclusive evidence, inclines us to the belief that they had been Johnson's, and it may be that some of them were drawn by him. Altogether the figures form a heterogeneous collection of no outstanding merit, largely of British plants but by no means exclusively so, and most of them are copies of those already in the herbals, including the 'Gerard' of Johnson himself.

At the present day there appear to be few copies of the *Pinax* of 1666 extant,[5] and the reason for this is evident when the following facts are noted. The Great Fire of London raged from 2 September until 6 September 1666, and as Merret signed the epistle dedicatory of the *Pinax* 'Aug. 66', the book was probably published shortly before the conflagration. The imprint on the title-page reads: 'Londini impensis Cave Pulleyn ad insigne Rosæ in cæmeterio Divi Pauli, typis F. & T. Warren, anno 1666.' Although no information appears to be available concerning Cave Pulleyn, it is known that the premises of another bookseller, Octavian Pulleyn, whose address was also the Rose in St. Paul's Churchyard, were destroyed in the Fire.[6] Furthermore, the printing-house in Foster Lane of the printers Francis and Thomas

---

[1] 'At present the world is glutted with Dr. Merrett's bungling "Pinax",' wrote John Ray, on 18 June 1667, to Martin Lister, Fellow of St. John's College, Cambridge. *Further correspondence of John Ray. Edited by R. W. T. Gunther*, 112 (1928).

[2] *Pinax*, etc. (1666) (Preface).

[3] Pressmark 441.i.6.

[4] Kew (H. W.) and Powell (H. E.), *Thomas Johnson*, etc. 126–7 (1932).

[5] The copy in the Brit. Mus. (Bloomsbury) (pressmark 976.b.3) is interleaved and contains MS. notes, possibly by the author.

[6] Plomer (H. R.), *A dictionary of the booksellers and printers who were at work in England, Scotland and Ireland from 1641 to 1667*, pp. 149–50 (1907).

Warren was also probably burnt down, as 'a list of the several printing houses taken on July 24th, 1668' records that 'amongst the master printers returned as ruined by the Fire of London was Mr. Warren ['Domestic state papers', Charles II, vol. 243. 126¹]'.[2] From this evidence it is reasonable to assume that most copies of the *Pinax* were lost in the Fire.

The *Pinax* was published again in 1667, when a number of spelling mistakes and other errors were corrected and the type in the text reset. Some copies of this edition contain a cancel title-page with a statement reading 'Editio secunda'. An advertisement in the *Philosophical Transactions* of 8 April 1667[3] announces that Christopher Merret, M.D., wishes to inform the public 'that within the space of four moneths, he shall re-publish his *Pinax rerum naturalium britannicarum*, with many additions, and in his proposed new method; and that he wholly disclaims a second edition of that book, as being printed and published without his knowledge'. This new enlarged edition was never published.

We have mentioned that Merret was a Fellow of the Royal Society and, indeed, many botanical books have been written by men who were Fellows of this, the oldest scientific society in Great Britain. Although 1660 is the year of the establishment of the Royal Society, it is first traceable about 1645 when a group of men met weekly in London to discuss matters of scientific interest.[4] The influence of the philosophy of Francis Bacon (1561–1621) as expressed in his writings was making itself felt, and these meetings were the outcome of the growing feeling of dissatisfaction with the theories of the past, and a desire for new knowledge through inquiry and experiment.[5] About 1648 the above group of men divided, some of its members settling in Oxford, while the rest remained in London.[6] At the Restoration the London group was strengthened by other men of like interest, and on 28 November 1660 this body decided to form itself into a society.[7] A list of forty names was drawn up and a weekly subscription fixed. On 15 July 1662 Charles II granted the new society a Royal charter of incorporation and conferred on it the name of the Royal Society.[8] A second charter was granted on 22 April 1663, and in this charter the King declared himself to be the Founder and Patron of the Society.[9] At two meetings held on 20 May 1663 and the following 22 June respectively, a total of 119 persons were declared to be members, and these members 'constituted the original Fellows of the Royal society'.[10]

---

[1] In The Public Record Office, Chancery Lane, London.

[2] Plomer (H. R.), op. cit. 189 (1907).

[3] p. 448.

[4] *The Record of the Royal society of London ... Fourth edition*, 4–5 (1940).

[5] 'The foundation of the Royal society was one of the earliest practical fruits of the philosophical labours of Francis Bacon' (*The Record of the Royal society of London*, etc. 1 (1940)). See also Singer (C. J.), *A short history of science to the nineteenth century*, 229 (1941), Oxford.

[6] *The Record of the Royal society of London*, etc. 5 (1940).

[7] Ibid. 7–8.

[8] Ibid. 13–14.

[9] Ibid. 14–15.

[10] Ibid. 15.

Birch, in his *History of the Royal society*, 4 vols. (1756–7), gives brief records of meetings held from 1660 until the end of 1687, and Raven has drawn attention to the great variety of the subjects discussed and the experiments performed at these meetings.[1] The first recorded lecture on a botanical subject appears to have been given on 23 January 1660 [i.e. 1661], when Sir Kenelm Digby gave a discourse 'concerning the vegetation of plants'.[2] This was afterwards published, apparently some time early in the following August. When the book was printed, the author presented 'some copies' to the Royal Society at their meeting held on the 14th of this month.[3] This gift was also noted by John Evelyn who, after attending the above meeting, wrote in his *Diary* under the 14th August:[4] 'This day Sir Kenh⟨e⟩lme Digby presented every one of us his Discourse of the vegetation of plants.' In this work Digby drew attention to the fact that 'there is in the aire a hidden food of life' necessary to every plant.[5] He thus suspected the relationship of plant growth to the gases in the air.

The 'handsome, charming, versatile, and unique Sir Kenelm Digby (1603–65), a wandering planet whose orbit one crosses at every turn in the period',[6] was author, courtier, and traveller. He was also a collector of books and manuscripts, and a patron of learning.[7] Science attracted him, and he was a keen observer of nature, but also a believer in astrology and alchemy. He was married to the famous beauty, Venetia Stanley. Weld, one-time Assistant-secretary and Librarian of the Royal Society, wrote of him:[8] 'Digby delighted in the marvellous, and was, probably, the most superstitious of the early Fellows of the Society.[9] It is related of him, that he fed his wife on capons fattened with the flesh of vipers, in order to preserve her beauty.'

John Evelyn (1620–1706), another of the early Fellows of the Royal Society,[10] was responsible for the first important book to be published in this country on forest trees. The work originated in the following way.

During the sixteenth and seventeenth centuries the growing shortage of timber in England was causing considerable anxiety. Timber was being extravagantly used for domestic fuel, and large quantities of wood in the form

[1] Raven (C. E.), *John Ray, naturalist*, 146 (1950), Cambridge.

[2] Birch (T.), *The history of the Royal society of London*, etc. **1**, 13 (1756).

[3] Ibid. **1**, 41.

[4] *The diary of John Evelyn . . . printed . . . from the manuscripts belonging to Mr. John Evelyn and edited by E. S. de Beer*, **3**, 294 (1955), Oxford.

[5] Digby (Sir K.), *A discourse concerning the vegetation of plants*, 64 (1661).

[6] Bush (J. N. D.), *English literature in the earlier seventeenth century 1600–1660*, p. 228 (1945), Oxford (Oxford History of English Literature, vol. **5**).

[7] Regarding Digby as a book collector and patron of learning see Fulton (J. F.), *Sir Kenelm Digby, writer, bibliophile and protagonist of William Harvey*, 39, etc. (1937), New York.

[8] Weld (C. R.), *A history of the Royal society*, etc. **1**, 103, footnote 8 (1848).

[9] Sir Kenelm Digby was elected into the Society 12 Dec. 1660. He was elected a member of the first Council in the Charter of 1662, and renominated as a member of the Council in the Charter of 1663.

[10] Regarding the date of Evelyn's election into the Society see *The diary of John Evelyn . . . edited by E. S. de Beer*, **3**, 266 and footnote 6 (1955).

of charcoal were being consumed by the iron industry and also by the glass workers.[1] These industries migrated to new centres as their supply of timber became exhausted, and in spite of the general destruction and waste of wood, little was done in the way of replanting. Furthermore, land was becoming increasingly converted to corn and pasture. Therefore, after the Restoration, when attention was directed towards increasing our shipping, difficulty was experienced in obtaining the necessary wood for the building of the ships and, as a result, the Commissioners of the Navy sent to the Royal Society for their consideration a paper with proposals for 'the improvement and planting of timber'. This was read on 17 September 1662, and passed for further attention to the following four Fellows: John Evelyn, Dr. Jonathan Goddard, Dr. Christopher Merret, and John Winthrop, Governor of Connecticut.[2] In due course Goddard, Merret, and Winthrop each presented a paper with their views on the matter and, on 1 October, Evelyn was asked to study them, add his own observations, and then make a digest of the whole.[3] After Evelyn had done this he wrote in his *Diary* under 15 October 1662:[4] 'I this day delivered my discourse concerning forest-trees to our Society upon occasion of certaine queries sent us by the Commissioners of His Majesties navy.' Subsequently papers were communicated to the Royal Society concerning cider and the cultivation of fruit-trees for making this drink, and on 21 January 1663 Evelyn was requested to read over and prepare a digest of the available material.[5] On 18 March, after the task was completed, it was resolved that 'Mr. Evelyn's treatise concerning timber-trees and fruit-trees be printed by order of the Royal society upon perusal of it by Dr. Wilkins, Dr. Goddard, and Dr. Merret'.[6] In his *Diary* under the same date, Evelyn wrote:[7] 'To Lond: our Council of R: So: ordered their printer to print my *Sylva*.'

After the above resolution was passed Evelyn's work had to wait until the Society appointed its own printers. This was done on 2 November 1663 when John Martyn and James Allestry received the appointment.[8] The following 21 December it was resolved that no book be printed by order of the Council which had not been examined by two members of the Council, and it was ordered 'that Dr. Goddard and Dr. Merret peruse Mr. Evelyn's book called *Sylva*, together with The appendix of fruit-trees, and the Calendarium hortense'.[9] At the same meeting Evelyn was given permission to print five discourses on cider formerly read at several of the Society's meetings. When

[1] Lipson (E.), *The economic history of England*, 2, 156–9; 3, 368 (1956).

[2] Birch (T.), *The history of the Royal society of London*, etc. 1, 111 (1756).

[3] Ibid. 1, 114.

[4] *The diary of John Evelyn . . . edited by E. S. de Beer*, 3, 340 (1955).

[5] Birch (T.), op. cit. 1, 179.

[6] Ibid. 1, 212.

[7] *The diary of John Evelyn . . . edited by E. S. de Beer*, 3, 353 (1955).

[8] Birch (T.), *The history of the Royal society of London*, etc. 1, 323–4 (1756).

[9] Ibid. 1, 347.

Evelyn's book was finally published it bore the *imprimatur* of the Council of the Royal Society, signed by Viscount Brouncker as President, and dated 3 February 1664. It consisted of *Sylva*, to which was appended 'Pomona or, an appendix concerning fruit-trees in relation to cider; the making and several ways of ordering it[1] . . . Also Kalendarium hortense; or, gard'ners almanac'. The work had the distinction of being the first book ever written and published by the express order of the Royal Society.[2]

On 16 February 1664 Evelyn presented a copy of his *Sylva* to the Royal Society,[3] and on the next day he gave copies to Charles II, the Lord Treasurer, and the Lord Chancellor. The King, to whom the work is dedicated, appears to have acknowledged the gift on 26 February, and later in the same year, on 28 October, he thanked Evelyn again 'before divers Lords & noble men'.[4]

The book received Royal approval; it also aroused great public interest. In the dedication to Charles II in the second edition (1669),[5] Evelyn informed the King that 'more than a thousand copies had been bought up . . . of the first impression, in much lesse time than two years' which according to booksellers was 'a very extraordinary thing in volumes of this bulk'. Evelyn also told the King: 'it has been the sole occasion of furnishing your almost exhausted dominions, with more (I dare say) than two millions of timber-trees; besides infinite others, which have been propagated within the three nations, at the instigation, and by the direction of this work.'

Evelyn's *Sylva* received publicity on the Continent through being advertised in the autumn catalogue of books exhibited in 1670 at the famous Frankfurt fair (*Catalogus universalis pro nundinis Francofurtensibus autumnalibus de anno MDCLXX*). It is entered in the catalogue under the heading of 'Libri futuris nundinis prodituri', as follows: 'Joann. Evelini dissertatio de arboribus & propagatione lignorum, accessit appendix de arboribus fructiferis & Kalendarium hortense'. The work was advertised again, under the same heading, in the autumn catalogue of 1671.[6] The importance of these lists has been stressed by Colin Clair, who writes:[7]

No doubt many of these catalogues were intended for distribution among the booksellers who frequented the celebrated Frankfurt fair . . . This 'shop-window of the Muses', as Henri Estienne termed it, became the Mecca of the book trade as early as

---

[1] 'Pomona' consists of a treatise on the cultivation of fruit-trees followed by discourses read at several meetings of the Royal Society by Mr. [John] Beale (referred to by Evelyn on p. 1 of 'Pomona' as 'the most excellently learned Mr. Beale of Yeavill in Somersetshire'), Sir Paul Neile, John Newburgh, Esq., Dr. Smith, and Capt. Taylor.

[2] *Phil. Trans.* **4**: 1071–2 (15 Nov. 1669).

[3] *The diary of John Evelyn . . . edited by E. S. de Beer*, **3**, 369 (1955).

[4] Ibid. **3**, 369, 386–7.

[5] Although the date on the title-page is 1670 this edition is noticed in *Phil. Trans.* **4**, 1071–4 (15 Nov. 1669). Evelyn also wrote in his *Diary* under 8 Dec. 1669: 'To Lond: upon the second edition of my Sylva, which I presented to the R: Society'. See *The diary of John Evelyn . . . edited by E. S. de Beer*, **3**, 541 (1955).

[6] Copies of these catalogues are preserved in the Brit. Mus. (Bloomsbury), pressmark C.106.g.1.

[7] Clair (C.), *Christopher Plantin*, 204 (1960).

SYLVA,

Or A DISCOURSE of
FOREST-TREES,

AND THE
Propagation of Timber

In His MAJESTIES Dominions.

By *J. E.* Esq;

As it was Deliver'd in the *ROYAL SOCIETY* the xv[th] of
October, CIↃIↃCLXII. upon Occasion of certain *Quæries*
Propounded to that *Illustrious Assembly*, by the *Honorable* the Principal
Officers, and *Commissioners* of the *Navy*.

To which is annexed

POMONA Or, An *Appendix* concerning *Fruit-Trees* in relation to *CIDER*;
The *Making* and several ways of *Ordering* it.

Published by express Order *of the* ROYAL SOCIETY.

ALSO
KALENDARIUM HORTENSE; Or, *Gard'ners Almanac*;
Directing *what* he is to do *Monethly* throughout the *Year*.

————*Tibi res antiquæ laudis & artis*
Ingredior, tantos ausus recludere fonteis. Virg.

LONDON, Printed by *Jo. Martyn,* and *Ja. Allestry,* Printers to the *Royal
Society,* and are to be sold at their Shop at the *Bell* in S. *Paul's* Church-yard,
MDCLXIV.

the end of the fifteenth century, and the twice-yearly fair, held in spring and autumn, was attended by booksellers from all over Europe, as well as by scholars of all nations, who came to Frankfurt to meet publishers and to inspect and buy the latest books.

It appears from correspondence addressed to Evelyn's father-in-law, Sir Richard Browne, that *Sylva* was included in the above Frankfurt catalogue through the enterprise and enthusiasm of Sir William Curtius.[1] Curtius wrote to Browne on more than one occasion about Evelyn's book[2] and in a letter of 4 March 1670 written from 'Umbst.' he informed Browne: 'Je fairay mettre son livre dans le catalogue vernal qui va par toute l'Europe, esperant que quelqu'un l'interpretera aux estrangers.' Shortly afterwards in a letter, dated 30 April 1670, from Frankfurt, Curtius wrote to Browne again about Evelyn's treatise, saying: 'Le titre . . . de cette aggreable Sylva fera une autre chamade publique à tous les curieux au catalogue de septembre', and on 19 August 1670 he told Browne in a letter addressed from 'Umbst.':

Nos marchands sont retournés de Londres sans s'estre chargés du livre de Monsr Evelyn. J'en suis marry . . . que l'on n'en trouvera pas si tost le translateur. Au moins je voudrois faire iustice à l'autheur & le faire conoistre par le catalogue de la foire. Vous suppliant de m'envoyer au plustost & dans le pacquet de Monsr Williamson un petit billet seulement, portant le titre de cette seconde edition de Sylva & je le fairay mettre au catalogue susdit qui s'en va trouver les curieux de toute l'Europe.

In a letter dated Umbstat. 30 November [16]70 Sir William Curtius wrote to John Evelyn at Sayes Court about the newly published second edition of *Sylva*:[3]

Vous m'avez fait la grace de me mander le titre de votre seconde impression. Comme j'ay desia fait mettre le premier au catalogue universel de la foire, ainsi sera-il fait du second, et quidem in forma. Il seroit à souhaitter que nous eûssions le livre mesme. Nous luy trouverions possible un interprète, à l'imitation de celuy de la Societé Royalle . . .

C'est une marque de la guerre et des [sic] ses reliques que nos libraires n'entretraffi-quent plus comme en tems de paix, où il y avoit plusieurs boutiques de Londres ouvertes et inscrites à nostre foire . . .

Un homme docte m'escrit que si les Anglois continuent à n'escrire ces belles choses qu'en leur langue, ils nous obligeront de l'apprendre comme à Rome on faisoit du Grec . . .[4]

[1] Sir William Curtius was English Minister Resident and special envoy in Frankfurt am Main from 1654 until his death in 1678 (information supplied by Archivdirektor, Dr. Andernacht of Frankfurt am Main, in epist. 27.xi.67).
[2] See letters addressed by Sir William Curtius to Sir Richard Browne, preserved in the Evelyn loan collection (Browne letters, Box A–C) in Christ Church, Oxford.
[3] Several letters written by Sir William Curtius during the period Nov. 1667 to Dec. 1670 are dated from 'Umbstad.', 'Umbst.', or 'Umbstat.' Umstadt, now called Groß Umstadt, is a town in Hesse a few miles south of Frankfurt am Main and Curtius may have lived there.
[4] This quotation was copied from Sotheby's sale catalogue of the collection of MSS. formed by Sir Thomas Phillipps (item 597, in the sale of 26 June 1967). The MS. is now in the Houghton collection in Harvard University.

◁ 34. Evelyn's *Sylva*, 1664. Title-page with engraving of the arms of the Royal Society above the imprint. 10·7 × 5·4".

In the dedication of the third edition (1679) of *Sylva*, again addressed to Charles II, Evelyn told the King: 'I need not acquaint your Majesty how many millions of timber-trees (besides infinite others) have been propagated, and planted throughout your vast dominions, at the instigation, and by the sole direction of this work; because your gracious Majesty, has been pleas'd to own it publickly, for my encouragement.' When Evelyn found his *Sylva* was proving such a success he was sorry that he had not arranged for the Royal Society to benefit from its sales. On 11 July 1679 he voiced his regret in a letter to John Beale, F.R.S., in the following way:[1] 'I am onely vexed that it proving so popular as in so few yeares to passe so many impressions, and (as I heare) gratifie the avaricious printer with some hundreds of pounds; there had not ben some course taken in it for the benefit of our Society. It is apparent that nere £500 has ben already gotten by it; but we are not yet oeconomists.'

Further reference to the book's success is found in a letter, dated 4 August 1690, addressed by Evelyn to the Countess of Sunderland.[2] Here Evelyn writes of

my *Sylva*, which . . . is now . . . calling for a fourth impression, and has ben the occasion of propagating many millions of usefull timber-trees thro'out this nation, as I may justifie (without im'odesty) from ye many letters of acknowledgement receiv'd from gentlemen of the first quality, and others altogether strangers to me. His late Ma^ty Cha. the 2d. was sometimes graciously pleas'd to take notice of it to me, & that I had by that booke alone incited a world of planters to repaire their broken estates & woodes, which the greedy rebells had wasted & made such havock of.

The fourth edition of *Sylva* (spelt in this edition and subsequent editions with an *i* instead of a *y*) was published in 1706, the year of Evelyn's death.[3] This edition contains a frontispiece consisting of an engraved portrait of the author at the age of thirty, executed in Paris by his 'particular friend'[4] Robert Nanteuil (1623?–78).[5] Evelyn recorded the event in his *Diary* under 13 June 1650:[6] 'I sate to the famous sculptor Nanteuil . . . who engraved my picture in coper.' *Sylva* was published a fifth time in 1729. This edition, however, contains no portrait. All five editions, the fifth edition being issued in 1729, contain the two appendices entitled 'Pomona, or an appendix concerning fruit-trees, in relation to cider', and 'Kalendarium hortense'. The

[1] *Diary of John Evelyn . . . edited from the original MSS. by W. Bray . . . A new edition . . .* by H. B. Wheatley, **3**, 191 (1906) (Appendix).
[2] Ibid. **3**, 463–4 (1906) (Epistolary correspondence). The recipient of this letter was Anne, wife of Robert Spencer, second Earl of Sunderland.
[3] Evelyn died 27 Feb. 1706, and the fourth edition of *Sylva* appeared shortly after the author's death. See *The diary of John Evelyn . . .* edited by E. S. de Beer, **1**, 16 (1955) (Introduction).
[4] Evelyn (J.), *Sculptura*, etc. 92 (1662).
[5] This engraving is found in several states. See Keynes (G.), *John Evelyn a study in bibliophily and a bibliography of his writings*, 132–3 (1937), Cambridge.
[6] *The diary of John Evelyn . . . edited by E. S. de Beer*, **3**, 9–10 (1955).

latter treatise was also frequently published as a separate work.[1] The influence of 'Pomona' on fruit cultivation in this country appears to have been considerable, as is shown in a notice concerning the second edition of *Sylva*, published in the *Philosophical Transactions*. Here we read regarding the appended treatise:[2] 'And together with His Majesties great example, Pomona hath already encourag'd the plantation of many hundreds of nurseries, or orchards in England, which by this time begin to reward the industrious owners with a salubrious liquor, perhaps more agreeable to our English temperament, than the grapes of some countries do afford.' Although 'Pomona' was printed in all five editions of *Sylva*, it was never, according to Keynes,[3] published by itself. To the third edition of *Sylva* was added the author's 'Philosophical discourse of earth', which first appeared in 1676 as a separate publication, and to the fourth edition was appended 'Acetaria. A discourse of sallets', published separately in 1699 and 1706.[4]

Arboriculture was an endless source of interest and delight to Evelyn. Throughout his life he was constantly adding to his knowledge on the subject, from his own experience in the planting of trees, from observations made during his travels at home and abroad, and from other men's writings. From 1664 until 1706 Evelyn published four editions of *Sylva* and on each occasion the work was expanded. It contains an enormous amount of information concerning the cultivation of the various kinds of forest trees, and the uses of their timber, together with facts and anecdotes obtained from books, both classical and contemporary. The work was a success from the start. Its publication gave a great stimulus to planting in Britain, Charles II setting the example with the replenishing of the Royal forests.

In writing of *Sylva* and its influence on British forestry the poet Robert Southey (1774–1843) said that in his opinion it was 'one of the few books in the world which completely effected what it was designed to do'.[5] Southey, however, while praising the work points out that it contains various errors. He states that in spite of *Sylva* having 'no beauties of style to recommend it . . . he who opens the volume is led on insensibly from page to page, and catches something of the delight which made the author enter with his whole heart and all his faculties into the subject'.[6] Dendrology, wrote Southey, was to Evelyn

an object of unwearied curiosity and interest; he was continually adding to his store of

---

[1] See below, Bibliography, under Evelyn (J.), 1699, etc. 8°.

[2] *Phil. Trans.* 4, 1072 (15 Nov. 1669).

[3] Keynes (G.), *John Evelyn a study in bibliophily and a bibliography of his writings*, 144 (1937).

[4] See below, Bibliography, under Evelyn (J.), 1699, etc. 8°.

[5] *Quarterly Review*, 19, 47 (Apr. 1818) (Review [by Robert Southey] of 'Memoirs, illustrative of the life and writings of John Evelyn . . . Edited by W. Bray', 2 vols., 1818). This article is attributed to R. Southey by Shine (H.) and Shine (H. C.), *The Quarterly Review under Gifford, identification of contributors 1809–1824*, p. 60 (1949), University of North Carolina Press, Chapel Hill.

[6] *Quarterly Review*, 19, 47–8.

facts and observations in this his favourite pursuit; and thinking with Erasmus, that *ut homines, ita libros, indies seipsis* [sic] *meliores fieri oportet*, he laboured till the end of his long life in perfecting his great work. He speaks of his 'too great affection and application to it', when he was in the eighty-fourth year of his age. But by this constant care he made it perfect, according to the knowledge of that age. It is a great repository of all that was then known concerning the forest trees of Great Britain, their growth and culture, and their uses and qualities real or imaginary; and he has enlivened it with all the pertinent facts and anecdotes which occurred to him in his reading.[1]

Seventy years after Evelyn's death a new edition of *Sylva* was published, with extensive notes by Dr. Alexander Hunter of York. Four further editions of this were issued in 1786, 1801, 1812, and 1825 respectively.

There can be little doubt that, throughout the period covered by the present *History*, no other work on arboriculture exerted a greater influence on forestry in this country than Evelyn's *Sylva*, and certainly no other book on the subject was so often quoted. Among a few of the seventeenth- and eighteenth-century authors who, when writing of trees, included Evelyn's observations on the subject, were Moses Cook, T. Langford, John Reid, Richard Bradley, Stephen Switzer, Batty Langley, James Justice, the Earl of Haddington, William Boutcher, William Marshall, and Samuel Hayes. When Boutcher published his *Treatise on forest-trees* in 1775 he had just heard of the forthcoming publication of the new edition of Evelyn's *Sylva*, with notes, by A. Hunter. Boutcher voiced his opinion concerning its value as follows:[2]

Having mentioned Mr Evelyn, I must here express the sensible pleasure I feel, from hearing a fine impression of his *Silva*, with notes by some gentlemen of approved learning, and knowledge of gardening, is now printing. His observations on the culture of young plants in the seed-bed and nursery, tho' the best published before or during his time, are since then much improved, and they now become the least valuable part of his work; but the additions and remarks on these, with the other essential improvements that will apparently be made, must render it the most valuable book on the subject ever appeared. His just encomiums on the pleasures and advantages arising from well-cultivated plantations, if attentively read by young men of education and fortune, must animate all but the most tasteless and dull to the pursuits of gardening; and some of his chapters to that purpose, ought to be recorded in capital letters of gold, and hung up in the dining-rooms of all rich men who love their country, or mean to give the most striking example of true patriotism to the present and succeeding generations.

During the eighteenth century the demand for timber in the country, and the serious outlook with regard to future supplies, continued to be a reason for concern and, as we shall see later, by the time Hunter published his edition of Evelyn's *Sylva* in 1776, various writers such as Batty Langley, James Wheeler, William Watkins, and William Hanbury had drawn attention to the gravity of the situation. These writers pointed out that while vast quantities

---

[1] *Quarterly Review*, **19**, 48.   [2] *A treatise on forest-trees*, etc., pp. xxiii–xxiv.

The Oak Tree

Publish'd Jan.^t 1st 1776 by A. Hunter, M.D. as the Act directs.

J. Miller del. & Sculp.

35. 'The Oak Tree'. Drawn and engraved by John Miller. From Alexander Hunter's edition, 1776, of Evelyn's *Sylva*. Plate facing p. 69. 9·2×7·2". *Quercus robur* L., Common oak.

of timber were being felled for use by the Navy, as well as for civilian needs, little was being done with regard to replanting. In his preface Hunter writes: 'Soon after the publication of the *Silva* . . . in 1664 . . . the spirit for planting increased to a high degree; and there is reason to believe that many of our ships . . . in the last war . . . were constructed from oaks planted at this time', a reference presumably to the Seven Years War (1756–63). The five editions of *Sylva*, edited by Hunter, were issued between 1776 and 1825, a period during which we were for many years at war with France, and when much of the timber planted in Evelyn's day was rapidly becoming exhausted. However, in the words of the anonymous author of a review of the fourth edition (1812) of Hunter's book:[1] Hunter's 're-publication of the *Sylva* revived the ardour which the first edition had excited, and while forests were laid prostrate to protect our shores from the insults of the enemy, the nobility and gentry began once more to sow the seeds of future navies'. The second half of the eighteenth century saw the making of extensive plantations both in England and in Scotland. Landowners planted for patriotic reasons and for the value of timber as a long-term investment. They also followed the fashion, which became increasingly popular during the century, of using trees in a general plan for the embellishment of estates. Thus, Dr. Hunter chose a most appropriate time to republish *Sylva*.

Alexander Hunter (1729–1809) was born in Edinburgh. He received his early education at the grammar school in that city, and was afterwards entered at the University. During the last three years of his course medicine was his chief study. He continued his medical studies in London, Rouen, and Paris, before graduating Doctor of Medicine in Edinburgh in 1753. Subsequently, he practised his profession first at Gainsborough and then at Beverley, before going to York in 1763, where he remained until his death. Hunter took a prominent part in establishing the York lunatic asylum, and after the building was completed in 1777 was appointed physician. He was a Fellow of the Royal Societies of London[2] and Edinburgh.[3] As well as carrying out his duties as a successful physician, with an extensive practice, Hunter took a great interest in rural economy and played an active part in founding the Agricultural Society of York in 1770. Some of the papers read before this Society were edited by Hunter in four volumes under the title of *Georgical essays*. These volumes, published in London from 1770 until 1772, consist of essays 'in which the food of plants is particularly considered, several new composts recommended, and other important articles of husbandry explained, upon the principles of vegetation'. Many of the essays in

[1] *Quarterly Review*, **9**, 50–1 (Mar. 1813). The name of the anonymous author is Thomas Dunham Whitaker. See Shine (H.) and Shine (H. C.), *The Quarterly Review under Gifford, identification of contributors 1809–1824*, p. 35 (1949).

[2] Elected 2 Feb. 1775.

[3] According to the *D.N.B.* Hunter was elected in 1790.

the first two volumes are by Hunter himself.[1] Later editions of this work appeared in 1773 and 1777, and, in the nineteenth century, after the York Agricultural Society had ceased to exist, the work was greatly enlarged. To this edition, which was published at York (6 vols., 1803–4), Hunter added new essays on agricultural subjects, many of which had previously appeared 'in different periodical works'.[2]

Hunter's edition of *Sylva* (spelt *Silva*), a handsome quarto volume with extensive notes to bring it up to date and illustrated with a number of whole-page engravings, was published by private subscription, and the long list of several hundreds of subscribers indicates the wide interest in the work by persons and institutions, not only in England but also in Scotland and Ireland. One subscription came from as far away as the library of South Carolina. The price of each volume was two guineas and some copies contain the original printed receipt, dated 'York, August 20, 1776'. Of especial interest to planters must have been the valuable hints on raising trees from seed. Also the excellent account by William Speechly, gardener to the third Duke of Portland, 'describing the method of forming plantations upon the Duke's estate in the county of Nottingham'.[3]

The work is dedicated to John Evelyn's great-great-grandson, Sir Frederick Evelyn (1733–1812) of Wotton. A portrait of John Evelyn, drawn and engraved by Bartolozzi, faces the title-page. The numerous whole-page illustrations depicting the foliage, flower, and fruit of the trees described are drawn and engraved by John Miller, otherwise Johann Sebastian Mueller, the noted eighteenth-century botanical draughtsman and engraver. The excellence of these figures resulted in their being used to illustrate later works on silviculture, even up to the present day.[4] Other plates include a 'winter view of the Cowthorpe oak, near Wetherby, Yorkshire, by John Miller, who signs the plate 'J: M: fecit'.[5] This was made from a drawing by Hunter's friend William Burgh (1741–1808), the controversialist and Irish landowner, who lived nearly forty years of his life at York. There are also two views of the famous Greendale oak at the Duke of Portland's estate at Welbeck engraved by Thomas Vivares and A. Rooker respectively, from drawings made in 1775 by Samuel Hieronymus Grimm (1733–94), a Swiss landscape and social artist who came to England in 1768 and who worked here for the remainder of his life.[6] As stated earlier, Hunter's *Silva* appeared in five editions, the editions of 1812 and 1825 appearing after his death. Some copies of the first

---

[1] See *Georgical essays* [edited by A. Hunter], **4**, pp. i–ii (1772). The essays by Hunter in these two volumes 'do not bear a signature'.

[2] See *Georgical essays*, **1**, pp. viii–ix (1803).

[3] pp. 90–100.

[4] e.g. Miller's figures were copied and used to illustrate A[ikin]. (J.), *The woodland companion*, etc. (1802), and Edlin (H. L.), *British woodland trees* (1944).

[5] John Miller is given as the engraver of this plate by Davies (R.), *A memoir of the York Press*, etc. 275 (1868), Westminster.

[6] See Clay (R. M.), *Samuel Hieronymus Grimm of Burgdorf in Switzerland* (1941).

JOANNES EVELYN ARMᴿ

F.Bartolozzi del.et sculp.1776

36. Hunter's edition, 1776, of Evelyn's *Sylva*. Frontispiece portrait of John Evelyn, drawn and
engraved by Francesco Bartolozzi. 9·3 × 6·6″.

Wm Burgh Esqr delin.

A Winter View of the Cowthorpe Oak.

J. Miller sculp.

37. A winter view of the Cowthorpe oak, near Wetherby. Etched by John Miller after a drawing by William Burgh. From Alexander Hunter's edition, 1776, of Evelyn's *Sylva*, folding plate facing p. 500. 11·0 × 15·8″.

two editions have the plates coloured by hand. To the second (1786) and
subsequent editions of *Silva* was added 'Terra: a philosophical discourse of
earth'.

Although Evelyn's *Silva* was the most important book to appear during the
seventeenth century on forestry, there were other works of less note that
dealt with the planting and care of trees, including two small treatises by
Arthur Standish, published in 1611 and 1613 respectively.

The earlier of these two works is only partly concerned with this subject
as is revealed by the title which reads: *The commons complaint. Wherein is
contained two speciall grievances. The first is, the generall destruction and waste
of woods in this kingdome, with a remedie for the same . . . The second grievance
is, the extreame dearth of victuals. Foure remedies for the same.* This treatise,
dedicated to King James I, appeared in four editions in its first year of
publication. The threatened shortage of timber was a matter of great concern,
and Standish's treatise with 'some proiects for the increasing of woods'
received Royal approval, the King being pleased to grant the author sole
rights in the publication of his work. The Royal sanction, given on 1 August
1611,[1] is published in all editions seen by the present writer except the
earliest. The author appears to have been a man of some position as he is
referred to as 'Arthur Standish gentleman'.[2] Regarding his family home there
seems to be a certain amount of mystery. In the earliest edition of the work,
published in 1611, we read: 'at Avener, the house from whence I descended'.[3]
In the corrected copy of this edition in the British Museum (Bloomsbury)[4]
the name of the house is erased. In the next edition of 1611 is found the
statement 'at the house from whence I descended'[5] and finally, in another
edition of 1611,[6] and in the edition of 1612[7] the author refers to 'Standish
hall, the house from whence I descended'. Standish spent many years in the
study of forestry and for this purpose travelled 'through some parts of most
of the countries of this kingdome'.[8] In his own words his treatise was the
fruits of his 'old age and travell'.

This work was followed in 1613 by the same author's *New directions of
experience . . . for the planting of timber and fire-wood.* It is one of the first
treatises to be published in this country entirely devoted to forestry and,
again, as in the case of the earlier book, it received Royal approval.[9] In this

[1] 'Given under our signet . . . the first day of August, in the ninth yeere of our reigne of England, Fraunce, and Ireland, and of Scotland the five and fortieth'.

[2] Standish (A.), *The commons complaint*, etc. (1611) (King's approval).

[3] See copy in the Bodleian Library, Oxford (pressmark Tanner 820(1)), p. 20.

[4] Pressmark 809.d.3(1).

[5] See copy in the Bodleian Library, Oxford (pressmark Pamph. 9(3)), p. 20.

[6] Copies in Brit. Mus. (Bloomsbury) (pressmark 1028.i.1.(1)), and the Bodleian Library, Oxford (pressmark 4°.A.9(6) Art. B.S.). See p. 25.

[7] Copy in Brit. Mus. (Bloomsbury) (pressmark 1507/1410), p. 23 (i.e. F4ᵃ).

[8] Standish (A.), *The commons complaint*, etc. (1611) ('Epistle dedicatorie').

[9] The Royal approval for printing and publishing is the same as was used in *The commons complaint*, 1611, etc.

work Standish was severe in his condemnation of the vast amount of timber
used by certain industries; 'the making of yron and glasse', he writes, 'hath
beene, and is the greatest decay of wood.'[1] Another, more famous, critic of
this devastation of the forests was the poet Michael Drayton who wrote in
his *Poly-olbion*,[2] published only one year earlier:

> These yron times breed none, that minde posteritie.
>
> .   .   .   .
>
> Ioves oke, the warlike ash, veyn'd elme, the softer beech,
> Short hazell, maple plaine, light aspe, the bending wych,
> Tough holly, and smooth birch, must altogether burne:
> What should the builder serve, supplies the forgers turne;
> When under publike good, base private gaine takes holde,
> And we poore woefull woods, to ruine lastly solde.

Shortly before the publication of Standish's *New directions of experience*,
another work on the planting of trees had appeared by an author who had
been employed in the 'surveyes and sales of divers His Maiesties copies and
woods'. During the execution of his duties this writer found 'lamentable
scarcitie, and exceeding abuses', and he decided that it might be very bene-
ficial to the realm if he published a book compiled from notes he had made
during the course of his work.[3] Thus originated a treatise published in 1612,
entitled *An olde thrift newly revived. Wherein is declared the manner of planting,
preserving, and husbanding yong trees of divers kindes for timber and fuell.* The
text is written in the form of a dialogue 'betweene a surveyour, woodward,
gentleman, and a farmer'.[4] No author's name appears in this work, but the
title-page states that it is 'by R. C.' and the preface is signed 'R. Ch.' As the
author was apparently a surveyor, and as it is known that about 1608 the
King's surveyor to Lord Salisbury was called Rocke Church,[5] it seems highly
probable that Church was the writer of *An olde thrift newly revived*.

A treatise was published in 1670 entitled *England's improvement reviv'd:
digested into six books*, with an imprint reading 'In the Savoy. Printed by
Tho. Newcomb for the author'. This is yet another publication which drew
attention to 'the great wasts and decay of all woods and timber in England',
and the need for replanting.[6] It is by Captain John Smith and it deals chiefly
with forestry, a branch of husbandry which the author 'much delighted in,
and endevoured to know above 30 years'.[7] The dedication, addressed to
Viscount Brouncker, first President of the Royal Society and one of the

[1] Standish (A.), *New directions of experience*, etc. 4 (1613).
[2] Drayton (M.), *Poly-olbion*, 266 [1612] ('The seventeenth song').
[3] Ch. (R.), *An olde thrift newly revived*, etc. (1612) (Preface).
[4] Ibid. (1612) (title-page).
[5] See *Calendar of State papers, domestic series, of the reign of James I. 1603–1610 . . . Edited by M. A. E. Green*, 479 (1857).
[6] Smith (J.), *England's improvement reviv'd*, etc. (1670) (To the reader).
[7] Ibid. (1670) (To the reader).

Commissioners of the Navy,[1] is followed by a report of the work by John Evelyn, written at the request of the Royal Society. This commendatory letter is signed by Evelyn and dated 10 February 1668, from his home Sayes Court, at Deptford. The treatise was apparently finished, 'at least the first and biggest part', about three years before it appeared in print, the delay in publication being due to lack of funds.[2] Besides dealing with forestry, the book is concerned with livestock and the reclamation of waste land. The sixth 'book' contains an interesting description of the islands of Orkney and Shetland, and the fishing industry in those parts. This, however, is only another edition of Smith's treatise of 1661, entitled: *The trade & fishing of Great-Britain displayed: with a description of the islands of Orkney and Shotland.* John Smith visited the Shetlands in 1633, having been sent by the Earl of Pembroke to make a report of their trade and industries.[3] He remained in the Orkney and Shetland islands for at least a year,[4] and during these months studied their chief industry which was the fishing trade. At the time that he was sent to these Scottish islands, Smith was an apprentice 'to Mr. Matthew Cradock of London merchant, one of the Society for the fishing trade of Great-Britain'.[5]

In 1676 appeared *The manner of raising, ordering, and improving forrest-trees,* a popular treatise by the noted gardener Moses Cook, or Cooke as his name is sometimes spelt.[6] It is dedicated by the author to his master, Arthur Capel, Earl of Essex (1632–83).[7] Regarding Cook, John Evelyn wrote after a visit on 18 April 1680 to the Earl of Essex:[8]

upon the earnest invitation of the Earle of Essex went with him to his house of Cassioberie in Hartford-shire[9] . . . no man has ben more industrious than this noble lord in planting about his seate, adorn'd with walkes, ponds, & other rural elegancies . . . the gardens are likewise very rare, & cannot be otherwise, having so skillfull an artist to governe them as Mr. Cooke, who is as to the mechanic part not ignorant in mathematics, & pretends to astrologie: here is an incomparable collection of the choicest fruits.

Cook's treatise, a small quarto volume, contains much practical informa-

[1] William Brouncker, second Viscount Brouncker of Lyons, in the province of Leinster, Ireland (1620–84). President of the Royal Society 1663–77; Commissioner of the Navy 1664–79; a Lord of the Admiralty 1680–3.
[2] Smith (J.), op. cit. (1670) ('A farther advertisement to the reader').
[3] Ibid. 249. Philip Herbert, Earl of Montgomery and fourth Earl of Pembroke (1584–1650) established, at the King's request, 'the Association of Royal fishings in 1632'. See C[okayne]. (G. E.), *The complete peerage,* etc. **10**, 416 (1945).
[4] Smith (J.), op. cit. 252.
[5] Ibid. 249.
[6] The dates of Cook's birth and death are

not known. Stephen Switzer in *The Nobleman, gentleman, and gardener's recreation,* 47 (1715) writes of Cook as 'yet living'.
[7] Arthur Capel, eldest son and heir of Arthur, first Baron Capel of Hadham. His mother was Elizabeth, daughter and heir of Sir Charles Morrison, Bart., of Cassiobury Park, Hertfordshire. He was created, on 20 Apr. 1661, Viscount Malden of Essex, and Earl of Essex.
[8] *The diary of John Evelyn . . . edited by E. S. de Beer,* **4**, 199–200 (1955).
[9] Cassiobury Park is one mile NW. of Watford. For details see Britton (J.), *The history and description, with graphic illustrations, of Cassiobury park, Hertfordshire,* etc. (1837).

38. Cook: *The manner of raising . . . forrest-trees*, 1717. Engraved
frontispiece of second edition. 6·4 × 4″.

tion; it also includes many tables and mathematical calculations. 'I have used
arithmetick the more', says the author, 'because it is so usefull to the
ingenious planter.'[1] Appended to the 1679 edition of the work is a treatise by

---

[1] Cook (M.), *The manner of raising . . . forrest-trees*, etc. (1676) (To the reader).

the agricultural writer Gabriel Plattes[1] that was first published in 1639. It has no botanical interest except for a brief mention how to obtain dyes from plants and wood. *The manner of raising, ordering, and improving forrest-trees* was published in several editions, the last in 1724. As an example of the high praise it received from later authors on the subject, the following passage from *The practical husbandman and planter*[2] published in two volumes during 1733 and 1734, nearly sixty years after the first appearance of Cook's work, is of interest. In this publication, which was edited by the noted eighteenth-century gardener, Stephen Switzer, we read: 'Cooke's is indeed an excellent book, and one that has done more good in the nursery and forest way than any other that I know of.'

[1] i.e. '*A discovery of subterranean treasure: (viz.) of all manner of mines and minerals, from the gold to the coal; with . . . directions . . . for the finding . . . melting, refining, and assaying of them . . . Also a . . . way to try what colour any berry, leaf . . . or wood will give: with a . . . way to make colours that they shall not stain nor fade*, etc., London, Peter Parker (1679).

[2] See vol. **1**, p. xlv (Introduction).

III

EARLY SCIENTIFIC AND FLORISTIC WORKS
(continued)

THE seventeenth century was a time of great scientific activity, and during this period England produced famous pioneers in almost every department of science. We have already mentioned that the end of the century saw botany becoming increasingly scientific. This subject rapidly developed with the work of Robert Morison and John Ray in the systematic field, and of Nehemiah Grew, who with the Italian Marcello Malpighi laid the foundations for the knowledge of plant anatomy.

Robert Morison, the first distinguished Scottish botanist, was born at Aberdeen in 1620.[1] In 1635 he entered Marischal College[2] and in 1638 graduated as Master of Arts.[3] Later he fought for the Royalists against the Covenanters at the battle of the Bridge of Dee, when he was severely wounded. On his recovery he fled to France and studied the medical sciences at Paris. He took the degree of Doctor of Medicine at Angers in 1648. After this he devoted himself almost entirely to botany, and in 1650 he was appointed by Gaston Duc d'Orléans[4] to join Abel Brunyer and Nicolas Marchant[5] in taking charge of the Royal garden at Blois. He received the appointment through the recommendation of his friend Vespasien Robin,[6] botanist to the French King. In 1660 Morison returned to England and was appointed by Charles II to be King's physician and Royal Professor of Botany. His first published work, the *Præludia botanica*, appeared in 1669, and on 16 December of the same year he was elected Professor of Botany at Oxford, receiving the appointment partly on account of the reputation which his small octavo volume had gained for him. Apart from his professional duties, much of Morison's time at Oxford was spent in 'prosecuting his large design of publishing the universal knowledge of simples',[7] the *Plantarum historia*

[1] For a life of Morison and an appreciation of his works see Vines (S. H.) and Druce (G. C.), *An account of the Morisonian herbarium*, etc., pp. xxiv–lii (1914).

[2] Anderson (P. J.), *Fasti Academiae mariscallanae aberdonensis . . . MDXCIII–MDCCCLX*, vol. 2, 210 (1898), Aberdeen.

[3] Vines (S. H.) and Druce (G. C.), op. cit., p. xxv (1914).

[4] Gaston Jean-Baptiste de France, Duc d'Orléans (1608–60), younger son of Henry IV and brother of Louis XIII.

[5] Abel Brunyer (1573–1665) and Nicolas Marchant (d. 1678) were both members of the household of Gaston d'Orléans. The former being Gaston's physician and the latter his botanist. [6] Born 1579, died 1662.

[7] Wood (A. à), *Athenæ oxonienses . . . To which are added the Fasti . . . A new edition . . . by Philip Bliss*, 4 (1820) (see *Fasti*, Pt. 2, col. 315).

universalis oxoniensis. Unfortunately Morison was unable to finish this great undertaking as, on visiting London in November 1683 to attend to business concerned with his *Historia*, he was knocked down in the Strand by the pole of a coach. He died the following day from his injuries.

The *Prœludia botanica* is composed of two parts. The 'Pars prior', entitled 'Hortus regius blesensis auctus', is dedicated to Charles II, and consists of an alphabetical list of the plants in the Royal garden at Blois. It is based upon previous catalogues of the plants in this garden that had been published in Paris in 1653 and 1655.[1] These were compiled by Morison's colleague, Abel Brunyer. At the end of the second part of the *Prœludia* is an address to Abel Brunyer and Nicolas Marchant, in which Morison describes the Paris editions of the catalogue as being the joint work of himself and his two colleagues. It is possible that Morison assisted with the preparation of the first and second editions, but as pointed out by Franchet[2] it was to Brunyer alone that the work was officially entrusted.

The 'Pars altera' is dedicated to James, Duke of York and Albany, afterwards James II. It consists of a list of mistakes ('Hallucinationes') made by Gaspard Bauhin in his *Pinax* (1623), with Morison's corrections; followed by criticisms ('Animadversiones') of Jean Bauhin's *Historia plantarum universalis* (1650, 1651). It was only natural that the 'Pars altera' aroused a certain amount of indignation at the time, and that exception was taken to the expression 'Hallucinationes'. Although Morison's criticisms are, on the whole, justified, the Bauhins were illustrious botanists and scarcely deserved such unsympathetic treatment. Haller,[3] writing just over a century later, called the treatise 'invidiosum opus'.

The *Prœludia* concludes with a dialogue between the author, as Botanographus Regius, and a Fellow of the Royal Society, on the classification of plants. Morison alludes in this dialogue, in a very critical manner, to a recently published method of classification. No author's name is mentioned, but the method criticized had appeared in a chapter giving tables of plants, contributed by John Ray to Dr. John Wilkins's *Essay towards a real character, and a philosophical language* (1668). This attack by Morison was the beginning of a permanent estrangement between the two botanists.

In 1674 Morison was the editor of Paul Boccone's *Icones & descriptiones rariorum plantarum Siciliæ, Melitæ, Galliæ, & Italiæ,* with nearly 120 figures of plants shown on fifty-two plates in the text. Morison wrote a dedication for this work, dated 4 October 1673, which he addressed to the

---

[1] A copy of the 1655 Paris edition of the *Hortus regius blesensis* with MS. notes by Morison is on loan to the Bodleian Library, Oxford (pressmark MS. Sherard 28). This copy, the property of the University Department of Botany, is described by Vines and Druce in their *Account of the Morisonian herbarium,* etc., p. xxxiii (1914).

[2] Franchet (A.), *Flore de Loir-et-Cher,* etc., pp. xiii–xiv (1885), Blois.

[3] Haller (A. von), *Bibliotheca botanica,* etc. **1**, 543 (1771), Tiguri.

Hon. Charles Hatton, second son of Christopher, first Baron Hatton. Paul Boccone (1633–1704), author of a number of works on natural history, was a native of Palermo, Sicily. He was especially fond of botany and travelled widely in Europe in his search for plants. He also got into touch with men interested in natural science. In 1673 he visited England, and on 7 May attended a meeting in London of the Royal Society.[1] In 1682 he joined the order of Cistercians and took the name, in religion, of Silvio.[2]

The manuscript of the above work, together with the plates, was sent to Morison by Charles Hatton at Boccone's request. Hatton had been a pupil of Morison's during his residence in France. Morison had the work printed at Oxford. He found the plates to be not very accurate and had the last seven redrawn from dried specimens, and engraved at Hatton's expense.[3] The title-page bears the Sheldonian device, and the imprint: 'e Theatro Sheldoniano'.

Three copies of Boccone's *Icones* seen by the present writer contain a leaf with a second dedication. This is signed by Boccone and dated from Paris, 7 April 1673. It is addressed to the Royal Society.[4] Mr. Harry Carter, Archivist to the Oxford University Press, has told the present writer that the factotum initial in this inscription is not known in Oxford printing nor are any of the types. The type used for the text is the double pica, roman and italic, by François Guyot, of Antwerp, which was common in London printing, but not used by the University Press at Oxford. The canon type used in the heading is also used by many London printers but not at Oxford. None of the types or the factotum initial would have been found in Paris.

One of the three copies of the *Icones* seen by the present writer, containing the above dedication, is in the library of the Royal Society, while the other two copies are in the library at the Chelsea Physic Garden and in the writer's own library respectively. The copy in the Society's library has a manuscript note on the title-page, reading: 'Liber nomine authoris exhibitus Societati Regiæ d. 28 Maji 1674.' An entry in the *Journal book of the Royal society*, under 4 June 1674, reads: 'The Secretary [i.e. Henry Oldenburg] presented to the Society four books . . . the third . . . by Signr Boccone . . . called, Icones et descriptiones rariarum [*sic*] plantarum Siciliæ Melitæ Galliliæ et Italiæ, dedicated to the R. Society.' A reference to the *Icones* and to this dedication is found in a work by Boccone published at Amsterdam in 1674 under

[1] Birch (T.), *The history of the Royal society of London*, etc. **3**, 87 (1757).

[2] *Biographie universelle, ancienne et moderne*, etc. **4**, 626 (1811), Paris.

[3] Boccone (P.), *Icones*, etc. (1674) (Morison's dedication).

[4] In a letter dated from the Hague, 6 Sept. 1673, and written by Boccone to the Secretary of the Royal Society, Henry Oldenburg, Boccone writes that he takes the opportunity of sending Oldenburg 'l'epistre dedicatoire'. He also says: 'Je suis, Monsieur, entierement soumis a vos ordres, et mesme à votre naif jugement touchant mon ouvrage, et de cette dedicatoire, et je vous prie de vouloir changer tous les mots qui vous parroient choquer.' The author may be referring in this paragraph to the *Icones*. This letter is preserved in the library of the Royal Society. See *Letter book, Supplement*.

the title of *Recherches et observations naturelles*. Here the author writes:[1] 'Vous serés aussi bien aise d'apprendre qu'une partie des plantes rares, qui j'ay trouvé en Sicile ont esté imprimées à Oxford. L'ouvrage a quelques figures en taille douce, il est intitulé *Icones, & descriptiones rariorum plantarum Siciliæ, Melitæ, Galliæ, & Italiæ*, & je l'ay dedié à la Societé Royale de Londres.'[2]

Boccone addressed his dedication to the Royal Society in a very flattering tone and hoped, perhaps, that he would be given help with the publication of his work. There is, however, no record in the Society's account books that he received any financial help from this institution. On the other hand Charles Hatton was a generous patron whose assistance is acknowledged by Morison. It may be that Morison and Boccone disagreed over the inclusion of the latter's inscription which resulted in it being withdrawn. This would account for its rarity.

As already stated Morison spent much of his time at Oxford working on the history of plants. In the dedication addressed to Charles II in the *Præludia botanica* it is learnt that the author first decided to write such a work, which was to illustrate his system of classification, whilst he was at Blois, and that he had hoped for assistance in his undertaking from Gaston d'Orléans. Unfortunately, Gaston died in 1660. However, in spite of the loss of his rich patron, Morison continued his project, and in 1672 a specimen of the work he was preparing appeared under the title of *Plantarum umbelliferarum distributio nova*. There are two dedications, the first to James, Duke of Ormonde, Chancellor of the University, and the second to the Vice-Chancellor and the University. The Umbelliferæ constituted 'Sectio IX' among the fifteen sections into which Morison divided herbaceous plants, and the work is of interest as being the first monograph to be published of a definite group of plants. It is noteworthy for its twelve copper plates which give careful representation of separate parts of plants. Each plate was the gift of a donor, and bears his name with his office and heraldic arms. The work was printed by the Oxford Press, the imprint on the title-page reading: 'Oxonii, e Theatro Sheldoniano.' The Press had only been installed in the Sheldonian Theatre, built through the munificence of Archbishop Sheldon, in 1669,[3] where it remained until 1713 when it moved to the new Clarendon building near by. On 30 March 1669 David Loggan (1633 or 1635–92) was appointed 'Public sculptor' to the University ('Publicus academiæ sculptor', i.e. engraver)[4] and, in the opinion of Madan,[5] the above-mentioned twelve copper plates were engraved by this eminent draughtsman and engraver.

[1] p. 223.
[2] This passage appears in a letter addressed by Boccone to 'Monsieur Ange Matth. Buonfanti de Casserinis'.
[3] *Some account of the Oxford University Press 1468–1926*, p. 16 (1926), Oxford.
[4] Madan (F.), *Oxford books*, etc. **3**, p. xxxv (1931), Oxford.
[5] Op. cit. **3**, 264, Entry 2917 (1931).

The first part of Morison's *Historia* was to have been on trees and shrubs, but it was never printed. A statement by Schelhammer in a work published in 1687 gave rise to the idea that the manuscript once existed. Schelhammer[1] said he had seen the whole of Morison's work about eleven years previously, almost completed, with all its engraved illustrations in the possession of the author. This statement, however, lacks confirmation.

Thus the first volume of the *Historia* to be published was the 'Pars secunda'. It was printed by the Oxford Press under the title of *Plantarum historiæ universalis oxoniensis pars secunda*. This first volume, published in 1680, deals with herbaceous plants, and the author records in the preface that he started with this large and difficult group so as to finish it in his life-time. Only five, however, out of the fifteen sections into which Morison arranged herbaceous plants are dealt with in this volume, and he was able to complete only four more sections before he died.

The 'Pars secunda' contains 126 plates with a number of small figures of plants on each; a method of illustration common at the time but having little artistic merit. The figures are considered by Pulteney[2] to have been 'chiefly copied from other authors', and Vines and Druce[3] record that 'some of them, at any rate, were taken from the "Ecphrasis" of Fabio Colonna (1616)'. Most of the plates give no artist's name, although a few are signed by Francis Barlow, and a number by William Sunman (or Sonmans). Sunman was a Dutch portrait painter who came to England during the reign of Charles II. He spent part of his life at Oxford where he was employed by the University. Many of the plates are signed by well-known engravers of the period, such as David Loggan, Robert White who was Loggan's talented pupil, Abraham Blooteling the eminent Dutch engraver who lived in England for only two or three years, and William Faithorne. A number of the plates are also engraved by the Dutchmen Michael Burghers, who lived chiefly at Oxford and was employed by the University, and Frederik Hendrik van Hove. The cost of the 126 plates was provided for by a large number of friends, and on each plate is engraved the name and heraldic arms of the donor.

Large illustrated books were costly to produce and the *Historia* was the cause of considerable personal expense to the author. This is evident from a letter, dated 17 January 1681 [i.e. 1682], addressed to William Sancroft, Archbishop of Canterbury, in which Morison complains of 'the great charges' to which he had been put 'in setting out the first volume'.[4] John Johnson and Strickland Gibson in *Print and privilege at Oxford to the year 1700*

[1] *Hermanni Conringii in universam artem medicam singulasq: ejus partes introductio . . . Cura ac studio Guntheri Christophori Schelhammeri*, 351 (1687), Helmestadii.

[2] Pulteney (R.), *Historical and biographical sketches of the progress of botany in England*, etc.

1, 310 (1790).

[3] Vines (S. H.) and Druce (G. C.), *An account of the Morisonian herbarium*, etc., p. xliii (1914), Oxford.

[4] Letter in the Bodleian Library, Oxford (Tanner MS. 36, fol. 216).

record a number of interesting details concerning the publication of Morison's *Historia*.[1] For example, 'the University' "lent and layd out" no less a sum than £2,153 6s. on the work, whereas on the credit side "Dr. Morison received for 126 books which were subscribed for by noblemen and other persons of quality at £5 per book £630 besides 18 or 20 books disposed of to the libraries in the University" (S.E.P., Z.28 [of the University Archives])'.

The 'Pars tertia', with a dedication to the University of Oxford, was published in 1699, under the editorship of Jacob Bobart the Younger who had succeeded his father as Keeper of the Oxford physic garden.[2] The University had asked this skilled botanist to complete Morison's work, and they granted him a salary for the job.[3] Prefixed to this volume is an interesting 'Vita Roberti Morisoni M.D.' compiled by an unknown author. During 1697 and 1698 the eminent Scottish physician Dr. Archibald Pitcairne (1652–1713) corresponded with Dr. Robert Gray on a life of Morison, and a study of this correspondence, now preserved in the British Museum (Bloomsbury),[4] suggests that Pitcairne in collaboration with Gray wrote the 'Vita' of 1699.

On 18 May 1709 the antiquary Thomas Hearne (1678–1735) recorded in his diary[5] the following information concerning the preface to the 'Pars tertia'.

It must be noted that after Mr. Jacob Bobart had finish'd his volume of the History of plants, he writ a preface to it, which he shew'd the Delegates of the Press; but they not approving of it, because of the barbarity of the Latin, advis'd him to get somebody to mend it, & some of them pitch'd upon Mr. (now Dr.) Hudson;[6] accordingly the preface was put into Mr. Hudson's hands, & he drew it up in proper Latin, & return'd it. 'Twas compos'd as Mr. Hudson worded it, & a very few copies printed off, particularly there is one of them before Mr. Dyer's copy of ye book at Oriel college; but Bobart, for reasons best known to himself, had a quite different one printed, drawn up partly by himself & partly by others, wch is prefixed to all ye copies except those very few before mention'd.

Unfortunately, Mr. Dyer's copy of the *Historia* is no longer at Oriel College, and the present writer has, so far, been able to find one version only of the preface in all copies of the book examined.

Facing the title-page of the 'Pars tertia' is a portrait of Morison looking to the right and holding a scroll, in an oval frame of flowers on a pedestal. This

[1] pp. 139–41, footnote 3 (1946), Oxford.
[2] See above, p. 96.
[3] See Vita Roberti Morisoni in *Plantarum historiæ universalis oxoniensis pars tertia*, b2 (1699).
[4] See Sloane MS. 3198, ff. 19–29.
[5] *Remarks and collections of Thomas Hearne . . . Edited by C. E. Doble*, 200 (1886) (Oxford Hist. Soc., vol. 2).
[6] i.e. John Hudson (1662–1719), a classical scholar. In Apr. 1701 he was elected Librarian of the Bodleian Library, Oxford, and the following June received the degree of Doctor of Divinity.

Su̅ma̅n Pinxit.

R. White Sculpsit.

ROBERTUS
Natus Aberdoniæ
Anno 1620.

MORISON M:D
Obiit Londini
Anno 1683.

Quæ **Morifone** *viro potuit contingere major*
Gloria, **Pæonium** *quam superaſſe genus?*
Ipſe tibi palmam **Phœbus** *concedit* **Apollo,**
Laureaque est capiti quælibet herba tuo.

Poſuit Archibaldus Pitcarn. M D

39. Morison's *Historia*, Part 3, 1699. Frontispiece portrait of Robert Morison engraved by Robert White after a painting by William Sunman. 13·5 × 8·5″.

line engraving, made from a painting by William Sunman, is by Robert White (1645–1703) who was responsible for a very large number of engraved portraits made both from his own drawings and from those of other draughtsmen. Among his subjects, writes Colvin,[1] 'were nearly all the most interesting characters of his time in England'. The 166 botanical plates represent many hundreds of species of plants, and the greater number of the plates are signed by F. H. van Hove or Michael Burghers. Regarding the last six plates which are all engraved by Burghers, Pulteney says:[2] 'The six tables of mosses, fuci, corallines, and corals, . . . are, except the few wooden cuts of Gerard, the first of the kind graved in England, and have great merit as the productions of that time.' The cost of the 'Pars tertia' appears to have been borne mainly by the University.[3] Some of the illustrations, however, were presented by persons interested in the project, and sixty-nine of the 166 plates bear the names of donors and their heraldic arms.

Many years after Morison's death appeared an anonymous pamphlet entitled *Historiæ naturalis sciagraphia*, with an imprint reading 'Oxon M. DCC. XX'. The device on the title-page, a shield with hollow sides, would indicate that the pamphlet was printed by one of the small surviving printers of Oxford and not at the University Press proper.[4] This tract, attributed to Jacob Bobart the Younger,[5] is important as it gives the only full statement of Morison's method of classification with, however, some modifications, considered by Vines and Druce to have been introduced by Bobart under the influence of Ray's *Methodus*. The outline of the classification of trees and shrubs contained in the first seven pages agrees with that in a work in Bobart's handwriting on loan to the Bodleian Library, Oxford,[6] and 'its special value', Vines and Druce point out,[7] 'is that it includes the classification of trees and shrubs in accordance with which the unpublished "Pars prima" of the "Historia" should have been written'. The last five pages of the *Sciagraphia* (i.e. pp. 8–12) are a reprint of the 'Botanologiæ summarium', giving an outline of the classification of herbaceous plants in fifteen 'Sectiones' according to Morison's method, prefixed by Bobart to the 'Pars tertia' of the *Historia*. The *Sciagraphia* is a very rare work,[8] and for this reason it was

[1] Colvin (S.), *Early engraving and engravers in England (1545–1695)*, p. 137 (1905).

[2] Pulteney (R.), *Historical and biographical sketches of the progress of botany in England*, etc. **1**, 310 (1790).

[3] Vines (S. H.) and Druce (G. C.), *An account of the Morisonian herbarium*, etc., pp. lx–lxi (1914). Regarding financial agreements made between Morison's widow and the Delegates of the Press, concerning the *Historia* see Johnson (J.) and Gibson (S.), *Print and privilege at Oxford to the year 1700*, pp. 139–41, and footnote 3 on p. 139 and continuing on p. 140 (1946).

[4] According to Dr. John Johnson, formerly Printer to the University of Oxford, in epist. 4.v.51.

[5] See below, Bibliography, under Historiæ naturalis sciagraphia, 1720, 8°.

[6] Pressmark MS. Sherard 34 (this manuscript is the property of the Department of Botany of the University of Oxford).

[7] Op. cit., p. lix.

[8] The only copy known to the present writer is in the Bodleian Library, Oxford (pressmark Sherard 296 (3)).

reprinted verbatim by Vines and Druce, in 1914, in their *Account of the Morisonian herbarium.*[1]

Let us now consider the other great British systematic botanist of this era—John Ray.[2]

Ray was born in 1627 at Black Notley, near Braintree, Essex, the son of a village blacksmith. When still a child he drew attention to himself by his unusual intellectual ability, and after attending Braintree Grammar School he was sent to Cambridge, largely because of the interest taken in him by Samuel Collins, Vicar of Braintree.[3] Ray was admitted on 12 May 1644 as a sizar at Trinity College. He migrated on 28 June 1644 to Catherine Hall, and on 21 November was readmitted to Trinity. At the University Ray showed 'great diligence, learning, and virtue'.[4] He graduated Bachelor of Arts in 1647–8, and in 1649 was elected to a fellowship. Afterwards he held a succession of college appointments as well as becoming tutor 'to many gentlemen of honourable birth and attainments'.[5] In order to hold his fellowship it was necessary for Ray to be ordained and thus on 23 December 1660 he took Holy Orders, being ordained in London by Robert Sanderson, Bishop of Lincoln. Unfortunately, Ray's academic career came to an abrupt end in 1662 because, being unwilling to subscribe to the Act of Uniformity, he was forced to give up his fellowship and college appointments. Ray left Cambridge and from then on much of his life was spent in the study of natural history and in the writing of books. He was elected a Fellow of the Royal Society on 7 November 1667,[6] and after the death of Henry Oldenburg on 5 September 1677 was invited to be Secretary of this institution.[7] This honour, however, Ray was not prepared to accept. In 1673 Ray married, and when his mother died six years later he and his wife went to live in her house, the Dewlands, at Black Notley. Ray remained there until his death in 1705.

Ray's first botanical work was published in 1660.[8] This was an alphabetically arranged catalogue of Cambridge plants written in Latin, for unlike Morison, who in Ray's opinion did not know how to write Latin,[9] Ray was a master of that language. He conceived the idea of writing this book at a time when he developed a great interest in botany. This was about nine years previous to its publication when, according to the preface, he was physically and mentally sick and resting from more serious study. He was helped in the

[1] pp. xliv–l.

[2] Much has been written on Ray and his works; e.g. see Raven (C. E.), *John Ray . . . his life and works* (1942), Cambridge, ed. 2 (1950); Keynes (G.), *John Ray a bibliography* (1951), Cambridge, ed. 2 (1968), Oxford.

[3] Raven (C. E.), op. cit. 18–19 (1942).

[4] Derham (W.), *Select remains of . . . John Ray*, etc. 3 (1760).

[5] Pulteney (R.), *Historical and biographical sketches of the progress of botany in England*, etc.

1, 193 (1790).

[6] *The Record of the Royal society of London,* etc. 380 (1940).

[7] *The diary of Robert Hooke . . . 1672–1680 . . . Edited by H. W. Robinson and W. Adams,* 316 (1935).

[8] *Catalogus plantarum circa Cantabrigiam nascentium.*

[9] See letter written by John Ray to Martin Lister in *The correspondence of John Ray . . . Edited by E. Lankester,* 42 (1848).

preparation of the work by his great friend John Nidd, a Senior Fellow of Trinity College who died shortly before the catalogue was completed, and by two younger men, Francis Willughby (1635–72),[1] and the latter's cousin, Peter Courthope. An appendix was published in 1663 of which a second edition appeared in 1685. Regarding the latter Raven states that 'it is not Ray's work, nor is it mentioned in his letters'.[2] It appears to have been chiefly compiled by one of Ray's friends, a Cambridge apothecary named Peter Dent.

During the period 1658 until 1672 Ray made a number of botanical journeys through various parts of England and Wales, and he also visited the Isle of Man and Scotland. In addition, from April 1663 until April 1666, he spent three years on the Continent when he visited the Low Countries, Germany, Switzerland, Italy, Malta, and France. On this tour Ray added to his knowledge of natural history, particularly in the field of botany, and observed and collected a great many plants.[3]

As a result of his tours in Britain Ray acquired a first-hand knowledge of our native flora and he was able to use the material he gathered during these journeys in preparing his *Catalogus plantarum Angliæ, et insularum adjacentium*, published by John Martyn, publisher to the Royal Society. It appeared in 1670 dedicated to Ray's friend Francis Willughby. Up to now Ray had spelt his name Wray, but the catalogue appeared under the authorship of Joannes Raius. In a letter to the naturalist Dr. Martin Lister, Ray gives the following reason for this alteration of spelling:[4] 'You will notice that in the title and dedication of the catalogue I have rejected the initial letter W. of my name. That you may not be surprised, I confess that I adopted it formerly without any good reason, thereby altering the ancient and paternal spelling.' The English catalogue is written in Latin and is alphabetically arranged with the Cambridge plants marked with a capital C. A marked feature of the work is the amount of space devoted to the medical uses of herbs. We have already dealt with the popular and widely read herbals published during the seventeenth century on astrological botany and the doctrine of signatures.[5] Ray had no sympathy with the many superstitious beliefs connected with plants, and both in his Cambridge catalogue and his English catalogue he attacked such credulousness. In the opinion of Raven,[6] Ray's attention to this subject 'did

---

[1] Francis Willughby, only son of Sir Francis Willughby of Middleton Hall, Warwickshire. Educated at Trinity College, Cambridge. Interested in natural history, especially entomology. Elected a Fellow of the Royal Society in 1663. Accompanied Ray on several journeys in Britain, and during 1663–4 was with Ray at the commencement of his continental tour.

[2] Raven (C. E.), *John Ray . . . his life and works*, 122, footnote 2 (1942).

[3] Ray's herbarium of European plants is preserved in the British Museum (Natural History).

[4] *The correspondence of John Ray . . . Edited by E. Lankester*, 65 (1848). The letter is in Latin. The present writer is indebted to Mr. H. Sellers, sometime Assistant Keeper in the British Museum (Bloomsbury) for a translation.

[5] See above, pp. 82–92.

[6] Raven (C. E.), *John Ray . . . his life and works*, 159 (1942).

important service in promoting the scientific investigation of the medical use of plants, and in combating its age-long association with superstition'.

A copy of the second edition (1677) of the English catalogue preserved in the British Museum (Bloomsbury) contains manuscript notes by Ray,[1] and is considered by Keynes to be 'the author's copy prepared for a third revised edition'.[2] However, although Ray planned a third edition it was never published. The publisher, John Martyn, died and, according to Ray,[3] his successors refused to give payment for any revision and enlargement of the work. The latter also threatened to take proceedings against any other publisher who undertook its production. Ray, therefore, gave up the idea of a third edition and he issued instead a supplement entitled *Fasciculus stirpium britannicarum*. This was published in 1688 by Henry Faithorne, Martyn's successor as publisher to the Royal Society, and it appeared under the authorship of 'Joanne Raio & ab amicis'.

Reference has already been made to Ray's first venture at a system of classification, the tables of plants that he contributed to Wilkins's *Essay towards a real character and a philosophical language* (1668).[4] His first comprehensive attempt, however, did not appear until 1682, when his *Methodus plantarum nova* was published by Faithorne and Kersey. This octavo volume is dedicated to Charles Hatton who was also the friend of Robert Morison.[5] A second edition of this work, giving the final form of Ray's system of classification, appeared in 1703 under the title of *Methodus plantarum emendata et aucta*. This book had been completed some time before it was published as in a letter, dated 19 February 1700 [i.e. 1701], addressed by Ray to Dr. (later Sir) Hans Sloane,[6] we read:[7] 'As to my "Methodus emendata", it lies by me finished, and ready for the press, but I believe will hardly ever be printed. No bookseller will undertake it.' This work, considered to be a real improvement on that of 1682, might never have been published but for the kindness of the Professor of Botany at Leyden, Dr. Peter Hotton (1648–1709), who arranged for the printing to be done in Holland.[8] Although it was published by Jansson–Waesberg of Amsterdam, the imprint on the title-page describes the book as being published in London by Samuel Smith and Benjamin Walford. This was done against the author's wish by the Waesbergs who thought it would be to their advantage.[9] On 20 January 1702 [i.e. 1703] Ray wrote to Hans Sloane:[10] 'I have a small present for you, which I entreat you to accept as *magni affectus e[x]iguum effectum*. It is my "Methodus

[1] Pressmark C.112.aa.6.
[2] Keynes (G.), *John Ray a bibliography*, 17 (1951).
[3] Ray (J.), *Fasciculus stirpium britannicarum* (1688) (Preface).
[4] See above, p. 120.
[5] See above, p. 121.
[6] Hans Sloane was created a baronet in 1716.
[7] *The correspondence of John Ray . . . Edited by E. Lankester*, 370 (1848).
[8] Derham (W.), *Select remains of . . . John Ray . . . with his life*, 76 (1760).
[9] Ibid. 77.
[10] *The correspondence of John Ray . . . Edited by E. Lankester*, 409 (1848).

plantarum emendata et aucta'', of which I have desired Mr. Smith to send or deliver you two copies, one in the larger, and the other in the common paper.' Ray showed his gratitude to Dr. Hotton by dedicating the work to him.

40. Ray: *Methodus plantarum emendata et aucta*, 1703. Frontispiece portrait of John Ray engraved by Abraham de Blois after a painting by William Faithorne. 6·6 × 3·9".

The frontispiece consists of a portrait of the author by William Faithorne, engraved by the Dutch engraver Abraham de Blois. The same portrait, engraved by William Elder, had already appeared in 1694 in Ray's *Stirpium europæarum . . . sylloge.*

On 15 March 1682 [i.e. 1683] the physician and naturalist Dr. (later Sir) Tancred Robinson wrote to Dr. Martin Lister:[1] 'Your friend Mr. Ray is about writing a generall herball, which must needs be very accurate.' This is the first information we have regarding Ray's most outstanding contribution to botany—his *Historia plantarum*, published in three volumes in 1686, 1688, and 1704 respectively. It contains the descriptions of all the plants known at that time, arranged according to the author's system of classification. The first fifty-eight pages of Volume 1 contain an introduction to botanical science that includes a survey of plant classification, morphology, and physiology. 'The mass of information in these thirty chapters', writes Raven,[2] 'is masterfully handled; the evidence is skilfully set out and its bearing on the sequence of the argument clearly shown; the result is an exposition of the best theoretical and experimental knowledge of the time.' In the preface Ray tells his readers that he originally started collecting material for the work at the suggestion of his friend Francis Willughby, but on the latter's death in 1672 he decided to give up the task. In addition Ray knew that Morison was working on a similar project. However, when Morison died Ray was persuaded by Charles Hatton and other friends to continue his project. The Royal Society approved of the work and in September 1685 the Council ordered 'that Henry Faithorne should print Ray's *Historia plantarum*'.[3] The following year saw the publication of Volume 1 and Birch records,[4] that on 7 July 'Mr. Faithorne, the bookseller, presented the Society with the first tome of Mr. Ray's *Historia plantarum* of the best paper fairly bound'.

Although the second volume is dated on the title-page 1688 it was evidently issued the previous year, as on 6 December 1687 Tancred Robinson wrote to Hans Sloane:[5] 'Mr Ray's second volume is now finished, and I have one for you which I will order Mr. Faithorne to send you by the first shipping.' Ray acknowledged in the preface the assistance given him by four helpers, including Leonard Plukenet and James Petiver. Later, further reference will be made to Plukenet and Petiver and to their own publications, including the latter's *Catalogue of Mr Ray's English herbal illustrated with figures on folio copper plates* [1713, 1715].

Considerable delay was experienced in the publication of the third volume,

[1] *Further correspondence of John Ray. Edited by R. W. T. Gunther*, 136–7 (1928).

[2] Raven (C. E.), *John Ray . . . his life and works*, 222 (1942).

[3] *Further correspondence of John Ray. Edited by R. W. T. Gunther*, 154 (1928).

[4] Birch (T.), *The history of the Royal society of London*, etc. 4, 493 (1757).

[5] *Further correspondence of John Ray. Edited by R. W. T. Gunther*, 155 (1928).

or supplement, to the *Historia plantarum*. Although negotiations between Ray and the printer started in 1698,[1] the volume was not published until 1704, the year before the author's death. With this last volume the record of all known plants was brought up to date, and it included more than 10,000 new entries.[2] This was a wonderful achievement when it is remembered that we know from Ray's correspondence that, during the last period of his life, he was a very sick man, and that, towards the end of the preparation of this volume, his strength was failing rapidly.

The *Historia plantarum* was not illustrated, and the author may well have felt a certain amount of envy when he looked at the fine figures in Morison's *Historia*, many of which bear the name and heraldic arms of a donor. Ray, however, intended to have plates as is evident both from a letter he addressed on 16 June 1684 to Dr. Tancred Robinson,[3] and from the notice headed: 'De iconibus sculpendis admonitio' at the end of the first volume. But engravings would have been a great additional expense and by 2 August 1689 we find Ray writing to his friend Edward Llwyd:[4] 'As for cutts to my History of plants there are none to be expected; the book sells not so well as to encourage the undertakers to be at any further charge about it. The times indeed of late have not been very propitious to the booksellers trade.' Many years later, at the beginning of the nineteenth century, the celebrated botanist Sir James Edward Smith wrote about the *Historia plantarum*:[5] 'This vast and critical compilation is still in use as a book of reference.' But regarding the lack of illustrations the same authority continues: 'So ample a transcript of the practical knowledge of such a botanist cannot but be a treasure; yet it is now much neglected, few persons being learned enough to use it with facility, for want of figures and a popular nomenclature.'

In 1688 in the preface to the *Fasciculus stirpium britannicarum* Ray had said: 'Next Spring if God give me strength and health I have decided to publish a *Synopsis stirpium britannicarum* with brief and characteristic notes not only of the genera but of all particular species.'[6] This promised work appeared in 1690, with the *imprimatur* dated 22 January 1689 [i.e. 1690] and signed by John Hoskyns, Vice-President of the Royal Society. According to Ray's correspondence the printing of the *Synopsis* was first in the hands of Mr. Motte,[7] but difficulties arose and the work was later transferred to Samuel Smith, the bookseller whose name appears in the imprint. The work is

[1] For details of these negotiations see Raven (C. E.), *John Ray . . . his life and works*, 300 (1942).

[2] Raven (C. E.), op. cit. 304 (1942).

[3] *The correspondence of John Ray . . . Edited by E. Lankester*, 146 (1848).

[4] *Further correspondence of John Ray. Edited by R. W. T. Gunther*, 191 (1928).

[5] See The life of John Ray . . . by Sir J. E. Smith (from Rees's *Cyclopædia* [1819]) in *Memorials of John Ray . . . Edited by E. Lankester*, 77 (1846).

[6] Translation by Canon Raven. See Raven (C. E.), *John Ray . . . his life and works*, 247 (1942).

[7] *Further correspondence of John Ray. Edited by R. W. T. Gunther*, 202, 204, 292-3 (1928).

dedicated to Sir Thomas Willughby (c. 1670–1729), the younger son of Ray's late friend Francis Willughby.[1]

On 17 August 1691 Ray told Edward Llwyd that he was 'revising & enlargeing' the *Synopsis*.[2] He was prepared, therefore, when in the summer of 1694 the publisher, Samuel Smith, called upon him for a second edition.[3] This edition, published in 1696, has received high praise from biographers. In 1819 Sir James Edward Smith wrote:[4] 'Of all the systematical and practical floras of any country, the second edition of Ray's *Synopsis* is the most perfect that ever came under our observation.' In recent years Raven expressed equally high praise, when he stated that:[5]

In the *Synopsis*, apart from the Linnean nomenclature, we have a modern hand-book. The survey of species is remarkably accurate, at least in the flowering plants. The country has been adequately explored. The names and brief descriptions make identification easy. The classification, if not scientifically perfect, follows a natural sequence and is as easy to use as the modern scheme. British botany has been given a secure and intelligible foundation.

A third edition of the *Synopsis* was published in 1724, nearly twenty years after Ray's death. Although no editor's name appears on the title-page or in the work, the editor was in fact Johannes Jacobus Dillenius (1684–1747),[6] who became in 1734 the first Sherardian Professor of Botany at Oxford.[7] Born at Darmstadt, Dillenius was a German botanist who came to England in 1721 at the invitation of William Sherard, to whom further reference will be made. It appears that the *Synopsis* was published without mentioning the editor because people were 'unwilling a foreigner shou'd put his name to it'.[8] This may have been due to jealousy or prejudice. The work contains many species new to Britain, especially among the cryptogams, and it is illustrated with twenty-four engravings executed from drawings by the editor.[9] A copy of this publication in the British Museum (Bloomsbury)[10] contains the plates only, all carefully coloured by hand, and according to an inscription, on a leaf preceding the plates, the figures are 'Illuminated by the editor, Joh: Ja: Dillenius, M.D.&c.'[11]

[1] Thomas Willughby succeeded his brother as second baronet in September 1688. In Jan. 1711 [i.e. 1712] he was created Baron Middleton.

[2] *Further correspondence of John Ray. Edited by R. W. T. Gunther*, 220 (1928).

[3] Ibid. 247.

[4] See The life of John Ray . . . by Sir J. E. Smith (from Rees's *Cyclopædia* [1819]) in *Memorials of John Ray . . . Edited by E. Lankester*, 78 (1846).

[5] Raven (C. E.), *John Ray . . . his life and works*, 258–9 (1942).

[6] Dillenius was born 22 Dec. 1684 at Darmstadt. He died at Oxford 2 Apr. 1747. See *Neue deutsche Biographie*, **3**, 718–19 (1957), Berlin, under Dillenius, Johann Jakob.

[7] Gunther (R. W. T.), *Oxford gardens*, etc. 17 and 171 (1912), Oxford.

[8] *Extracts from the literary and scientific correspondence of Richard Richardson*, etc. [edited by D. Turner], 204 (1835), Yarmouth.

[9] Druce (G. C.), *The Dillenian herbaria . . . Edited . . . by S. H. Vines*, p. xx (1907) (biography of Dillenius).

[10] Pressmark 969.f.23.

[11] Another copy of the 1724 edition of the *Synopsis* with an inscription saying the plates are coloured by Dillenius is in the Bodleian Library Oxford (pressmark MS. Sherard 211).

In 1673 appeared Ray's *Observations topographical, moral, & physiological; made in a journey through part of the Low-countries, Germany, Italy, and France: with a catalogue of plants not native of England.* A number of years later, in 1694, a revision of the catalogue of foreign plants was published under the title of *Stirpium europæarum extra britannias nascentium sylloge.* The frontispiece of this octavo volume is a portrait of the author by Faithorne, engraved by William Elder.[1] In the opinion of Raven,[2] the importance of the *Sylloge* for the history of botany, and of Ray's work, lies in the preface in which the author discusses classification, defending his own system against that of August Quirinus Rivinus (Bachmann).

On 3 February 1695 [i.e. 1696] Ray wrote to Hans Sloane:[3] 'I am now upon a little treatise concerning the method of plants, wherein I shall give a more particular account of the several methods that have been attempted, and especially of my own, with an answer to what Monsieur Tournefort hath objected against it.' The 'little treatise' mentioned in this letter was published in 1796 under the title of *Joannis Raii de variis plantarum methodis dissertatio brevis.* This brief dissertation is chiefly an answer to the criticism made by the French botanist Joseph Pitton de Tournefort in his work entitled *Élémens de botanique,* published in Paris in 1694.[4]

[1] See above, p. 131.

[2] Raven (C. E.), *John Ray . . . his life and works,* 283–5 (1942).

[3] *The correspondence of John Ray . . . Edited by E. Lankester,* 286 (1848).

[4] For an account of the history and development of this controversy between Ray and Tournefort see Raven (C. E.), op. cit. 288–91 (1942).

IV

EARLY SCIENTIFIC AND FLORISTIC WORKS
continued

Two authors are frequently referred to by Ray in the *Historia plantarum*: Nehemiah Grew and Marcello Malpighi, the pioneers in England and Italy respectively, in the field of microscopic botany, and the creators of the science of plant anatomy.

Nehemiah Grew (1641–1712), after receiving his early education at Coventry, was admitted at the age of seventeen a pensioner at Pembroke Hall, Cambridge. He graduated Bachelor of Arts in 1661. Later he went to Leyden where in July 1671 he took his doctor's degree in medicine. It appears that on his return to England Grew set up in practice at Coventry, but that soon afterwards he moved to London. He was evidently successful in his profession for in 1680 he was admitted an honorary Fellow of the College of Physicians. Grew first turned his attention to the study of plant structure in 1664.[1] His reason for doing this was as follows.[2] He had noticed that while the 'anatomy of animals' had been studied since early times, that of plants had been hardly 'so much as thought upon'. 'But', he writes, 'considering that both came at first out of the same hand, and are therefore the contrivances of the same wisdom; I thence fully assured my self, that it could not be a vain design, though possibly unsuccessful, to seek it in both.' Thereupon Grew made a study of the structure of plants, and by 1670 he had written his first treatise on the subject.[3] His investigations were presented to a meeting of the Royal Society by John Wilkins, Bishop of Chester. His work was approved, and on 11 May 1671 the Council of the Society issued an order for *The anatomy of vegetables begun* to be printed by the Society's printer. A few months later, on 7 December 1671, four copies of the printed book were delivered complete by the printer, Spencer Hickman, to the Royal Society. These were presented on Grew's behalf for distribution: 'One for the Society, one for the President, and two for the two Secretaries.'[4]

While Grew was making a study of plant anatomy in England, Marcello

---

[1] Grew (N.), *The anatomy of plants*, etc. (1682) (Preface).

[2] Grew (N.), *The anatomy of vegetables begun*, etc. (1672) (Preface).

[3] Grew (N.), *The anatomy of plants*, etc.

(1682) (Preface).

[4] Birch (T.), *The history of the Royal society of London*, etc. **2**, 498 (1756). It is of interest to note that the title-page of Grew's work is dated 1672.

Malpighi (1628–94) was working, apparently unknown to Grew, on the same subject in Italy. This eminent Italian physician and naturalist was a native of Crevalcore, near Bologna. He studied philosophy and medicine at Bologna University where from 1661 to 1691 he was Professor of Medicine. In 1691, on becoming chief physician to Pope Innocent XII, he moved to Rome, where he died soon afterwards. Now the Royal Society received communications of scientific interest not only from Englishmen but also from foreigners, and Malpighi was a regular correspondent of this illustrious body of which he had been elected a Fellow on 4 March 1668 [i.e. 1669].[1] By a strange coincidence, at the same meeting of the Royal Society at which Hickman, the printer, presented the above-mentioned four copies of Grew's *Anatomy of vegetables begun*, the Society's Secretary, Henry Oldenburg, read a letter from Malpighi, dated 'Bologna Nov. 1, 1671'. This accompanied a manuscript containing an abstract of his observations and considerations of the structure of plants, which, he said, he intended to 'inlarge and to illustrate with figures, if he should find, that the Society approved of his attempt'.[2] The Englishman and the Italian must have started working on this subject at about the same time. Later, controversy arose over the question of priority, but as Grew's manuscript had been received by the Royal Society several months before that of Malpighi, the honour of priority can be fairly claimed for the Englishman.[3]

Henry Oldenburg, as Secretary of the Royal Society, was asked to reply to Malpighi's letter, and to state that the Society would be very glad to see his work on the structure of plants 'brought to that perfection, which was intended by him'.[4] With this encouragement Malpighi continued his project. His preliminary sketch, or 'Anatome plantarum idea' as it was called, was later prefixed to his enlarged treatise on the subject, the *Anatome plantarum*.[5] This work received the Royal Society's *imprimatur* signed by Lord Brouncker, as President of the Society, on 24 June 1675, and it was published in the same year. A 'Pars altera' was published in 1679. Both parts contain the same allegorical half-title, engraved by Robert White. It consists of cupids playing with three leopards, and garlands of fruit, with two cupids on a tree behind picking fruit. Malpighi acquired great skill as a microscopist; he was also an accurate draughtsman, and his figures of plant anatomy illustrating his work are outstanding. As Miall remarks,[6] 'we are often astonished that so early an investigator should have seen so much and understood so well what he saw'. The original drawings for the half-title and for the figures of all the plates in both parts, as well as the original manuscript of the work of 1675, are

[1] *The Record of the Royal society of London*, etc. 381 (1940).

[2] Birch (T.), *The history of the Royal society of London*, etc. **2**, 499 (1756).

[3] Arber (A.), Nehemiah Grew 1641–1712 in *Makers of British botany . . . edited by F. W.* *Oliver*, 48 (1913), Cambridge.

[4] Birch (T.), op. cit. **2**, 499 (1756).

[5] The author's *De ovo incubato* was added as an appendix to this work.

[6] Miall (L. C.), *The early naturalists their lives and work (1530–1789)*, p. 150 (1912).

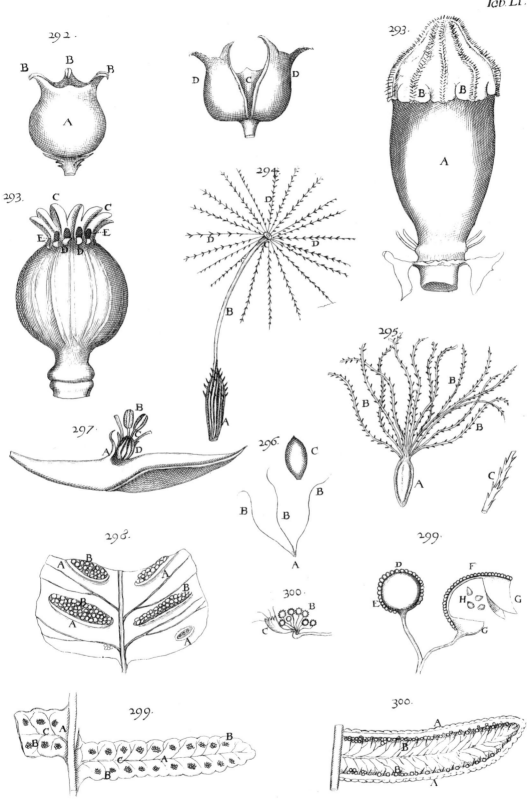

41. Malpighi: *Anatome plantarum*, 1675. Plate 51 illustrating variation in the form of fruiting and spore-bearing bodies. 12·5 × 8·4″.

preserved in the library of the Royal Society. The drawings are executed in red chalk.

On the 16 November 1671, shortly before his first treatise was published, Grew was elected a Fellow of the Royal Society,[1] and at a meeting of the Society on the following 10 April the 'Bishop of Chester proposed Dr. Grew to be a Curator of the Society for the anatomy [of] plants for a year, upon subscriptions, amounting to fifty pounds, to be made by such members as should be willing to contribute thereto'.[2] This proposal was approved, and Grew thus received both encouragement and money from the Society for the continuance of his work. In 1673 his second treatise was published under the title of *An idea of a phytological history propounded. Together with a continuation of the anatomy of vegetables, particularly prosecuted upon roots. And an account of the vegetation of roots grounded chiefly thereupon.* Grew's third botanical work, *The comparative anatomy of trunks,* appeared in 1675. Regarding the annotated copy of this book in the British Museum (Bloomsbury),[3] Arber has pointed out that from internal evidence 'it seems almost certain that this is the author's copy, corrected in his own handwriting'.[4]

In 1682 Grew's three treatises, much revised, were published in a folio volume, dedicated to Charles II, and entitled *The anatomy of plants. With an idea of a philosophical history of plants. And several other lectures, read before the Royal society.* The work contains eighty-three plates with carefully executed figures. The author, in his preface, shows his anxiety to make his text as clear as possible by the use of good illustrations, and states:

> In the plates, for the clearer conception of the part described, I have represented it, generally, as entire, as its being magnified to some good degree, would bear. So, for instance, not the barque, wood, or pith of a root or tree, by it self; but at least, some portion of all three together: whereby, both their texture, and also their relation one to another, and the fabrick of the whole, may be observed at one view.

This excellent method of illustration led Arber to remark:[5] 'One cannot help wishing that botanists of the present day would more often take the trouble to illustrate their papers on this principle.'

Grew and Malpighi, together, are regarded as the founders of the science of plant anatomy. These two men wrote on a subject that could hardly have existed before their day, and it was only natural that time should prove them mistaken in many of their conclusions. Nevertheless according to Gilmour,[6] 'Grew, in the meagre leisure of a London physician, contrived, with Malpighi, to sketch a picture of plant anatomy, the main outlines of which still

[1] Birch (T.), *The history of the Royal society of London,* etc. 2, 490 (1756).

[2] Birch (T.), op. cit. 3, 42 (1757). On 15 Jan. 1672 [i.e. 1673] the Society recommended that the subscriptions should be continued (Birch (T.), op. cit. 3, 72 (1757)).

[3] Pressmark 972.a.10.

[4] Arber (A.), Nehemiah Grew 1641–1712 in *Makers of British botany . . . edited by F. W. Oliver,* 51 and plate VI (1913).

[5] Arber (A.), op. cit. 52 (1913).

[6] Gilmour (J.), *British botanists,* 22 (1944).

Part of a Vine Branch cut transversly, and
split half way downe $\stackrel{e}{y}$ midle.

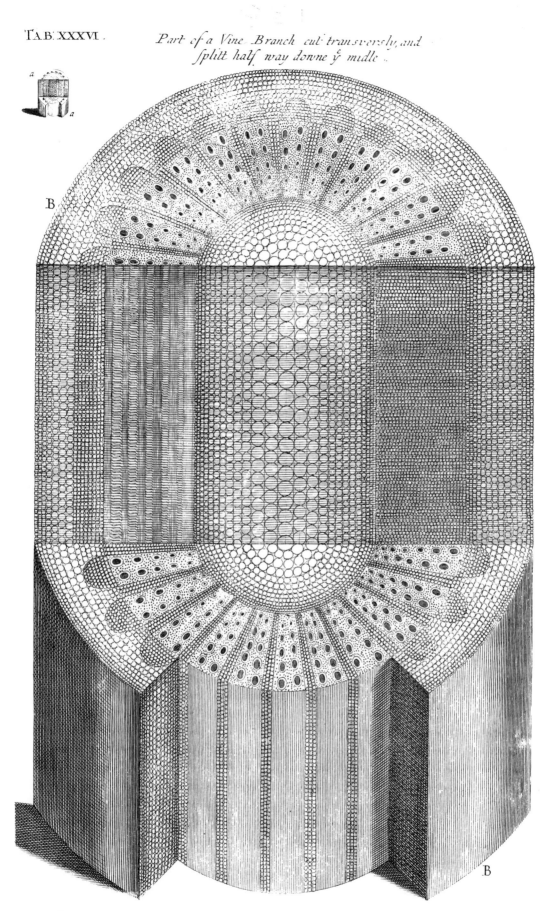

42. Grew: *The anatomy of plants*, 1682. An illustration by Nehemiah Grew of 'Part of a vine
branch cut transversly, and splitt half way downe $\stackrel{e}{y}$ midle'. Plate 36. 10·6 × 6·5".

serve as the framework of the science'. Grew has been accused at various times of having plagiarized from the writings of Malpighi, but these accusations have been shown to be without foundation.[1] 'There is now practically no doubt', Arber wrote,[2] 'that Grew was an independent worker, and was only definitely indebted to Malpighi, in so far as he himself acknowledges it.' The two botanists themselves appear to have been always on the best of terms. This is evident when studying the correspondence of Grew, Malpighi, and Oldenburg the Secretary of the Royal Society. A letter illustrating the cordiality existing between the two men is published by Carruthers in the *Journal of the Royal microscopical Society*.[3]

As stated earlier, before Grew plant anatomy had been hardly 'so much as thought upon'. In the preface to his *Anatomy of plants* (1682) Grew says that in the preparation of his researches he had only a few writings which offered him any assistance, namely Nathaniel Highmore's *History of generation* (1651), Robert Sharrock's *History of the propagation and improvement of vegetables* (1659),[4] and afterwards, in 1665, Robert Hooke's *Micrographia*. Sharrock's book, the only one of these three treatises to concern us here, was published at Oxford. The dedication is addressed to Robert Boyle. Its chief interest lies in the fact that Robert Sharrock (1630–84) was one of the earliest writers to be interested in the scientific study of plant cultivation, and his work was referred to by both Grew[5] and Ray.[6] This author was a Fellow of New College, Oxford.[7] In 1684 he became Archdeacon of Winchester, 'being then', according to Wood,[8] 'accounted learned in divinity, in the civ. and com. law, and very knowing in vegetables and all pertaining thereunto'.

Among those who assisted John Ray in the preparation of the second volume of his *Historia plantarum* was Dr. Leonard Plukenet (1642–1706).[9] Of the life history of this 'learned, critical, and laborious botanist'[10] little is known. It seems likely that he received his early education at Westminster School.[11] He matriculated in 1662, aged twenty, at Hart Hall, Oxford.[12] His portrait as a middle-aged man is prefixed to his *Phytographia* (1691–6) and beneath is inscribed: 'Leonardi Plukenett. D.M. effigies ætat: suæ 48 año

[1] See Carruthers (W.), On the life and work of Nehemiah Grew, *J. R. micr. Soc.* 137–41 (1902), also Arber (A.), The relation of Nehemiah Grew and Marcello Malpighi. *Chron. Bot.* 6, 391–2 (1941).

[2] Arber (A.), Nehemiah Grew 1641–1712 in *Makers of British botany . . . edited by F. W. Oliver*, 48 (1913).

[3] pp. 140–1 (1902). Reprinted in *J. Bot.* (London), 40, 199–200 (1902).

[4] The date on the title-page is 1660. See below, Bibliography, under Sharrock (R.), 1660 [1659], 8°.

[5] Grew (N.), *The anatomy of plants*, etc. (1682) (Preface).

[6] e.g. see p. 15, etc., of Ray's *Historia plantarum*, etc. 1 (1686).

[7] Elected 5 Mar. 1648 [i.e. 1649].

[8] Wood (A. à.): *Athenæ oxonienses . . . A New edition . . . by Philip Bliss*, 4, col. 147 (1820).

[9] Ray (J.), *Historia plantarum*, etc. 2 (1688) (Preface).

[10] Pulteney (R.), *Historical and biographical sketches of the progress of botany in England*, etc. 2, 18 (1790).

[11] Jackson (B. D.), Dr. Leonard Plukenet, *J. Bot.* (London), 32, 248 (1894).

[12] Foster (J.), *Alumni oxoniensis*, etc., vol. 3, early series, 1172 (1892).

LEONARDI PLUKENETT. D.M.
EFFIGIES Ætat:suæ 48 Año Dom:1690

Collins sculp.

43. Plukenet's *Phytographia*, Part 1, 1691. Frontispiece portrait of Leonard Plukenet engraved by John Collins. 7·6 × 5·7″.

Dom: 1690', but, so far, his biographers have failed to discover where he took his degree. About 1672 Plukenet was living in St. Margaret's Lane, near Old Palace Yard, Westminster, and there he seems to have resided for the rest of his life.[1] It appears that a few years before he died Plukenet was appointed Superintendent of the Royal garden at Hampton Court, his patron being Queen Mary, consort of William III, who also granted him the title of Queen's Botanist.[2]

The first known reference to Plukenet as a botanist is found in a letter written 11 February 1684 [i.e. 1685] by John Ray to Hans Sloane.[3] His collection of dried plants was notable, and Trimen and Dyer record[4] that after his death 'Plukenet's vast herbarium of more than 8,000 plants, mostly passed into the hands of Dr. Moore, Bishop of Norwich . . . from Dr. Moore they were purchased by Sir Hans Sloane.' Now they form part of the collection of *horti sicci* in the Sloane herbarium of the British Museum (Natural History).[5]

Plukenet did not publish any botanical work until he had reached middle age. His *Phytographia*, *Almagestum botanicum*, *Almagesti botanici mantissa*, and the *Amaltheum botanicum*, four books which may be considered as one great catalogue of plants, with figures of new and rare species, were published during the years 1691–1705 inclusive. The *Phytographia*, the first of these works, was published in four parts between 1691 and 1696, and contains plates only. The *Almagestum botanicum* consists of letterpress only, and was published in 1696. The *Almagesti botanici mantissa*, or appendix to the *Almagestum*, appeared in 1700, and the *Amaltheum botanicum*, the author's last work, was issued in 1705. Many of the plants figured and described in these works were from Plukenet's own herbarium. He obtained his specimens through the help of correspondents in all parts of the world, and also from the gardens about London which were daily being enriched by new and rare plants from abroad.

The *Phytographia* is referred to by Linnæus as 'Opus incomparabile'.[6] The frontispiece portrait of this volume is engraved by John Collins. The title-page is printed from two plates: a plate with the title which is etched and a plate with a small oblong illustration engraved by John Collins. This illustration shows a scholar, probably intended to be the author, sitting at a table with his books, and above is a motto reading: 'Ut pene nullus sic ardeo. Alijs inserviendo consumor.' The first five words form an

[1] Trimen (H.) and Dyer (W. T. T.), *Flora of Middlesex*, etc. 374 (1869).

[2] Jackson (B. D.), Leonard Plukenet, 'Queen's botanist', *J. Bot.* (London), **20**, 340 (1882).

[3] *The correspondence of John Ray . . . Edited by E. Lankester*, 139 (1848).

[4] Op. cit. 376 (1869).

[5] For details regarding the volumes of Plukenet's herbarium see Britten (J.), *The Sloane herbarium . . . revised and edited by J. E. Dandy*, 184–7 (1958).

[6] *Caroli Linnæi . . . Bibliotheca botanica . . . editio altera*, etc. 27 (1751) Amstelodami.

LEONARDI PLUKENETY

PHYTOGRAPHIA,

Sive

Stirpium Illustriorum, & minus cognitarum

ICONES,

TABULIS ÆNEIS,

Summâ diligentiâ elaboratæ;
Quarum unaquæg. Titulis descriptorys
ex Notis Suis propriis, & Characteristicis
desumptis, insignitâ; ab alijs ejusdem
Sortis, facile discriminatur.

PARS PRIOR.

MEMINISSE JUVABIT.

I Collins fec:

Ἐμπειρον εἶναι συμβάλλω ἰητρόν ἒι διοτε
πάντων φυτῶν. Gal. de Antidot. lib. 1. cap. 15.

LONDINI, MDCXCI.

SUMPTIBUS AUTORIS.

44. Plukenet's _Phytographia_, Part 1, 1691. Etched title-page with small oblong design engraved by John Collins. 9·2×6·2″.

anagram of the author's name, Leonardus Plucenetius. The first part of the *Phytographia* is dedicated to Henry Compton (1632–1713),[1] who, during the years he held office as Bishop of London, made the gardens at Fulham famous for their collection of exotic trees and plants. Of this prelate's love of gardening Stephen Switzer, the noted eighteenth-century gardener and author, relates:[2]

This Reverend Father was one of the first that encouraged the importation, raising, and increase of exoticks, in which he was the most curious man in that time, or perhaps will be in any age; and by the recommendation of chaplains into foreign parts, had likewise greater advantages of improving it than any other gentleman could. He had above 1000 species of exotick plants in his stoves and gardens, in which last place he had endenizon'd a great many that have been formerly thought too tender for this cold climate. There were few days in the year, till towards the latter part of his life, but he was actually in his garden ordering and directing the removal and replacing of his trees and plants. A virtuous and laudable pattern, and a person by whom gard'ning has not a little been recommended to the world.[3]

The second part of the *Phytographia* is dedicated to Hans Willem Bentinck (1649–1709), first Earl of Portland, who from 1689 until 1700 held the office of Superintendent of the King's gardens;[4] the third part is inscribed to William III, who spent so much time designing and planting to his taste the gardens of Hampton Court and Kensington Palace.

The *Almagestum botanicum*, published in 1696, was criticized by John Ray, who wrote on 17 July 1696 to Hans Sloane:[5]

I have gotten a sight of Dr. Plukenet's 'Almagæstum bot.,' though as yet he hath not presented me with a copy of it; I find in it many mistakes in the language, and in the composition of Greek names; and I doubt not but there are many in the matter. It is impossible but that a man who relies wholly upon dried specimens of plants (be he never so cunning) should often mistake and multiply . . . As far as I am able to judge, he is often out in his conjectural synonymes.

The plates in the *Phytographia*, *Mantissa*, and *Amaltheum botanicum* contain 'upwards of 2740 figures' of plants,[6] most of which were drawn from dried specimens. As was the custom of the time the figures are small, several

---

[1] Henry Compton, Bishop of London from 1675 until 1713, was the youngest son of Spencer Compton, second Earl of Northampton.

[2] *Ichnographia rustica*, **1**, 70–1 (1718).

[3] Bishop Compton was noted for his generosity in allowing botanists free access to his garden, and in willingly communicating to them such plants and seeds as he possessed. Among botanical authors who acknowledge assistance received from Dr. Compton in the preparation of their works are John Ray, Leonard Plukenet, and James Petiver. For 'An

account of the Bishop of London's garden at Fulham' read to the Royal Society on 27 June 1751 by Mr. (later Sir) William Watson, F.R.S. see *Phil. Trans.* **47** (for 1751 and 1752), 241–7 (1753).

[4] C[okayne]. (G. E.), *The complete peerage*, etc. **10**, 589–90 (1945).

[5] *The correspondence of John Ray . . . Edited by E. Lankester*, 297 (1848).

[6] Pulteney (R.), *Historical and biographical sketches of the progress of botany in England*, etc. **2**, 27 (1790).

being included on one plate. They were executed on copper by different engravers. Many are signed by Michael van der Gucht (1660–1725). This native of Antwerp came to England when quite young and studied under David Loggan. His work met with considerable success and he stayed in this country until his death, being chiefly employed by the booksellers.

Plukenet published his first three books himself, the imprint on the title-page of each work reading: 'Sumptibus autoris.' He was assisted in the cost of producing the *Amaltheum* by eleven eminent men of the day who each sub-scribed five guineas for single copies of the work.[1] The names included Dr. Moore, Bishop of Norwich, who purchased Plukenet's herbarium after the latter's death, and Henry Compton, Bishop of London.

Plukenet's work suffers from various errors and imperfections. 'It is, not-withstanding', writes Pulteney,[2] 'a large magazine of botanical stores; inas-much as, no work before published by one man, ever exhibited so great a number of new plants. And as many of the English species are here figured, for the first time, it has been equally acceptable to the lovers of indigenous, as of exotic botany.' Plukenet received high praise from Linnæus who said in his *Bibliotheca botanica*:[3] 'Nullus botanicorum plures novas plantas detexit, quam ille qui, ut fere nullus, sic ardebat ad locupletandam botanicen.'

The famous Swede held Plukenet's work in great esteem, and, as pointed out by Jackson,[4] 'nearly every page of Linnæus's *Species plantarum* refers to some one or other of his works'. A Linnæan key to Plukenet's works was published at Hamburg in 1779, compiled by the German physician and botanist, Paul Dietrich Giseke (1745–96).[5]

Plukenet is severely critical in the *Mantissa* of the writings of Sir Hans Sloane and James Petiver. But Sir James Edward Smith, in his biography of Plukenet,[6] whilst lamenting this botanist's 'severity of stricture on the literary labours of Sloane and Petiver', considers that 'his criticisms, how-ever severe, are not unjust'. These three authors were often at variance, and Sloane and Petiver, in their respective works, were often equally harsh in their strictures on Plukenet. Britten and Dandy in their guide to the contents of the Sloane herbarium, with historical information about the contributors,[7] have pointed out that 'the publications of the three men—Sloane, Petiver and Plukenet—whose collections now form part of one whole, and are thus available for comparison with their reciprocal criticisms, abound in strictures couched in terms of considerable severity'.

---

[1] See list of subscribers on leaf facing the title-page of the *Amaltheum*.

[2] Pulteney (R.), *Historical and biographical sketches of the progress of botany in England*, etc. **2**, 27–8 (1790).

[3] p. 60 (1736), Amstelodami.

[4] Jackson (B. D.), Leonard Plukenet, 'Queen's botanist', *J. Bot.* (London), **20**, 338 (1882).

[5] *Index Linnæanus in Leonhardi Plukenetii, M. D. Opera botanica*, etc.

[6] In Rees (A.), *The cyclopædia*, etc. **27** (1819).

[7] Britten (J.), *The Sloane herbarium . . . revised and edited by J. E. Dandy*, 183 (1958).

Sir Hans Sloane (1660–1753), an eminent and successful physician of his day, is chiefly remembered by posterity as a collector, and as a founder of the British Museum.[1] He was also an enthusiastic and outstanding naturalist, taking an interest in this subject even in boyhood. 'I had from my youth', he tells us,[2] 'been very much pleas'd with the study of plants, and other parts of nature.' Sloane was born at Killyleagh in County Down, Ireland, and after spending his childhood in his native country came to London in 1679 to study medicine.[3] Here he was able to continue his favourite pastime of botany in the physic garden at Chelsea which had been established by the Society of Apothecaries only a few years earlier. In the spring of 1683 Sloane went to France and continued his medical training in Paris. Here he was able to study botany under the famous Joseph Pitton de Tournefort (1656–1708). On 28 July 1683 Sloane received his doctor's degree at the University of Orange, near Avignon, and afterwards went on to Montpellier, armed with letters of introduction from Tournefort to M. Pierre Chirac, Professor at that University and its Chancellor. On 23 May 1684 Sloane left Montpellier and after staying for a time in Paris returned to London. On 21 January 1684 [i.e. 1685] he was elected a fellow of the Royal Society, and just over two years later he was admitted as a Fellow of the Royal College of Physicians. About this time Sloane was invited to be physician in the suite of the newly appointed Governor of Jamaica, Christopher Monck, second Duke of Albemarle (1653?–88). He accepted the invitation, set sail from England in September 1687, and arrived at Jamaica the following December. Soon afterwards, in the autumn of 1688, the Duke died, and in the following year Sloane accompanied the widowed Duchess back to England, arriving in London in May 1689.

When he returned to England Sloane brought with him a rich harvest of his activities as a scientific collector. On the outward journey he was able to collect plants from Madeira, Barbados, Nevis, and St. Kitts, and his time in Jamaica gave him a wonderful opportunity in which to search and examine the natural history of that island. Regarding the large collections made by Sloane during these months, John Evelyn, on 16 April 1691, noted in his *Diary*:[4]

I went to see Dr. Sloans curiosities, being an universal collection of the natural productions of Jamaica consisting of plants, [fruits,] corralls, minerals, [stones,] earth, shells, animals, insects &c: collected by him with greate judgement, several folios of

[1] For details of the first founders of the British Museum see Edwards (E.), *Lives of the founders of the British museum . . . 1570–1870* (1870).

[2] Sloane (Sir H.), *A voyage to the islands Madera . . . and Jamaica*, etc. 1 (1707) (Preface).

[3] For a detailed life of Sir Hans Sloane see Beer (Sir G. R. de), *Sir Hans Sloane and the British museum* (1953). Also Brooks (W. E. St. John), *Sir Hans Sloane the great collector and his circle* (1954).

[4] *The diary of John Evelyn . . . edited by E. S. de Beer*, 5, 48 (1955).

dried plants & one which had about 80: severall sorts of fernes, & another of grasses: &c: the Jamaica pepper in branch, leaves, flowers, fruits &c: [which] with his journal, & other philosophical and naturall discourses & observations is indeede very extraordinary and copious, sufficient to furnish an excellent history of that iland, to which I encouraged him, & exceedingly approved his industry.

The 'history' that Evelyn had encouraged appeared in two volumes in 1707 and 1725 respectively, under the title of: *A voyage to the islands Madera, Barbados, Nieves, S. Christophers*[1] *and Jamaica, with the natural history . . . of the last of those islands.* Only part of this 'Natural history of Jamaica', as it is generally called, deals with plants, and it is not included in the present *Bibliography.* It may be noted, however, that before it was published, Sloane generously placed his manuscript at the disposal of Ray who extracted details of the new species of Jamaican plants for use in the third volume (1704), or Supplement, to his *Historia plantarum.*[2] Regarding this kindness Ray wrote in 1697 to Edward Llwyd:[3] 'Dr. Sloane's History of Jamaica plants, wch he hath frankly contributed to my work, is indeed a great treasure, he having very exactly described every species; it will make up a 3d part of the Supplement. He described all in English, so that I am at the pains of turning it into Latine.'

Previous to the appearance of the 'Natural history of Jamaica', was published Sloane's *Catalogus plantarum quæ in insula Jamaica sponte proveniunt* of 1696. This small octavo volume received the following appreciative review in the *Philosophical Transactions,*[4] from John Ray: 'The author of this catalogue doth not present the reader with titles of plants collected out of other mens writings, or of which he had seen only dryed specimens, but of such as himself saw growing in their native places: among which there are a great multitude of new and non-descript species.' The work was also held in high esteem by Linnæus.[5] Plukenet, however, with whom Sloane was often at variance in botanical matters, attacked in his *Almagesti botanici mantissa* (1700), many statements in Sloane's catalogue,[6] and as pointed out by Edwards,[7] 'sometimes on well-grounded objections; more often upon exceptions rather captious than just, and with that bitterness of expression which is the unfailing finger-post of envy'. Sloane bided his time before answering his critic, and the publication of his 'Natural history of Jamaica' gave him his opportunity. In this work the author not only defended himself against Plukenet's strictures but also, in his turn, often criticized his assailant.[8]

There are extant two issues of Sloane's catalogue. These are identical

[1] Or St. Kitts.
[2] Raven (C. E.), *John Ray . . . his life and works,* 301 (1942).
[3] *Further correspondence of John Ray.* Edited by R. W. T. Gunther, 271 (1928).
[4] No. 221, pp. 293–6 (for June–Aug. 1696).
[5] See *Caroli Linæi . . . Bibliotheca botanica . . editio altera,* etc. 140 (1751), Amstelodami.
[6] e.g. p. 174, etc.
[7] Edwards (E.), *Lives of the founders of the British museum . . . 1570–1870,* pp. 282–3 (1870).
[8] e.g. vol. 1, 160, etc.

Feb. 26. 1695.

IIn Concilio Regiæ Societatis Londini ad Scientiam Naturalem promovendam inftitutæ ; Liber cui Titulus, *Catalogus Plantarum,* quæ in Infulâ Jamaicâ fponte proveniunt, &c. *Autore Hans Sloane, M.D. Reg. Soc. & Colleg. Reg. Med. Lond. Socio,* Imprimatur.

Robertus Southwell,

V. P. R. S.

TRactatum hunc, cui Titulus *Catalogus Plantarum* quæ in Infula Jamaica fponte proveniunt, &c. dignum Judicamus qui Imprimatur.

Datum in Comitiis Cenforiis ex ædibus Collegii noftri, Mart. 6. 1695.

Samuel Collins, Præfes.
Tho. Burwell,
Rich. Torleffe,
Will. Dawes, Cenfores:
Tho. Gill.

CATALOGUS
PLANTARUM
QUÆ IN
INSULA JAMAICA

Sponte proveniunt, vel vulgò coluntur, cum earundem Synonymis & locis natalibus ; adjectis aliis quibufdam

QUÆ IN

Infulis Maderæ, Barbados, Nieves, & Sancti Chriftophori nafcuntur.

Seu Prodromi

Hiftoriæ Naturalis Jamaicæ
Pars Prima.

Autore *HANS SLOANE,* M. D. Coll. Reg. Med. Lond. nec non Soc. Reg. Lond. Soc.

LONDINI:
Impenfis *D. Brown,* ad Infigne Cygni & Bibliorum extra Portam vulgò dictam *Temple-Bar.*
MDCXCVI.

45. Sloane: *Catalogus plantarum quæ in insula Jamaica sponte proveniunt,* 1696. The title-page, 5·8 × 3·1″, and the verso of the leaf immediately preceding it, 4·9 × 3·0″. By mistake of the printer 'the licence of the Royal Society was placed before that of the President and Censors of the College of Physicians'.

Illuftriffimis Doctiffimifque Viris

Præfidi, Concilio, & Sociis

Clariffimæ Societatis Regiæ Londi-

nenfis ad promovendam Scientiam

Naturalem inftitutæ,

NEC NON

Præfidi, Electoribus, Cenforibus

E T

Sociis Celeberrimi Coll. Reg. Med. Lond.

Quorum aufpiciis Hiftoria Naturalis & Medica

quotidiè augetur, hunc qualemcunque

Tractatulum in Obfervantiæ &

Gratitudinis Teftimonium

Dedicat

AUTOR.

A   PRÆ-

46. Sloane: *Catalogus plantarum quæ in insula Jamaica sponte proveniunt*, 1696. The recto of the leaf immediately following the title-page. 5·7 × 3·1″. This leaf together with the leaf preceding the title-page were removed in all but a very few copies of the work.

except that the first issue contains two leaves which were removed later. In the original issue a leaf precedes the title-page with a half-title on the recto, and on the verso the Royal Society's *imprimatur* beneath which is the *imprimatur* of the President, and Censors of the College of Physicians. The title-page is followed by a leaf containing a dedication addressed by the author to the Royal Society and to the College of Physicians, the dedication to the Society preceding that to the College. These two leaves are only found in one of the five copies of the work in the British Museum (Bloomsbury), that is in the copy that originally belonged to Sir Joseph Banks.[1] They are also found in the copy of the work in the library of the Royal College of Surgeons of England, and in one of the two copies in the Botany School, Cambridge, namely the copy that belonged to John Martyn, Professor of Botany at Cambridge from 1733 until 1762. The copy in the library of the Royal Society, presented by Sloane on 17 June 1696,[2] and the copy in the library at the Chelsea Physic Garden,[3] contain the second of the two leaves only, while a copy in the library of the Royal College of Physicians has the first leaf with the top half, containing the *imprimatur* of the Royal Society cut away.[4]

Of the second issue, identical with the first, but not containing the above-mentioned two leaves, many copies are extant. For long the present writer could find no reason for these two issues, or for the copies in the libraries of the Royal Society, the College of Physicians, and the Chelsea Physic Garden, being apparently imperfect. Finally the matter was made clear through the assistance of Mr. L. M. Payne, Librarian of the Royal College of Physicians, who wrote as follows:[5]

For a short time at the end of the 17th century the College had the power of licensing medical books, power which originally rested with the Archbishop of Canterbury. On 5th June 1696 (I quote now from the *Annals*)[6] 'Dr. Sloan presented his book . . . to the President, Censors and one for the College and acquainted them that by mistake of the printer, the licence of the Royal society was placed before that of the President, and Censors of the College of physicians, upon which the Board was very angry and ordered him either to have it reprinted to place the licence of the President and Censors before that of the Royall society or leave both out, which he promised to do.'

After Sloane returned from the West Indies he settled in London as a

[1] Pressmark 450.c.15. Of the other four copies, all of which contain MS. notes by the original owners, one (C.60.e.10) originally belonged to Sir Hans Sloane, one (968.f.16) to Leonard Plukenet, and two (968, f. 15 and 968, f. 18) to James Petiver.

[2] The entry in the *Journal book of the Royal society*, 8, 359 (1690–6) under 17 June 1696, reads: 'Doctor Sloan's book of the plants of Jamaica was this day presented to the Society for which he had thanks ordered him, and the book was put into the library.'

[3] This copy was originally in the library of the Society of Apothecaries, and it seems likely that it is a presentation copy from the author.

[4] This copy has no leaf with the author dedication. It also lacks the preface.

[5] In epist. 15.vii.64.

[6] Quoted from the *Annals* by permission of the Registrar of the Royal College of Physicians.

physician, and as time went on his professional reputation steadily increased. He also became the recipient of many honours. In 1716 he was created a baronet by George I, almost the first physician to receive that honour, the first medical baronet being Sir Edward Greaves, M.D. (1608–80).[1] In 1719 Sloane was elected President of the Royal College of Physicians, and in 1727 he succeeded Sir Isaac Newton in the Chair of the Royal Society.

Sloane died 11 January 1753, and in his will he directed that his museum was to be offered to the King for the nation, on condition of a payment of £20,000 to his heirs. The legacy was accepted, and in June 1753 an Act of Parliament was passed to purchase the collection of Sir Hans Sloane, the Harleian collection of manuscripts,[2] and a suitable house to put them in, together with the Cottonian library which was already the property of the nation but inadequately housed.[3] Montagu House on the north side of Great Russell Street, built about the year 1680 by Ralph Montagu, first Duke of Montagu,[4] was acquired as a suitable building to house the collections. It was opened to the public on 15 January 1759, and thus was founded the British Museum.[5]

Sloane's large herbarium, now in the British Museum (Natural History) comprises not only the plants collected by himself but also a number of herbaria that he acquired, including those of Philip Miller, James Petiver, and Leonard Plukenet.[6] Of his library which was said to consist of 40,000 or 50,000 printed books,[7] Arundell Esdaile, formerly Assistant Keeper in the Department of Printed Books, of the British Museum (Bloomsbury), recorded:[8]

Sloane collected . . . medical and scientific, and especially botanical literature, both practically and historically, and was rich in the publications of continental academies. But he threw his net wider, and was in fact omnivorous. So far as is known, the Museum owes to Sloane few if any of its rarer monuments of literature or typography; but it does owe to him a very solid foundation-stone of a great library of universal scope.

Among his other activities Sloane took a great interest in the Apothecaries', or physic, garden at Chelsea, the scene of his botanical studies when he first

[1] Greaves practised physic at Oxford, and was honoured with a baronetcy in 1645 by Charles I, see C[okayne]. (G. E.), *Complete baronetage*, 2, 244 (1902).

[2] The Harleian manuscripts were from the collection started by Robert Harley, first Earl of Oxford (1661–1724) and continued by his son Edward (1689–1741), the second Earl.

[3] The collection of manuscripts and books in the Cottonian library had been made by Sir Robert Cotton (1571–1631).

[4] Ralph Montagu, first Duke of Montagu (1638?–1709), succeeded his father as third Baron Montagu of Boughton 10 Jan. 1684.

Created Earl of Montagu 9 Apr. 1689 and became Duke of Montagu 14 Apr. 1705.

[5] For further details see Brooks (W. E. St. John), *Sir Hans Sloane the great collector and his circle*, 218–23 (1954).

[6] For details see Britten (J.), *The Sloane herbarium . . . revised and edited by J. E. Dandy* (1958).

[7] Francis (F. C.), The Sloane collection of printed books, *Brit. Mus. Quarterly*, **18**, 4 (1953).

[8] Esdaile (A.), *The British museum library*, 177 (1946).

came to England as a young man, and it is largely due to Sloane's munificence that this famous garden is still in existence at the present day. The ground of this garden was originally leased in 1673 from Charles Cheyne, later Viscount Newhaven,[1] by the Society of Apothecaries for a term of sixty-one years. In 1712, however, Sloane purchased the Manor of Chelsea, including the physic garden, from William Cheyne, second Viscount Newhaven (1657–1728), and on 20 February 1721 [i.e. 1722] signed a deed of conveyance by which for a yearly rent of £5 he transferred to the Society of Apothecaries the ground of the garden, with its greenhouse and other erections, for them to have and to hold in perpetuity, provided certain specified conditions were duly observed and complied with. The indenture states that release was granted

to the end that the said garden may at all times hereafter be continued as a physick garden and for the better encouraging and enabling the said Society to support the charge thereof for the manifestation of the power wisdom and glory of God in the workes of the Creation and that their apprentices and others may the better distinguish good and usefull plants from those that bear resemblance to them and yett are hurtfull and other the like good purposes.

The document further specifies that the Society of Apothecaries is to present yearly to the Royal Society of London:

Fifty specimens or samples of distinct plants well dryed and preserved and which grew in the said garden the same year together with their respective names or reputed names and so as the specimens or samples of such plants be different or specifically distinct and no one offered twice untill the compleat number of two thousand plants have been delived [sic] as afores.[d][2]

Later, when considering British botanical books published between 1700 and 1800, we shall refer a number of times to the Apothecaries' garden at Chelsea, and to the botanists and horticulturists who were associated with it during this period. Among some of the men connected with this garden during the eighteenth century the following were all authors of note, William Curtis, William Hudson, Joseph Miller, Philip Miller, and Isaac Rand.

The earliest botanical work to be published in Scotland appeared at Edinburgh in 1683. It is the *Hortus medicus edinburgensis: or, a catalogue of the plants in the physical garden at Edinburgh*, compiled by the 'Intendant

---

[1] Charles Cheyne (1625–98), created 17 May 1681 Viscount Newhaven and Lord Cheyne. He purchased the Chelsea estate in 1657 (C[okayne]. (G. E.), *The complete peerage*, etc. 9, 539 (1936)).

[2] The deed of conveyance of the garden at Chelsea from Sir Hans Sloane is now preserved in the Guildhall Library, London (MS. 8268). The most important covenants contained in this conveyance are recorded by Field (H.),

Memoirs of the Botanic garden at Chelsea belonging to the Society of apothecaries of London . . . Revised by R. H. Semple, etc., 35–8 (1878), The document has been printed in full in *Trans. bot. Soc. Edinburgh*, **41**, 293–307 (1972) in a paper by W. T. Stearn entitled: 'Philip Miller and the plants from the Chelsea physic garden presented to the Royal society of London, 1723–1796'.

over the garden'[1] James Sutherland. This garden owed its inception to Andrew Balfour (1630–94) and Robert Sibbald (1641–1722), two Edinburgh physicians who took a prominent part in the foundation of the Royal College of Physicians at Edinburgh in 1681. Both men received recognition for their contribution to science by being knighted in 1682. About 1670 they started a physic garden for the study of medicinal plants on a small piece of ground near Holyrood House,[2] which they stocked with plants from their own private gardens, and from the garden of their friend the keen and wealthy plant collector, Patrick Murray, Laird of Livingstone. Meanwhile, they had become acquainted with James Sutherland, a youth who had attained, through his own industry, a good knowledge of plants, and he undertook the care of the garden. In 1675, the same physicians, with others, acquired of the Town Council of Edinburgh a lease to James Sutherland for nineteen years 'of the garden belonging to Trinity hospitall, and adjacent to it'.[3] The following year the Town Council officially appointed Sutherland 'Intendant' of the garden.[4] The plants were transferred from Holyrood to the new garden, and the former was then apparently abandoned.[5]

Sutherland was an expert gardener, a learned botanist, an accomplished Latin scholar, and a good man of business, and under his care the garden thrived and became famous throughout Europe. He not only collected plants native to Scotland, but also by correspondence acquired seeds and plants from many countries abroad, including 'the Levant, Italy, Spain, France, Holland, England' and the East and West Indies.[6] Robert Sibbald devoted a chapter to this garden in his *Scotia illustrata*, published in 1684,[7] and a translation from the original, which is in Latin, is given by John Macqueen Cowan in his 'History of the Royal botanic garden, Edinburgh'.[8] Sibbald was writing, apparently about 1682. The following passage is quoted from Cowan's translation:

There are in the garden not only quite a number of plants indigenous to this country, but also plants from both hemispheres, especially those which have been distributed through all countries, for the cure of sickness and disease . . . The total number of all the plants is approximately two thousand, of which, the worthy keeper of the garden, James Sutherland, Master of Arts and student of medicine, will shortly issue a catalogue.

[1] Sutherland (J.), *Hortus medicus edinburgensis*, etc. (1683) (Epistle dedicatory).

[2] Cowan (J. M.), The history of the Royal botanic garden, Edinburgh, *Notes R. bot. garden Edinburgh*, **19**, 11 (1933). For an account of the inception of this garden, with Sutherland's appointment as first 'Intendant' see *The memoirs of Sir Robert Sibbald (1641–1722) Edited . . . by F. P. Hett*, 65–6 (1932).

[3] Sutherland obtained a lease of this garden 7 July 1675; see Cowan (J. M.), *Notes R. bot. garden Edinburgh* **19**, 12 and 14 (1933).

[4] Sutherland (J.), *Hortus medicus edinburgensis*, etc. (1683) (Epistle dedicatory).

[5] Cowan (J. M.), *Notes R. bot. garden Edinburgh*, **19**, 31 (1933).

[6] Sutherland (J.), *Hortus medicus edinburgensis*, etc. (1683) (Epistle dedicatory).

[7] Sibbald (R.), *Scotia illustrata sive prodromus historiæ naturalis*, etc., Pt. 2, 65–6 (1684), Edinburgi (chapter entitled 'Horti medici edinburgensis descriptio').

[8] *Notes R. bot. garden Edinburgh*, **19**, 16–18 (1933).

Sutherland's *Hortus medicus edinburgensis: or, a catalogue of the plants in the physical garden at Edinburgh* was issued in 1683 and, as pointed out by Cowan,[1] this work most fortunately preserves for us an accurate and detailed list of the plants grown in this seventeenth-century garden, and thus supplements the account given by Sibbald.

Apart from the above catalogue, Sutherland appears to have published nothing further. He continued, however, to be a successful gardener and botanist, and for a time was in charge of three distinct botanic or physic gardens in Edinburgh. These were the garden around Trinity Hospital, the Town's garden referred to above, and two gardens started for the cultivation of medicinal plants in 1695, namely: the College garden[2] beside the College, and a part of the Royal garden at Holyrood, known as the King's garden.[3] In 1695 the Town Council appointed Sutherland to be the first Professor of Botany in the Town's College,[4] now the University of Edinburgh, and in 1699, after he took charge of part of the Royal garden at Holyrood as a physic garden, he became King's Botanist for Scotland.[5] In 1706 Sutherland resigned the care of the Town's garden and the College garden, as well as his Professorship in the University, but continued to be King's Botanist, Keeper of the Royal garden, and Regius Professor of Botany until the death of Queen Anne in 1714.[6] He died 24 June 1719 'aged above 80 years'.[7]

[1] *Notes R. bot. garden Edinburgh*, **19**, 18.
[2] Ibid. 27–9.
[3] Ibid. 31.
[4] Ibid. 27.
[5] Ibid. 33.
[6] Ibid. 54, 56. Sutherland became King's Botanist under a warrant of William III, dated 12 January 1699, and Regius Professor of Botany under a warrant of Queen Anne, dated 17 March 1710.
[7] Ibid. 57.

V

GARDENING BOOKS AND WORKS ON CULTIVATION

THE sixteenth century had seen the publication in England of comparatively few gardening books. Ignorant beliefs and medieval assertions were still current, and writers of such books were, on the whole, men of little learning. In the seventeenth century, however, as progress gradually took place in all branches of gardening and cultivation, the literature on these subjects increased in quantity and worth. After the Restoration, when England was much influenced by foreign horticulturists and garden designers, a number of translations were produced made from the works of contemporary foreign authors on gardening. Let us now consider some of these books published in the seventeenth century, beginning with the writings of Sir Hugh Platt.

Sir Hugh Platt[1] (1552–1608), held by Richard Weston[2] to be 'the most ingenious husbandman of the age he lived in', was the son of Richard Platt, a wealthy brewer, and a Sheriff of London. Hugh Platt matriculated as a pensioner of St. John's College, Cambridge, in 1568, and graduated Bachelor of Arts in 1571 [i.e. 1572]. Soon afterwards he was admitted at Lincoln's Inn. Much of his life was devoted to literary work and to the study of husbandry and gardening. He was also interested in all kinds of inventions and experiments, and in consideration of his services in this field was knighted by James I on 22 May 1605.[3] Platt describes a number of his inventions, together with 'sundry new experiments in the art of husbandry, distillation, and moulding' in his *Jewell house of art and nature*, first published in 1594. In 1600 appeared Platt's *New and admirable arte of setting of corne*, a treatise in which this author advocates growing corn by setting the seed at regular distances apart, the usual method of sowing corn at that time being by broadcast. On the title-page of this small quarto volume is a woodcut of a growing plant of corn, over which is a spade lying in a scroll bearing the words 'Adams toole revived'. Some early writers on husbandry, including

[1] Platt's name is found spelt Plat, Platt, or Platte. The present writer has used the form 'Platt' as given in Mundy (R.), *Middlesex pedigrees . . . Edited by Sir G. J. Armytage* (1914) (Harleian Society, publications, **65**, 55).

[2] Weston (R.), *Tracts on practical agriculture and gardening . . . The second edition*, 14 (1773) (A catalogue of English authors, etc.).

[3] *D.N.B.* (under Plat or Platt, Sir Hugh).

John Worlidge,[1] refer to the book under this title. The work was published several times in 1600, and once the following year, and 'about 1852' Richard Prosser of Birmingham issued a private reprint of the edition of 1601.[2]

In 1594 Platt lived at Bishops Hall,[3] Bethnal Green, Middlesex, but he also owned property near St. Albans in Hertfordshire.[4] His work on gardening entitled *Floraes paradise, beautified and adorned with sundry sorts of delicate fruites and flowers* appeared in 1608, the year of his death. He dated the preface from 'Bednall-greene, neere London, this 2. of July. 1608'. Platt had a garden at this address[5] and another in St. Martins-lane,[6] and he wrote his book from his own practical experience as well as from information supplied to him by other gardeners. Platt, unlike many authors of his day, freely acknowledged any help given to him and the people he named throughout his *Floraes paradise* make a delightful assembly, they include: 'Mr. Stutfield that married my L. Norths brothers daughter', 'Maister Jacob of the glasse-house',[7] 'Maister Hunt, the good horsman', 'Mistresse Hill', 'my coosen Mathew of Wales', 'Garret the apothecary, and Pigot the gardener', 'Maister Pointer of Twickenham', 'Parson Simson', and the 'Right honourable my Lorde Zouch', whose garden was at Hackney.[8]

Floraes paradise continued to be published after the author's death but with the new title of *The garden of Eden* and edited by Charles Bellingham who refers to Platt as 'my ever honoured kinsman'.[9] In 1660 was issued *The second part of The garden of Eden . . . By . . . Sir Hugh Plat*. Readers who questioned the authenticity of this work were invited to 'see the original manuscript under the authors own hand, which is too well known to undergo the suspition of a counterfeit'.[10]

In 1604 a small quarto volume was published anonymously under the title of *The fruiterers secrets*. This treatise consists of methods of gathering, packing, carrying, and storing fruits and, as pointed out by Brotherston,[11] remained for many years the best work to appear in England on this branch of gardening. Nothing seems to be known of the author except that he was 'Irish-borne', and that as the result of long practical experience was well

[1] W[orlidge]. (J.), *Systema agriculturæ*, etc. 43 (1669).
[2] See MS. note at end of copy of the reprint in Brit. Mus. (Bloomsbury) (pressmark 7074.ccc.19).
[3] Platt (Sir H.), *The jewell house of art and nature*, etc. 52 (1594) (Second book).
[4] Platt (Sir H.), op. cit. 34 (1594) (Second book).
[5] Platt (Sir H.), *Floraes paradise*, etc. 91–2 (1608).
[6] Platt (Sir H.), *The second part of The garden of Eden*, etc. 49 (1660).
[7] At one time there was a glass-house in 'the parish of St. Botolph, Aldersgate'. See Maitland (W.), *The history and survey of London from its foundation to the present time*, etc. 2, 1351 (1756).
[8] This was the Lord Zouche whose physic garden at Hackney was at one time under the charge of Matthias de l'Obel. See above, p. 31.
[9] See Platt (Sir H.), *The garden of Eden*, etc. [edited by C. Bellingham] (1653), etc. (Dedication, and 'The publisher to the reader').
[10] Platt (Sir H.), *The second part of The garden of Eden*, etc. (1660) (To the reader).
[11] B[rotherston]. (R. P.), The fruiterer's secrets. *Gard. Chron.*, Series III, vol. 36, 262 (1904).

acquainted with the subject upon which he wrote.[1] He dedicated his work to Charles Blount, Earl of Devonshire and eighth Lord Mountjoy (*c.* 1562–1606), who had been appointed Lord Lieutenant of Ireland by James I, on 25 April 1603. Both the dedication and the epistle to the reader are signed N.F., whose identity the present writer has, so far, been unable to trace.

In the epistle to the reader details are given concerning a famous orchard at Tenham in Kent. This was started by a native of Ireland, one Richard Harris of London, 'fruiterer to King Henry the eight'.[2] Harris planted his orchard with pippin grafts which he fetched out of France, and with cherry and pear grafts from the Low Countries, and, according to 'N. F', 'afore that these said grafts were fetched out of Fraunce, and the Lowe Countries, although that there was some store of fruite in England, yet there wanted both rare fruite, and lasting fine fruite'. This orchard, known as 'the New-garden',[3] was apparently still flourishing at the time of Michael Drayton, as in the eighteenth song of his *Poly-olbion* [1612][4] this poet refers to it thus:

> Rich Tenham undertakes thy closets to suffize
> With cherries.

In 1609 appeared a short treatise entitled *Instructions for the increasing of mulberie trees, and the breeding of silke-wormes, for the making of silke in this kingdome.* The imprint on the title-page reads 'London printed by E[dward]. A[llde]. for Eleazar Edgar', and the address to the reader is signed with the initials W. S.

Preceding the *Instructions* is printed a letter sent by James I to the Lords Lieutenant of the several shires of England, dated 16 November 1608. The King, impressed by the work done during the reign of Henri IV (1589–1610) to promote the silk industry in France, made an attempt to establish the native growth of silk in this country.[5] With this end in view he wrote the above-mentioned letter in which he requested the Lord Lieutenant of each shire to make public the announcement that 10,000 mulberry trees were to be sent to each county town and that all those who were able were required to purchase them at three farthings the plant, or six shillings the hundred. Moreover, the following March or April each county was to receive a good quantity of mulberry seed. In the meantime there was going to be published 'a plaine instruction and direction' for the growing of mulberry trees and the breeding of silkworms.

One of the leading English silkworm breeders of the day was 'Comptroller

[1] N. (F.), *The fruiterers secrets*, etc. (1604) (Dedication).

[2] N. (F.), op. cit. (1604) (Epistle to the reader).

[3] Ibid.

[4] pp. 297–8.

[5] Stow (J.), *The annales, or generall chronicle of England . . . continued and augmented . . . by Edmond Howes*, 895 (1615).

of the custome house', William Stallenge, who had 'taken ingenious paynes in breeding wormes, and making of fine silke for all uses: he had a patent far seaven yeers, to bring in mulberry seed, and this yeere (1609) he z Monsieur Verton by order from the King planted mulberry trees in most shires of England'.[1] Stallenge was also in charge of the King's garden that had been made on '4 acres of land taken in for His Majesty's use, near to his Palace of Westminster, for the planting of mulberry trees'.[2] His importance as a silkworm breeder is manifest in looking through the Issues of the Exchequer during the reign of James I, when several large payments are found to have been made to William Stallenge in connection with mulberry culture and silkworm breeding.[3] Under the circumstances it seems reasonable to assume that the initials at the end of the address to the reader in the *Instructions* of 1609 are those of William Stallenge. The present writer has been unable to find any absolute proof confirming this supposition, but Stallenge is ascribed as the author both in the *Catalogue of printed books in the British museum* (*Bloomsbury*), and in the *Short title catalogue*.

The three illustrations published in the *Instructions* had already appeared in 1607 in *The perfect use of silk-wormes, and their benefit. With the exact planting . . . of mulberrie trees*, an English translation by Nicholas Geffe of the French original by Olivier de Serres. These three woodcuts are degraded copies of parts of two plates of a series of six published at Antwerp? in 1600? under the title of 'Vermis sericus'.[4] These six engravings are made from drawings by Jan van der Straet, an artist born at Bruges in 1523 and who died at Florence in 1605.

The *Instructions* were published a second time in 1609, when no imprint appeared on the title-page, only the statement 'Newly printed. 1609', and with the address to the reader unsigned.[5] Although the King's letter to the Lords Lieutenant is now dated 19 January 1608 [i.e. 1609] the text, apart from the spelling, is identical with the earlier communication. In 1726, Richard Bradley reprinted in his *General treatise of husbandry and gardening* the letter of 16 November 1608, with the following remark:[6] 'This letter had so good an effect, that several people began to propagate silk-worms; but for want of good order among them, their labours came to little.'

The earliest published work on gardening in the north of England is William Lawson's *A new orchard and garden*, first issued in 1618. The dedication is addressed to Sir Henry Bellasis, or Belasyse (d. 1624),[7] a baronet who

[1] Stow (J.), op. cit. (1615).
[2] Devon (F.), *Issues of the Exchequer; being payments made out of His Majesty's revenue during the reign of King James I*, etc. 98 (1836).
[3] See Devon (F.), op. cit. 88, 98, 138, 162 (1836).
[4] See copy in Dept. of Prints and Drawings, Brit. Mus. (Bloomsbury) (pressmark 157*.a.38).

[5] This edition of the *Instructions*, with the omission of the last two paragraphs and without the illustrations, was reprinted in *The Harleian miscellany*, 2, 218–23 (1809).
[6] Vol. 1, 353.
[7] C[okayne]. (G. E.), *Complete baronetage*, 1, 43 (1900).

A
NEW ORCHARD
and Garden :

OR

The beſt way for planting, grafting, and to make
any ground good, for a rich Orchard : Particularly in the North,
and generally for the whole kingdome of *England,* as in nature,
reaſon, ſituation, and all probabilitie, may and doth appeare.

With the Country Houſewifes Garden for herbes of common vſe, their
vertues, ſeaſons, profits, ornaments, varietie of knots, models for trees, and
plots for the beſt ordering of Grounds and Walkes.

AS ALSO

The Husbandry of Bees, with their ſeuerall vſes and annoyances, all being the
experience of 48. yeeres labour, and now the ſecond time corrected and
much enlarged, by *William Lawſon.*

Whereunto is newly added the Art of propagating Plants, with the true ordering
of all manner of Fruits, in their gathering, carrying home, and preſeruation.

Printed at *London* by *I. H.* for ROGER IACKSON, and are to be ſold at his
ſhop neere Fleet-ſtreet Conduit, 1623.

47. Lawson: *A new orchard and garden . . . now the second time corrected and much*
enlarged, 1623. Title-page. 7·1 × 4·7".

lived at Newborough in Yorkshire, a town east-south-east of Ripon, now called Boroughbridge.[1] Little is known of the author, William Lawson, who was the owner of a 'northerne orchard and country garden',[2] probably near Teesmouth, as he refers to a sea monster that landed 'at Teesmouth in Yorke shiere, hard by us'.[3] He wrote from experience acquired over more than forty-eight years in the north of England,[4] and his book displays his great love of gardening. Appended to *A new orchard and garden*, with the signatures continuous, but with separate pagination, is another work by Lawson entitled 'The countrie housewifes garden . . . Together with the husbandry of bees'. This treatise has its own title-page, dated 1617, and has the distinction of being the first book written in this country avowedly for women gardeners. It is full of practical information for the lady of the house concerning the herb and kitchen gardens, including various illustrations of flower knots, and offering advice on the husbandry of bees.

A new orchard and garden . . . with The country housewifes garden was published again in 1623 with the statement on the title-page: 'now the second time corrected and much enlarged', and in 1626 with a statement reading 'now the third time corrected . . .'. Both these editions contain sections headed respectively 'The art of propagating plants' and 'The husband-mans fruitfull orchard'. The first treatise is by Simon Harward, while the second has no author's name. The latter, however, is only a rewritten and abbreviated version of *The fruiterers secrets*, first published in 1604 with the dedication and epistle to the reader signed with the initials N. F.[5]

In 1623 *A new orchard and garden* was included in Gervase Markham's compilation entitled *A way to get wealth*, and it was published for more than seventy years in the many subsequent editions of this book.[6] Although Lawson's treatise gives much useful horticultural information, it is not without a number of ridiculous assertions, and John Beale drew attention to some of these in his *Herefordshire orchards* (1657).[7] In 1927 *A new orchard and garden . . . reprinted from the third edition with a preface by Eleanour Sinclair Rohde*, was published by the Cresset Press.

Only a passing reference need be made to a small tract 'printed for John Marriott' and issued in 1623 under the title of *Certaine excellent and new invented knots and mazes, for plots for gardens*. The author of a notice to the reader, which is signed 'I. M.', was evidently the bookseller who published the work, and he writes of his intention to publish shortly 'a most perfect and exact booke of the art of planting, grafting, and gardening'. So

[1] Wilson (J. M.), *The imperial gazetteer of England and Wales*, etc. Vols. **1** and **2** [1866–9] (see under Newborough and Boroughbridge).

[2] Lawson (W.), *A new orchard and garden*, etc. (1618) (Dedication).

[3] Ibid. 42.

[4] Ibid. (the Preface).

[5] See above, pp. 156–7.

[6] i.e. in 1631, 1638, 1648, 1657, 1660, 1668, 1676, 1683.

[7] B[eale]. (J.), *Herefordshire orchards*, etc. 13, etc. (1657).

far, however, the present writer has been unable to discover if such a treatise was ever published by Marriott.

In an earlier chapter we referred to John Parkinson's *Paradisus* (1629),[1] a famous horticultural book of which further notice must now be taken. It was printed by Humfrey Lownes and Robert Young, and its title *Paradisi in sole paradisus terrestris*, meaning the terrestrial paradise of the park in the sun, is a pun upon the author's name.[2]

The *Paradisus* is dedicated to the consort of Charles I, Queen Henrietta Maria. The title-page is a woodcut and consists of a design in an upright oval with the title contained in a cartouche below. The name of the wood-cutter, Switzer, appears in the lower right-hand corner with a large capital A above it, but it is uncertain whether this is an initial or not, as so far as is known Switzer's Christian name was Christopher. The design portrays the Garden of Eden with Adam and Eve tending the flowers, with a repre-sentative of the legendary 'plant-animal', known as the 'vegetable lamb of Tartary', in the middle distance.[3] Above the garden is the name of Jehovah in Hebrew characters. Prefixed to the *Paradisus* is a portrait of the author at the age of sixty-two. The illustrations of plants were printed from whole-page woodblocks, each composed of a number of species. These appear to be mostly new figures but some are copied from previous works, including the *Hortus floridus* of Crispian van de Passe the Younger, first published at Arnhemij in 1614.[4] The figures in the *Paradisus* do not bear the cutter's name but, they seem to be by the same hand as the title-page. In his *Sculptura* of 1662 John Evelyn, in referring to English engravers, states:[5] 'We have . . . Switzer for cutting in wood, the son of a father who sufficiently discover'd his dexterity in the herbals set forth by Mr. Parkinson, Lobel, and divers other works'. The elder Switzer was presumably the Christopher Switzer who made the woodcuts of coins and seals for John Speed's *History of Great Britaine* (1611), and who was called by this historian 'the most exquisit and curious hand of our age'.[6] Besides being a woodcutter this craftsman worked, during the years 1595 to 1605, as a line-engraver.[7] It was presumably on the authority of Evelyn's statement that

[1] See above, pp. 79–80.

[2] For details regarding the translation of this title see *Notes and Queries*, Series VI, **9**, 114 (1884).

[3] The legend of this 'lamb' met with almost universal credence from the thirteenth to the seventeenth centuries. See Lee (H.), *The vegetable lamb of Tartary*, etc. (1887).

[4] e.g. compare *Paradisus*, p. 29, fig. 2 (Lilium persicum), and p. 75, fig. 3 (Narcissus medio purpureus) with the figures of these plants in the *Hortus floridus*, Pt. I (1614), Arnhemij on pls. 25 and 19 (Book I). For other

works containing copies of the *Hortus floridus* engravings see Savage (S.), The Hortus floridus of Crispijn vande Pas the Younger, *The Library*, Series IV, vol. **4**, 206 (1924). (*Trans. bibl. Soc.*, Series II, vol. **4**).

[5] Evelyn (J.), *Sculptura*, etc. 100 (1662).

[6] Speed (J.), *The history of Great Britaine*, etc. (1611) (A summary conclusion of the whole).

[7] See Hind (A. M.), *Engraving in England in the sixteenth and seventeenth centuries*, etc., Pt. I, 229–30 (1952), Cambridge.

PARADISI IN SOLE
Paradisus Terrestris.
Or
A Garden of all sorts of pleasant flowers which our
English ayre will permitt to be noursed vp:
with
A Kitchen garden of all manner of herbes, rootes, & fruites,
for meate or sause vsed with vs,
and
An Orchard of all sorte of fruitbearing Trees
and shrubbes fit for our Land
together
With the right orderinge planting & preseruing
of them and their vses & vertues
Collected by Iohn Parkinson
Apothecary of London
1629

Qui veut parangonner l'artifice a Nature,
Et nos parcs a l'Eden, indiscret il mesure.

Le pas de l'elephant par le pas du ciron,
Et de l'Aigle le vol par cil du mouscheron.

49. Parkinson: *Paradisi in sole paradisus terrestris*, 1629. Portrait of John Parkinson. Woodcut on p. [xii]. 6·5 × 4·1″.

Wornum, in his edition of Horace Walpole's *Anecdotes of painting in England*, wrote in a footnote concerning Christopher Switzer that this woodcutter 'probably engraved the botanic figures for Lobel's "Observations", and the plates for Parkinson's "Paradisus terrestris", 1629'.[1]

[1] Walpole (H.), *Anecdotes of painting in England . . . With . . . Vertue's . . . Catalogue of engravers . . . A new edition by R. N. Wornum*, **3**, 130, footnote 5 (1888).

◁ 48. Parkinson: *Paradisi in sole paradisus terrestris*, 1629. Title-page. Woodcut. 12·2 × 7·5″. A woodcutter's knife is depicted beneath the Signature 'Switzer' in the bottom right-hand corner.

The *Paradisus* is divided into three parts dealing respectively with the flower garden, the kitchen garden, and the orchard, and in 1633 Thomas Johnson in his edition of Gerard's *Herball*[1] praises the work and remarks that Parkinson 'hath not superficially handled these things, but accurately descended to the very varieties in each species'. Regarding the section on flowers, Parkinson confesses that he had seen many herbals and divers books on flowers but no work devoted exclusively to the description of plants suitable for 'a garden of delight and pleasure'.[2] He therefore undertook the *Paradisus* in which he here 'selected and set forth a garden of all the chiefest for choyce, and fairest for shew, from among all the severall tribes and kindreds of natures beauty'.[3]

Part of the charm of the *Paradisus* lies in the author's love of plants and his sensibility of their beauty, feelings strongly reflected throughout his writing. His book is of interest and value as a record of the state of horticulture in England at the beginning of the seventeenth century, and as pointed out by Canon Raven in his survey of the work,[4] Parkinson's knowledge 'is not merely that of a working druggist and gardener: he has real botanical science'. Parkinson describes a great number of plants many of which grew in his own garden in Long Acre, and in his book refers frequently to contemporary botanists and gardeners. The second part, dealing with the kitchen garden, is of especial interest as it contains the names and descriptions of 'herbes and rootes' commonly grown in the gardens of the period for 'sallets' and other dishes.

Regarding the later history of the *Paradisus* the following details are of interest. In 1880 an article appeared in the monthly review *The Nineteenth Century*, in which Mrs. Kegan Paul condemned the prim flower gardens of the period with their monotonous 'carpet-bedding' and suggested a return to 'a garden of delight' as described by Parkinson.[5] Shortly afterwards Mrs. Ewing, the popular children's writer, wrote a serial story that was published in the numbers of *Aunt Judy's Magazine* from November 1883 to March 1884.[6] Here some children read Parkinson's book and afterwards decided to play a game to be called 'the game of the earthly paradise', in which they collected plants and seeds of pretty flowers in order to grow them in hedges and waste places. This serial proved so popular that in 1886 it was published in book form under the title of *Mary's meadow*. Moreover it created such interest in the plants mentioned that in 1884 a 'Parkinson society' was formed, whose objects were to search out and cultivate old garden flowers

[1] Gerard (J.), *The herball or generall historie of plantes . . . amended by Thomas Johnson* (1633) (Epistle to the reader).
[2] Parkinson (J.), *Paradisi in sole paradisus terrestris* (1629) (Epistle to the reader).
[3] Ibid.
[4] Raven (C. E.), *English naturalists from Neckam to Ray*, etc. 255 (1947).
[5] Paul (M. A.), Old-fashioned gardening, *The Nineteenth Century*, 7, 128–35 (1880).
[6] Ewing (J. H.), *Mary's meadow*, etc. [edited by H. K. F. Gatty] [1886] (Preface).

50. 'Flos Africanus', Woodcut from Parkinson: ▷ *Paradisi in sole paradisus terrestris*, p. 305, 1629. 11·5×6·3". *Tagetes erecta* L., French Marigold.

1 *Flos Africanus maximus multiplex.* The greatest double French Marigold. 2 *Flos Africanus maior multiplex.* The greater double French Marigold.
3 *Flos Africanus maximus simplex* The greatest single French Marigold. 4 *Flos Africanus multiplex fistulosus.* The double hollow French Marigold.
5 *Flos Africanus simplex fistulosus.* The single hollow French Marigold. 6 *Flos Africanus minor multiplex.* The smaller double French Marigold. 7 *Flos Africanus minor multiplex alter.* Another sort of the lesser double French Marigold. 8 *Flos Africanus minor simplex.* The lesser single French Marigold.

which had become rare; to exchange seeds and plants; to plant waste places with hardy flowers, and to circulate books on gardening amongst the members. Mrs. Ewing was the first President of the Society and after her death in 1885, this office was held by Professor Daniel Oliver, Keeper of the Herbarium in the Royal Botanic Gardens, Kew.[1] The attention thus focused on Parkinson and his book resulted in various writings by other authors about the *Paradisus*, and with so much publicity the market value of the work naturally rose. For example, it is found that in 1867 Messrs. Wheldon and Wesley offered a copy of the *Paradisus* of 1629, bound in calf gilt for 12s. (Catalogue 65, item 522), and in 1901 the same bookseller had a copy, with the last pages of the index imperfect, for £13. 13s. 0d. (Catalogue N.S. 9, item 508). In 1904 Methuen published a reprint of the edition of 1629 at £2. 2s. 0d., with thirty copies bound in Japanese vellum at £10. 10s. 0d.[2]

There are numerous passages in the *Paradisus* in which Parkinson mentions his friend John Tradescant (d. 1638).[3] This gardener visited the Low Countries, France, Russia, the Island of Rhé, Algiers, and the Mediterranean, and after each journey returned home with new varieties of plants to enrich our gardens. The journeys made by Tradescant and his son John (1608–62), who also became a gardener and collector, and the plants these two men procured from abroad, are described by Miss Mea Allan in her book *The Tradescants their plants, gardens and museum 1570–1662*, published in 1964. In 1626 Tradescant went to live at South Lambeth, then in the county of Surrey, and in his new home, called 'Tradescants Ark' he had the first public museum in Britain. Here he displayed his 'collection of rarities', the accumulation of a lifetime, which included birds, animals, fishes, minerals, fruits, instruments, garments, utensils, and other treasures. This museum and Tradescant's Lambeth garden became famous throughout the western world. In the Bodleian Library, Oxford, is preserved Tradescant's own copy of Parkinson's *Paradisus* of 1629 in which, on a few blank pages at the end of the book, Tradescant made notes of plants added to his garden from the time the book was published until 1633. The following year was published *Plantarum in horto Johannem [sic] Tradescanti nascentium catalogus*. The only known copy of this list of plants grown by Tradescant in his Lambeth garden is in the library of Magdalen College, Oxford, in the collection of books bequeathed to the College by John Goodyer.[4] After Tradescant's death the Lambeth museum and garden continued to flourish under the care of John Tradescant the Younger, and in 1656 a much more extensive 'Catalogus

[1] Ewing (J. H.), op. cit. [1886] (Preface).

[2] One of the thirty copies printed on Japanese vellum is in the Brit. Mus. (Bloomsbury) (pressmark LR.30.c.1.)

[3] For a list of the passages in the *Paradisus* in which Parkinson mentions Tradescant see

Boulger (G. S.), A seventeenth-century botanist friendship, *J. Bot.* (London), 56, 200–2 (1918).

[4] This catalogue of 1634 was reprinted, with footnotes added by R. W. T. Gunther, in his *Early British botanists and their gardens*, etc. 334–45 (1922).

plantarum in horto Johannis Tredescanti nascentium' was published at the end of the *Musæum Tradescantianum*. The above mentioned copy of the *Paradisus* with Tradescant's manuscript notes was later acquired by the antiquary Elias Ashmole who also used it as a notebook, recording 'Trees found in Mrs. Tredescants ground when it came into my possession'. This was in 1679, the year after the death in 1678 of Hester Tradescant, second wife of John the Younger.[1]

In 1640 appeared *The country-mans recreation*, a small quarto volume consisting of the three following sixteenth-century treatises: *A booke of the art and maner, howe to plante and graffe all sortes of trees*, a translation by Leonard Mascall of the French by Davy Brossard; *A perfite platforme of a hoppe garden* by Reginald Scot; and the anonymous treatise entitled *The orchard, and the garden*. In *The country-mans recreation*, the names of Mascall and Scot are omitted, and *The orchard, and the garden* is given the new title of *The expert gardener*. In 1640, soon after the appearance of this compilation, the Civil War broke out, and from then until the time of the Commonwealth no further book on gardening or cultivation appeared in England. From 1642, until the establishment of the Commonwealth in 1649, only one botanical book of any description appears to have been published in this country, namely the *Catalogus plantarum Horti medici oxoniensis* (1648). Mumby has pointed out that, although a number of important literary works were published during this period, the book trade, 'as sensitive then as now to outside disturbance, was naturally affected during these years of strife. Most of the reading matter of the day took the form of controversial pamphlets or news-sheets, each side having its own organs, published two or three times a week in the more stirring stages of the wars.'[2]

[1] See Allan (M.), *The Tradescants*, etc. 215 (1964).
[2] Mumby (F. A.), *Publishing and bookselling. A history from the earliest times to the present day*, 109–10 (1949).

VI

GARDENING BOOKS AND WORKS ON
CULTIVATION
continued

COMPARED with the years 1600–50, the second half of the seventeenth century in England witnessed a great increase in the number of gardening books published. As a large percentage were on fruit culture, owing to the movement started during the Commonwealth towards the improvement of orchards, we will begin by considering some of the various works on this subject.

In 1653 appeared an anonymous treatise entitled *A designe for plentie, by an universall planting of fruit-trees.* The preface is by Samuel Hartlib who here states that the writer of the work was not known to him and that moreover he was unable to discover his name. However, it was said that he was 'an aged minister of the Gospel' of Loving-land near Yarmouth, who spent his leisure over a period of many years in the study of fruit culture.[1] He wrote his treatise as the result of the knowledge he thus acquired but died before the work could be published. For himself, Hartlib claims nothing 'but the contentment to be the publisher thereof'.[2]

Samuel Hartlib (d. 1670?),[3] a great promoter of husbandry and the author of several publications in relation to this subject, was the son of a Polish merchant who, in order to escape persecution by the Jesuits, had settled at Elbing in Prussia.[4] Samuel Hartlib came to England about 1628,[5] became a friend of John Milton, and corresponded with many learned and eminent men of the day, including Robert Boyle.[6]

In his *English improver improved* of 1652, the agricultural writer, Walter Blith, notes that he had learnt from Samuel Hartlib that 'an Oxford gentleman, called Ra. Austen, an artist both learned and experienced, had finished a work fit for the presse, of approved experiments in planting late fruit'.[7] This work, which was also announced as a forthcoming attraction by Hartlib himself in his preface to *A designe for plentie*, finally appeared in 1653, entitled *A treatise of fruit-trees*, and with an imprint reading 'Oxford printed

[1] *A designe for plentie*, etc. [1653] (Preface).
[2] Ibid. (1653) (Preface).
[3] *D.N.B.* (under Hartlib, Samuel).
[4] Dircks (H.), *A biographical memoir of* *Samuel Hartlib*, etc. 2 [1865].
[5] Ibid. 5.
[6] See Dircks (H.), op. cit. 6, 14, 44, etc.
[7] p. 259 (i.e. Mm2ᵃ).

for Tho: Robinson'. The dedication is addressed by the author, Ralph Austen, to his much honoured friend, Samuel Hartlib. The title-page is engraved by John Goddard, who worked as an engraver during the years 1645 to 1673.[1] Above the title are clasped hands, illustrating 'Profits' shaking hands with 'Pleasures', and beneath the title is a plan of a neatly planted orchard. Although the beginning of the work is interspersed with texts from the Bible, and is typical of the puritanical style of the day, the *Treatise* as a whole contains much useful information on the planting and care of trees. Of particular interest is a section headed 'Errors discovered'.[2] Here the author exposes a number of the old superstitions to be found in garden literature and also draws attention to some of the errors practised by gardeners. Together with *A treatise of fruit-trees* was published 'The spirituall use of an orchard', but this tract is so full of references to the Scriptures that it contains little of value to the practical gardener. A second edition of the *Treatise* with its appended tract appeared in 1657. According to one writer,[3] 'it is very probable that the said book might have been printed more than twice had not he, the author, added to, and bound with it, another treatise as big as the former entit. "The spiritual use of an orchard, or garden of fruit-trees," etc., which being all divinity and nothing therein of the practice part of gardening, many therefore did refuse to buy it'. This conclusion was probably correct for in 1665 the *Treatise* was published a third time, but without 'The spirituall use of an orchard'. However, the 1657 edition of the latter was reprinted in Victorian times, in 1847, by William Pamplin, as a separate work.

Austen was the author of two other works. The first, published in 1658 at Oxford, is his *Observations upon some part of Sr Francis Bacon's Naturall history as it concernes, fruit-trees, fruits and flowers*. This treatise with a commendatory letter by Robert Sharrock, Fellow of New College, Oxford,[4] is dedicated to Robert Boyle. The second work appeared at Oxford in 1676, the year of the author's death, and is the rarest of Austen's publications. It is *A dialogue, or familiar discourse, and conference betweene the husbandman, and fruit-trees*, and was printed by Henry Hall, printer to the University, for Thomas Bowman.

Ralph Austen, gardener and author, was a native of Staffordshire, who apparently lived much of his life at Oxford.[5] In this city he became Registrary

[1] Johnson (A. F.), *A catalogue of engraved and etched English title-pages down to ... 1691*, p. 24 (1934 for 1933).

[2] See pp. 78–97.

[3] Wood (A. à), *Athenæ oxonienses ... To which are added the Fasti ... A new edition ... by Philip Bliss*, 4 (1820). (See *Fasti*, Pt. 2, col. 174.)

[4] Robert Sharrock was the author of *The history of the propagation and improvement of vegetables*, etc. (1659).

[5] Wood (A. à), *Athenæ oxonienses ... To which are added the Fasti ... A new edition ... by Philip Bliss*, 4 (1820). (See *Fasti*, Pt. 2, col. 174.) In the *D.N.B.* this Ralph Austen who died at Oxford on 26 Oct. 1676, is confused with Ralph Austen the Oxford scholar. See Foster (J.), *Alumni oxonienses ... 1500–1714*, etc. 1, 45 (1891).

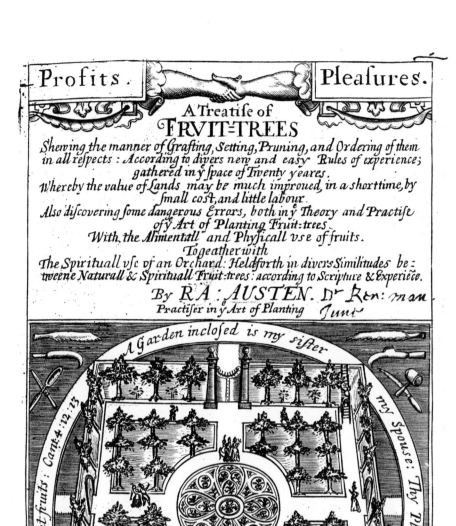

Profits. Pleasures.

A Treatise of
FRVIT=TREES
Shewing the manner of Grafting, Setting, Pruning, and Ordering of them
in all respects : According to divers new and easy Rules of experience;
gathered in y̆ space of Twenty yeares.
Whereby the value of Lands may be much improued, in a shorttime, by
small cost, and little labour.
Also discovering some dangerous Errors, both in y̆ Theory and Practise
of y̆ Art of Planting Fruit=trees.
With, the Alimentall and Physicall vse of fruits.
Togeather with
The Spirituall vse of an Orchard: Held forth in divers Similitudes be=
tweene Naturall & Spirituall Fruit=trees: according to Scripture & Experiēce.
By RA: AUSTEN. Dr Ren: man
Practiser in y̆ Art of Planting Juni

A Garden inclosed is my sister

pleasant fruits : Cant 4 :12 :13

my Spouse; Thy Plants are

an Orchard of Pomgranads, with

Oxford printed for Tho: Robinson 1653.

I: Goddard sculp:

51. Austen: *A treatise of fruit-trees*, 1653. Title-page engraved by John
Goddard. 6·7 × 4·3″.

to the Visitors.[1] In 1652 he was 'entred a student into the public library [the Bodleian Library], to the end that he might find materials for the composition of a book which he was then meditating'—i.e. for the book called *A treatise of fruit-trees*. Anthony à Wood refers to Austen as 'a very useful man' who spent all his time in Oxford until his death in 1676, in planting gardens in, and near it, and in raising fruit-trees. At the time of his death Austen had been 'a practiser in gardening' for fifty years. His work as gardener at Oxford is highly commended by Anthony Lawrence in a letter published in 1677, in a treatise entitled *Nurseries, orchards, profitable gardens, and vineyards encouraged*.[2] This letter addressed by Lawrence to Henry Oldenburg, Secretary of the Royal Society, was apparently partly written in order to advertise the fact that Austen had 'very lately taken-in twenty seven acres of ground, to enlarge his former nurseries, and for new plantations'.[3]

Another writer who helped to encourage fruit growing was John Beale, D.D. (1603–82?),[4] who was especially interested in the propagation of cider fruit in Herefordshire and other parts of England, and who corresponded on this subject with Boyle, Evelyn, Hartlib, and the Secretary of the Royal Society, Henry Oldenburg.[5]

John Beale, a Fellow of the Royal Society,[6] was a native of Herefordshire. He was educated at Eton, where he was a scholar,[7] and at King's College, Cambridge. He graduated Bachelor of Arts in 1632 [i.e. 1633], took his degree of Master of Arts in 1636, and was a Fellow of King's College from 1632 until 1640. From 1638 until 1682 Beale was Rector of Sock in Somerset and from 1660 until 1682 was also Rector of Yeovil. It is recorded that after graduating Master of Arts he was ordained. Subsequently Beale received the degree of Doctor of Divinity.[8] In 1665 he received the appointment of Chaplain to Charles II.

Beale's published works include 'Aphorisms concerning cider', printed in Evelyn's *Sylva* (1664), and a small octavo volume published in 1657 with the title of *Herefordshire orchards, a pattern for all England*. This work, published under the author's initials J. B., consists of two letters on orcharding in Herefordshire, written on the 3rd and 13th May 1656, respectively, by John Beale to his friend Samuel Hartlib. These letters were published at the desire

[1] Wood (A. à), *Athenæ oxonienses . . . To which are added the Fasti . . . A new edition . . . by Philip Bliss*, **4** (1820). (See *Fasti*, Pt. 2, col. 174.)

[2] See pp. 5–8.

[3] See p. 8.

[4] Regarding the probable year of Beale's death see Venn (J.) and Venn (J. A.), *Alumni cantabrigienses . . . Part I . . . to 1751*, **1**, 116 (1922) and *D.N.B.* (under Beale, J.).

[5] e.g. see *The works of . . . Robert Boyle . . . A new edition*, **6** (1772), and *Supplement to the Royal society's Letter books*, vol. **1**.

[6] Beale 'was elected a Fellow of the Society' 21 Jan. 1662 [i.e. 1663]. See Birch (T.), *The history of the Royal society of London*, etc. **1**, 179 (1756).

[7] Venn (J.) and Venn (J. A.), *Alumni cantabrigienses*, etc. **1**, 116 (1922).

[8] Hutchinson (J.), *Herefordshire biographies*, 12 (1890). The present writer has been unable to find from which University Beale received his doctorate.

of Samuel Hartlib,[1] and the book is dedicated to him. The imprint on the title-page of the work reads 'London, printed by Roger Daniel'. Regarding this publication Beale wrote on 6 December 1672:[2]

It was anno 1656 that I permitted two . . . letters . . . to be printed by Daniel who was then printer both to Cambridge & for London. The print was very fair, but very false, & much to my prejudice, and with J. B. in the front, contrary to my convention with Mr. H., tis intitled: *Herefordshire orchards a pattern for all England*: since which time Herefordshire hath gotten some hundred of thousands sterling, by the fame of their orchards.

In 1724 Beale's excellent tract was published again, both as a separate work and also printed in Richard Bradley's *New improvements of planting and gardening*.

Another letter written by Beale, on orchards and vineyards, was published in 1677 in *Nurseries, orchards, profitable gardens, and vineyards encouraged*. This thin quarto volume contains letters written by Beale, and by Anthony Lawrence, addressed to Henry Oldenburg. Concerning Anthony Lawrence little appears to be known. He must, however, have been very interested in fruit growing, as in a letter referring to the above tract of 1677, dated from Yeovil, 29 November 1676, Beale told Robert Boyle:[3]

I dare say, that Anthony Lawrence can do more for propagation of orchards in five years, than Mr. Austen hath done in fifty-two years, as he numbers them. Yea, I can prove and shew, that he hath done so before our eyes very lately, only by transporting many thousands of grafts of apples and pears of the best cyder fruit out of Herefordshire and Worcestershire, into Somersetshire, Dorsetshire, Devonshire, and Cornwall; and by sending grafts to London, and by riding up and down to give instructions and encouragements.

In a letter published in the above work of 1677, Anthony Lawrence recommends *The French gardiner* and Le Gendre's *The manner of ordering fruit-trees* for their 'accurate directions' concerning the growing of wall fruits.[4] The first of these two works, a translation by John Evelyn, will be discussed later.[5] Of the second treatise, John Beale wrote on 26 October 1672 to Robert Boyle:[6]

And because I have seen your fair and large walls, I recommend to you, and for your man, the Sieur Le Gendre's manner of ordering fruit trees, printed for Humphrey Moseley at Prince's arms, Paul's, 1660, written with the greatest judgment, that ever

[1] B[eale]. (J.), *Herefordshire orchards*, etc. 59–60 (1657).
[2] See letter from Beale to Oldenburg? in *Supplement to the Royal society's Letter books*, 1, 466–7.
[3] *The works of . . . Robert Boyle . . . A new edition*, 6, 439 (1772).
[4] *Nurseries, orchards, profitable gardens, and vineyards encouraged*, etc. 13 (1677).
[5] See below, pp. 186–7.
[6] *The works of . . . Robert Boyle . . . A new edition*, 6, 435–6 (1772).

I saw any, after about fifty years experience,[1] and a full knowledge of all the best gardens in France, translated (as I guess by the stile) by Mr Evelyn.

The book referred to by Lawrence and Beale is a translation of '*La manière de cultiver les arbres fruitiers . . . où il est traitté des pépinières, des espaliers, des contr'espaliers des arbres en buisson & à haute tige*' by Antoine Le Gendre, curé d'Hénouville, a work first published in Paris in 1652. Until recently, perhaps on the authority of Quérard,[2] some biographers have considered the real author of this work to be Robert Arnauld d'Andilly, a member of the celebrated family who played a leading role in the religious movement during the seventeenth century at Port-Royal. However, Mademoiselle Madier of the Muséum National d'Histoire Naturelle, in Paris, has been able to send the present writer, with the permission of Monsieur Auguste Chevalier, Honorary Professor of the Museum, the following informative details concerning the real authorship of the work:[3]

. . . une recherche biographique récente effectuée par M. Auguste Chevalier, professeur honoraire au Muséum, nous a permis de rétablir la vérité: Antoine Le Gendre, né en 1590, mort en 1665 a bien existé; il fut inspecteur des jardins de Louis XIII en même temps qu'aumonier du Roi; nommé curé d'Hénouville en 1622 il y resta jusqu'à sa mort. Il est bien l'auteur du petit traité d'arboriculture.

In 1952 Monsieur Auguste Chevalier drew attention to the enlightened views on fruit culture held by Le Gendre, and the latter's friendship with Pierre Corneille, the celebrated French writer who was in the habit of visiting 'le presbytère d'Hénouville' which was so noted for the excellency of its fruit.[4]

The French editions of this work, and also the English version, state that the author was the curé of Hénonville.[5] Le Gendre, however, was definitely the curé of Hénouville, a parish lying in the fertile Normandy country, a few miles west-north-west of Rouen,[6] and he appears to have had no connection with Hénonville, a village several miles north-north-west of Pontoise, in the Canton of Méru.

Beale, as we noted earlier, considered *The manner of ordering fruit-trees* to be a translation by Evelyn, and in recent years F. E. Budd has put forward grounds for accepting this attribution.[7] But Hiscock considers that Budd has

[1] '. . . by an experience of almost fifty years' (the Preface).
[2] Quérard (J. M.), *Les supercheries littéraires dévoilées . . . seconde édition . . . par G. Brunet et P. Jannet*, etc. **2**, col. 729 (1870), Paris.
[3] In epist. 18.v.53.
[4] Chevalier (A.), Histoire des sciences.— D'où viennent les pommiers à bons fruits de nos jardins et de nos vergers?: *Comptes rendus Acad. Sci.* **234**, 2126–7 (26 May 1952), Paris. See also Hecht (Y.), L'œuvre d'Antoine Le Gendre 'Inspecteur des arbres fruitiers' du

roi Louis XIII et curé d'Hénouville: *Paris–Normandie*, 1 (2 June 1952), Rouen.
[5] This statement is found not only on the title-page but also at the end of the Epistle dedicatory to the various French editions and the English version.
[6] Bunel (J.), *Géographie du département de la Seine-Inférieure*, 257–60 (1879), Rouen.
[7] Budd (F. E.), A translation attributed to Evelyn: The manner of ordering fruit-trees (1660), *The Review of English studies*, **14**, 285–97 (1938).

not proved conclusively that Evelyn was the translator of the work,[1] and the same authority adds further doubt to this attribution by writing:[2] 'Moreover, it is curious that Evelyn did not possess a copy of the translation. It does not appear in his list of publications sent to Dr. Plot on 16 March 1683'.[3] Hiscock, however, did not add that according to the catalogue of his library Evelyn possessed a copy of the second (1653) Paris edition from which the translation was made.[4] 'The fact that Evelyn did not mention the book in his Diary or elsewhere', writes Keynes,[5] 'does not make the attribution less probable, since there are other instances of fully authenticated books against which the same objection could be raised.' 'It seems reasonable, therefore', he continues, 'to admit *The manner of ordering fruit-trees* to the Evelyn canon', and Keynes has included the translation in the new edition, published in 1968, of his work entitled *John Evelyn a study in bibliophily with a bibliography of his writings*.[6]

The frontispiece in the English version is not found in the French editions. It consists of the title and imprint of the book surrounded by four small compartments with illustrations depicting the art of grafting and pruning, and the shaping of horizontally trained fruit trees.

In 1665 and 1666 two books were published on viticulture, a subject which attracted considerable attention during the reign of Charles II. The first of these works, entitled *The compleat vineyard*, is by William Hughes. This author gives information on the planting and care of vines, on the gathering of grapes, and on the making of wine, according to methods practised in England, Germany, and France. The second book, *The English vineyard vindicated*, is stated on the title-page to be 'by John Rose gard'ner to His Majesty, at his Royal garden in St. James's', and the treatise is dedicated by John Rose to his master, the King. It appears, however, that although Rose supplied the matter for this work, it was actually written by John Evelyn, who signed the preface under the pseudonym of Philocepos. Evelyn's identity is revealed at the end of the preface when he refers to his *Sylva*, published under his name two years earlier. Regarding the origin of *The English vineyard*, Evelyn recounts in the preface:

Being one day refreshing my self in the garden at Essex-house, and amongst other things falling into discourse with Mr. Rose, (then gard'ner to her Grace the Dutchess of Somerset) about vines, and particularly the cause of the neglect of vineyards of late in England; he reason'd so pertinently upon that subject (as indeed he does upon all things,

[1] Hiscock (W. G.), *John Evelyn and his family circle*, 243 (1955).

[2] Ibid.

[3] Hiscock's reference is 'Letter book, Evelyn MS. 39, p. 37' in the Evelyn collection at Christ Church, Oxford.

[4] This copy is now preserved in the Brit.

Mus. (Bloomsbury) (pressmark 1506/640); a note on the fly-leaf reads: 'From Evelyn collection Jan. 1814, Upcott–⁸1–'.

[5] Keynes (G.), *John Evelyn a study in bibliophily with a bibliography of his writings*, 83 (1968).

[6] See pp. vii, 82–4.

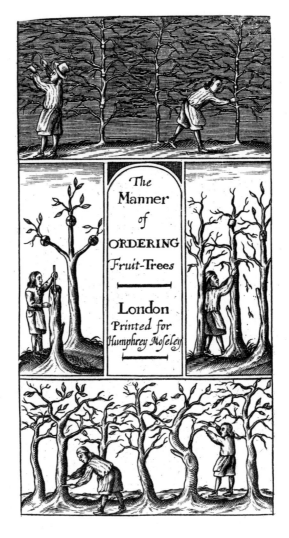

52. Le Gendre: *The manner of ordering fruit-trees*, 1660.
Engraved frontispiece. 5·2 × 2·7″.

which concern his hortulan profession) that . . . I was easily perswaded to gratifie his modest and charitable inclinations, to have them communicated to the world. The matter therefore of the ensuing discourse being totally his, receives from me onely its forme, and the putting of his conceptions together; which I have dress'd up in as rural a garbe as I thought might best become, and recommend them for practice.

John Rose[1] had become Keeper of the Royal garden in St. James's Park

---

[1] John Rose was born presumably in 1622 'as the Wiltshire Record Office have the Amesbury Court Rolls with his succession to a small copyhold of his father, Stephen Rose, dead by 20/9/1638, when John Rose was stated to be aged 16' (information supplied to the present writer by Mr. John Harvey in epist. 17. viii. 72).

only a short time before the above work was published.[1] There is some confusion as to the appointments he held previous to this. According to Switzer,[2]
Rose 'was first gardener to the Lord Essex at Essex-house in the Strand'—
a reference presumably to Robert Devereux, third Earl of Essex (1591–1646)
whose sister Frances (1599–1674) became the second wife of William Seymour, second Duke of Somerset (1587–1660). In 1639 William Seymour and
his wife bought a ninety-nine years' lease of a moiety of Essex House from
the Earl of Essex,[3] the house being shared by the two parties. On Robert
Devereux's death the earldom became extinct, and it seems likely that Rose
then became gardener to William Seymour. The latter, who in September
1660 became Duke of Somerset, died at Essex House on 24 October 1660,[4]
and Evelyn's visit to the gardens may have been shortly after this event,
as he refers to Rose being 'then gard'ner to her Grace the Dutchess of
Somerset'.[5]

The Duchess's son, Henry Seymour, Lord Beauchamp, married in 1648
Mary, daughter of the first Baron Capel of Hadham. It is possible, therefore,
that Rose, who 'was esteemed to be the best of his profession in those days',[6]
was asked by Lord Capel to assist with the laying out of the gardens at Cassiobury. It will be remembered that when Evelyn visited these noted gardens,
in 1680, at the time of Lord Capel's son, Arthur Capel, first Earl of Essex,
they were under the care of the eminent gardener Moses Cook, who in 1676
had published a popular treatise on *The manner of raising, ordering and
improving forrest-trees*.[7] It is learnt from Daines Barrington in his letter on
the progress of gardening, published in *Archæologia*[8] that: 'Lord Essex . . .
sent his gardener Rose to study the then much celebrated beauties of Versailles. Upon Rose's return Charles the second appointed him Royal
gardener.' It appears, therefore, that Rose also served as gardener to Arthur
Capel, Earl of Essex. John Rose died in September 1677.[9]

The English vineyard was printed for the London bookseller John Crook

[1] In the *Calendar of State papers, domestic
series, of the reign of Charles II. 1665–1666 . . .
Edited by M. A. E. Green*, 237 (1864) under
8 Feb. 1666, is an 'Order for a warrant to pay
to John Rose, appointed Keeper of St. James's
garden, in place of Andrew and Gabriel Mollet,
deceased, 24ol. a year for wages, for keeping the
said garden', and under 21 Feb. 1666, a 'warrant to pay John Rose, Keeper of St. James's
park gardens . . . 24ol. a year', ibid. 261 (1864).
[2] Switzer (S.), *Ichnographia rustica*, etc. 1, 68
(1718).
[3] C[okayne]. (G. E.), *The complete peerage*,
etc. 12, 73, footnote d (1953).
[4] *Calendar of State papers, domestic series, of
the reign of Charles II. 1660–1661 . . . Edited by
M. A. E. Green*, 324 (1860) (under 26 Oct.

1660).
[5] *The English vineyard* (1666) (Preface).
[6] Switzer (S.), *Ichnographia rustica*, etc. 1,
68–9 (1718).
[7] See above, pp. 116–18.
[8] **7**, 122 (1785).
[9] See the *Calendar of State papers, domestic
series, March 1st, 1677, to February 28th, 1678
. . . Edited by F. H. Blackburne Daniell*, 633
(1911), where under 7 February 1678 we read
of, '. . . Rose dying 10 Sept., three weeks
before last Michaelmas'.
   See also Wills Hale, 93, Prob. 11/354/93
will of John Rose of Parish in St. Martin's in
the Fields 22 February 1676 [i.e. 1677]. (Will
in the Public Record Office.)

(or Crooke), whose address from 1640 until 1666 was the Ship in St. Paul's
Churchyard. His stock of the work, therefore, was probably lost in the Great
Fire of 1666, and this would account for the rarity of this little volume.[1]
According to Keynes,[2] *The English vineyard* was not published again as
a separate work, but it was appended to the second and subsequent editions
of *The French gardiner*, 1669, etc.

Although both *The compleat vineyard* and *The English vineyard vindicated*
were published with the obvious intention of encouraging the planting of
vineyards and the manufacture of wine in this country, the result they
achieved appears to have been disappointing. This is evident from the
following passage found in a letter by John Beale published in 1677 in
Nurseries, orchards, profitable gardens, and vineyards encouraged.[3]

> But yet I have much to say for the wine of the grape, though with some disparagement
> to our own country-men, who have done so little for it, after they have had such bright
> instructions, and such lively encouragements from Mr. Evelyn and Mr. Rose in their
> English Vineyards, published anno 1666. Mr. Rose then offering all that desire it with
> sets and plants of the best vines (sufficiently tried in our own soyl and climate) at
> reasonable rates: and Mr. Hughes enlarging (in his 'Compleat vineyard',) as the manner
> is in Germany.

Among other eighteenth-century English writers on fruit culture is Francis
Drope, whose *Short and sure guid in the practice of raising and ordering of
fruit-trees*, was published posthumously in 1672. This treatise was written
from the author's 'own experience',[4] and according to Wood[5] it is on a subject Drope 'much delighted in' and on which he spent 'a considerable part
of his time'. The work is edited by the author's brother, Edward.[6] Francis
Drope (1629?–71), was a Fellow of Magdalen College, Oxford, a Bachelor
of Divinity, and a Canon of Lincoln. He may well have received early
encouragement in the study of pomology from William Browne, part author
of the Oxford catalogue of 1658.[7] The two men were contemporaries at
Magdalen, Browne becoming a demy of that college in 1644, and Drope
in 1645.

Until a few years ago it was generally considered that *The planters manual*,
a small octavo volume published in 1675, was an original work by Charles
Cotton (1630–87), the English poet and friend of Izaak Walton. In 1918, however, Edward Bunyard pointed out that, although the name of the author
appears on the title-page as Charles Cotton, the book is in reality a translation

[1] There are two copies in the Brit. Mus. (Bloomsbury), but only one of these copies (Pressmark C. 118. b. 22) is perfect.

[2] Keynes (G.), *John Evelyn a study of biblio-phily and a bibliography of his writings*, 178 (1937).

[3] p. 21.

[4] Drope (F.), *A short and sure guid*, etc. (1672) (Preface).

[5] Wood (A. à), *Athenæ oxonienses . . . A new edition . . . by Philip Bliss*, 3, col. 941 (1817).

[6] Drope (F.), op. cit. (1672) (Preface).

[7] See above, pp. 96–7.

of the French *Instructions pour les arbres fruictiers. Par M.R.T.P.D.S.M.*, first published in 1653 by Antoine Bertier of Paris.[1] Cotton was responsible for a number of translations from the French, including Montaigne's 'Essays', and he was also no doubt the translator of *The planters manual*. He may well have first seen the French original in France when he visited that country as a young man. As noted above the author is referred to on the title-page of the French work by the initials M.R.T.P.D.S.M., and he is again alluded to by these letters in this volume in the 'Privilège du Roy', where it is learnt that they stand for M[onsieur] R. Triquel, Prieur de Saint Marc. Bunyard considers that R. Triquel is not the author of the book but the editor, and that it was actually written by François Vautier, physician to Louis XIV. Cardew, however, has supplied data proving that this statement is incorrect, and that although the manuscript was found after Vautier's death 'amongst his most treasured books', this physician could not have been its author.[2] 'There can be no doubt', states Cardew,[3] 'that this book was the work of R. Triquet, or Triquel, Prior of St. Mark's.'[4]

The title-page of *The planters manual* shows various scenes illustrating agricultural pursuits. The engraver of this title, Frederik Hendrik van Hove (1628–98), was a native of The Hague who lived much of his life in England. He was also responsible, it will be remembered, for a number of the engravings of plants in the second and third parts of Morison's 'Historia' (1680, 1699).

In 1681 appeared *Plain and full instructions to raise all sorts of fruit-trees that prosper in England* by 'T. Langford, Gent.'. The imprint reads 'London, printed by J. M. for Rich. Chiswel', and following the epistle to the reader is a commendatory letter addressed to Mr. Chiswel by John Evelyn, in which the latter writes: 'I have read the treatise of fruit-trees, &c. which you lately put into my hand, and . . . I know of nothing extant which exceeds it, so nor do I of any thing which needs be added to it.' Equally high in his praise of this work is the horticulturist Samuel Gilbert, who pronounced in his *Florists vade-mecum* of 1682,[5] 'I meddle not at present with fruit trees, it being well done by Mr. Langford in a pocket volume of easie price'. Langford's treatise sold well, and in 1696 it was published in a new and enlarged edition with a dedication addressed by the author to his 'honoured master, Sir Samuel Grimston, Bar.'.[6] From this inscription it is apparent that Langford worked for Sir Samuel, but in what capacity the reader is not told. Sir Samuel

[1] Bunyard (E. A.), Cotton's *'Planter's manual'*, *Gard. Chron.*, Series III, vol. **63**, 174–5 (Apr. 1918).

[2] Cardew (F.), M.R.T.P.D.S.M.: 'Instructions pour les arbres fruictiers', *J. Soc. Bibl. nat. Hist.* **2**, 206–7 (1950).

[3] Op. cit. **2**, 206.

[4] R. Triquet is also given as the author by Barbier (A. A.), *Dictionnaire des ouvrages anonymes . . . troisième édition*, etc. **2**, col. 936 (1874), Paris.

[5] See Epistle to the reader.

[6] Langford (T.), *Plain and full instructions*, etc. (1696) (Dedication).

The Planters Manuell

Bij Charles Cotton eqs

London Printed for Henry Brome 1675

F. H. van Hove fec:

53. Cotton: *The planters manual*, 1675. Frontispiece engraved by Frederik Hendrik van Hove. 5·6 × 3·4″.

Grimston (1643–1700) of Gorhambury, in Hertfordshire, was for many years Member of Parliament for St. Albans.[1] To the 1696 edition of the work was added a section headed 'Of greens and green-houses in general',[2] followed by eleven pages consisting of 'A catalogue of choice fruits . . . and also of greens and blossoming shrubs: to be had at Brompton park, near Kensington'.[3] As we shall be referring a number of times to this famous nursery garden let us pause and consider a few points of interest in its history.

[1] C[okayne]. (G. E.), *Complete baronetage*, **1**, 107 (1900).
[2] pp. 171–209. Green = 'a tree, herb, or plant. Also specifically, an evergreen (mostly in plural)' (*The Oxford English dictionary*, **4** (1933)).
[3] pp. 210–20.

Brompton Park nursery was founded in 1681 by four gardeners:[1] Roger Looker, 'gardener to her Ma:^{tie},[2] Moses Cook (or Cooke), gardener to Arthur Capel, Earl of Essex, at Cassiobury, and the author of the excellent work published in 1676 on *The manner of raising, ordering, and improving forrest-trees*, John Field (or Feild), gardener to William Russell, fifth Earl of Bedford, at Woburn Abbey in Bedfordshire, and George London, gardener to Henry Compton, Bishop of London, at Fulham Palace. Looker died in 1685 and Field in 1687.[3] In 1689 Cook disposed of his share to Henry Wise, and in the following year George London and Henry Wise went into partnership. During the next quarter of a century these two men, who apparently had known each other for some years,[4] built up Brompton Park to be the foremost nursery garden in the country. Furthermore, they became the leading garden designers of the period, belonging to the school of formal gardening of which Le Nôtre was the chief exponent. Chatsworth, Castle Howard, and Melbourne are but three of the famous gardens with which these men's names are associated. In addition London and Wise achieved literary success with their abridgement of John Evelyn's *The compleat gard'ner* (1699) and *The retir'd gard'ner* of 1706, two works which will be referred to later. George London (d. 1714),[5] who held the appointment of Master Gardener and Deputy Superintendent of the Royal gardens, during the reign of William III,[6] received his early training under John Rose who sent his pupil, at the end of four or five years, to further his studies in France. 'Soon after the peace of Ryswick' London went again to France.[7] On this occasion he stayed several months and 'is said to have visited Chantilly, Fontainebleau, Versailles, and Vaux, and to have been shown the gardens by Le Nôtre himself'.[8] It has been recorded that Henry Wise (1653–1738) also was an apprentice of John Rose, but regarding this there appears to be no definite proof.[9] During the reign of Queen Anne, Wise was responsible for the upkeep of the Royal parks and

[1] The four gardeners gave their reasons for entering into a partnership and also for acquiring about twenty-four acres of ground 'comonly called Brompton Parke in the parishes of Kensington and Westminster in the county of Mddx' as a nursery garden, in a notice of 1681 to be found in Harley MS. 6273, ff. 50–56.

[2] According to Switzer (S.), *Ichnographia rustica*, etc. 1, 78 (1718) Looker (sometimes spelt Lucre or Lukar) was 'gardener to Queen-Dowager at Somerset-house'. He may, therefore, have been gardener to the Dowager Queen Henrietta Maria (d. 1669) at some period before she finally left England in 1665. But in 1681 when he himself gave his occupation as 'gardener to her Ma:^{tie}', Looker was presumably referring to Catherine of Braganza, the consort of Charles II.

[3] For further details concerning Field see Thomson (G. S.), *Life in a noble household 1641–1700* (1937)(Chapter XIII, The gardens).

[4] See Green (D.), *Gardener to Queen Anne. Henry Wise (1653–1738) and the formal garden*, 5 (1956).

[5] Regarding the date of London's death see Brotherston (R. P.), Brompton park nursery, *Gard. Chron.*, Series III, vol. 74, 218 (1923).

[6] 'The Earl of Portland was, during the reign of William III, Superintendent of the Royal gardens. George London was Master Gardener and Deputy Superintendent.' Green (D.), *Gardener to Queen Anne. Henry Wise (1653–1738) and the formal garden*, 55, footnote 1 (1956) (quoted by Green from *Wren Society*, **4**, 30).

[7] Switzer (S.), *Ichnographia rustica*, etc. **1**, 80 (1718). The Treaty of Ryswick was in 1697.

[8] Green (D.), op. cit. 17 (1956).

[9] Ibid., p. xiii (1956).

gardens, and regarding his work as Royal gardener, the part he played in the running of Brompton Park, and the magnificent gardens he made throughout the country, the reader must turn to Mr. David Green's informative book about Henry Wise published in 1956 by the Oxford University Press, under the title of *Gardener to Queen Anne. Henry Wise (1653–1738) and the formal garden.*

In 1685 appeared an anonymous work entitled *The compleat planter & cyderist.* Also *The art of pruning fruit-trees*, an English translation of *L'Art de tailler les arbres fruitiers* published in Paris in 1683. Nicolas Venette (1633–98), the author of this French treatise, was a physician of La Rochelle.[1] In 1690 *The compleat planter & cyderist* and *The art of pruning fruit-trees* were published together in one volume.

During the seventeenth century attention was turned to the growing of oranges and lemons, and special glass-fronted houses were built for the shelter of these trees. The plants were generally placed in pots or cases which were left in the open during the summer months and taken indoors during the winter. After the Restoration these conservatories, orangeries, or greenhouses, as they were variously called, became more general, and an increased interest developed in the growing of tender plants. Books were published giving information on the growing of citrus fruits, myrtles, and other 'exotic greens'.[2] In 1683 an English version of Jan Commelin's *Nederlantze Hesperides* appeared as a small octavo volume, entitled *The Belgick, or Netherlandish Hesperides. That is: The management, ordering, and use of the limon and orange trees, fitted to the . . . climate of the Netherlands.* Jan Commelin (1629–92) was a citizen and wealthy merchant of Amsterdam. He took charge of the city's new botanic garden and under his care it became one of the most renowned in Europe. His *Nederlantze Hesperides*, first published in 1676 at Amsterdam, is a fine folio volume with many copper plates. The English translator, known only by the initials G. V. N.,[3] dedicated his book to Thomas Belasyse, second Viscount Fauconberg of Henknowle (1628–1700).[4] This nobleman had a house at Sutton Court, in the parish of Chiswick, Middlesex, with a noted garden and a greenhouse 'very well furnished with good greens'.[5]

[1] Hoefer (J. C. F.), *Nouvelle biographie générale*, etc. 45, cols. 1079–80 (1866), Paris.

[2] e.g. in the second edition of his *Plain and full instructions to raise all sorts of fruit-trees* (1696), Langford includes a section 'Of greens and green-houses in general'.

[3] On the title-page of *The Belgick, or Nether-* *landish Hesperides* is the statement: 'Made English by G. V. N.' The dedication is also signed G. V. N.

[4] In 1689 created Earl Fauconberg.

[5] A short account of several gardens near London . . . upon a view of them (by J. Gibson) in Dec. 1691, *Archæologia* 12, 184 (1796).

VII

GARDENING BOOKS AND WORKS ON CULTIVATION
continued

THE most famous writer on gardening and planting during the second half of the seventeenth century was John Evelyn. He was a man of many interests and the author of books on such varied subjects as architecture, engraving, gardening, history, numismatics, painting, planting, and politics. In Wheatley's opinion Evelyn,[1] 'was not a professed author, although he was a prolific writer, and his publications were mostly intended to meet a want which he had descried'. He was certainly correct in his judgement concerning the need for practical books on planting and gardening as is evident from the many editions in which were published his *Sylva, Kalendarium hortense*, and *French gardiner*, a translation from the French of N. de Bonnefons. Earlier, reference was made to his famous *Sylva*, a work of national importance which gave an enormous stimulus to planting in Britain. Now we must discuss some of his works on gardening, but first we will record a few of the many details found in his *Diary*, and other works, indicating his great enthusiasm for gardening, for the laying out of plantations and ornamental gardens, and for his interest and knowledge of plants, especially trees.

John Evelyn was born in 1620 at his father's house of Wotton in Surrey, which he describes as being 'large and antient, suitable to those hospitable times, and so sweetely environ'd with those delicious streames and venerable woods, as in the judgment of strangers, as well as English-men, it may be compared to one of the most tempting and pleasant seates in the nation . . .'.[2] Evelyn's early interest in horticulture is shown to us during his stay in Holland in 1641 when he visited the Leyden physic garden which, he writes,[3] 'was indeede well stor'd with exotic plants, if the Catalogue presented to me by the gardiner be a faithful register'. He also went to Antwerp where he was 'ravished' by the 'delicious shades and walkes of stately trees'.[4] During a

---

[1] *Diary of John Evelyn . . . edited from the original MSS. by W. Bray . . . A new edition . . . with a life of the author . . . by H. B. Wheatley,* **1**, xv (1906).

[2] *The diary of John Evelyn . . . edited by E. S. de Beer,* **2**, 4 (1955).
[3] Ibid. 52–3.
[4] Ibid. 67.

sojourn abroad from November 1643 until October 1647 Evelyn became familiar with the gardens of France and Italy. His attention was drawn to every sort of garden, both large and small, and in Geneva on his homeward journey, he was 'invited to a little garden . . . where were many rare tulips, anemonies & other choice flowers'.[1] Among the many gardens Evelyn visited at home was the Oxford physic garden. He went there on 12 July 1654 and subsequently recorded in his *Diary* that in this garden there 'grew canes, olive tres, rhubarb, but no extraordinary curiosities, besides very good fruit'.[2] Ten years later, on 25 October 1664, Evelyn was again at this garden on which occasion he noted 'some rare plants under the culture of old Bobart',[3] this being Jacob Bobart the Elder who, at this time, had the care of the Oxford physic garden.

In 1652 Evelyn settled at Sayes Court, Deptford, belonging to his father-in-law, Sir Richard Browne,[4] which remained his home for more than forty years. Almost at once, on 17 January 1653, he 'began to set out the ovall garden at Says court, which was before a rude ortchard . . . & this was the beginning of all the succeeding gardens, walkes, groves, enclosures & plantations there'.[5] In 1683 he 'planted all the out limites of the garden, & long walkes, with holly'.[6] Evelyn was very enthusiastic about holly as a hedge plant and in his *Sylva* of 1706 writes:[7] 'Is there under Heaven a more glorious and refreshing object of the kind, than an impregnable hedge of about four hundred foot in length, nine foot high, and five in diameter; which I can shew in my now ruin'd gardens at Say's-court, (thanks to the Czar of Moscovy)[8] at any time of the year, glitt'ring with its arm'd and varnish'd leaves?' During the years he was making this garden Evelyn received advice on gardening matters and also gifts of plants from his friend Sir Thomas Hanmer (1612–78) of Bettisfield, Flintshire.[9] A Royalist, Hanmer took up gardening during the years previous to the Restoration, and became one of the great horticulturists of his day. His *Garden book* printed from the manuscript volume of 1659, with an introduction by Eleanour Sinclair Rohde, was published in 1933. Hanmer numbered among his friends another keen gardener, John Rea, author in 1665 of *Flora: seu, de florum cultura. Or a complete florilege*. As well as receiving plants from friends in this country

---

[1] *The diary of John Evelyn . . . edited by* E. S. de Beer, **2**, 528.

[2] Ibid. **3**, 109–10.

[3] Ibid. 386.

[4] In Evelyn's day the Sayes Court estate occupied many acres. Now the land is mostly built over except for a park of 3·88 acres, administered by the Greater London Council. (Information supplied by the Lewisham Borough Librarian in epist. 6.vii.66.)

[5] *The diary of John Evelyn . . . edited by E. S. de Beer*, **3**, 80 (1955).

[6] Ibid. **4**, 312.

[7] p. 182.

[8] In 1696 Sayes Court was let to Admiral Benbow and in 1698 it was occupied by Peter the Great, then visiting the Deptford dockyard. During the Czar's stay of three months much damage was done to the garden.

[9] See *The garden book of Sir Thomas Hanmer Bart. With an introduction by E. S. Rohde*, pp. xiv–xv (1933) (two letters written by Hanmer to Evelyn, dated 22 Aug. 1668 and 21 Aug. 1671 respectively).

Evelyn endeavoured to obtain seeds and plants from abroad, and on one occasion was offered assistance in procuring rare plants by a Captain Nicholson who was 'going to command some forces in New-England'. Evelyn accepted the Captain's offer and made out a list of his requirements.[1]

In 1932 was published by the Nonesuch Press Evelyn's *Directions for the gardiner at Says-court*, printed from the original manuscript and edited by Geoffrey Keynes. This work, with its many observations connected with the care of a garden, its various lists of plants, details concerning fruit trees planted at Sayes Court, and a list of 'Tooles & instruments necessary for a gardiner', not only shows the very active interest Evelyn took in the care and running of his garden but also his considerable knowledge of gardening matters.

Besides his own grounds at Sayes Court Evelyn assisted in the designing and laying out of the gardens of several other houses, including the gardens of the family seat of the Evelyns, Wotton, in Surrey, where he helped his brother carry out alterations in 1652.[2] In 1694 Evelyn left Sayes Court and settled with his brother at Wotton, succeeding to this estate on the latter's death in 1699. Evelyn also made a design in 1667 for the garden of Henry Howard (1628–84), later sixth Duke of Norfolk, at Albury in Surrey,[3] and the terraces as laid out at that time are still the finest feature of the garden.[4]

From Samuel Pepys it is learnt that Evelyn made a collection of dried plants. Under the date 5 November 1665 Pepys entered in his *Diary*:[5] 'By water to Deptford, and there made a visit to Mr. Evelyn . . . He showed me his *Hortus hyemalis*; leaves laid up in a book of several plants kept dry, which preserve colour, however, and look very finely, better than any herball.' Evelyn may have called this *hortus siccus* by the fancy name *Hortus hyemalis* (winter garden) because he enjoyed studying the specimens during the winter months when there was nothing much to see in the garden. It is of interest to note that Evelyn included a chapter on the making of a herbarium under the title: 'Of composing the *Hortus hyemalis*, and making books of naturall arid plants and flowers, with other curious wayes of preserving them in their natural' in the synopsis of his 'Elysium britannicum',[6] a projected

---

[1] Evelyn met Captain Nicholson when dining one day with Samuel Pepys. Afterwards Evelyn wrote to Pepys a letter, dated 1 Sept. 1786, enclosing a note for Captain Nicholson with a list of seeds and plants he required. The letter and its enclosure are printed in *A history of gardening in England by the Hon. Mrs. Evelyn Cecil (The Hon. Alicia Amherst)*, 168–9 (1910).

[2] *The diary of John Evelyn . . . edited by E. S. de Beer*, **3**, 60–1 (1955).

[3] Ibid. 496. For further reference to Evelyn's planning of this garden see ibid. 561–2; **4**, 111, 558.

[4] For an excellent description of the gardens as designed by Evelyn and the alterations subsequently made. See *Country Life*, **108**, 598–602 (25 Aug. 1950).

[5] *The diary of Samuel Pepys . . . Edited . . . by H. B. Wheatley*, **5**, 129 (1952).

[6] See copy in the Brit. Mus. (Bloomsbury) Add. MS. 15950, f. 143. Another version of this sketch of the 'Elysium britannicum', under the title of 'The plan of a Royal garden' appears in the preliminary matter of Evelyn's *Acetaria*. See below, p. 191.

work which was to treat of gardening in all its aspects, but which was never completed.[1]

Although Evelyn achieved his greatest literary success with the publication of his *Sylva*, a work which as shown earlier did so much to revive the spirit of planting in this country, there can be no doubt that during his lifetime he also exerted, through his works on gardening, a great influence on horticulture. His publications on this subject were popular as well as useful, and they had the distinction of being much quoted by contemporary authors. The eighteenth-century gardener, Stephen Switzer, wrote in his *Nobleman, gentleman, and gardener's recreation* of 1715:[2]

John Evelyn esq; one of the greatest writers we have had in gard'ning, as well as in several other matters . . .

This ingenious and learned person . . . was appointed for the retrieving the calamities of England, and re-animating the spirit of planting and sowing of woods in his countrymen . . . How he has acquitted himself is very well known at present, his books being almost in all hands; and, 'tis to be hop'd, will be continued down to the farthest posterity, amongst the most ingenious and useful writings of that age.

Neither was his labour less in matters nearer relating to gard'ning, in his translations, and in his *Kalendarium hortense* . . . He translated Quintinye's *Compleat gardener*, with another smaller tract, from French;[3] was in his time the best linguist, and to him it is owing that gardening can speak proper English. His *Philosophical discourse of earth* is accounted amongst the best writings of the Royal society.

As he begun, so he continued till his death, a great lover and observer of gard'ning; and tho' not at his own expense, yet in his readiness to give advice, he merited general thanks. In short, if he was not the greatest master in practice,[4] 'tis to him is due the theoretical part of gard'ning.

But I need say no more, his own works, which are publick, are a clearer demonstration of the greatness of his genius, than any monument I can raise to his memory.

The first work on horticulture attempted by Evelyn is a translation of '*Le jardinier françois*', a treatise first published in Paris in 1651.[5] No author's name appears in this work but the 'Epistre aux dames' is signed R.D.C.D.W.B.D.N. After Evelyn had accomplished his task he wrote in his *Diary* under 6 December 1658:[6] 'Now was publishd my *French gardiner* the first & best of that kind that introducd the use of the olitorie garden[7] to any purpose.' The title of *The French gardiner* describes it as 'An accom-

[1] About one-third of the manuscript of this work is preserved in the Evelyn collection in the library of Christ Church, Oxford.

[2] pp. 44–5.

[3] This is presumably a reference to *The French gardiner*, a translation by Evelyn from the French of N. de Bonnefons.

[4] Switzer considered the best professional gardener in Evelyn's day was John Rose, Keeper of the Royal garden in St. James's Park (*The nobleman, gentleman, and gardener's recreation*, etc. 51 (1715)).

[5] 'A passage in the translation (pp. 74–5) shows that it was made from one of the later editions of the French work' (*The diary of John Evelyn . . . edited by E. S. de Beer*, 3, 225, footnote 3 (1955).

[6] *The diary of John Evelyn . . . edited by E. S. de Beer*, 3, 225 (1955).

[7] i.e. kitchen garden.

plished piece, first written by R.D.C.D.W.B.D.N. and now transplanted into English by Philocepos'. According to Quérard[1] these initials when placed in reverse stand for Nicolas de Bonnefons, valet de chambre du Roi—the word valet being spelt with a W instead of a V. Evelyn dedicated his translation to Thomas Henshaw (1618–1700) who suggested that the former should undertake the work.[2] The two men were old friends and fellow travellers, having spent more than a year in each other's company in Italy from October 1644.[3] Both were original Fellows of the Royal Society, and on 30 November 1668 Henshaw was elected Secretary,[4] a position to which Evelyn succeeded on 30 November 1672.[5] The plates in *The French gardiner* are copies by A. Hertochs of the plates in the original work by François Chauveau (1613–76). Hertochs was an engraver from Holland who worked in England from 1626 until 1672.[6]

To his *Sylva* of 1664 Evelyn appended *Kalendarium hortense*, this being the first gardener's calendar to be published in this country. The second edition of the *Kalendarium* was issued in 1666 as a small octavo volume. Subsequently, the work was published both with the *Sylva* in folio, and separately in octavo. The imprint of the second edition reads 'London, printed by Jo. Martyn and Ja. Allestry, printers to the Royal society, and are to be sold at their shops in St. Paul's church-yard. MDCLXVI'. Few copies of this edition appear to be extant[7] and this may be explained by the fact that in the Great Fire of 1666 the premises of James Allestry were destroyed, and this well-known London bookseller 'was almost ruined'.[8] Evelyn dedicated the *Kalendarium* of 1666 to Abraham Cowley who replied in an essay in verse and prose entitled 'The garden'. Cowley's work was printed in the 1691 octavo edition of the *Kalendarium*, and also in subsequent editions. In a letter to the Countess of Sunderland, dated from Deptford on 4 August 1690, Evelyn wrote:[9]

As for the 'Kalendar' y[r] L[p] mentions, what ever assistance it may be to some novice gardiner, sure I am his Lo[p] will find nothing in it worth his notice but an old inclination to an innocent diversion, & the acceptance it found with my deare (and while he liv'd) worthy friend Mr. Cowley, upon whose reputation only it has survived seaven impressions,

[1] Quérard (J. M.), *Les supercheries littéraires dévoilées*, etc. 3, col. 345 (1870), Paris.
[2] *The French gardiner*, etc., A2ª (1658) (Dedication).
[3] Evelyn travelled in Italy from 1644 until the spring of 1646. He met Henshaw at Pisa on 20 Oct. 1644 and from that date he never parted from the company of his friend 'till more then a yeare after'. See *The diary of John Evelyn . . . edited by E. S. de Beer*, 2, 179 (1955).
[4] *The Record of the Royal society of London*, etc. 342 (1940).
[5] Ibid. 342.

[6] Thieme (U.) and Becker (F.), *Allgemeines Lexikon der bildenden Künstler von der Antike bis zur Gegenwart*, 16, 558 (1923), Leipzig.
[7] A presentation copy from Evelyn to Lord Arlington is in the Brit. Mus. (Bloomsbury) (pressmark G. 2299).
[8] Plomer (H. R.), *A dictionary of the booksellers and printers . . . at work in England, Scotland and Ireland from 1641 to 1667*, p. 3 (1907).
[9] *Diary of John Evelyn . . . A new edition . . . by H. B. Wheatley*, 3, 463 (1906) (Epistolary correspondence).

(a)

(b)

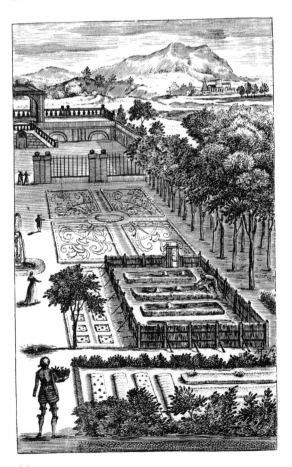

(c)

(d)

& is now entering on the eighth with some considerable improvements, more agreeable to the present curiosity. 'Tis now, Mad^me, almost fourty yeares since first I writ it, when horticulture was not much advanc'd in England, and neere thirty since first 'twas publish'd, which consideration will I hope excuse its many defects. If in the meane time it deserve the name of no un-usefull trifle, 'tis all it is capable of.

In 1693 appeared *The compleat gard'ner . . . Made English by John Evelyn*, a translation from the French *Instruction pour les jardins fruitiers et potagers* by Jean de La Quintinie (1626–88),[1] 'Chief director of all the gardens of the French King' Louis XIV.[2] In the opinion of Hiscock[3] the translation, as a whole, was undoubtedly the work of the King's gardener George London who, together with Henry Wise, was responsible for a popular abridged version of *The compleat gard'ner* first published in 1699. It is possible that Evelyn did little more than read the translation before publication and allow his name to appear on the title-page. It would appear, however, that he may have been partly responsible for the translation, as on 24 March 1693 he sent a copy of this book to his brother George, with the following note:

I do not attribute the whole to my self; the toil of mere translating would have been very ungratefull to one who had not so much time to spend in thrashing: but as a considerable part of it has, and the rest under my care, the publishers and printers will have it go under my name, altogether against my intentions.[4]

Evelyn was personally acquainted with La Quintinie who had visited him at his house, Sayes Court, at Deptford, more than twenty years before the publication of *The compleat gard'ner*.[5] On his return to Paris the Frenchman gratified Evelyn by sending him some directions 'concerning the ordering of melons'.[6] These directions Evelyn translated into English and distributed to his friends, and he also included them in his translation of 1693.

The compleat gard'ner contains copies of the frontispiece, and illustrations of garden scenes, used in the original work. The frontispiece, engraved by William Elder,[7] consists of a portrait in an oval of La Quintinie by the French painter Florent de La Mare-Richart (*c.* 1630–1718), and on a pediment below the oval are engraved four Latin lines by Santolius Victorinus. The dedication, signed by Matthew Gillyflower and James Partridge, the publishers of the work, is addressed to Henry Capel, Baron Capel of Tewkesbury (1638–96).[8] Capel, like his brother the Earl of Essex,[9] was very interested in

[1] This work was first published in Paris in 1690.

[2] La Quintinie (J. de), *The compleat gard'ner . . . Made English by John Evelyn* (1693) (title-page).

[3] Hiscock (W. G.), *John Evelyn and his family circle*, 168–9 (1955).

[4] Quotation as given by Hiscock, op. cit. 168 (1955).

[5] La Quintinie (J. de), *The compleat gard'ner . . . Made English by John Evelyn*, 1 (1693)

(Directions concerning melons).

[6] Ibid.

[7] Elder also engraved the portrait frontispiece to John Ray's *Sylloge* of 1694. See above, p. 131.

[8] Henry Capel, created Baron Capel of Tewkesbury 11 Apr. 1692.

[9] i.e. Arthur Capel, Earl of Essex, who had a famous garden at Cassiobury Park in Hertfordshire. See above, p. 116.

◁ 54. *The French gardiner*, 1658, a translation by John Evelyn, illustrated with four plates engraved by A. Hertochs.
(a) the frontispiece, (b) and (c) garden scenes, (d) women cooking and conserving fruits. Each plate 4·5 × 2·7″.

gardening, and he had a noted garden at Kew. 'I went ⟨to⟩ my worthy friends Sir. Hen: Capels', wrote John Evelyn on 27 August 1678 in his *Diary*,[1] '. . . it is an old timber house, but his garden has certainly the choicest fruite of any plantation in England, as he is the most industrious, & understanding in it.' A fuller description of this garden is given by J. Gibson, after he visited it in December 1691 when he noted a number of interesting trees and plants, and also found the garden 'as well kept as any about London'.[2]

The preface to *The compleat gard'ner* is followed by an 'Advertisement' signed by John Evelyn. This consists of a eulogy on the merits of the Brompton Park nursery and its two industrious owners, George London and Henry Wise.

Evelyn's *Compleat gard'ner* was not reprinted. This handsome folio volume with its portrait frontispiece and many copper-plate engravings must have been an expensive book to produce and also costly to purchase—a copy bound in contemporary calf in the library of the present writer has an inscription on the fly-leaf reading 'Bought from Mr. Bulton on Newcastle-bridge Feb. 1694. Cost 20 shil.'. The astute Mr. London and Mr. Wise, however, appear to have realized that a book based on this work and condensed so as to present only the most useful of the information would be of greater value to the practical gardener, and at the same time have a much wider popular appeal. Thus in 1699 we find Matthew Gillyflower publishing an octavo volume with a title reading *The compleat gard'ner . . . by Monsieur de La Quintinye. Now compendiously abridg'd, and made of more use, with very considerable improvements. By George London, and Henry Wise.* Evelyn's name does not appear on the title-page, nor did the abridgers consider it necessary to give him any acknowledgement. His signed 'Advertisement' concerning the Brompton Park nursery, however, is reprinted in full on two leaves inserted between pages xiv and xv. It was omitted from a few copies of the first edition, possibly because London and Wise did not at first realize its value to their business.

About 1659,[3] Evelyn began to write his 'Elysium britannicum' a work that was intended to describe and show 'the amplitude, and extent of that part of georgicks, which belongs to horticulture'.[4] Ten years later, in November 1669, the *Philosophical Transactions* announced the author as busy and preparing this book for the press.[5] This announcement was premature. Although Evelyn was occasionally occupied with this undertaking for more than forty-five years it was never completed or published.

This manuscript treated of gardening in all its aspects [writes Hiscock],[6] and comprised

[1] *The diary of John Evelyn . . . edited by E. S. de Beer*, **4**, 144 (1955).

[2] A short account of several gardens near London . . . upon a view of them (by J. Gibson) in Dec. 1691, *Archæologia*, **12**, 185 (1796).

[3] E[velyn]. (J.), *Acetaria*, etc. (1699) (Preface).

[4] Ibid. (The plan of a Royal garden).

[5] *Phil. Trans.* **4**, 1073 (15 Nov. 1669).

[6] Hiscock (W. G.), *John Evelyn and his family circle*, 33 (1955).

nearly 900 folio pages, of which 342 have survived. Evelyn had this by him for the rest of his life, always expanding, amending, and including new facts, or things read: perfection was unattainable. As time went on, the work got out of hand; the inexhaustible number of insertions put all out of scale and it never got into print.

Although the 'Elysium britannicum' was never completed, the author decided, towards the end of his life, that he would publish the chapter in the work dealing with salads. Thus, in 1699 appeared his *Acetaria. A discourse of sallets*. The possibility of publishing this had occurred to Evelyn many years before. Twenty years previously, on 11 July 1679, he had informed Dr. Beale:[1]

> I have sometimes thought of publishing a treatise of Acetaria, which (tho' but one of the chapters of 'Elysium britannicum') would make a competent volume, accompanied with other necessaries, according to my manner; but whilst I as often think of performing my so long-since promis'd (more universal) hortulan work, I know not how to take that chapter out, and single it for the presse, without some blemish to the rest.

Evelyn included a brief synopsis of his projected 'Elysium britannicum', under the title of 'The plan of a Royal garden', in the preliminary matter of his *Acetaria*. This synopsis he divided into three books and forty-two chapters. *Acetaria* consists of the twentieth chapter, entitled 'Of sallets', of Book II. A slightly different version of this summary is found printed on a single leaf headed 'Elysium britannicum' and signed with the author's initials 'J. E.'. A copy of this version is in the Department of Manuscripts of the British Museum (Bloomsbury).[2]

Evelyn dedicated *Acetaria* to John Lord Somers of Evesham, Lord High Chancellor of England and President of the Royal Society. Ordinary copies of the work were printed on paper which has now become badly foxed. There were, however, some copies printed on a good quality paper which has remained white. 'These', writes Keynes,[3] 'are in pretty gold-tooled bindings of calf or morocco, and the pages are rubricated throughout.' 'Their uniformity', continues the same authority, 'shews that they were bound to Evelyn's order in the same shop at the same time.'

We now turn to a small book published in 1658[4] under the title of *Adam out of Eden, or, an abstract of divers excellent experiments touching the advancement of husbandry*. Although the author's name appears on the title-page as 'Ad. Speed' and he is sometimes referred to as Adam Speed, his Christian name was in fact Adolphus, and George Thomason's copy of Speed's anonymous *General accommodations by address*,[5] is signed by the author 'Att

---

[1] *Diary of John Evelyn . . . A new edition . . . by H. B. Wheatley*, **3**, 190 (1906) (Appendix).

[2] Add. MS. 15950, f. 143. This version is divided into three books and forty-one chapters.

[3] Keynes (G.), *John Evelyn*, etc. 235 (1937), Cambridge.

[4] In the imprint on the title-page the date is

1659. See below, Bibliography, under Speed (A.), Adam out of Eden, etc. 1659 [1658], 8°.

[5] In the Brit. Mus. (Bloomsbury) (press-mark E.599(1)). This work is undated but the Museum copy bears the date 'April 26. 1650' in Thomason's hand on the title-page.

M[er] Fisshers house in Kin[g] street w[th]in the Covent garde[n] Adolphus
Speed'. Little is known concerning this writer. He was apparently not a
rich man, as Walter Blith tells us that Samuel Hartlib maintained Speed
for 'divers moneths together' while the latter was making some of his experiments.[1] Blith attacked Speed for his far-fetched schemes for the improvement
of agriculture,[2] and although *Adam out of Eden* contains a few interesting
remarks, Speed's assertions regarding the results of some of his horticultural
experiments are as ludicrous as the 'errors' in gardening condemned some
years earlier by Ralph Austen in his *Treatise of fruit-trees* (1653).[3]

After the middle of the seventeenth century the attention of the Royal
Society was directed to the economic importance of the potato, and during
this period several eminent Fellows advocated its cultivation as a means of
preventing famine.[4] 'It is no longer as a strange and costly food that it
finds favour', writes Salaman,[5] 'but rather because of the hope it holds out
of being a veritable manna for the poor.' In 1664 appeared *Englands happiness
increased, or a sure and easie remedy against all succeeding dear years; by a
plantation of the roots called potatoes.* This treatise, which is the first to be
devoted exclusively to the potato, is by John Forster of Hanslop in Bucking-
hamshire.[6] It is dedicated to Charles II. Forster's avowed object in publishing
this work was to recommend the potato as a food for the poor,[7] and after
giving details concerning its cultivation he suggests various methods in which
to cook potatoes, and gives directions for the making of potato bread, pud-
dings, custards, and cheese cakes. He also outlines a plan for the planting of
potatoes, which he points out would be of benefit not only to the poor but
also to the Crown. Very briefly this plan was as follows. Potatoes were to be
grown in plantations in the different parishes throughout the country.[8]
For every hundred families there was to be one planter only, and 'for his
license and authority to plant and sell the said roots' he had to pay £5 a
year to the King.[9] In Forster's estimation the number of planters might be
about 10,000 and the Crown would thus derive a revenue of £50,000 per
annum.[10]

In 1671 an interesting little tract was published under the title of *St.
foine improved: a discourse shewing the utility and benefit which England hath
and may receive by the grasse called St. foine.* This anonymous treatise, with

[1] Blith (W.), *The English improver improved*,
etc. 176 (1652).

[2] Blith writes of Speed and his experiments
in ibid. 173–6, 260–1 (1652).

[3] Note, for example, Speed's method (1) to
make red roses white (p. 150) (2) to make white
lilies red (p. 152).

[4] Salaman (R. N.), *The history and social
influence of the potato*, 445–9 (1949), Cambridge.

[5] Op. cit. 445.

[6] Forster (J.), *Englands happiness increased*,
etc. (1664) (To the reader).

[7] On the title-page is the statement 'Invented
and published for the good of the poorer sort,
by John Forster Gent.'

[8] Forster (J.), *Englands happiness increased*,
etc. 14–16 (1664).

[9] Ibid. 15–16.

[10] Ibid. 16–17.

a statement on the title-page reading: 'Written by a person of honour lately deceased', is attributed by Richard Weston to Sir John Pettus.[1] The validity of this statement, however, is questionable, as Pettus died in 1690, and no other authority has corroborated Weston's statement. Whoever the author was, he certainly knew what he was talking about, and, as pointed out by McDonald,[2] he 'had evidently made himself thoroughly acquainted with the peculiarities and value of the plant as a farmer's crop'.

Another tract of economic interest, issued in 1691, is the anonymous *Englands improvement, and seasonable advice to all gentlemen and farmers, how to prepare the ground fit for sowing hemp and flax-seed; the nature of it, with directions how to sow it*. This is the first work, known to the present writer, to be published in this country to deal exclusively with hemp and flax. In the eighteenth century, as will be noted later, a number of works were published on this subject, not only in England, but also in Scotland and Ireland.

In 1664 appeared *The compleat gardener's practice*, a small quarto volume by a gardener named Stephen Blake. On the 23 November of the same year John Evelyn mentioned in a letter that 'one Rhea has published a very usefull book concerning the culture of flowers'.[3] This is a reference presumably to John Rea's *Flora: seu, de florum cultura. Or, a complete florilege*, a work that appeared, according to the title-page, in 1665. John Rea (or Rhea), who by 1665 had been a gardener for at least forty years,[4] received high praise for his skill as a horticulturist from other seventeenth-century writers. For example, in a letter addressed by Samuel Hartlib on 12 April 1659 to Robert Boyle there is a reference[5] to 'Mr. Pitt and Sir Thomas Hanmer of Flintshire, and Mr. Rea of Shropshire, all three exquisite florists'. Again, Samuel Gilbert, author of the popular *Florists vade-mecum* of 1682, wrote of his knowledge as a horticulturist having been 'inform'd by my long converse with the best florist of his time, Mr. John Rea, my father-in-law, whose skill and collections were alike famous'.[6] It is not known whereabouts in Shropshire Rea lived. Later he resided in Worcestershire, for he signed the epistle to the reader of the 1676 edition of his *Flora*: 'From my house at Kinlet near Bewdly in Worcestershire', and when he died in November 1681 he bequeathed his holding at Kinlet to his daughter Minerva, the wife of Samuel Gilbert.[7]

[1] Weston (R.), *Tracts on practical agriculture and gardening . . . The second edition*, 41 (1773) (A catalogue of English authors, etc.). Sir John Pettus (1613–90), Deputy-governor of the Royal mines, knighted in 1641, published miscellaneous works.

[2] McDonald (D.), *Agricultural writers from . . . 1200–1800*, etc. 110 (1908).

[3] *Diary of John Evelyn . . . A new edition . . . by H. B. Wheatley*, 3, 192 (1906) (Appendix).

[4] 'Fourty years are now compleated, since first I began to be a planter.' (Rea (J.), *Flora: seu, de florum cultura*, etc. (1665) (To the reader).)

[5] *The works of . . . Robert Boyle . . . A new edition*, 6, 119 (1772).

[6] Gilbert (S.), *Florists vade-mecum*, etc. (1682) (To the reader).

[7] Revd. Samuel Gilbert, *Journ. Hort.* New series, 30, 172 (1876).

This Figure reprefents Lines how they ought to be layde
before you begin to drawe a large Knott but efpecially
that following, And allfo note that thefe Lines are not
to be ftirred till the Knott be finifht, and fo by the ufe of thefe
Lines and two lines more you may draw any Knott. This figure is fup-
pofed to contayne 18: yards fquare & allowing 21:Inches to each footpath.

1

(a)

(b)

55. Blake: *The compleat gardeners practice . . .
with variety of artificial knots for the beautifying of a garden*, 1664. (a) Ground marked out
in preparation for making a large knot, or
flower-bed. 5·8 × 4·5″. (b) The completed knot.
4·4 × 4·3″.

It seems that Rea undertook the writing of his book for the following reason. He had found that Parkinson's *Paradisus* now needed 'the addition of many noble things of newer discovery, and that a multitude of those there set out, were by time grown stale, and for unworthiness turned out of every good garden'.[1] Rea therefore considered preparing a new edition, but afterwards decided that it would be better to write an entirely new work. This, when it appeared, proved to be the most important English treatise on gardening to be published during the second half of the seventeenth century. It is a small folio volume with an engraved, as well as a letterpress, title-page. The former is by David Loggan who, it will be remembered, engraved many of the figures of plants in Morison's *Historia*. This title-page represents Flora seated on a pediment, with Ceres standing on a plinth below against a pillar on the left, and Pomona similarly on the right. Displayed on a banner between the pillars is the title *Flora Ceres & Pomona*. The purport of this engraving is explained on a separate leaf, in four verses headed 'The mind of the front'.[2] Apart from eight plates with diagrams of gardens, the work has no illustrations.

Rea's *Flora* contains two dedicatory letters, the first of which the author addressed to Charles Gerard, fourth Baron Gerard of Gerard's Bromley (d. 1667), whose garden at Gerard's Bromley in Staffordshire Rea had designed.[3] The second Rea addressed to Sir Thomas Hanmer, Baronet, of Bettisfield in Flintshire. This famous horticulturist appears to have been much interested in Rea's literary project, and he generously supplied him 'with many noble and new varieties' from his own 'incomparable' collection of plants.[4] The opening words of this dedicatory letter are as follows: 'These papers which have long lain by neglected, are at last made publick.' This delay in publication is explained, perhaps, by a passage written by a correspondent to Samuel Hartlib, and repeated by the latter in his letter of 12 April 1659 addressed to Robert Boyle.[5] Here we read: 'Mr Rea brought up his hortulan labours to London. It required many costly cuts, which so affrighted the stationers, that they offered him but thirty pounds for his pains. This displeased him so much, that he brought home his manuscripts.' When Rea's *Flora* was finally published it contained, as already noted, no botanical figures, and in the preface to this work the author excuses the lack of illustrations in the following manner.

As for the cutting the figures of every plant, especially in wood, as Mr. Parkinson hath done, I hold to be altogether needless; such artless things, being good for nothing, unless

[1] Rea (J.), *Flora: seu, de florum cultura*, etc. (1665) (To the reader).

[2] Seventeenth-century engraved titles were often provided with such explanatory verses. See Johnson (A. F.), *A catalogue of engraved and etched English title-pages down to . . . 1691*, pp. viii–ix (1934 for 1933).

[3] Rea (J.), *Flora: seu, de florum cultura*, etc. (1665) (Dedication to Charles Lord Gerard).

[4] Ibid. (Dedication to Sir Thomas Hanmer).

[5] *The works of . . . Robert Boyle . . . A new edition*, 6, 119 (1772).

FLORA
CERES &
POMONA
by
IOHN REA
gent:
London printed for Richard Marriott
& are to bee sold at his shopp in fleetstreet
under y.e kings head Taverne. 1665.

FLOS speculum vitæ modo vernat et interit ama,
FLORIS imago fugax rapidi nos admonet ævi.
FLORI par iuvenis tener est crescentibus annis,
FLOREM si ostendet, feret ipso tempore fractum,
OFLOS sic vernans iuvenili ætate, pudorem
A FLORE accipias, et honeste vivere discas.

D: Loggan sculp:

F. H. van Hove fec:

57. Rea: *Flora: seu, de florum cultura, Or, a complete florilege . . . The second impression*, 1676. Head-piece on p. 1, engraved by Frederik Hendrik van Hove. 5·5 × 4·6".

to raise the price of the book, serving neither for ornament or information, but rather to puzzle and affright the spectator into an aversion, than direct or invite their affections; for did his flowers appear no fairer on their stalks in the garden, than they do on the leaves of his book, few ladies would be in love with them, much more than they are with his lovely picture. I have therefore spared my self and others such unnecessary charge, and onely added some draughts for flower-gardens.

From this passage it seems that Rea, after finding that his *Flora* could not be published with 'many costly cuts', decided to condemn the illustrations in the only other important English book on florists' flowers, namely Parkinson's

56. Rea: *Flora: seu, de florum cultura. Or, a complete florilege*, 1665. Title-page engraved by David Loggan. 10·1 × 6·1".

Paradisus.[1] Parkinson's portrait in the latter work has considerable merit as a woodcut, and many of the botanical figures, though poorly designed are well executed.

After Rea's death most of his famous collection of plants passed into the hands of his son-in-law, Samuel Gilbert,[2] who was Rector of Quatt in Shropshire, and Chaplain to Jane, Baroness Gerard of Gerard's Bromley (d. 1703).[3] It was during the lifetime of this lady's husband[4] that Rea planned the gardens of Gerard's Bromley. Earlier it was stated that Gilbert was the author of *The florists vade-mecum* (1682). The frontispiece of this work consists of a portrait of the author with the title of 'Philomusus'.[5] It is from an engraving by the noted engraver Robert White. The dedication is addressed to James Fleetwood, D.D. (1603–83), Bishop of Worcester, a prelate referred to by Gilbert as 'the greatest florist amongst the chiefest pillars of our church'.[6] It is evident from this little treatise that Gilbert's favourite flower was the auricula, and he records that he had the finest collection of these plants to be seen in Shropshire.[7] Among other auricula enthusiasts Gilbert mentions Jacob Bobart, 'who keeps the physick garden in Oxford',[8] and Peter Egerton of Boughton, near Chester, whom Gilbert considered to be the 'best' florist in Cheshire,[9] and also in Lancashire.[10] Gilbert praises the auriculas to be found 'in the Pallace garden at Worcester, belonging to Mr Thomas Newton, gentleman to my very good Lord, the Right Reverend Father in God James Lord Bishop of Worcester', Newton being famous in Worcestershire for his skill as a florist.[11] Gilbert also draws attention to the great care paid at this time to the cultivation of the tulip, and he proudly states that he himself has 'an hundred sorts'.[12] After giving the names and details of some of the best tulips, Gilbert writes:[13] 'Those that are desirous of more descriptions of tulips, I refer to Mr Reas *Flora*: wherein he is ample enough and had the largest collection of any man in England, some of which I lost by being beyond sea at his death.'

In 1651 appeared at Stockholm *Le jardin de plaisir*, a handsome folio volume dedicated to Queen Christina of Sweden.[14] The preface is followed

---

[1] This popular book was first published in 1629 and subsequently in 1635 and 1656.

[2] Gilbert (S.), *The florists vade-mecum*, etc. (1682) (To the reader).

[3] Gilbert (S.), *Fons sanitatis: or the healing spring at Willowbridge in Stafford-shire. Found out by ... Lady Jane Gerard Baroness of Bromley ... Published by ... S. Gilbert*, etc. (1796) (Title-page).

[4] Charles Gerard, fourth Baron Gerard of Gerard's Bromley (d. 1667).

[5] 'Philomusus', loving the Muses. One evidence that Gilbert was entitled to this designation is the fact that he wrote poetry, a number of his verses being found throughout his works.

[6] Gilbert (S.), *The florists vade-mecum*, etc. (1682) (Dedication).

[7] Ibid. (Appendix).   [8] Ibid. 47.

[9] Ibid. (Appendix).

[10] Peter Egerton moved later to his estate at Shaw Hall, near Manchester in Lancashire (Gilbert (S.), op. cit. (Appendix)).

[11] Ibid.   [12] Ibid. 65.

[13] Ibid. 74.

[14] Christina was the daughter and successor of Gustavus II Adolphus who died in 1732. She took over the reins of government on reaching her majority in 1644. In 1654 she abdicated the throne in favour of her cousin Karl Gustav of Pfalz-Zweibrücken.

Philo   mufus.

58. Gilbert: *The florist's vade mecum*, 1683. Frontispiece
portrait of Samuel Gilbert from an engraving by Robert White.
4·7 × 2·8″ (cropped). An earlier and finer impression is found
in the Department of Prints and Drawings of the British Museum
(Bloomsbury).

by eleven chapters of text in which various kinds of fruits, herbs, and flowers
suitable for 'a garden of pleasure' are described. Information is also included
on grafting and viticulture. The work contains many plates with designs for
gardens which are described in Chapter XI. The author, André Mollet, is
referred to on the title-page as 'Maistre des jardins de la . . . Reine de Suede'.[1]
Nearly twenty years later, in 1670, was published in London *The garden of
pleasure, containing several draughts of gardens both in embroyder'd-ground-
works, knot-works of grass, as likewise in wildernesses, and others.* This publication

[1] Mollet wrote *Le jardin de plaisir* in three
languages, French, German, and Swedish (see
'Extraict du privilege'). A copy in French and
German is in the Brit. Mus. (Bloomsbury)
(pressmark 441.k.3).

consists of a dedication to the King, Charles II, a preface, a commendatory letter addressed to the author, signed 'Belon', followed by details concerning the plates. The latter are the same as those in the Stockholm publication with the addition of six further plates of garden designs. A statement on the title-page reads 'By Andrew Mollet, Master of His Majesty of Englands gardens in his park of St. James's'.

André Mollet was a member of a family of outstanding French gardeners. His father, Claude Mollet, who died about 1613, had been chief gardener to Henri IV and later Louis XIII. His brother, Gabriel, worked in the Royal gardens, St. James's Park, and another brother, Charles, became 'Maitre des jardins du Louvre'.[1] André, whose designs show him to have been a gifted garden planner, went to Sweden after having practised the art of gardening not only in France, but also in England, and Holland. He recorded in his dedication to Queen Christina: 'Après avoir . . . servi quelques années le Roy & la Reine de la grande Bretaigne; ensuite M.:r le Prince d'Orenge, il ayr pleu a V :te Maté faire choix de ma personne, pour la servir en lornement de ses maisons Royales.'

Soon after the Restoration André and his brother Gabriel were employed as gardeners in the service of Charles II.[2] Some interesting details concerning the two men are to be found in the *Calendar of State papers, domestic series*. Here we find that in June 1661 a warrant was issued 'to pay to Andrew and Gabriel Mollett 240 l. yearly, for wages as the King's gardeners, and for them to have the lodgings in St. James's park belonging to the gardeners'.[3] Gabriel, however, appears to have died soon after this for there is a petition dated Whitehall 27 February 1662 [i.e. 1663] 'of Charles Mollett to the King, for payment of 115 l. due for flowers brought from France by his late brother Gabriel, and planted in the Royal gardens, St. James's park'.[4] Subsequently, in an undated petition of 1663 ? we find André referred to as 'Chief gardener in St. James's park',[5] but he did not long survive his brother for on 8 February 1666, there was an 'Order for a warrant to pay to John Rose, appointed Keeper of St. James's garden, in place of Andrew and Gabriel Mollet, deceased, 240 l. a year for wages, for keeping the said garden'.[6] As the Plague was at its worst during 1665, it seems possible that André Mollet's death was due to this disease.

[1] *La grande encyclopédie*, 24, 33 (vols. 1–31, 1887–1902), Paris.

[2] It appears that André Mollet and his brother Gabriel also worked in England at the time of the Commonwealth, for on 29 June 1658 warrants were issued by the Protector and Council 'For And. Mollet, wife, and servant, to Hamburg' and on 1 July of the same year 'For Gab. Mollett and 1 servant beyond seas'. (See *Calendar of State papers, domestic series, 1658–59*, p. 577 (1885).)

[3] Op. cit. 'of the reign of Charles II. 1661–1662', p. 25 (1861).

[4] Op. cit. 'of the reign of Charles II. 1663–1664', p. 57 (1862).

[5] Op. cit. 422 (1862).

[6] Op. cit. 'of the reign of Charles II. 1665–1666', p. 237 (1864). The warrant 'to pay to John Rose, Keeper of St. James' park gardens, in place of the late Gabriel and And. Mollett, 240 l. a year' was issued 21 Feb. 1666. Op. cit. 261 (1864).

The garden of pleasure, therefore, was published some years after André Mollet's death. This suggests that Mollet did not write the dedication to the King, even though it is signed by him. It is also unlikely that he was responsible for the preface, in which tribute is paid to the improvements made by Charles II at St. James's, Hampton Court, and Greenwich: '. . . where this mighty Prince hath made more notable changes, and added more Royal decorations since the 10 years of his happy Restoration, then any of his ancestors ever thought on in the space of a whole age'. When André Mollet died the Monarchy had been restored only about five years.

The imprint on the title-page of *The garden of pleasure* reads 'In the Savoy. Printed by T. N. for John Martyn . . . and Henry Herringman . . .'. The initials T. N. may stand for Thomas Newcombe, whose printing-house was one of the largest in London, and whose address from 1649, until his death in 1681, was 'The Kings printing house in the Savoy'.[1] Most of the engravings illustrating the work are signed with Mollet's initials A. M. (in the shape of a monogram), followed by the letters I. F. (i.e. André Mollet invenit et fecit), and the preface contains a translation from a passage in the work of 1651, which reads: 'I have composed this book, whose designs are all of my own invention, and drawn with my own hand.' The plates also bear the inscription 'I. V. Velde sculp a Stockholm',[2] or the abbreviation 'Velde', or the inscription 'Wolffgang Hardman sculp'. The second design in the book, one that had already been published by Mollet in *Le jardin de plaisir* of 1651, shows a moated chateau standing in extensive grounds. The back of the building overlooks a fine parterre at the end of which is a semicircle of trees from which radiate three great avenues of trees forming a *patte d'oie*, or goose-foot. This distinctive form of a *patte d'oie* in which avenues and, or, canals radiate from semicircles of trees designed to carry the eye outwards in several directions is found in plans of the two Royal parks of St. James's and Hampton Court, which Charles II began to remodel soon after his return from exile in 1660. Two other examples are found in plans of Drottningholm Castle in Sweden, where alterations began to be made in 1661, and of Fredensborg in Denmark where a start was made at about the same date in laying out the grounds.[3] Although it is known that Charles II invited Le Nôtre, gardener to Louis XIV, to come to England to advise him on the planning of the Royal gardens, especially at Greenwich, there is no record that he ever came. He did, however, make a plan for a formal garden at Greenwich but no

[1] Plomer (H. R.), *A dictionary of the booksellers and printers . . . at work in England, Scotland and Ireland from 1641 to 1667*, p. 136 (1907).

[2] This may have been Jan van de Velde, a goldsmith and map engraver who worked in Amsterdam, Haarlem, and Stockholm. He is considered by Hind to have engraved a portrait

of Christina of Sweden, executed about 1650, and signed 'Velde sculp.' (*A history of engraving and etching*, etc. 169, footnote 1 (1927)).

[3] See Gothein (M. L.), *A history of garden art*, etc. 2, fig. 442 (Hampton Court), fig. 444 (St. James's Park), fig. 518 (Drottningholm), and fig. 522 (Fredensborg) (1928).

Zolde.

⊢——⊣——⊣——⊣——⊣——⊣ Ioſes. M. I. f.
1 2   3   4   5

59. Mollet: *The garden of pleasure*, design 7, 1670. A design for a parterre 'partly embroidery, and partly knots of grass and flowers'. 5·3 × 10".

evidence exists that the design was ever carried out.[1] It would be interesting
to know to what extent Mollet was responsible for the planning of the Royal
parks in which the above distinctive pattern of planting was used. Although
Le Nôtre also employed the *patte d'oie* it was not in Mollet's form combined
with a semicircle of trees—since Le Nôtre could not tolerate any interruption
of the view.[2]

Another interesting engraving in *The garden of pleasure*, and this had not
appeared in the Stockholm work of 1651, is a plan[3] of a Royal garden '200
toises in length, and 50 in breadth',[4] stated to have been 'contrived by His
Majesties order in his park at St. James's'.[5] The Hon. Mrs. Evelyn Cecil
(Hon. A. Amherst) who has given a transcription of the description of this
plan,[6] has drawn attention to the fact that it is 'for a garden, and does not
embrace the canal, which was 100 feet broad and 2,800 feet long, and ran
through the centre of the park'. This garden may be the one shown in Kip's
plan (*c.* 1700) of St. James's Palace and Park[7] in which a long parterre
appears at the side of the palace. Most of the engravings in Mollet's book are
designs for parterres of embroidery, grass knots, labyrinths, and mazes. An
attractive parterre of embroidery, stated to have been carried out at Stockholm
before the palace 'of the late Queen Mother of Sweden',[8] introduces into the
design the three crowns in the Swedish coat of arms.[9]

The garden of pleasure appears to be an exceedingly rare work. It is possible
that it was being prepared by the author at the time of his death. Later the
manuscript and plates may have come into the hands of the English publishers
John Martyn and Henry Herringman who decided to add a preface and
publish the work, without mentioning that Mollet was dead.

In 1670 appeared *The English gardener* by Leonard Meager, a treatise
dedicated to Philip Hollman of Warkworth in Northamptonshire, in whose
service the author had at one time studied and practised the art of gardening.[10]
From the epistle to the reader it is learnt that Meager had been hampered
in the execution of his book through 'multiplicity of business, together with
the want of learning'. However, in spite of these difficulties he produced a
useful work giving much practical information on the management of the
fruit, kitchen, and flower garden, and illustrated with engravings 'of knots,
and wilderness-work'.[11] Included is a catalogue of herbs for growing in the

[1] Platts (B.), Origins of Greenwich park, *Country Life*, **138**, 866–7 (7 Oct. 1965).

[2] Green (D.), *Gardener to Queen Anne, Henry Wise (1653–1738) and the formal garden*, 61, footnote 1 (1956).

[3] This plan, numbered 25, is printed from two plates.

[4] In giving measurements Mollet uses the French 'toise', or fathom, containing six feet.

[5] *The garden of pleasure*, etc. 11 (1670).

[6] *A history of gardening in England*, 185 (1910).

[7] See *Britannia illustrata*, etc. [Drawings by L. Knyff and others, engraved by J. Kip and others], **1**, pl. 3 (1720).

[8] See *The garden of pleasure*, design 6 and its description on p. 5 (1670).

[9] The Royal arms of Sweden are azure (blue) three open crowns gold which appear in the first and fourth quarter of the official State arms.

[10] Meager (L.), *The English gardener*, etc. (1670) (Dedication).

[11] *Ibid.* (title-page).

kitchen garden and another of plants suitable for adorning the flower garden or for picking when making nosegays. Furthermore, as house plants were a popular form of decoration various plants suitable for growing in pots are also listed. In addition there is a 'Catalogue of divers sorts of fruit, which', Meager writes, 'I had of my very loving friend Captain Garrle, dwelling at the great nursery between Spittle-fields and White-chappel, a very eminent and ingenious nursery-man.'[1] This publication was issued in many editions, a tenth edition appearing in 1704. Another popular work by Meager was issued in 1697 under the title of *The new art of gardening*. This has an attractive frontispiece depicting a small formal garden of the period. Meager was also the author of *The mystery of husbandry* (1697).

Mention has already been made of *The compleat vineyard* (1665) by William Hughes. Two other works by this author may now be noted: *The flower-garden* first published in 1671, and *The American physitian; or, a treatise of the roots, plants, trees, shrubs, fruit, herbs, &c. growing in the English plantations in America*, issued in 1672. The first of these works proved so popular that all copies of the first impression were sold in three months.[2] Little is known concerning Hughes. According to the dedication in the 1670 edition of *The compleat vineyard*, addressed to 'Edward Lord Viscount Conway and Kilulta',[3] Hughes worked at one time at Ragley, in Warwickshire, in the service of Conway's mother. In the preface to the same treatise Hughes states that he had been 'in many parts of England, as also in other places elsewhere', and it appears possible that he visited some of the vineyards in Europe. His *American physitian* was composed in the West Indies and regarding this work he tells us that it was not written 'in a closet or study, in the corner of a house, amongst many books; but . . . rather in travelling the woods, and other parts' during his free time ashore whilst serving on 'one of His Majesties ships of war'.[4] His design in writing this treatise was to give details 'concerning certain trees, fruits, herbs, roots, &c.', that he had used in the West Indies and especially in the island of Jamaica, for food and medicine.[5]

The West Indies were much in the news during the seventeenth century. In 1655 England had acquired Jamaica, and the possession of this island,

[1] Meager, (L.), op. cit. 82–8. The nursery gardener referred to was Leonard Gurle, sometimes called Captain Gurle or Garrle, whose name was also written Gerle and Quarle. His garden was pre-eminently one for fruit trees of the finer and rarer sorts. See Thomson (G. S.), *Life in a noble household 1641–1700*, pp. 248–51 (1937) Paperback edition. After the death, in September 1677, of John Rose, Leonard Gurle became Keeper of the Royal garden in St. James's Park. He still held this post on 2 September 1684, but by 3 August 1685, he was dead. See *Calendar of Treasury books*, **5**, Pt. 1, p. 828 (under 31 December 1677); **7**, Pt. 2, p. 1321 (under 2 September 1684), **8**, Pt. 1, p. 290 (under 3 August 1685).

[2] Hughes (W.), *The flower garden and compleat vineyard. In two parts*, etc. (1683) (To the reader Pt. 1).

[3] Edward Conway, Viscount Conway of Conway Castle and Baron Conway of Ragley, also Viscount Killultagh (*c.* 1623–83).

[4] Hughes (W.), *The American physitian*, etc. (1672) (To the reader).

[5] Ibid. (1672).

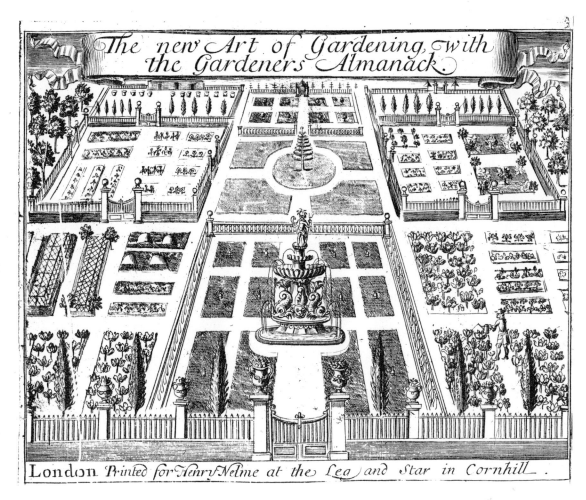

The new Art of Gardening, with the Gardeners Almanack.

London Printed for Henry Nelme at the Lea and Star in Cornhill.

60. Meager: *The new art of gardening*, 1697. Engraved frontispiece. 6·5 × 8.

together with Barbados and other settlements in the West Indies, helped to increase her commerce in that part of the world. Lipson tells us that England traded with Virginia, Maryland, Barbados, and Jamaica for 'commodities such as tobacco, sugar, cotton, cocoa, ginger and dyeing woods'.[1] The contents of Hughes's little book, therefore, struck a note of topicality. Among his descriptions he gives a discourse on the sugar-cane and the process of making sugar.[2] He also includes accounts of the cotton-tree and cotton-bush,[3] but the longest section in the work is devoted to the 'cacoa-tree' and the making of chocolate.[4]

John Worlidge was responsible for a small octavo volume published in 1677 under the title of *Systema horti-culturæ: or, the art of gardening*. This

[1] Lipson (E.), *The economic history of England*, **3**, 157 (1948).
[2] p. 27, etc.
[3] p. 68, etc.
[4] p. 102, etc.

popular treatise, with a title-page and three plates engraved by F. H. van Hove, contains much useful advice and information for the practical gardener. The author, referred to by John Houghton[1] as 'the ingenious Mr. John Worlidge of Petersfield in Hampshire', is generally considered one of the most enlightened of the seventeenth-century writers on gardening and husbandry, his most important works on the latter subject being *Systema agriculturæ, the mystery of husbandry discovered* (1669) and *Vinetum britannicum: or, a treatise of cider* (1676). When writing of gardens in his *Systema horti-culturæ* Worlidge makes the following statement:[2]

> Neither is there a noble or pleasant seat in England but hath its gardens for pleasure and delight; scarce an ingenious citizen that by his confinement to a shop, being denied the priviledge of having a real garden, but hath his boxes, pots, or other receptacles for flowers, plants, &c . . . there is scarce a cottage in most of the southern parts of England but hath its proportionable garden, so great a delight do most of men take in it; that they may not only please themselves with the view of the flowers, herbs and trees, as they grow, but furnish themselves and their neighbours upon extraordinary occasions, as nuptials, feasts, and funerals, with the proper products of their gardens.

In view of this general interest in horticulture, it is not surprising that the number of books published in England on practical gardening increased rapidly during the second half of the seventeenth century. The majority of these publications were convenient in size and small in price, and the fact that so many of them appeared in several editions[3] is proof of their popularity.

The first book to be written for gardeners in Scotland was *The Scots gard'ner*, which was published in 1683 at Edinburgh.[4] The author, John Reid, was gardener to Sir George Mackenzie (1636–91) of Rosehaugh in Ross-shire,[5] Lord Advocate and chief founder of the Advocates' Library, now the National Library of Scotland. It appears that when Nicholas Carlisle wrote his *Topographical dictionary of Scotland* of 1813, this house at Avoch was then 'surrounded with extensive plantations, and well cultivated grounds',[6] and their beauty, suggests Hyatt, was probably due to the care bestowed upon them by John Reid.[7] Reid's excellent little book was republished in 1721. Later editions issued in 1756 and 1766 were 'carefully corrected . . . by an eminent hand', and enlarged with the addition of several works by other writers. These include the Earl of Haddington's *Treatise on forest-trees*, an

---

[1] *A collection of letters for the improvement of husbandry & trade,* [edited] *by John Houghton,* **1**, 136 and 163 (1681).

[2] W[orlidge]. (J.), *Systema horti-culturæ: or, the art of gardening,* etc. 4–5 (1677).

[3] e.g. see below, Bibliography, under Gilbert (S.), Hughes (W.), Meager (L.), and Worlidge (J.).

[4] In 1907 *The Scots gard'ner* of 1683, edited

by Alfred H. Hyatt, was published as vol. **4** of The garden lover's series.

[5] On the title-pages of the 1756 and 1766 editions of the work is the statement: 'originally by John Reid, gardiner to Sir George Mackenzie of Rosehaugh'.

[6] Vol. **1** (see under Avoch).

[7] *The Scots gard'ner . . . edited by Alfred H. Hyatt* (1907) (Editor's note).

interesting publication on planting in Scotland to which further reference will be made.[1]

At this time, poets, too, wrote on gardening. During the decade 1660 to 1670 the English poet and essayist Abraham Cowley (1618–67), and the French Jesuit writer, René Rapin (1621–87), each wrote a famous poem devoted to a botanical subject.

Abraham Cowley's Latin poem *Plantarum libri duo* was published in 1662, and in 1668 this was included in the author's *Poemata latina. In quibus continentur; sex libri plantarum . . . et unus miscellaneorum.* The origin of this work is told by Thomas Sprat in his *Life and writings of Mr Abraham Cowley.*[2] On 2 December 1657 Cowley was created Doctor of Medicine at Oxford,[3] and during his studies for this profession:

after many anatomical dissertations he proceeded to the consideration of simples; and having furnish'd himself with books of that nature, he retir'd into a fruitful part of Kent, where every field and wood might shew him the real figures of those plants, of which he read. Thus he speedily master'd that part of the art of medicine. But then, as one of the antients did before him in the study of law, instead of employing his skill for practice and profit, he presently digested it into that form which we behold [i.e. in the form of his Latin poem on plants].

The first two books of this poem are on the qualities of herbs, the third and fourth books are on the beauties of flowers, and the fifth and sixth are on the uses of trees.

Cowley dedicated his poem to Trinity College, Cambridge, where he received his education and where he was elected a Fellow in 1640. It possesses neither botanical nor gardening value, but being written by an eminent poet it was read by many including the intellectuals of the day, and it must have done much to further the interest in botany and gardening in England during the reign of Charles II. To the complete work of 1668 is prefixed a portrait of the author by William Faithorne, and a short account of Cowley's life and writings by his friend Thomas Sprat in a communication to Martin Clifford.[4] The work remained popular for many years and in 1795 an English translation by Nahum Tate 'and others'[5] was published together in one volume with James Gardiner's translation of Rapin's poem *Of gardens.* The title of this publication is, *Cowley's history of plants, a poem in six books: with Rapin's disposition of gardens, a poem in four books.*

[1] See below, 2, 569–71.

[2] See *The works of Mr Abraham Cowley*, etc. [edited, with an account of the life and writings of Cowley, by Thomas Sprat] (1668). Thomas Sprat (1635–1713) became Dean of Westminster in 1683, and Bishop of Rochester in 1684. He was one of the 'original Fellows' of the Royal Society and in 1667 was the author of the earliest published 'History' of that institution.

[3] Foster (J.), *Alumni oxonienses*, etc. vol. 1, Early series, 338 (1891).

[4] Martin Clifford (d. 1677). Elected in 1671 Master of the Charterhouse.

[5] Nahum Tate (1652–1715), English poet and dramatist; appointed poet laureate in 1692; wrote mainly as an editor or translator. Tate

61. Cowley: *Poemata latina*, 1668. Frontispiece portrait of Abraham
Cowley engraved by William Faithorne. 6·3 × 4·1″.

René Rapin's Latin poem *Hortorum libri IV* first appeared in Paris in
1665. It was published in a number of editions in France and was also issued
at Leyden (1668), Utrecht (1672), and Amsterdam (1782). An English
translated Books IV and V only of Cowley's poem on plants. Books I and II are translated by 'J.O.', Book III by the poet C. Cleve and Book VI by the dramatist and novelist Aphra Behn (1640–1689).

translation by John Evelyn the Younger (1655–99) appeared in London in 1672, and in the eighteenth century a version by James Gardiner, Fellow of Jesus College, Cambridge, was issued.[1] Evelyn's name does not appear on the title-page of his translation, only his initials 'J. E.'. The dedication to Henry Bennet, first Earl of Arlington (*c.* 1620–85) is signed 'J. Evelyn'. Under the date 5 January 1672 [i.e. 1673] the elder Evelyn wrote in his *Diary*:[2] 'My sonn now publish'd his version of 'Rapinus Hortorum' &c dedicated to the Ear: of Arlington.'[3] Although the dedication is reprinted by William Upcott in *The miscellaneous writings of John Evelyn, Esq. F.R.S.* (pp. 623–4 (1825)) as the work of Evelyn the Elder, Keynes[4] has pointed out that the book 'is entirely by John Evelyn, Junior', as is evident from a perusal of the dedication. The younger Evelyn was only eighteen when his translation was published and he had already shown promise as a classical scholar with the set of Greek lines published in the second edition (1670) of his father's *Sylva*.[5]

A Latin poem was published in 1699 entitled *Ric. Ricardsoni . . . de cultu hortorum . . . carmen*, and dedicated to William III. Richard Richardson, the author of various works in Latin, was admitted in 1652 as a sizar at Emmanuel College, Cambridge.[6] He graduated Master of Arts in 1660 and proceeded Bachelor of Divinity in 1671. In 1673 he was incorporated as a member of the University of Oxford. In 1663 he became Vicar of Brixworth, a place described by his contemporary, Anthony à Wood, as 'the most pleasant village of Brixworth in Northamptonshire'.[7] In 1699 Richardson was appointed Rector of Lamport in the same county. He was buried at Lamport on 6 January 1705 [i.e. 1706]. A reference to Brixworth is found in the author's poem.[8]

It should be noted that Richard Richardson lived during the same time as Richard Richardson (1663–1741), the physician of North Bierley, in Yorkshire. The latter was a Fellow of the Royal Society, an eminent botanist and antiquary, and the owner of a valuable library of botanical and historical works. He corresponded with Sir Hans Sloane, James Petiver, Johannes Jacobus Dillenius, and other leading men of the day. The fact that Richardson the divine and Richardson the physician had the same Christian name resulted in confusion at least once over the authorship of the above Latin poem of 1699, as on 19 August 1727 the celebrated eighteenth-century

[1] Gardiner's version first appeared in [1706].

[2] *The diary of John Evelyn . . . edited by E. S. de Beer*, 4, 1 (1955).

[3] The elder Evelyn reprinted Book II ('Woods') of his son's translation of Rapin's poem, in the third edition (1679) of *Sylva* (see pp. 276–81).

[4] Keynes (G.), *John Evelyn a study in biblio-*

phily and a bibliography of his writings, 283 (1937).

[5] See d2[b].

[6] Venn (J.) and Venn (J. A.), *Alumni cantabrigienses . . . Part I . . . to 1751*, 3, 453 (1924).

[7] Wood (A. à), *Athenæ oxonienses . . . A new edition . . . by Philip Bliss*, 3, col. 209 (1817).

[8] See p. 21 (1699).

gardener Philip Miller wrote to Dr. Richardson of Bierley:[1] 'A gentleman the other day surpris'd me with a fine piece, which, upon reading, I found you to be the author of: the title is, if I remember right, *De cultu hortorum*. Pray if it is to be had, give me directions where I may procure it.'

During the second half of the seventeenth century three drinks, coffee, chocolate, and tea, gradually became fashionable in England,[2] and books were written on the history and nature of these beverages. One such work was published in 1682 under the title of *The natural history of coffee, thee, chocolate*. Included in this treatise is a chapter on the natural history of tobacco, and another giving details concerning elderberries and juniper berries. The work, although of considerable interest, is an acknowledged compilation 'from the writings of the best physicians, and modern travellers'.[3]

In 1699 there appeared *An essay upon the nature and qualities of tea*.[4] The author, John Ovington, M.A., was Chaplain to the King,[5] and in his dedication, addressed to the Countess of Grantham,[6] he delivered an elaborate eulogy on the virtues of tea. In concluding his dedication Ovington writes: 'But in pity, Madam, to this tender leaf, I must cease from panegyrick, lest it should create a satyr, and the innocent praises of it be eccho'd back in sharp invectives.' Ovington did not escape being ridiculed, for in 1733 there appeared in Dublin John Waldron's *Satyr against tea. Or, Ovington's Essay upon the nature and qualities of tea, &c., dissected, and burlesq'd.*

[1] *Extracts from the literary and scientific correspondence of Richard Richardson*, etc. [edited by D. Turner], 275 (1835).

[2] Mitchell (R. J.) and Leys (M. D. R.), *A history of the English people*, 255, 478–9 (1950).

[3] Title-page.

[4] In 1928 a facsimile reprint of this work of 1699 was published in London by the Institute of Certificated Grocers.

[5] 'By J. Ovington, M.A., Chaplain to His Majesty' (Title-page).

[6] This was Henrietta (d. 1724), wife of Henry d'Auverquerque, first Earl of Grantham.

62. Rea: *Flora: seu, de florum cultura. Or, a complete florilege . . . The second impression.* 1676. Engraved head-piece on p. 169. 5·5 × 5·3″.

CONCLUSION

FINALLY, there are some points of general interest concerning the production and illustration of these seventeenth-century books. From 1600 to 1650, a time that included several outbreaks of the plague[1] and a long period of civil war, comparatively few botanical or horticultural works were published. Among those issued, however, are three notable publications: Parkinson's *Paradisus* (1629); Johnson's edition of Gerard's *Herball* (1633); and Parkinson's *Theatrum botanicum* (1640).

Apart from the title-pages and portraits, most of the illustrations in seventeenth-century English botanical and horticultural books are woodcuts. After 1590 copper-plate engravings became increasingly popular in this country,[2] but except for titles and portraits their first appearance in books included in the present undertaking was not until 1658 when John Evelyn's *French gardiner* appeared with an engraved frontispiece and three engraved plates.

Johnson recorded[3] that in England the engraved title-page belongs especially to the Stuart period, and the following five botanical books may be noted for having interesting examples of these; the herbals of 1633 and 1640 mentioned above, Austen's *Treatise of fruit-trees* (1653), Rea's *Flora Ceres & Pomona* (1665), and Cotton's *Planters manual* (1675). The herbal of 1640, Rea's book and Cotton's manual each display the seventeenth-century custom for the engraved plate to be in addition to a type-set title-page.[4] Among the engraved portraits, by far the most outstanding is that of Robert Morison prefixed to the 'Pars tertia' of his *Historia* (1699).

With the arrival of the Commonwealth England enjoyed more settled conditions and there was a revival of the book trade.[5] This was followed by the Restoration and a time of great development in scientific botany as well as an advancement in horticulture. Therefore, as noted in our Introduction to seventeenth-century books, the number of works published during this period rapidly increased. The second half of the century saw the publication of Morison's *Plantarum umbelliferarum* (1672) and the second and third parts of the same author's *Historia* (1680, 1699), three fine folio volumes which have the distinction of being among the first of the great works to be published

---

[1] 'On the accession of Charles I plague paralysed trade and made gaps in the ranks of the Stationers' Company' (Plomer (H. R.), *A short history of English printing 1476–1900*, p. 138 (1915)).

[2] Pollard (A. W.), Some notes on English illustrated books, *Trans. bibl. Soc.* **6**, 29 (1903).

[3] Johnson (A. F.), *A catalogue of engraved and etched English title-pages down to . . . 1691*, p. viii (1934 for 1933).

[4] Ibid. p. ix.

[5] Pollard (A. W.), *Fine books*, 289 (1912).

by the Oxford University Press.[1] The total number of plates in these three books exceeds three hundred. Illustrations then, as now, were a very costly item in book production, and other authors were less fortunate than Morison. It will be remembered that because of expense the florist John Rea had to forgo publishing a work with 'many costly cuts',[2] and for the same reason the great botanist John Ray was unable to illustrate his *Historia*.[3]

Although an increasing number of horticultural books were published during the second half of the seventeenth century, only a few of these works such as Rea's *Flora Ceres & Pomona* (1665), Mollet's *Garden of pleasure* (1670), and *The compleat gard'ner . . . Made English by John Evelyn* (1693), were folio volumes. The majority were duodecimo, octavo, or small quarto volumes. In the 1665 edition of his *Treatise of fruit-trees* Ralph Austen advocates that books of this nature should 'be of small bulk and price; because great volumns . . . are of too great a price for mean husband-men to buy'.[4] The truth of this statement, which was later echo'd by other writers, including Worlidge in 1677[5] and Langford in 1681,[6] is evident when the popularity of Evelyn's *Compleat gard'ner* (1693) is compared with London and Wise's abridged version published in 1699. The former appeared in only one edition and the latter in seven. The majority of the illustrations in seventeenth-century English horticultural books consist of mathematical diagrams and garden plans. Occasionally garden scenes are depicted. So far in our *History* there has been no botanical or horticultural work of any kind with outstanding illustrations. England had to wait until the eighteenth century before such books were published with original and beautiful plates.

[1] Madan (F.), *Oxford Books*, etc. **3**, p. xxii (1931).
[2] See above, p. 195.
[3] See above, p. 132.
[4] Austen (R.), *A treatise of fruit-trees*, etc. (1665) (Dedication to Robert Boyle).
[5] W[orlidge]. (J.), *Systema horti-culturæ: or, the art of gardening*, etc. (1777) (Preface).
[6] Langford (T.), *Plain and full instructions to raise all sorts of fruit-trees*, etc. (1681) (To the reader).

BIBLIOGRAPHY

EXPLANATORY NOTES

FOR THE USE OF THIS *BIBLIOGRAPHY*

(Note that some of the examples will be found in Volume III.)

Headings and Arrangement

THE headings in the *Bibliography* are in alphabetical order and consist primarily of the names of the authors of the various works. Headings such as those used for anonymous works and for official institutions, societies, or national bodies are included in the same alphabetical sequence.

Cross-references are made from the names of editors and translators.

Works written in conjunction by two authors are entered under the names of both authors conjointly in the order in which they appear on the title-page, with a cross-reference from the names of the authors placed in reverse.

Where the part written by each author is specified the name of the first is taken as the heading. Both names are included in the title-entry and a cross-reference is made from the name of the second author.

e.g. GENTIL (FRANÇOIS) Le jardinier solitaire, the solitary or Carthusian gard'ner . . . by Francis Gentil . . . Also The compleat florist . . . By . . . Louis Liger.

When a work is published under initials which apparently denote an author's name these are adopted as a heading, the last initial being placed first. A cross-reference is made from the full name when known.

e.g. S., R. The gardener's pocket-book . . . by R. S.

Titles of honour are shown in the heading. In the case of foreign titles the practice of the British Museum (Bloomsbury) in their Catalogue of printed books is followed, the portion of the epithet indicating the rank being given in English.

e.g. COVOLO (GIOVAMBATISTA DAL) *Count.*

If an author wrote under a name known to be fictitious his work is entered under the pseudonym followed by the abbreviation 'pseud.' and his real name, if known, is added within square brackets. A cross-reference is made from the real name.

e.g. MOUNTAIN (DIDYMUS) pseud. [i.e. THOMAS HILL.]

Where an author wrote under a descriptive name it is taken as a heading if it consists of a single word, otherwise the work is treated as an anonymous publication. A cross-reference is made from the real name, if known.

e.g. LADY. Botanical dialogues . . . by a lady [i.e. MARIA E. JACKSON.]

e.g. COMPLEAT CYDERMAN. The compleat cyderman . . . By experienc'd hands.

Anonymous works concerning a person named in the title are entered under his name.

e.g. BROWN (PHILIP) A catalogue of . . . plants, collected by . . . Philip Brown . . . deceased.

e.g. COWELL (JOHN) A true account of the Alöe americana . . . now in blossom in Mr. Cowell's garden.

If no author's name, real or assumed, is given anywhere in the book, the work is entered under the first word, or words, of the title, omitting the article if there is one. Occasionally, such works are entered under the first substantive in the title.

e.g. TRACTS. Tracts on practical agriculture and gardening.

e.g. POETICAL FLOWER GARDEN. The poetical flower garden, with moral reflections.

e.g. BOOK. Here begynneth the boke of the arte . . . of . . . plantyng of trees.

Anonymous works concerning a place named in the title are entered under the heading proper to such place. A cross-reference is made from the author, if known.

e.g. CAMBRIDGE. Catalogus plantarum circa Cantabrigiam nascentium, etc. [By John Ray].

A work concerning an official institution, society, or national body is entered under the name of the author of the work. A cross-reference is made from the name of the institution, society, or body. If no author's name is given on the title-page or elsewhere in the book the work is entered under the heading proper to such an institution, society, or body.

Official institutions are entered under the name of the place where they are situated, societies and national bodies directly under their proper name.

e.g. EDINBURGH.—*Royal botanic garden.*

e.g. SOCIETY OF APOTHECARIES OF LONDON.

e.g. COMMISSIONERS AND TRUSTEES FOR IMPROVING FISHERIES AND MANUFACTURES IN SCOTLAND.

Commercial firms are entered under their names.

e.g. GORDON, DERMER AND CO.

A translation which contains the name of the author of the original work is entered under his name, otherwise it is treated as an anonymous work.

Magazines are entered under the first words of the title, omitting the article if there is one.

On occasion the above rules have been relaxed.

e.g. The anonymous work first printed in 1525 by the London printer Richard Banckes, with the title reading 'Here begynnyth a new mater . . . the whiche is called an herball' and its many editions with their various titles, including those bearing the names or initials Macer, Askham, and W. C., respectively, are all entered under the heading HERBAL. Cross-references are made from the names and initials Macer, Askham, and W. C.

The arrangement of the entries under each heading is alphabetical. Successive editions and issues of each work immediately succeed the first in chronological order. To denote the number of the edition stated on the title-page the abbreviation 'Ed.' is used followed by the requisite numeral in arabic. e.g. Ed. 2.

Description: Title-pages

An omission made in transcribing from a title-page is shown thus . . . except at the end of a title when etc. is used. No attempt has been made to reproduce title-page capitalization and the use of capitals has been kept down to the absolute minimum.[1] The spelling and punctuation of the title have been carefully followed. Obvious errors and misprints are indicated by *sic* enclosed in square brackets.

The practice of the early printers regarding the use of the letters I, J, U, and V has been followed for all books until about 1640. Thus, capital I is used for letters now represented by I and J and lower-case j is transcribed as such when used by the printer following i, e.g. vij. The printer's use of capital V for upper-case U and V has been observed and so has the use of lower-case u and v, lower-case u being always used in the middle of a word and v at the beginning. The letter W when represented by the printer by a double V has been transcribed as such.

The name of the author of a work is not repeated in the title-entry except (*a*) where necessary for the sake of clearness, (*b*) if a work is by a nurseryman or florist, when not only his name but also his address is transcribed.

e.g. DICKSONS AND CO. A catalogue of . . . plants . . . by Dicksons & Co. nursery-men, seedsmen, and florists, Edinburgh.

e.g. LEE (James) An introduction to botany . . . By James Lee, nursery man, at The vineyard, at Hammersmith.

Additions to the title-entry if supplied by the compiler are enclosed in square brackets. If the author's name does not appear on the title-page but if his name or initials are given in some other part of the book the information is supplied in square brackets at the end of the entry.

e.g. [The address to the reader is signed W. B. Coyte.]

e.g. [With an advertisement by M. E. J., i.e. M. E. Jackson.]

If the author or editor of an anonymous work is known, his name is supplied in square brackets at the end of the title-entry and the reason for the attribution is given in a footnote.

e.g. Phytologia britannica. [By William How.]

Title-page imprints

The following particulars are given at the end of the title-entry.

The place of publication or if this is not indicated the place of printing.

In the case of early books, defined as those before 1700, the name of the printer or bookseller is stated, or a combination of both if indicated.

[1] For reason *see* Preface in Vol. I.

e.g. London, T. Este, for Thomas Wight.

e.g. London, R. B., solde for Roger Jackson.

After 1700 the name of the publisher only is stated or failing such indication the name of the printer.

e.g. London, John Ryall.

e.g. Manchester, printed by J. Harrop.

The statement 'printed for the author' when occurring in the imprint is taken to indicate the publisher and is given thus: 'London, the author.'

When the names of several publishers occur in the imprint the first three only are generally given, followed by etc.

e.g. Dublin, Richard Gunne, George Risk, George Ewing, etc.

In the case of a firm having a large number of names the first three only are given followed by etc. enclosed in square brackets.

e.g. London, Longman, Hurst, Rees, [etc.].

When two or more places of publication occur with equal prominence all are stated.

e.g. Hull, printed and sold by Rawson and Co. sold also by J. Johnson . . . London; and W. Creech, Edinburgh.

When the place of printing and the place of publication occur with equal prominence both are generally given.

e.g. Birmingham, printed by M. Swinney; for T. Cadel and P. Elmsley, and G. Robinson, London.

Colophon imprints

Particulars are given from the colophon when the name of the printer and the place and date of publication are not to be found elsewhere, or if a book contains both title-page imprint and colophon imprint and the two are contradictory or supplementary to one another.

See entry under HERBAL. The grete herball (1526).

See entry under GERARD (John). The herball (1597).

Date of publication

The date of publication is stated in arabic numerals. When the year of publication does not appear in a work and it has been obtained by means of an external source it is supplied enclosed in square brackets. A date taken from the dedication, preface, or some other part of the work is also enclosed in brackets. The source of the information is given in a note.

Dimensions

The measurements of the height and breadth of a book are given to the nearest centimetre. But this can only be a rough guide as the dimensions are always those of the leaves

as left by the binder who trimmed off the rough edges of the leaves. No two copies, therefore, will necessarily measure exactly the same.

Format

The format is stated as fol., folio; 4°, quarto; 8°, octavo; 12°, duodecimo, etc.

Collation

The format of the book is followed by a statement of pagination or, if the leaves are
numbered and not the pages, by a statement of foliation. If a book is without pagination
or foliation the signatures are specified.

In the statement of pagination the printer's method of numeration is followed,
including the use of roman numerals.

For the parts of a book without pagination the total number of pages is noted in
square brackets (preliminaries in roman, the actual text in arabic).

Blank leaves at the beginning and the end of the work (i.e. the first leaf of the first
gathering and the last of the last gathering) are normally ignored, except when the first
leaf is included by the printer in the pagination.[1] Other blank leaves are included in the
collation. The presence of blank leaves when included in a statement of pagination is
made the subject of a note.

e.g. LOCKE (JOHN) Observations upon . . . vines.
pp. xv, [i], 73, [1].
Leaf A1 (i.e. pp. i–ii) is blank.

e.g. AUSTEN (RALPH) A dialogue, or familiar discourse.
pp. [xxxii], 87, [1].
Leaf A8 (i.e. pp. [xxxi–xxxii]) is blank.

Booksellers' advertisements are included in the pagination if they form part of a
gathering.

Pagination is recorded as it stands and if this differs from the number of pages ascer-
tained by counting, the figure thus obtained preceded by the abbreviation, i.e. is given
in square brackets.

e.g. pp. [xiv], 255 [i.e. 159], [5].

With some plate books, instead of the usual collation, the contents of the works have
been briefly described. Among these works, all of which are difficult to collate, are:
BLACKWELL (ELIZABETH) A curious herbal.
STUART (JOHN) *Earl of Bute* Botanical tables.
CURTIS (WILLIAM) Flora londinensis.
MARTYN (THOMAS) Flora rustica.
MUELLER (JOHANN SEBASTIAN) Illustratio systematis sexualis Linnæi.

[1] They are also included when a collation by signatures is given, e.g. Signn. A–K⁸. Leaf K8 is
blank.

Illustrative matter

If there are two title-pages one of which is engraved the description is taken from the letterpress title and the following information is given in a note:

'There is an additional title-page, engraved.'

e.g. **See under** PARKINSON (John) Theatrum botanicum.

Illustrations in a book are indicated in the collation in the following order and form: frontis., pls., illust. As here used illust. stands for illustration or illustrations in the text as distinguished from plates which are printed separately from the rest of the book and do not form part of either the preliminary or the main sequence of pages.

The abbreviation pls. col. is used for both plates printed in colour and coloured by hand. Details regarding works with plates printed in colour are given in the *History*.

In the case of books that were sold with the plates either uncoloured, or coloured by hand, only the latter fact is specified in the collation.

In the case of works published in one volume only the total number of plates is given. If the plates are numbered and the numeral on the last plate differs from the figure obtained by counting the plates, the figure thus obtained, preceded by the abbreviation i.e., is stated in square brackets.

e.g. 43 [i.e. 44] pls.

Occasionally, when the numbering of the plates is confused or irregular, a statement is made of the plate numbers. For examples **see under**:

LANGLEY (Batty) Pomona: or, the fruit-garden illustrated.
MOLLET (André) The garden of pleasure.
TOURNEFORT (Joseph Pitton de) The compleat herbal.

Botanical volumes of general works

If one volume only of a work of two or more volumes is devoted to a subject of botanical interest it is included in the present *Bibliography*, if it is separately paged and separately signed.

e.g. BERKENHOUT (John) Outlines of the natural history of Great Britain and Ireland. Vol. II. Comprehending the vegetable kingdom.

The title and date of publication of the remaining volume, or volumes, are given in a note.

Books divided into parts

If the constituent parts of a single volume, on the title of which their presence is proclaimed, have separate title-pages and pagination, the fact is indicated in a note together with the dates of the separate parts, if these differ from that on the general title-page.

e.g. **See** LAURENCE (John) Gardening improv'd: containing I. The clergyman's recreation . . . II. The gentleman's recreation . . . III. The fruit-garden kalendar . . . The lady's recreation, etc.

Location of copies

The writer has located copies of every book included in the *Bibliography*. Locations are shown by symbols given in a note beneath each item. Lists of libraries and of the symbols used to denote them follow on at the end of these Explanatory Notes. Unless stated otherwise every item has been personally examined by the compiler. The *Bibliography* is not intended as a census of copies in each of the various libraries visited. The libraries whose collections are best represented are those situated in London and within easy reach of the capital. If a required edition has not been found in these libraries every effort has been made to locate a copy elsewhere in England, or in Scotland or Ireland.

If several copies of a work have been examined they have, as a rule, all been recorded. But it would be wrong to assume that a work is rare if one location only has been given, as other copies may be available in libraries not visited by the writer.

Material has been inspected in private libraries and also in antiquarian bookshops. Locations of copies in private libraries have not generally been recorded, and similarly references have only occasionally been given to books passing through the hands of the antiquarian book trade.

This *Bibliography* includes all editions of works published during the period concerned located by the writer in Britain, Ireland, and in Paris. The Bibliothèque Nationale in Paris has a fine collection of English botanical books, especially of those by Sir John Hill. As the writer makes frequent visits to France she was able to search the catalogues of Paris libraries for wanted and rare editions.

LIST OF LIBRARIES AND THEIR SYMBOLS

LIBRARIES represented by symbols in square brackets have works included in the *Bibliography* that have not been seen by the compiler; collations of such works have been supplied by members of the staffs of the libraries concerned, or by other individuals.

Bibliothèque du Muséum National d'Histoire Naturelle, Paris	PMHN
Bibliothèque Nationale, Paris	PBN
Birmingham Public Library	BPL
Bodleian Library, Oxford	OBL
British Museum (i.e. British Library Reference Division)	LBM
British Museum (Natural History)	LBMNH
Chelsea Physic Garden, London	LCPG
Chelsea Public Library, London	LCPL
Corpus Christi College, Oxford	OCCC
Edinburgh Public Library	EPL
Edinburgh University Library	EUL
Fitzwilliam Museum, Cambridge	CFM
Guildhall Library, London	LGL
Hammersmith Public Library, London	LHPL

Hancock Museum, Newcastle upon Tyne	NHM
Harvard College Library, Cambridge, Massachusetts	[Harv CL]
Harvard University: Arnold Arboretum, Jamaica Plain, Massachusetts	Harv (AA)L
Henry E. Huntington Library, San Marino, California	[HEHL]
India Office Library	LIO
King's College, Cambridge	CKC
Library of the Philosophical Society, Newcastle upon Tyne	NPS
Library of the Society of Friends, London	LSF
Linnean Society of London	LLS
London Library	LLL
McGill University, Osler Library, Montreal	[McGU(O)L]
Magdalen College, Oxford	OMaC
Manchester Public Library	MPL
Medical Society of London	LMS
Ministry of Agriculture, Fisheries and Food Library, London	LMA
Museum of the History of Science, Oxford	OMHS
National Library of Ireland	DNLI
National Library of Scotland	ENLS
Northamptonshire Record Office	NRO
Nottingham Subscription Library	NSL
Patent Office Library (being incorporated into the British Museum)	LPO (BM)
Pharmaceutical Society of Great Britain, London	LPS
Radcliffe Science Library, Oxford	ORSL
Rothamsted Experimental Station, Harpenden	HRES
Royal Agricultural Society of England	LRAS
Royal Botanic Garden, Edinburgh	ERBG
Royal Botanic Gardens, Kew	KRBG
Royal College of Physicians of Edinburgh	ERCP
Royal College of Physicians, London	LRCP
Royal College of Physicians and Surgeons of Glasgow	GRCPS
Royal College of Surgeons of England	LRCS
Royal Dublin Society	DRDS
Royal Horticultural Society: Lindley Library	LRHS
Royal Institute of British Architects	LRIBA
Royal Society of Arts	LRSA
Royal Society, London	LRS
Royal Society of Medicine	LRSM
Trinity Hall, Cambridge	CTH
University Botanic Garden, Cambridge	CUBG
University Library, Cambridge	CUL
University Library, Glasgow	GUL
University Library, Reading	RUL
University of Cambridge: Botany School Library	CBS
University of London Library (chiefly Goldsmiths' Library)	LUL
University of Manchester Medical Library	MUML

University of Oxford: Botany School Library   OBS
Victoria and Albert Museum, London   LVAM
Wadham College, Oxford   OWaC
Wellcome Historical Medical Library, London   LWML
Wisconsin University Library, Madison, Wisconsin   [WUL]
Yale University Library, New Haven, Connecticut   [YUL]

LIST OF PRIVATE LIBRARIES, BOOKSELLERS, AND SYMBOLS

Books seen at antiquarian booksellers, not Messrs. Quaritch   B
Miss Blanche Henrey   BH
Mr. A. E. Lownes   [AEL]
Mr. E. F. Croft-Murray   EC-M
Messrs. Quaritch   Q
Sir George Taylor   GT

LIST OF SYMBOLS AND LIBRARIES

BPL	Birmingham Public Library
CBS	University of Cambridge Botany School Library
CFM	Fitzwilliam Museum, Cambridge
CKC	King's College, Cambridge
CTH	Trinity Hall, Cambridge
CUBG	University Botanic Garden, Cambridge
CUL	University Library, Cambridge
DNLI	National Library of Ireland
DRDS	Royal Dublin Society
ENLS	National Library of Scotland
EPL	Edinburgh Public Library
ERBG	Royal Botanic Garden, Edinburgh
ERCP	Royal College of Physicians of Edinburgh
EUL	Edinburgh University Library
GRCPS	Royal College of Physicians and Surgeons of Glasgow
GUL	University Library, Glasgow
Harv (AA)L	Harvard University: Arnold Arboretum, Jamaica Plain, Massachusetts
[Harv CL]	Harvard College Library, Cambridge, Massachusetts
[HEHL]	Henry E. Huntington Library, San Marino, California
HRES	Rothamsted Experimental Station, Harpenden

KRBG	Royal Botanic Gardens, Kew
LBM	British Museum (i.e. British Library Reference Division)
LBMNH	British Museum (Natural History)
LCPG	Chelsea Physic Garden, London
LCPL	Chelsea Public Library, London
LGL	Guildhall Library, London
LHPL	Hammersmith Public Library, London
LIO	India Office Library
LLL	London Library
LLS	Linnean Society of London
LMA	Ministry of Agriculture, Fisheries and Food Library, London
LMS	Medical Society of London
LPO (BM)	Patent Office Library (being incorporated into the British Museum)
LPS	Pharmaceutical Society of Great Britain, London
LRAS	Royal Agricultural Society of England
LRCP	Royal College of Physicians, London
LRCS	Royal College of Surgeons of England
LRHS	Royal Horticultural Society: Lindley Library
LRIBA	Royal Institute of British Architects
LRS	Royal Society, London
LRSA	Royal Society of Arts
LRSM	Royal Society of Medicine
LSF	Library of the Society of Friends, London
LUL	University of London Library (chiefly Goldsmiths' Library)
LVAM	Victoria and Albert Museum, London
LWML	Wellcome Historical Medical Library, London
[McGU(O)L]	McGill University, Osler Library, Montreal
MPL	Manchester Public Library
MUML	University of Manchester Medical Library
NHM	Hancock Museum, Newcastle upon Tyne
NPS	Library of the Philosophical Society, Newcastle upon Tyne
NRO	Northamptonshire Record Office
NSL	Nottingham Subscription Library
OBL	Bodleian Library, Oxford
OBS	University of Oxford, Botany School Library
OCCC	Corpus Christi College, Oxford
OMaC	Magdalen College, Oxford
OMHS	Museum of the History of Science, Oxford
ORSL	Radcliffe Science Library, Oxford
OWaC	Wadham College, Oxford
PBN	Bibliothèque Nationale, Paris
PMHN	Bibliothèque du Muséum National d'Histoire Naturelle, Paris
RUL	University Library, Reading
[WUL]	Wisconsin University Library, Madison, Wisconsin
[YUL]	Yale University Library, New Haven, Connecticut

LIST OF SYMBOLS AND PRIVATE LIBRARIES AND BOOKSELLERS

B	Books seen at antiquarian booksellers, not Messrs. Quaritch
BH	Miss Blanche Henrey
[AEL]	Mr. A. E. Lownes
EC-M	Mr. E. F. Croft-Murray
Q	Messrs. Quaritch
GT	Sir George Taylor

ABBREVIATIONS AND SIGNS

b.	born	illust.	illustration, -s
𝔅.𝔏.	printed in black letter	In epist.	in letter, or letters
brs.	broadsheet	litho.	lithographic
c.	circa (about)	MS., MSS.	manuscript, -s
Cat.	catalogue	n.d.	no date (of publication)
cf.	confer (compare)	No.	number, -s
cm.	centimetre, -s	n.p.	no place (of printing or publication)
col., cols.	column, -s		
col.	coloured (when used in referring to plates e.g. pls. col.)	obl.	oblong
		orna.	ornamental
		p., pp.	page, -s
d.	died	pl., pls.	plate, -s
ded.	dedication	port.	portrait
Ed.	edition	pref.	preface
engr.	engraved, or engraving (includes engravings and etchings, or a combination of both)	pseud.	pseudonym
		Pt., Pts.	part, -s
		s.sh.	single-sheet
		sic	thus, so
engr. on tp.	engraving on a letterpress title-page	Sign., Signn.	signature, -s
		Suppl.	supplement
f., ff.	folio, or leaf; folios or leaves	tp.	title-page
Fasc.	fascicle, -s	uncol.	uncoloured
fig., figs.	figure, -s	Vol., vols.	volume, -s
frontis.	frontispiece		

→ after a date or the number of a volume or part signifies that the set was in progress in 1800

† after the number of a volume or part signifies that no more has been published

... denotes the omission of a word or words

( ) denotes information included in the transcription of a title-page that has been obtained from some other part of the work

[ ] encloses words, dates, etc. that have been supplied

⟨ ⟩ encloses unsigned leaves or gatherings, if the signature letter can be inferred

e.g. ⟨A⟩⁴ B–L⁴

encloses a dash if the signature letter cannot be inferred

e.g. ⟨—⟩² A–Z²

The following abbreviations are used for three works frequently referred to in footnotes:

Cat. works of Linnæus	*A catalogue of the works of Linnæus . . . preserved in the libraries of the British museum (Bloomsbury) and the British museum (Natural history)* (1933).
Dryander (J.), *Cat. bibl. Banks*	Jonas Dryander's *Catalogus bibliothecæ historico-naturalis Josephi Banks*, 5 vols. (1796–1800).
D.T.C.	The collection of copies of the correspondence of Sir Joseph Banks made for Dawson Turner, F.R.S. in 1833–4, preserved in the Department of Botany of the British Museum (Natural History).

BIBLIOGRAPHY FOR THE SIXTEENTH AND SEVENTEENTH CENTURIES

ART

1. The art of pruning fruit-trees . . . And a tract of the use of the fruits of trees, for preserving us in health, or for curing us when we are sick. Translated from the French original, set forth . . . by a physician of Rochelle [i.e. from 'L'Art de tailler les arbres fruitiers', by Nicolas Venette]. London, for Tho. Basset. 1685. 18×11 cm. 8°. pp. [viii], 104, [8]: illust.
Copies: LBM; LRHS; KRBG; HRES.

— **See** COMPLEAT PLANTER AND CYDERIST. The compleat planter & cyderist. Together with the art of pruning fruit-trees, etc. 1790. 8°.

ASKHAM (ANTHONY)

A lytel herball . . . newely amended . . . with certayne addicions at the ende of the boke . . . by Anthonye Askham, etc. **See** HERBAL. Here begynnyth a newe mater, etc. [Another edition.] A lytel herball, etc. 1550. 8°.

— [Another edition.] [1561?] 8°.

AUSTEN (RALPH) [–1676]

2. A dialogue, or familiar discourse, and conference betweene the husbandman, and fruit-trees; in his nurseries, orchards, and gardens, etc. Oxford, Hen. Hall, for Thomas Bowman. 1676. 17×11 cm. 8°. pp. [xxxii], 87, [1].
Leaf A8 (i.e. pp. [xxxi–xxxii]) is blank.
Copies: LPO (BM); LRHS; OBL.

3. Observations upon some part of Sʳ Francis Bacon's Naturall history as it concernes, fruit-trees, fruits, and flowers, etc. Oxford, Hen: Hall, for Thomas Robinson. 1658. 19×15 cm. 4°. pp. [viii], 46, [2].
Copies: LBM; LBMNH; KRBG; HRES.

4. The spirituall use of an orchard, or garden of fruit-trees. Set forth in divers similitudes . . . The second impression; with the addition of many similitudes, etc. Oxford, Hen: Hall, for Tho. Robinson. 1657. 19×14 cm. 4°. pp. [xx], 208.

In the preface to *The spirituall use of an orchard* reference is made to 'the first part of this work' i.e. Austen's *Treatise of fruit-trees* (1657). The two parts are distinct although, according to the title-page of the *Treatise* of 1657, the second part may be annexed to the first part. *See* Madan (F.), *Oxford books*, etc. **3**: Entry 2327 and 2328 (1931) Oxford.
Copy: BH.

5. A treatise of fruit-trees shewing the manner of grafting, setting, pruning, and ordering of them . . . With the alimentall and physicall vse of fruits. Togeather with the spirituall vse of an orchard, etc. Oxford, for Tho. Robinson. 1653. 19×14 cm. 4°. pp. [xxiv], 97 [i.e. 95], [1]; [xii], 41 [i.e. 39], [1].
The title-page is engraved.
'The spirituall vse of an orchard' has a separate title-page with no imprint or date, and its own pagination.
Copies: LBM; LRHS; HRES.

6. — A treatise of fruit-trees . . . With the alimentall, and physicall use of fruits . . . To which may be annexed the second part, viz. The spirituall use of an orchard . . . The second edition; with the addition of many new experiments, and observations, etc. Oxford, Henry Hall, for Thomas Robinson. 1657. 19×14 cm. 4°. pp. [xxiv], 140; [xx], 208.
The above edition (1657) has a letterpress title-page, and an additional title-page, engraved.
'The spirituall use of an orchard' has a separate title-page with imprint and date, and its own pagination.
Copies: LBM; LCPG; KRBG; HRES.

7. — A treatise of fruit-trees . . . Whereunto is annexed, Observations upon Sʳ Fran. Bacons Natural history, as it concerns fruit-trees, fruits, and flowers . . . The third impression, revised, with additions, etc. Oxford, William Hall, for Amos Curteyne. 1665. 14×9 cm. 8°. pp. [xlviii], 260; [x], 82.
On the verso of the leaf facing the title-page is a longitudinal half-title, reading 'Austen of fruit-trees', the recto of this leaf is blank.

'Observations upon Sᵣ Fran. Bacons Natural history' has a separate title-page and pagination.
Copies: LBM; CUL.

B., J.

8. Herefordshire orchards, a pattern for all England. Written in an epistolary address to Samuel Hartlib Esq; by J. B. [i.e. John Beale.] London, Roger Daniel. 1657. 15×9 cm. 8°. pp. [ii], 62.
Copies: LBM; OBL.

9. — [Another edition.] London, W. Mears. 1724. 20×13 cm. 8°. pp. [ii], 36.
Copies: LBM; LRHS; OBL.

10. — [Another edition.] Dublin, George Grierson. 1724. 19×12 cm. 8°. pp. 30, [2], 7, [1].
Copy: LBM.

— See BRADLEY (R.) New improvements of planting and gardening . . . To which is added . . . Herefordshire-orchards (by J. B. [i.e. J. Beale]). 1724, etc. 8°.

BACON (FRANCIS) Viscount St. Albans [1561–1626]

Observations upon some part of Sᵣ Francis Bacon's Naturall history as it concerns, fruit-trees, fruits, and flowers, etc. See AUSTEN (R.) 1658. 4°.

— See AUSTEN (R.) A treatise of fruit trees . . . Whereunto is annexed Observations upon Sᵣ Fran. Bacons Natural history, as it concerns fruit-trees fruits, and flowers, etc. 1665. 8°.

BEALE (JOHN) [1603–1682?]

Herefordshire orchards, a pattern for all England. Written in an epistolary address to Samuel Hartlib Esq; by J. B. [i.e. J. Beale.] See B., J. 1657. 8°.

— [Another edition.] 1724. 8°.

— [Another edition.] Dublin. 1724. 8°.

— See BRADLEY (R.) New improvements of planting and gardening . . . To which is added . . . Herefordshire-orchards (by J. B. [i.e. J. Beale]). 1724, etc. 8°.

Nurseries, orchards, profitable gardens, and vineyards encouraged . . . In several letters . . .

to Henry Oldenburgh . . . The first letter from Anthony Lawrence; all the rest from John Beale, etc. See LAWRENCE (A.) 1677. 4°.

BELLINGHAM (CHARLES)

The garden of Eden, etc. See PLATT (Sir H.) Floraes Paradise, etc. [Another edition.] The garden of Eden, etc. [Edited by C. Bellingham.] 1653, etc. 8°.

BLAGRAVE (JOSEPH) [1610–1682]

11. Blagrave's supplement or enlargement, to Mr. Nich. Culpeppers English physitian . . . To which is annexed, a new tract for the cure of wounds made by gun-shot or otherways, etc. London, for Obadiah Blagrave. 1674. 17×11 cm. 8°. pp. [iv], 237, [17], 46.
Copies: LBM; LWML; KRBG; CUL.

12. — The second impression. London, for Obadiah Blagrave. 1677. 16×10 cm. 8°. pp. [iv], 237, [17], 46: frontis.
'The second impression' consists of the original printed sheets with a new title-page and the addition of a frontispiece. Regarding an earlier appearance of the frontispiece, see above, History, p. 90.
The copy of this work of 1677 in the library of the Yale University School of Medicine has no frontispiece. (Information supplied by the Yale Historical Librarian in epist. 23.vii.68.)
Copies: GUL; [YUL].

BLAKE (STEPHEN)

13. The compleat gardeners practice, directing the exact way of gardening. In three parts. The garden of pleasure, physical garden, kitchin garden. How they are to be ordered for their best situation and improvement, with variety of artificial knots for the beautifying of a garden (all engraven in copper), etc. London, for Thomas Pierrepoint. 1664. 19×14 cm. 4°. pp. [xvi], 154, [6]: 30 pls.
Copies: LBM; LRHS; OBL; CUBG.

BOBART (JACOB) [1600?–1680]

Catologus [sic] plantarum Horti medici oxoniensis, etc. [By J. Bobart.] See OXFORD.— UNIVERSITY.—Botanic garden. 1648. 8°.

— [Another issue.] 1648. 8°.

— [Another edition.] Catalogus Horti botanici oxoniensis . . . Adhibitis . . . in consilium D.

Boberto, etc. **See** Oxford.—University.— *Botanic garden*. 1658. 8°.

BOBART (Jacob) *the Younger* [1641–1719]
Catalogus Horti botanici oxoniensis . . . Adhibitis . . . in consilium D. Boberto patre . . . ejusque filio, etc. **See** Oxford.—University.—*Botanic garden.* Catologus [*sic*] plantarum Horti medici oxoniensis, etc. [Another edition.] 1658. 8°.

Historiæ naturalis sciagraphia [by J. Bobart the Younger]. **See** Historiæ Naturalis Sciagraphia. 1720. 8°.

Plantarum historiæ universalis oxoniensis pars tertia seu herbarum distributio nova . . . post auctoris mortem . . . absolvit Jacobus Bobartius, etc. **See** Morison (R.) 1699. fol.

BOCCONE (Paolo, afterwards Silvio) [1633–1704]
14. Icones & descriptiones rariorum plantarum Siciliæ, Melitæ, Galliæ, & Italiæ, etc. [Edited, and with a dedication by Robert Morison.] [Oxford], e Theatro Sheldoniano. 1674. 23 × 17 cm. 4°. pp. [xvi], 96: engr. on tp., 52 engravings in text.
Copies: LBM; LBMNH; LRHS; LLS; LWML; LPS; KRBG; OBL; OMaC; CUL; PBN.
A few copies of the above work of 1674 contain an additional leaf bearing a dedication to the Royal Society signed by Boccone. The pagination of these copies is pp. [xviii], 96.
Copies: LRS; LCPG; BH.

BOCCONE (Silvio)
See Boccone (Paolo, afterwards Silvio)

BOKE.
See Book.

BONNEFONS (Nicolas de)
The French gardiner: instructing how to cultivate all sorts of fruit-trees, and herbs for the garden . . . first written [under the title of 'Le jardinier françois', etc.] by R.D.C.D.W.B.D.N. [i.e. N. de Bonnefons] and now transplanted into English by Philocepos [i.e. John Evelyn], etc. **See** N., R.D.C.D.W.B.D. 1658. 12°.

— [Another issue.] 1658. 12°.

— [Another issue.] 1658. 12°.

— [Another edition.] The French gardiner . . . written originally in French [by N. de Bonnefons], and now transplanted into English, by John Evelyn, etc. **See** French Gardiner. 1669. 8°.

— Ed. 3. 1672. 8°.

— Ed. 3. 1675. 8°.

— Ed. 4. 1691. 12°.

BOOK.
15. A booke of the art and maner, howe to plante and graffe all sortes of trees, how to set stones, and sow pepynes to make wylde trees to graffe on . . . with diuerse other newe practises, by one of the abbey of S. Vincent in Fraunce [i.e. D. Brossard] . . . With an addition . . . of certayne Dutche practises, sette forth and englished, by Leonarde Mascal. [A translation of 'L'Art & maniere de semer, ₹ faire pepinieres des sauuageaux, enter de toutes sortes darbres ₹ faire vergiers'.] London, Henry Bynneman for Iohn Wight. [1569.] 19 × 13 cm. 4°. pp. [xxiv], 90, [10]: woodcut on tp., illust., 𝔅.𝔏.
Some copies are dated '1589' on page [xxii] i.e. at the end of 'An exhortation to the planter and graffer'. Other copies have no date.
The book was entered in the Register of the Company of Stationers of London during the period 22 July 1568–22 July 1569.
Copies: LBM (imperfect); CFM; HRES.

16. — [Another edition.] London, Henrie Denham, for Iohn Wight. [1572.] 18 × 14 cm. 4°. pp. [xxiv], 90, [10]: woodcut on tp., illust., 𝔅.𝔏.
'An exhortation to the planter and graffer' (pp. [xix–xxii]) is dated 1572.
Copies: LBM; LRHS.

17. — [Another edition.] London, for Iohn VVight. 1575. 18 × 14 cm. 4°. pp. [xxii], 88, [10]: woodcut on tp., illust., 𝔅.𝔏.
Copies: LBM; HRES.

18. — [Another edition.] London, for Ihon Wight. 1582. 19 × 14 cm. 4°. pp. [xxiv], 84, [12]: woodcut on tp., illust., 𝔅.𝔏.
The last leaf P4 (i.e. pp. [11–12]) is blank, except for the publisher's device, with colophon below, on the recto.
Copies: LBM; HRES.

19. — [Another edition.] London, T. Este, for Thomas Wight. 1590. 19 × 14 cm. 4°. pp. [xxiv], 84, [10]: woodcut on tp., illust., 𝕭.𝕷.

Copy: CUL.

20. — [Another edition.] London, T. East, for Thomas VVight. 1592. 18 × 13 cm. 4°. pp. [xxiv], 84, [10]: woodcut on tp., illust., 𝕭.𝕷.

Copy: LBM.

21. — [Another edition.] London, 1596. 18 × 13 cm. 4°. pp. [xxiv], 84, [10]: woodcut on tp., illust., 𝕭.𝕷.

Copies: LBM; OCCC.

22. — [Another edition.] London, T. Este for Thomas Wight. 1599. 17 × 13 cm. 4°. pp. [xxiv], 84, [10]: woodcut on tp., illust., 𝕭.𝕷.

Copy: CTH.

— [Another edition.] The country-mans recreation . . . in three bookes. The first [by D. Brossard, translated by L. Mascall], etc. **See** COUNTRY-MANS RECREATION. 1640. 4°.

— [Another edition.] 1654. 4°.

— [Another edition.] The country-mans new art of planting and graffing, etc. [By D. Brossard, translated by L. Mascall.] **See** COUNTRY-MANS NEW ART. 1651. 4°.

— [Another edition.] 1651. 4°.

— [Another edition.] 1652. 4°.

— [Another edition.] 1656. 4°.

23. Here begynneth the boke of the arte or crafte of graffynge and plantyng of trees. [1565?] 18 × 14 cm. 4°. Signn. A–B⁴, woodcut on tp., 𝕭.𝕷.

Colophon: Imprinted at London in Lothbery . . . by me Wyllyam Copland.

Copy: HRES.

For earlier editions **see** CRAFT. The craft of graffing and planting of trees [1563?], etc. 4°.

BOOKE.

See BOOK.

BROSSARD (DAVY)

A booke of the art and maner, howe to plante and graffe all sortes of trees, how to set stones,

and sow pepynes to make wylde trees to graffe on . . . with diuerse other newe practises, by one of the abbey of S. Vincent in Fraunce [i.e. D. Brossard] . . . With an addition . . . of certayne Dutche practises, sette forth and englished, by Leonarde Mascal. [A translation of 'L'Art & maniere de semer, 𝑡 faire pepinieres de sauuageaux, enter de toutes sortes darbres 𝑡 faire vergiers'.] See BOOK. [1569.] 4°.

— [Another edition.] [1572.] 4°.

— [Another edition.] 1575. 4°.

— [Another edition.] 1582. 4°.

— [Another edition.] 1590. 4°.

— [Another edition.] 1592. 4°.

— [Another edition.] 1596. 4°.

— [Another edition.] 1599. 4°.

— [Another edition.] The country-mans recreation . . . in three bookes. The first [by D. Brossard, translated by L. Mascall], etc. **See** COUNTRY-MANS RECREATION. 1640. 4°.

— [Another edition.] 1654. 4°.

— [Another edition.] The country-mans new art of planting and graffing, etc. [By D. Brossard, translated by L. Mascall.] **See** COUNTRY-MANS NEW ART. 1651. 4°.

— [Another edition.] 1651. 4°.

— [Another edition.] 1652. 4°.

— [Another edition.] 1656. 4°.

BROWNE (WILLIAM) [1629?–1678] and STEPHENS (P.)

Catalogus Horti botanici oxoniensis . . . Curâ & operâ sociâ Philippi Stephani . . . et Gulielmi Brounei . . . Adhibitis etiam in consilium D. Boberto patre . . . ejusque filio, etc. **See** OXFORD.—UNIVERSITY.—*Botanic garden.* Catologus [*sic*] plantarum Horti medici oxoniensis, etc. [Another edition.] 1658. 8°.

C., W.

A booke of the properties of herbes, called an herball . . . Also a generall rule of all maner of herbes, drawen out of an auncient booke of

physycke by VV.C. **See** HERBAL. Here bygynnyth a newe mater, etc. [Another edition.]
A booke of the properties of herbes, etc.
[*c.* 1550.] 8°.

— [Another edition.] [1552?] 8°.

— [Another edition.] [1560?] 8°.

— [Another issue.] [1560?] 8°.

— [Another edition.] [1560?] 8°.

— [Another issue.] [1560?] 8°.

— [Another issue.] [1560?] 8°.

CAMBRIDGE.

24. Catalogus plantarum circa Cantabrigiam
nascentium: in qua exhibentur quotquot hactenus inventæ sunt, quæ vel sponte proveniunt,
vel in agris seruntur; una cum synonymis
selectioribus, locis natalibus & observationibus
quibusdam oppido raris. Adjiciuntur in gratiam
tyronum, index anglo-latinus, index locorum,
etymologia nominum, & explicatio quorundam
terminorum. [By John Ray.] Cantabrigiæ,
excudebat Joann. Field, impensis Gulielmi
Nealand. 1660. 14×9 cm. 8°. pp. [xxx], 182;
[ii], 103, [1].

Copies: LBM; LBMNH; LRS; OBL; CBS.

According to Keynes (G.), *John Ray, a bibliography*,
1–2 (1951), copies originally had the first leaf blank.
When the errors in the latinity of the title (on the
second leaf) were discovered, a cancel title-page was
printed on the first leaf, reading *Catalogus . . . in quo
exhibentur . . . index anglico*, etc.

Copies with both titles: LBM; LLS; CBS.

Copies with corrected title only: LBM; LRHS;
LLS; LCPG; KRBG; OBL; CBS.

25. — [Another issue.] Londini, apud Jo.
Martin, Ja. Allestry, Tho. Dicas. 1660.
14×9 cm. 8°. pp. [xxx], 182; [ii], 103, [1].

This issue has a cancel title-page.

Copies: LBM; LBMNH; OBL.

26. — Appendix ad catalogum plantarum circa
Cantabrigiam nascentium: continens addenda
et emendanda. [By John Ray.] Cantabrigiæ,
excudebat Joan. Field, impensis Gulielmi
Morden. 1663. 14×9 cm. 8°. Signn. ¶⁶T².

It was apparently intended to add this 'Appendix'
to unsold copies of the *Catalogus plantarum. See*
Keynes (G.), op. cit. 7.

Copies: LBM; OBL; CBS.

27. — Appendix ad catalogum plantarum circa
Cantabrigiam nascentium: continens addenda
& emendanda. Editio secunda, aucta plantis
sexaginta. Cantabrigiæ, ex officina Joh. Hayes.
1685. 14×9 cm. 8°. Signn. A–B⁸.

According to Raven (C. E.), *John Ray naturalist*,
122, footnote 2 (1950) this second edition of the
'Appendix' is not Ray's work.

Copies: LBM; LCPG; KRBG; CBS.

CERTAINE EXCELLENT AND NEW INVENTED KNOTS AND MAZES.

28. Certaine excellent and new inuented knots
and mazes, for plots for gardens, etc. ([colophon:]
London, for Iohn Marriott. 1623.) 18×14 cm.
4°. pp. 19, [1]: illust.

The above title appears at the head of page 1. There
is no title-page. The work consists of diagrams with
captions; there is no letterpress. The last page contains a notice to the reader, signed 'I. M.', and
beneath is the colophon reading 'London printed for
Iohn Marriott . . . 1623'.

Copies: LBM; OBL.

CH., R.

29. An olde thrift newly reuiued. Wherein is
declared the manner of planting, preseruing,
and husbanding yong trees of diuers kindes
for timber and fuell . . . also the vse of a small
portable instrument for measuring of board,
and the solid content and height of any tree
standing. Discoursed in dialogue betweene a
surueyour, woodward, gentleman, and a farmer
. . . by R. C., etc. [With a preface by R. Ch.,
i.e. Rocke Church?] London, W. S. for Richard
Moore. 1612. 18×13 cm. 4°. pp. [vi], 108,
[4]: 1 pl., illust., 𝔅.𝔏.

B2 (i.e. pp. 3–4), D3 (i.e. pp. 21–22), K3–4 (i.e.
pp. 69–72) were cancelled, and cancels substituted.
The compiler has not seen B2 or K3–4 in their
original state, but D3 was doubtless reprinted, as,
after the words 'odious to farmers' in line 21 on the
recto, there is an opprobrious passage of one and
a half lines, beginning 'as sharking catch-poles', etc.
(*See* copy in the Bodleian Library, Oxford, 4°. D. 17
Art.) The late Dr. F. S. Ferguson told the compiler
that in an auction room some years ago he saw a copy
of *An olde thrift newly reuiued* with an extra leaf
signed ✱. This contained an address 'To the friendly
reader', signed A. D., written from the Inner Temple,
10 Oct. 1612. A copy with such a leaf is in the
Arnold Arboretum collection, deposited in the
Houghton Library of Harvard University. This
work has been attributed in the Catalogue of the
Bodleian Library, Oxford, to R. Chambers, but the
attribution has, in the course of revising the Catalogue, been discarded for lack of supporting evidence.

It has also been attributed to R. Churton (*see* McDonald (D.), *Agricultural writers, from . . . 1200–1800, etc.* 202 (1908)) but the compiler can find no evidence for this attribution. She considers there is reason for supposing the author to be Rocke Church. *See above, History,* p. 115.

Copies: LBM; LUL; KRBG; HRES; OBL; [Harv CL].

CLARIDGE (JOHN)

The shepherd of Banbury's rules to judge of the changes of the weather . . . By John Claridge. **See** REID (J.) The Scots gardiner, etc. 1756, etc. 12°.

COLE (WILLIAM)

See COLES.

COLES (WILLIAM) [1626–1662]

30. Adam in Eden: or, natures paradise. The history of plants, fruits, herbs and flowers. With their several names, whether Greek, Latin or English; the places where they grow; their descriptions and kinds . . . also their several signatures, anatomical appropriations, and particular physical vertues; together with necessary observations on the seasons of planting, and gathering of our English simples, etc. London, J. Streater, for Nathaniel Brooke. 1657. 27 × 18 cm. fol. pp. [xx], 629 [i.e. 591], [25].

The last leaf (i.e. pp. [24–25]) contains a list of books 'printed for Nath. Brook', and is signed Rrrr instead of Pppp4, as would have been expected. On account of the pagination being very irregular, the following collation by signatures is given: A^2 [a]⁴ (b)⁴ B–T⁴ T^2 U–Z⁴ Aa–Tt⁴ Aaa–Ooo⁴ Ppp¹ Aaaa–Hhhh⁴ Iiii¹ Aaaaa–Kkkkk⁴ Lllll–Ooooo² Ppppp³ Rrrrr¹.

Copies: LBM; LBMNH; LRHS; LRCS; KRBG.

31. The art of simpling. An introduction to the knovvledge and gathering of plants . . . Whereunto is added, a discovery of the lesser world, etc. London, J. G. for Nath. Brook. 1656. 13 × 8 cm. 12°. pp. [xvi], 175, [1].

A 'discovery of the lesser world' has its own title-page reading: 'Perspicillum microcosmologicum: or, a prospective for the discovery of the lesser world. Wherein man is in a compendium; theologically, philosophically, and anatomically described, and compared with the universe.'

The collation of the above work has been made from the copy in the Thomason collection of tracts, Brit. Mus. (Bloomsbury) (E.1698). George Thomason wrote on the title-pages of many of his tracts the date when they came into his possession, and his

copy of *The art of simpling* (1656) is dated in manuscript 'March 25'.

The pagination of the work is very irregular, a collation by signatures reads as follows: A⁸ B–H¹² I⁴.

Copy: LBM.

32. — [Another edition.] London, J. G. for Nath: Brook. 1656. 13 × 8 cm. 12°. pp. [xxiv], 175, [1].

The above edition differs from the previous work of 1656 only in having a gathering of four leaves (a⁴), consisting of a dedication to Elias Ashmole and a list of errata, inserted between A1 and A2 (or sometimes between A8 and B1).

Copies: LBM (957.a.21); LWML; KRBG; OBL (Sherard 58); OMaC.

33. — [Another edition.] London, J. G. for Nath. Brook. 1656. 14 × 8 cm. 12°. pp. [xxiv], 175, [1].

In the above edition a1 (the first leaf of the dedication), B1 (i.e. pp. 1–2) and E2–4 (i.e. pp. 75–80) are all cancels; a1 is incorrectly signed a2, E2 is incorrectly signed E3; and E3 and E4 are unsigned.

Copies: LBMNH (D4, i.e. pp. 55–56, is cut out); LPS (the errata leaf a4 is wanting); OBL (Vet. A3. f. 7.—Douce. c. 365). In OBL (Douce. c. 365) the second tract entitled 'Perspicillum microcosmologicum' is wanting.

34. — [Another issue.] London, J. G. for Nath: Brook. 1657. 14 × 8 cm. 12°. pp. [xxiv], 175, [1].

The above issue is made up of the sheets and cancels of the previous issue. The title-page is from the same setting of type with the date changed to 1657.

For further bibliographical details concerning this work *see* Lownes (A. E.), The strange case of Coles vs. Culpeper. *Journ. New York bot. garden.* **41**: 158–166 (1940). *See also Catalogue of botanical books in the collection of Rachel McMasters Miller Hunt* **1**: item 266 (1958).

Copy: LWML.

The copy of the 1657 issue in the Yale University Library does not contain the a⁴ gathering.

COMMELIN (JAN) [1629–1692]

35. The Belgick, or Netherlandish Hesperides. That is. The management, ordering, and use of the limon and orange trees, fitted to the nature and climate of the Netherlands . . . Made English by G. V. N. [from 'Nederlantze Hesperides']. London, for J. Holford, sold by Langly Curtis. 1683. 18 × 11 cm. 8°. pp. [x], 194, [4].

Copies: LBM; LRHS; KRBG.

COMPLEAT PLANTER AND CYDERIST.

36. The compleat planter & cyderist: or, choice collections and observations for the propagating all manner of fruit-trees, and . . . methods . . . for the making and ordering of cyder, and other English-wines. By a lover of planting. London, for Tho. Basset. 1685. 18×12 cm. 8°. pp. [xvi], 256, [8]: illust.

Some authorities have ascribed the above work to William Ellis. The compiler, however, can find no supporting evidence for this attribution. According to G[ough]. (R.), *British topography*, etc. 1: 416 (1780) William Ellis of Little Gaddesden in Hert-fordshire was the author of 'The complete planter and cyderist, or a new method of planting cyder-apple and perry-pear trees, and the most approved way of making cyder', etc. London, 1757. 8°. The similarity between the opening words of these two titles may have caused some bibliographers to confuse the works.

Copy: LBM.

37. — [Another edition.] The compleat planter & cyderist. Together with The art of pruning fruit-trees. In two books . . . By a lover of planting. London, for Thomas Bassett. 1690. 18×11 cm. 8°. pp. [xvi], 256, [8]; [viii], 104, [8]: illust.

The second book has separate pagination, and a title-page reading 'The art of pruning fruit-trees . . . Translated from the French original [i.e. from 'L'Art de tailler les arbres fruitiers', by Nicolas Venette], etc. London, for Tho. Basset. 1685. This work was also published separately. See ART. 1685. 8°.

Copy: HRES.

COOK (MOSES)

38. The manner of raising, ordering, and improving forrest-trees: also, how to plant, make and keep woods, walks, avenues, lawns, hedges, etc. London, for Peter Parker. 1676. 20×15 cm. 4°. pp. [xvi], 204, [4]: 4 pls.

Copies: LBM; KRBG; HRES.

39. — [Another edition.] Whereunto is now added, that ingenious treatise of Mr. Gabriel Plattes, viz. A discovery of subterranean treasure. London, for Peter Parker. 1679. 20×15 cm. 4°. pp. [xvi], 204, [4]; [iv], 24: 4 pls.

'A discovery of subterranean treasure' has a separate title-page and pagination. This treatise did not appear in the 1717 or 1724 editions of Cook's work recorded below.

Copies: LBM; LRHS; HRES.

40. — Ed. 2, very much corrected. London, for Daniel Browne, Andrew Bell, John Darby, etc. 1717. 20×12 cm. 8°. pp. xix, [i], 276: frontis., 4 pls.

Copies: LBM; LRHS; KRBG.

41. — Ed. 3, corrected. London, for Eliz. Bell, John Darby, Arthur Bettesworth, etc. 1724. 19×12 cm. 8°. pp. xx, 273, [3]: frontis., 4 pls.

Copies: LBM; LBMNH.

COTTON (CHARLES) [1630–1687]

42. The planters manual: being instructions for the raising, planting, and cultivating all sorts of fruit-trees . . . By Charles Cotton Esq; [a translation of the French 'Instructions pour les arbres fruictiers. Par M[onsieur]. R. T[riquet]. P[rieur]. D[e]. S[aint]. M[arc]'.]. London, for Henry Brome. 1675. 16×9 cm. 8°. pp. [vi], 139, [5].

There is an additional title-page, engraved.

Copies: LBM; LRHS; KRBG; HRES.

COUNTRY-MANS NEW ART.

43. The country-mans new art of planting and graffing [by D. Brossard, translated by Leonard Mascall] . . . with divers other new experi-ments: practised by Leonard Mascall, etc. London, J. Bell. 1651. 18×14 cm. 4°. pp. [xii], 70: woodcut on tp., illust.

Copies: OBL; CUL.

44. — [Another edition.] London, J. Bell. 1651. 18×14 cm. 4°. pp. [xii], 70: woodcut on tp., illust.

Copies: LPO (BM); HRES.

45. — [Another edition.] London, Jane Bell. 1652. 18×14 cm. 4°. pp. [xii], 70: woodcut on tp., illust.

Copies: LBM; LRHS; KRBG.

46. — [Another edition.] London, Jane Bell. 1656. 18×14 cm. 4°. pp. [xii], 70: woodcut on tp., illust.

Copy: LBM.

For earlier editions see (1) BOOK. A booke of the art and maner, howe to plante and graffe all sortes of trees, etc. [1569], etc. (2) COUNTRY-MANS RECREA-TION. The country-mans recreation . . . in three bookes. The first [by D. Brossard, translated by L. Mascall], etc. 1640, etc.

COUNTRY-MANS RECREATION.

47. The country-mans recreation, or the art of planting, graffing, and gardening, in three bookes. The first [a translation by Leonard Mascall of Davy Brossard's 'L'Art & maniere de semer, *1* faire pepinieres de sauuageaux, enter de toutes sortes darbres *1* faire vergiers', etc.] declaring divers wayes of planting, and graffing . . . The second [Reginald Scot's 'A perfect platforme of a hoppe-garden'] treateth of the hop-garden . . . Whereunto is added, The expert gardener, etc. London, B. Allsop and T. Favvcet for Michael Young. 1640. 17×13 cm. 4°. pp. [xvi], 127, [1]; [ii], 54: illust.

The first book, a translation by L. Mascall, had previously been published under the title of 'A booke of the art and maner, howe to plante and graffe all sortes of trees'. **See** Book. [1569], etc. 4°. The second and third books entitled respectively 'A perfect platforme of a hoppe garden' and 'The expert gardener: or, a treatise containing certaine necessary, secret, and ordinary knowledges in grafting and gardening . . . Faithfully collected out of sundry Dutch and French authors' have separate title-pages, the latter work has also separate pagination. 'The expert gardener' had previously been published under the title of 'The orchard, and the garden'. **See** Orchard. 1594, etc. 4°.

Copies: LBM; LRCS; HRES.

48. — [Another edition.] The country-mans recreation . . . in three books. The first declaring divers waies of planting, and graffing . . . The second treateth of the hop-garden . . . with some directions for tabaco. Whereunto is added, The expert gardener . . . likewise . . . The art of angling [by Thomas Barker]. London, T. Mabb, for William Shears. 1654. 19×14 cm. 4°. pp. [xvi], 135, [1]; [ii], 54; [ii], 18: illust.

The second book ('A perfect platform of a hop-garden'), 'The expert gardener', and 'The art of angling' have separate title-pages dated 1653, 1654 and 1653 respectively, the last two works have also separate pagination.

Copies: LBM; HRES.

COWLEY (Abraham) [1618–1667]

49. A. Couleii plantarum libri duo, etc. [In verse.] Londini, typis J. Flesher, & prostant apud Nath. Brooks. 1662. 15×9 cm. 8°. pp. [xiv], 118.

Copy: LBM.

50. Abrahami Couleij Angli, poemata latina. In quibus continentur, sex libri plantarum, viz. duo herbarum, florum, sylvarum. Et unus miscellaneorum, etc. [Edited, with an introduction, by Thomas Sprat, Bishop of Rochester.] Londini, typis T. Roycroft, impensis Jo. Martyn. 1668. 18×11 cm. 8°. pp. [xxxiv], 420 [i.e. 416]: frontis. (port. of author).

Copies: LBM; LBMNH; LLL; KRBG; OBL.

51. — [Another edition.] Huic editioni secundæ accessit index rerum antehac desideratus. Londini, typis M. Clark, impensis Jo. Martyn. 1678. 15×9 cm. 12°. pp. [xxvi], 343 [i.e. 345], [13]: frontis. (port. of author).

Copies: LBM; OBL.

CRAFT.

52. The craft of graffing and planting of trees. [1563?] 17×13 cm. 4°. Signn. A–B⁴, woodcut on tp., **B.L.**

Colophon: Imprynted at London in Lothbery . . . by me Wyllyam Copland.

The compiler obtained the above details from the photographic facsimile of this work in the Brit. Mus. (Bloomsbury) taken from an original lent by Messrs. Quaritch in 1926. It is a later edition of a treatise in the Brit. Mus. (Bloomsbury) (C.122. bb.42), entitled *The crafte of graffynge 1 plantynge of trees* [n.p., n.d.]. This copy wants all after signature A4. According to information given to the compiler by the late Dr. F. S. Ferguson, the printer of this imperfect copy was Wynkyn de Worde, the publication date being about 1520. The ribbon factotum and type ornaments on the title-page, the initial letter T on the first page of the text, and the type, are all those used by Wynkyn de Worde.

— [Another edition.] **See** Book. Here begynneth the boke of the arte or crafte of graffynge and plantyng of trees. [1565?] 4°.

CULPEPER (Nicholas) [1616–1654]

53. The English physitian: or an astrologo-physical discourse of the vulgar herbs of this nation. Being a compleat method of physick, whereby a man may preserve his body in health; or cure himself, being sick, etc. London, Peter Cole. 1652. 26×17 cm. fol. pp. [xiv], 255 [i.e. 159], [5]: frontis. (port. of author).

Copies: LBM; LWML; LRCP; OMaC.

As far as possible with Culpeper's *English physitian* the compiler has checked line endings and pagination in each of the copies listed below. Quite frequently parts of certain copies appear to have been printed from standing type while other parts were newly set. Such copies have normally been described as 'another edition', rather than as 'another issue'.

54. — [Another edition.] London, William Bentley. 1652. 13×7 cm. 12°. pp. [xxiv], 266 [i.e. 276], [12]: frontis. (port. of author).

The above edition 'is in twelves, of the letter smal Bibles use to be printed on'. Thus wrote Culpeper in *The English physitian enlarged* (1653) (*see* 'To the reader', where the author also denounced this edition as being 'very falsly printed' and 'counterfet'). The above edition of 1652, and the issue below of 1652, are identical except for the imprint on the title-page. This was probably changed because the printer 'William Bentley' wished to conceal his name. The 276 pages of text are numbered 1–51, [52], 53–82, 81, 84–136, [137], 138–188, 179–214, 217, 216–266.

Copies: LWML; KRBG.

55. — [Another issue.] London, printed for the benefit of the commonwealth of England. 1652. 13×7 cm. 12°. pp. [xxiv], 266 [i.e. 276], [12]: frontis. (port. of author).

Copies: LBM; LBMNH; LWML; RSM.

56. — [Another edition.] London, printed for the commonwealth of England. 1652. 13×7 cm. 12°. pp. [xxiv], 266 [i.e. 276], [12].

In the above edition of 1652 the 276 pages of text are numbered 1–192, 183–266.

The only copy of this edition seen, so far, by the compiler, is in the library of the Royal College of Physicians of London. This copy has no frontispiece and it lacks Bb3–4 (i.e. pp. [5–8]). It is very badly printed and is possibly a counterfeit of the preceding pirated edition.

Copy: LRCP.

57. — [Another edition.] The English physitian enlarged: with three hundred, sixty, and nine medicines made of English herbs that were not in any impression until this, etc. London, Peter Cole. 1653. 17×11 cm. 8°. pp. [xxiv], 398 [i.e. 288], [16].

The first leaf B1 (i.e. pp. [i–ii]) is blank but for the printer's device on the verso. Leaf C8 (i.e. pp. [xxiii–xxiv]) is blank but for a longitudinal half-title on the recto, reading: 'Culpepers English physitian enlarged'.

The 288 pages of text are numbered 1–173, 284–286, 187–191, 292–398.

Copy: LBM.

From 1653 until 1790 inclusive a number of editions of *The English physitian* were issued with no signature A or with no signature B, while a few editions appeared with no signature A or B.

58. — [Another edition.] London, Peter Cole. 1653. 16×11 cm. 8°. pp. [xviii], 398 [i.e. 288], [16].

The collation of the above work of 1653 has been made from the copy in the Brit. Mus. (Bloomsbury) (988.a.7). Sign. B consists of four leaves, the first blank and therefore not included in the above collation. Sign. C consists of six leaves (i.e. pp. [vii–xviii]). The verso of C6 headed 'The names of several books printed by Peter Cole', etc., has a catchword 'Eight', while the first word on the recto of D1 (i.e. p. 1) is 'The'. In the copy of this edition in the Yale Historical Medical Library, Sign. C has seven leaves. The headline of C7 reads 'Books printed by Peter Cole', etc., and the first word of C7 (recto) is 'Eleven'. The catchword on C7 (verso) matches the first word on the recto of D1. (Information supplied to the compiler by the Librarian of the Yale historical collections, in epist. 16.vi.66.) A copy similar to that at Yale with an inserted engraved portrait of the author facing the title-page, was at one time in the library of the Society of Herbalists of London (*see* Sotheby's catalogue of books sold 13 March 1967, item 73). In this copy C8 (perhaps a longitudinal half-title) is indicated by a ragged stub between C7 and D1. Apart from the preliminary matter this work and the issues below of 1655 and 1656 are identical, and the 288 pages are numbered 1–131, 110, 133–173, 284–288, 189, 290–398.

Copies: LBM; [YUL].

59. — [Another issue.] London, Peter Cole. 1655. 17×11 cm. 8°. pp. [xx], 398 [i.e. 288].

The only copy of the work of 1655 seen, so far, by the compiler is in the Wellcome Historical Medical Library, a collation of which is given above. This copy is imperfect wanting the first leaf B1 (blank?), C8 indicated by a ragged stub between C7 and D1 (longitudinal half-title?), and all after p. 398. It appears that the title-page is a cancel.

Copy: LWML.

60. — [Another issue.] London, Peter Cole. 1656. 17×11 cm. 8°. pp. [xxiv], 398 [i.e. 288], [16].

Leaf C8 (i.e. pp. [xxiii–xxiv]) is blank but for a longitudinal half-title on the recto. It reads 'Culpepers English physitian enlarged'.

Copies: LWML; LRSM; LRCP; LPS.

61. — [Another edition.] London, Peter Cole, 1656. 17×10 cm. 8°. pp. [xxiv], 398 [i.e. 288]. [16].

The leaf preceding the title-page has on the recto a longitudinal half-title reading 'Culpepers English physitian enlarged'. The verso is blank. The 288 pages of text are numbered 1–106, 10, 108–173, 284–389, 393, 391–398.

Copies: LRSM; LRCS; OBL.

62. — [Another edition.] London, Peter Cole, 1656. 17×11 cm. 8°. pp. [xxiv], 398 [i.e. 288]. [16].

The 288 pages of text are numbered 1–173, 284–285, 176, 287–398.
Copies: LBM; LPS.

63. — [Another edition.] London, Peter Cole. 1656. 17 × 10 cm. 8°. pp. [xviii], 398 [i.e. 288], [16].

The collation of the above work of 1656 has been made from the copy in the Brit. Mus. (Bloomsbury).

The verso of the title-page is blank except for a line of printers' flowers beneath which is the heading 'To the reader' followed by the first five lines of this preface. The 288 pages are numbered 1–173, 184, 285, 176, 287–398. The same errors in pagination are found in the issue below of 1661 and in the work of 1665. In these two issues, however, the title-page (blank on the verso) is followed by three leaves with lists of books printed by Peter Cole, at the end of which are the opening lines of 'To the reader', making a total of twenty-four preliminary pages.
Copy: LBM.

64. — [Another issue.] London, Peter Cole. 1661. 17 × 10 cm. 8°. pp. [xxiv], 398 [i.e. 288], [16].

With a cancel gathering of preliminary leaves, B4.
Copy: LBM.

65. — [Another edition.] London, Peter Cole. 1661. 16 × 10 cm. 8°. pp. [xxiv], 398 [i.e. 288], [16].

The copy of the above work of 1661 in the Wellcome Historical Medical Library is imperfect, wanting C1–2 (i.e. pp. [ix–xii]) and X–Y8 (i.e. pp. 335–366). Apart from the preliminary matter the above edition of 1661 and the work below of 1662 are identical and the 288 pages are numbered 1–173, 284–285, 176, 287–398.
Copy: LWML.

66. — [Another issue.] London, Peter Cole. 1662. 17 × 10 cm. 8°. pp. [xxiv], 398 [i.e. 288], [16].
Copy: LWML.

67. — [Another edition.] London, Peter Cole. 1665. 17 × 11 cm. 8°. pp. [xxiv], 398 [i.e. 288], [16].

A reissue of the edition of 1656 which was subsequently reissued in 1661. It has a different cancel gathering of preliminary leaves, B4.
Copy: LBM.

68. — [Another edition.] London, John Streater. 1666. 17 × 11 cm. 8°. pp. [xiv], 285, [17].
Copies: LBM; LRSM; LRCS.

69. — [Another edition.] London, John Streater. 1669. 16 × 10 cm. 8°. pp. [xiv], 285, [19].
Copies: LBM; LWML.

70. — [Another edition.] London, John Streater. 1671. 17 × 11 cm. 8°. pp. [xiv], 285, [19].
Copy: LBM.

71. — [Another edition.] London, for George Sawbridge. 1674. 17 × 11 cm. 8°. pp. [xiv], 285, [19].
Copies: LBM; LWML; LRSM; LRCS.

72. — [Another edition.] London, for George Sawbridge. 1676. 17 × 11 cm. 8°. pp. [xiv], 285, [19].
Copies: LBM; LWML.

73. — [Another edition.] London, for George Sawbridge. 1681. 17 × 11 cm. 8°. pp. [xiv], 285, [19].
Copies: LBM; LWML; KRBG; OBL.

74. — [Another edition.] London, for Hannah Sawbridge, sold by Tho. Malthus. 1683. 17 × 11 cm. 8°. pp. [xiv], 285, [19].

In the above edition of 1683, and in the issue below of 1683, the 285 pages of text are numbered very irregularly.
Copy: LBM.

75. — [Another issue.] London, for Hannah Sawbridge. 1683. 18 × 11 cm. 8°. pp. [xiv], 285, [19].

The above issue of 1683 differs from the preceding work of 1683 only in the imprint. This reads 'London, printed for Hannah Sawbridge, and are to be sold at the Bible on Lud-gate-hill. 1683' instead of 'London, printed for Hannah Sawbridge, and are to be sold by Tho. Malthus at the Sun in the Poultrey, 1683'.
Copy: PBN.

76. — [Another issue.] London, for Hannah Sawbridge, sold by John Taylor. 1684. 17 × 11 cm. 8°. pp. [xiv], 285, [19].

The above issue has a cancel title-page. Apart from the title-page and further errors in pagination the above work of 1684 is identical with the previous two issues of 1683.
Copies: LWML; OBL.

77. — [Another edition.] London, for Hannah Sawbridge. 1684. 17 × 11 cm. 8°. pp. [xiv], 285, [17].

In this edition (1684) the pages are numbered con-
secutively 1–285. The copy in the library of the
Royal College of Surgeons of England originally
belonged to Rudyard Kipling who gave a portrayal
of Nicholas Culpeper, the physician-astrologer, in
'A doctor of medicine', one of the tales in *Rewards
and fairies* (1910).
Copy: LRCS.

78. — [Another edition.] London, for A. and
J. Churchill. 1695. 17×11 cm. 8°. pp. [xii],
284, [16].
Copies: LBM; LWML.

79. — [Another edition.] London, for A. and
J. Churchill. 1698. 17×11 cm. 8°. pp. [xii],
284, [16].
Copy: LWML.

80. — [Another edition.] London, for A. and
J. Churchill. 1703. 16×10 cm. 12°. pp. [xvi],
386, [10].
Copies: LRCP; KRBG.

81. — [Another edition.] London, for J.
Churchill. 1714. 16×10 cm. 12°. pp. [xvi],
386, [10].
Copies: LBM; LRHS; LWML; LPS.

82. — [Another edition.] London, for W.
Churchill. 1718. 16×10 cm. 12°. pp. [xvi], 386,
[10].
Copies: LBM; LWML; LUL; OBL.

83. — [Another edition.] London, for Tho.
Norris; A. Bettesworth; J. Batley, etc. 1725.
16×10 cm. 12°. pp. [xii], 386, [10].
Copies: LBM; LWML.

84. — [Another edition.] London, for A.
Bettesworth, C. Hitch, J. Battley, etc. 1733.
16×10 cm. 12°. pp. [xii], 386, [10].
Copies: LBM; LWML; CUL.

85. — [Another edition.] London, for S. Ballard,
R. Ware, S. Birt, etc. 1741. 16×10 cm. 12°.
pp. [xii], 387, [9].
Copies: LBM; LWML; LRCP.

86. — [Another edition.] London, for S. Ballard,
R. Ware, S. Birt, etc. 1752. 17×10 cm. 12°.
pp. [xii], 387, [9].
Copy: LWML.

87. — [Another edition.] London, for S. and

E. Ballard, C. Hitch and L. Hawes, etc. 1759.
17×10 cm. 12°. pp. [xii], 387, [9].
Copy: LBM.

88. — [Another issue.] London, for S. Ballard,
C. Hitch, L. Hawes, etc. [c. 1760.] 16×10 cm.
12°. pp. [xii], 387, [9].
*The Catalogue of printed books in the Wellcome
historical medical library* gives the date of the above
issue as [c. 1760]. It differs from the preceding work
of 1759 only in the title-page.
Copies: LBM; LWML.

89. — [Another edition.] London, for S. Ballard,
L. Hawes and Co., W. Johnston, etc. 1765.
16×10 cm. 12°. pp. [xii], 387, [9].
Copies: LWML; KRBG.

90. — [Another edition.] London, for E. Ballard,
W. Strahan, R. Baldwin, etc. 1770. 17×10 cm.
12°. pp. [xii], 387, [9].
Copy: LRSM.

91. — [Another issue.] London, for E. Ballard,
L. Hawes and Co., W. Johnston, etc. 1770.
16×10 cm. 12°. pp. [xii], 387, [9].
The above issue differs from the preceding work of
1770 only in the title-page.
Copies: LRCP; ORSL.

92. — [Another edition.] London, for E. Ballard,
L. Hawes and Co., W. Johnston, etc. 1775.
17×10 cm. 12°. pp. [xii], 387, [9].
Copies: LBM; LWML; LRSM; LLL.

93. — [Another edition.] London, for Lacking-
ton, and Denis. 1778. 17×10 cm. 12°. pp. [ii],
18, 407, [1].
Copies: LBM; LWML; LRSM.

94. — [Another issue.] Edinburgh, for Patrick
Anderson. 1778. 17×10 cm. 12°. pp. [ii], 18,
407, [1].
The above issue differs from the preceding work of
1778 only in the title-page.
Copy: LWML.

95. — [Another edition.] London, for J. Bruce,
D. Burnet, R. Hopper, etc. 1784. 18×10 cm.
12°. pp. [xii], 348.
Copies: LBM; LRSM.

96. — [Another edition.] London, printed for
the booksellers. 1785. 17×10 cm. 12°. pp. [xii],
345, [3].
Copies: LBM; LWML.

97. — [Another edition.] Dublin, H. Colbert. 1787. 17×10 cm. 12°. pp. [ii], iv, 418, [14].
Copy: LRCP.

98. — [Another edition.] London, for P. M'Queen, J. Laikington, J. Mathews. 1788. 18×10 cm. 12°. pp. xii, 371, [1].
Copies: LBM; LWML; ORSL.

99. — [Another edition.] London, for J. Barker; R. Banister; J. Deighton, etc. [1788?] 17×11 cm. 12°. pp. [xii], 348.

A copy of the above undated edition is in the Yale Historical Medical Library and the compiler is indebted to the Librarian of the historical collections for the above collation. The only copy of this edition seen, so far, by the compiler is in the Wellcome Historical Medical Library. This copy is imperfect, wanting all after p. 342. *The Catalogue of printed books in the Wellcome historical medical library* gives the date of this work as [1788?]. The Cataloguer of the Yale library has assigned a date of [1800?].

Copies: LWML; [YUL].

The Sibly editions, entitled *Culpeper's English physician; and complete herbal*, first published in 1789 in two quarto volumes bound in one, and *Culpeper's English family physician, etc.* 2 vols. 1792, have been listed for convenience, after *The English physician*. 1799. 12°.

100. — [Another edition.] London, for J. Walker. 1790. 17×10 cm. 12°. pp. [xii], 348.
Copy: LWML.

101. — [Another edition.] London, for A. Law, W. Millar, and R. Cater. 1792. 16×10 cm. 12°. pp. [xii], 345, [3].
A reissue of the edition of 1785.
Copy: LBM.

102. — [Another edition.] London, printed for the booksellers. 1799. 17×10 cm. 12°. pp. xii, 348.
Copies: LRSM; LRCP.

103. — [Another edition.] Leeds, for John Binns. 1799. 17×11 cm. 12°. pp. [xii], 346, [2].
Copy: LRCP.

104. — [Another edition.] Culpeper's English family physician; or, medical herbal enlarged, with several hundred additional plants, principally from Sir John Hill . . . and, A new dispensatory, from the MS. of the late Dr. Saunders . . . By Joshua Hamilton, etc. 2 vols. London, W. Locke. 1792. 21×13 cm. 8°.

1. pp. 186, *187–188*, 187–336, *337–338*, 337–456: frontis. (port. of author), 122 pls. (121 col., 1 uncol.).

2. pp. 72, *73–*74, 73–183, [1], [1], 184–429, [1], 331–378: 83 pls. col.

As suggested under the heading 'Index to the plates, including Directions to the binder' (*see* Vol. **2.** pp. 337 and 342) some copies of the work were bound with all the plates in a third volume, except for eleven plates specifically named for binding in Vol. **1.**

At the end of 'Index to the herbal' (Vol. **2.** p. 374) is a note reading: 'The common edition of this work having been sold at 1s. 6d. without the smallest regard to the colour of the plants, the publisher has, ever since he discovered the deception, printed his plates for colouring on fine white writing paper, wire marked. The common, being wove, and of a different colour, may be easily distinguished. Besides, some attention has been paid to nature, in the fine edition.'

Copies: LBM; LLS; LWML; LRCP; LLL; PBN.

105. — [Another edition.] Culpeper's English physician; and complete herbal. To which are now first added, upwards of one hundred additional herbs, with a display of their medicinal and occult properties . . . Beautified and enriched with engravings of upwards of four hundred and fifty different plants, and a set of anatomical figures. Illustrated with notes and observations . . . By E. Sibly, etc. 2 Vols. [in 1.] London, printed for the author, and sold at the British Directory office, etc. [1789.] 25×20 cm. 4°.

[Vol. **1.**] pp. xvi, 396 [i.e. 398]: frontis. (port. of author), 29 pls.

[Vol. **2.**] pp. [ii], 256: 13 pls.

Sibly's dedication is addressed to 'Thomas Dunckerly, Esq. Provincial Grand Master of the . . . fraternity of free and accepted Masons of Dorset, Essex', etc., and it is dated: 'in the year of Masonry 5793' [i.e. 1789].

The second volume has a separate title-page reading: 'Culpeper's English physician; and complete herbal . . . The medical part . . . London: printed for the author, and sold at the British Directory-office', etc. [n.d.].

In the above edition [1789] and in the issue below of 1789, the 398 pages (Vol. **1**) are numbered 1–74, 67, 76–79, 72, 81–124, 124–131, 131–396.

Copy: LWML.

This edition was apparently originally published in forty-two consecutive numbers or fascicles. Throughout the work at regular intervals are found special signatures. These read, in numerical order, 'No. 1' to 'No. 26' and without the prefixed abbreviation,

27–42. These special signatures which apparently mark the place of each 'number' in the series, are found not only in the above edition but also in all issues and editions of Sibly's work included in the present *Bibliography*. They are also found in the 1805 edition in which there is a notice giving directions 'for binding Dr. Sibly's works in four volumes', Vol. 3 to contain the herbal and Vol. 4 the medical part. In the directions readers are informed that: 'A general title for each volume . . . may be had gratis by those who have taken the whole in numbers and want to bind them uniform, by applying at the publishers.'

106. — [Another issue.] 2 Vols. [in 1.] London, printed for the proprietors, and sold by Green and Co. 1789. 26 × 21 cm. 4°.

[Vol. 1.] pp. xvi, 396 [i.e. 398]: frontis. (port. of author), 29 pls.

[Vol. 2.] pp. [ii], 256: 13 pls.

A reissue of the work of [1789] with a new title-page and the type of the Preface and Introduction reset. The title-page of the second volume is the same as that of the second volume, first issue.

Copies: LWML; CUL (Vol. 1 only).

107. — [Another edition.] 2 Vols. [in 1.] London, printed for the proprietors, and sold by Green and Co. 1789. 26 × 21 cm. 4°.

[Vol. 1.] pp. xvi, 398 [i.e. 400]: frontis. (port. of author), 29 pls. col.

Vol. 2. pp. [ii], 256: 13 pls. printed in red.

The title-page of the second volume reads: 'Culpeper's English physician; and complete herbal . . . Volume the second . . . London: printed for the author, and sold at the British Directory-office', etc. [n.d.].

In the above edition the 400 pages (Vol. 1) are numbered 1–74, 67, 76–79, 72, 81–124, 124–131, 131–398.

Although the errors in pagination in (Vol. 1) of the above edition of 1789 are the same as those in the previous work of 1789, much of the type, from p. 208 onwards (i.e. from No. 15), has been reset, and some omissions have been made (e.g. last 13 words at bottom of p. 244 of previous work omitted, also footnote at bottom of p. 248, and last sentence under heading 'Smallage' on p. 347).

The 'Index to the herbs and plants' (pp. 395–396) is different from this 'Index' in the previous work of 1789 and an 'Index of diseases' (pp. 397–398) has been added. Much of the type of Vol. 2 has been reset, some passages are partly rewritten and p. 197 is almost entirely rewritten.

Sibly's dedication is still dated 'in the year of Masonry 5793'.

Copy: LWML.

108. — [Another edition.] 2 Vols. [in 1.] London, printed for the author, and sold at the British Directory office, etc. [1794.] 27 × 21 cm. 4°.

[Vol. 1.] pp. xvi, 396 [i.e. 398]: frontis. (port. of author), 29 pls. col.

[Vol. 2.] pp. [ii], 256: 13 pls. printed in red.

Sibly's dedication to Thomas Dunckerly, Esq. is dated 'in the year of Masonry 5798'. According to the Librarian of the Grand Lodge Library (in epist. 31.xii.56) at this time Freemasons in England were using two forms of chronology, some adding 4,000 years to the Christian era, and others 4,004. In this particular instance, however, there can be no doubt upon the point as Thomas Dunckerly died late in 1795, and it may be safely assumed that the year of Masonry 5798 is identical with A.D. 1794.

The title-page of the second volume reads: 'Culpeper's English physician; and complete herbal . . . The medical part . . . London: printed for the author, and sold at the British Directory-office', etc.

The 398 pages (Vol. 1) are numbered 1–95, 95, 97–124, 124–127, 129–132, 131*–132*, 133–396.

The above collation was made from the copy of the work in the library of the Royal Botanic Gardens, Kew. Pages 397–398 with the 'Index of diseases', included in the previous edition of 1789, are not found in this copy.

Copy: KRBG.

Nearly every copy, seen by the compiler, of *Culpeper's English physician; and complete herbal . . . By E. Sibly*, with the imprint: 'London: printed for the author, and sold at the British Directory office', etc., and the dedication dated 'in the year of Masonry 5798' has a slightly different collation. Presumably parts were reprinted as necessary and copies were made up from whatever sheets were available at the time. The second volume of most of these copies has a title-page which reads: 'Culpeper's English physician; and complete herbal . . . Volume the second . . . London: printed for the author, and sold at the British Directory-office', etc. But the imprint on the title-page of Volume 2 in the Radcliffe Science Library, Oxford, reads: 'London: printed, by George Sidney, Green arbour court, Old Bailey, for the author, and sold at the British Directory-office', etc. The compiler has been unable to find when George Sidney was in business at this address and his name does not appear under the heading Green Arbour Court in the Sewer Rate Books of 1796, 1797 and 1799 for Faringdon without St. Andrews, Holborn precinct, preserved in the Guildhall Library, London. The only printing-house at this address during the years 1796–99 was that of Robert Hindmarsh. *Holden's triennial directory* 'corrected up to 28 January 1800' records George Sidney, printer, at 27, Leadenhall Street, and according to *Holden's . . . directory for 1805, 1806, 1807*, during these years he was at 1, Northumberland Street, Strand. As Sidney's name does not appear in any of the various rate books up to 1800, or in London directories published previous to this date, seen by the compiler, it appears that he had no business address before he was in Leadenhall Street. Before this time he may have been permitted to use the press of Robert Hindmarsh at Green Arbour Court, and to print the above volume using Hindmarsh's address in the imprint. The pagination of various copies of the first volume of *Culpeper's English physician*, with the imprint 'London: printed for the author, and sold at the British Directory office', is recorded below. The pagination of Vol. 2 including the title-page is [ii], 256, and the total number of plates in the two volumes is a frontispiece and 29 plates (Vol. 1) and 13 plates (Vol. 2).

(1) [Vol. 1.] pp. xvi, 1–52, 35, 54–95, 95, 97–132, 131*–132*, 133–398.

Copy: LWML (Title-page of Vol. 2 is wanting).

(2) [Vol. 1.] pp. xvi, 1–132, 131*–132*, 133–398.
Copy: LLL.

(3) [Vol. 1.] pp. xvi, 1–95, 95, 97–132, 131*–132*, 133–398.

Copy: LBMNH.

(4) [Vol. 1.] pp. xvi, 1–132, 131–194, 183–186, 199–398.

Copy: LPS.

(5) [Vol. 1.] pp. xvi, 1–124, 124–131, 131–132, 123, 134–194, 183–186, 199–210, 112, 212–398.

Copies: LWML (Title-page of Vol. 2 is wanting), Sotheby (sale of 13 March 1967).

(6) [Vol. 1.] pp. xvi, 1–132, 131–398.

Copies: ORSL; Sotheby (sale of 13 March 1967).

Another copy of *Culpeper's English physician* with Sibly's dedication to Thomas Dunckerly dated 'in the year of Masonry 5798', has the imprint 'London: printed for the proprietor, by Lewis and Roden, Paternoster-row; and sold at the British Directory office', etc., on the title-page of the first volume, and 'London: printed, by George Sidney, Green arbour court, Old Bailey, for the author, and sold at the British Directory-office', etc. on the title-page of the second volume. Records indicate that the partnership of Lewis and Roden was of short duration, the Sewer Rate Books date it 1801–2. The pagination of Vol. 2 and the total number of plates in each of the two volumes is the same as previously. The pagination of the first volume is: pp. xvi, 1–132, 131*–132*, 133–398.

Copy: LRHS.

Various editions of Culpeper's work continued to be published throughout the nineteenth century and during the twentieth century until the present day. Fine collections are to be found in this country in the Brit. Mus. (Bloomsbury), and in the Wellcome Historical Medical Library.

— See BLAGRAVE (J.) Blagrave's supplement or enlargement, to Mr. Nich. Culpeppers English physitian, etc. 1674. 8°.

— The second impression. 1677. 8°.

DETHICK (HENRY) [d. 1613?]

The gardeners labyrinth . . . by Dydymus Mountaine. [Completed by H. Dethick.] See MOUNTAIN (DIDYMUS) pseud. [i.e. THOMAS HILL.] 1577. 4°.

— [Another edition.] 1578. 4°.

— [Another edition.] 1586. 4°.

— [Another edition.] 1594. 4°.

— [Another edition.] 1608. 4°.

— [Another edition.] The gardeners labyrinth . . . By D. M. [i.e. Didymus MOUNTAIN.] See M., D. 1652. 4°.

— [Another edition.] 1656. 4°.

— [Another edition.] 1660. 4°.

DETHICKE (HENRY)
See DETHICK (H.)

DIGBY (Sir KENELM) [1603–1665]
109. A discourse concerning the vegetation of plants. Spoken by Sir Kenelme Digby, at Gresham college, on the 23. of January, 1660. At a meeting of the Society for promoting philosophical knowledge by experiments. London, J. G. for John Dakins. 1661. 12×7 cm. 12°. pp. [ii], 100, [2].
Copies: LBM; KRBG; OBL.

DILLENIUS (JOHANNES JACOBUS)
Joannis Raii Synopsis methodica stirpium britannicarum . . . Editio tertia multis locis emendata, etc. [Edited by J. J. Dillenius.] See RAY (J.) 1724. 8°.

— [Another issue.] 2 vols. 1724. 8°.

DODOENS (REMBERT) [1517–1585]
110. A nievve herball, or historie of plantes: wherin is contayned the vvhole discourse and perfect description of all sortes of herbes and plantes . . . First set foorth in the Doutche or Almaigne tongue . . . and nowe first translated out of French into English, by Henry Lyte Esquyer. At London by my [*sic*] Gerard Dewes . . . 1578. 30×19 cm. fol. pp. [xxiv], 779, [25]: title within a woodcut compartment, illust., B.L.

Colophon: Imrinted [*sic*] at Antwerpe, by me

Henry Loë bookeprinter, and are to be solde at London . . . by Gerard Devves.

In most copies of *A nievve herball* (1578) the words 'my' and 'Imrinted' in the imprint and colophon respectively, have been corrected by the printer.

The copy of this work in the Brit. Mus. (Nat. Hist.) has a cancel slip: 'I. H. in laudem tam auctoris', etc. inserted to cover the original verses headed: 'Iohannis Hardingi in laudem', etc.

Copies: LBM; LBMNH; LRHS; LCPG; LWML; KRBG; OBL; CUL; CBS.

111. — [Another edition.] London, Ninian Newton. 1586. 19×14 cm. 4°. pp. [xl], 916, [48]: 𝔅.𝔏.

Copies: LBM; CUL.

112. — [Another edition.] Corrected and amended. London, Edm. Bollifant. 1595. 19×13 cm. 4°. pp. [xl], 916, [48] 𝔅.𝔏.

Copies: LBM; LBMNH; HRES.

113. — [Another edition.] Corrected and amended. London, Edward Griffin. 1619. 29×19 cm. fol. pp. [xxiv], 564 [i.e. 562], [30]: title within a woodcut compartment, 𝔅.𝔏.

Copies: LBM; LBMNH; LRHS; LRCS; KRBG; CBS.

114. Rams little Dodeon. A briefe epitome of the new Herbal, or history of plants . . . translated into English by Henry Lyte . . . and now collected and abbridged by William Ram, etc. London, Simon Stafford. 1606. 18×14 cm. 4°. pp. [xliii], 213. 𝔅.𝔏.

Copies: LBM; LBMNH; LWML; KRBG; CUL.

DROPE (FRANCIS) [1629?–1671]

115. A short and sure guid in the practice of raising and ordering of fruit-trees. Being the many years recreation and experience of Francis Drope, etc. Oxford, for Ric. Davis. 1672. 16×10 cm. 8°. pp. [xiv], 120.

Copies: LBM; LRHS; LRCS; KRBG; CUL.

EDINBURGH. — *Royal botanic garden.* [Founded 1670.]

Hortus medicus edinburgensis, etc. **See** SUTHERLAND (J.) 1683. 8°.

ENGLANDS IMPROVEMENT.

116. Englands improvement, and seasonable advice to all gentlemen and farmers, how to prepare the ground fit for sowing hemp and flax-seed; the nature of it, with directions how to sow it . . . pull it, and preserve the seed . . . with directions for watering, breaking, swingling and preparing it fit to be hachell'd. London, to be had at the booksellers in Westminster-hall. 1691. 19×14 cm. 4°. pp. [ii], 16.

Copies: LBM; HRES.

EVELYN (JOHN) [1620–1706]

117. Acetaria. A discourse of sallers. By J. E., etc. [With a dedication signed: 'John Evelyn'.] London, for B. Tooke. 1699. 16×10 cm. 8°. pp. [xlii], 192, [48]: 1 table.

In some copies of the above work of 1699, and in the issue below of 1706, the errata leaf b4 (i.e. pp. [xli–xlii]) has been bound at the end of the book.

Copies: LBM; LBMNH; LRHS; CUL.

118. — Ed. 2. London, for B. Tooke. 1706. 16×10 cm. 8°. pp. [xlii], 192, [48]: 1 table.

'Ed. 2' (1706) consists of the sheets of the work of 1699 with a cancel title-page.

Copies: LBM; LRHS.

The compleat gard'ner . . . By . . . Monsʳ de La Quintinye . . . To which is added his treatise of orange-trees, with the raising of melons . . . Made English by John Evelyn, etc. **See** LA QUINTINIE (J. DE) 1693. fol.

The English vineyard vindicated, etc. [Edited, with a preface, by Philocepos, pseud., i.e. J. Evelyn.] **See** ROSE (J.) 1666. 8°.

The French gardiner: instructing how to cultivate all sorts of fruit-trees, and herbs for the garden . . . now transplanted into English by Philocepos [i.e. J. Evelyn, who signs the dedication J. E.], etc. **See** N., R.D.C.D.W.B.D. 1658. 12°.

— [Another issue.] 1658. 12°.

— [Another issue.] 1658. 12°.

— [Another edition.] The French gardiner . . . now transplanted into English, by John Evelyn, etc. **See** FRENCH GARDINER. 1669. 8°.

— Ed. 3. 1672. 8°.

— Ed. 3. 1675. 8°.

— Ed. 4. 1691. 12°.

119. Kalendarium hortense: or, the gard'ners almanac, directing what he is to do monethly throughout the year. And what fruits and flowers are in prime. The second edition, with many useful additions, etc. London, Jo. Martyn and Ja. Allestry. 1666. 15×10 cm. 8°. pp. [vi], 115, [1].

Copies: LBM; OBL.

The first edition of *Kalendarium hortense* was printed at the end of the first edition of Evelyn's *Sylva* (1664). *See* Keynes (G.), *John Evelyn a study in bibliophily*, etc. 152 (1937).

120. — Ed. 3, with many . . . additions. London, Jo. Martyn and Ja. Allestry. 1669. 16×10 cm. 8°. pp. 127, [15].

Leaf A1 (i.e. pp. 1–2) is blank.

Copies: HRES; OBL.

121. — Ed. 4, with many . . . additions. London, John Martyn. 1671. 15×10 cm. 8°. pp. 127, [15].

Leaf A1 (i.e. pp. 1–2) is blank.

Copies: LBM; CBS.

122. — Ed. 5, with many . . . additions. London, John Martyn. 1673. 15×9 cm. 8°. pp. 127, [9].

Leaf A1 (i.e. pp. 1–2) is blank.

Copies: LBM; LRHS; OBL.

123. — Ed. 6, with many . . . additions. London, John Martyn. 1676. 16×10 cm. 8°. pp. 127, [9]; 182.

Leaf A1 (i.e. pp. 1–2) is blank.

To this edition is added 'A philosophical discourse of earth', with a separate title-page and pagination. No mention of this work is made on the general title-page until the 'sixth edition' (1676) given below.

Copies: LRHS; HRES; OBL.

124. — Kalendarium hortense: or, the gard'ners almanac . . . To which is added, a discourse of earth . . . The sixth edition, with many . . . additions. London, John Martyn. 1676. 15×10 cm. 8°. pp. 127, [9]; 182.

Leaf A1 (i.e. pp. 1–2) is blank.

Copies: HRES; CUL.

125. — Ed. 7, with many . . . additions. London, for T. Sawbridge, G. Wells, and R. Bently. 1683. 15×9 cm. 8°. pp. 127, [9].

Leaf A1 (i.e. pp. 1–2) is blank.

Copies: LBM; LBMNH; OBL.

126. — Ed. 8, with many . . . additions. London, for R. Chiswell, T. Sawbridge, and R. Bently. 1691. 16×10 cm. 8°. pp. [xx], 175, [15]: frontis., illust.

To this edition is added a section entitled 'A new conservatory, or green-house' not mentioned on the title-page until the 'eighth edition' (1691) given below.

Copies: LBM; LRHS; LRCS.

127. — Kalendarium hortense: or, the gard'ners almanac . . . To which is now added in this eighth edition, a new conservatory, or green-house. With many other . . . additions. London, for Matthew Gillyflower, and James Partridge. 1691. 15×9 cm. 8°. pp. [xx], 175, [15]: frontis., illust.

The above work of 1691 consists of the sheets of the previous edition (i.e. eighth edition first issue) with a cancel title-page.

Copy: KRBG.

128. — Ed. 9, with many . . . additions. London, for Rob. Scott, Ri. Chiswell, Geo. Sawbridge, and Benj. Tooke. 1699. 15×9 cm. 8°. pp. [xx], 181, [17]: frontis., illust.

Copy: Q.

129. — Ed. 9, with many . . . additions. London, for George Huddleston. 1699. 16×10 cm. 8°. pp. [xx], 181, [17]: frontis., illust.

The above work of 1699 consists of the sheets of the previous edition (i.e. ninth edition first issue) with a cancel title-page.

Copies: LBM; OWaC.

130. — Ed. 9, with many . . . additions. London, for Francis Fawcet. 1699. 16×9 cm. 8°. pp. [xx], 181, [17]: frontis., illust.

The above work of 1699 consists of the sheets of the ninth edition (first issue) with a second cancel title-page. The ninth edition (third issue) of the *Kalendarium* is sometimes found bound up with the first edition of the author's *Acetaria* (1699). 8°.

Copies: OBL; CUL.

131. — Ed. 10, with many . . . additions. London, for Rob. Scot, Ric. Chiswell, George Sawbridge, etc. 1706. 16×10 cm. 8°. pp. [vi], ix, [xv], 170, [14]: frontis., illust.

The tenth edition of the *Kalendarium* is sometimes found bound up with the octavo edition of *Acetaria* published in 1706.

Copies: LBM; OBL; CUBG.

The manner of ordering fruit-trees. By the

Sieur Le Gendre . . . Written originally in French, and translated . . . into English [by J. Evelyn?], etc. **See** LE GENDRE 1660. 12°.

132. Sylva, or a discourse of forest-trees, and the propagation of timber in His Majesties Dominions. By J. E. [With a dedication signed: 'J. Evelyn'.] . . . To which is annexed Pomona; or, an appendix concerning fruit-trees in relation to cider . . . Also Kalendarium hortense; or, gard'ners almanac, etc. London, Jo. Martyn, and Ja. Allestry. 1664. 30×19 cm. fol. pp. [xvi], 120, [iv], 83 [i.e. 85], [3]: engr. arms on tp., illust.

'Pomona' and 'Kalendarium hortense' have separate title-pages, dated 1664.

Copies: LBM; LBMNH; LRHS; KRBG; HRES.

133. — Ed. 2, much inlarged and improved, etc. London, for Jo. Martyn, and Ja. Allestry. 1670 [1669]. 30×19 cm. fol. pp. [xlviii], 247 [i.e. 241], [1]; [iv], 67, [1]; 33, [3]: engr. arms on tp., illust.

Although the date on the title-page is 1670 this edition was apparently published at the end of 1669. *See above, History,* p. 103.

In this edition of *Sylva,* and in subsequent editions, the author's name appears on the title-page. The two appended treatises, 'Pomona', and 'Kalendarium hortense', have separate title-pages and are of the 'second edition' (1670) and 'third edition' (1669), respectively.

Copies: LBM; LBMNH; LRHS; LCPG; HRES.

134. — Sylva, or a discourse of forest trees . . . Terra, a philosophical essay of earth . . . To which is annexed Pomona . . . Also Kalendarium hortense . . . All which several treatises are in this third edition much inlarged, and improved, etc. London, for John Martyn. 1679. 31×19 cm. fol. pp. [lxx], 412; 38, [2]: illust.

Each treatise has a separate title-page. 'A philosophical discourse of earth' is of the 'second edition' (1678), 'Pomona' is of the 'third edition' (1678), and 'Kalendarium hortense' is of the 'fifth edition' (1679). To the above edition (1679) of *Sylva,* and to the editions of 1706 and 1729 recorded below, is added Abraham Cowley's poem 'The garden'.

Copies: LBM; LBMNH; LCPG; HRES.

135. — Silva, or a discourse of forest-trees . . . Together with an historical account of the sacredness and use of standing groves. Terra, a philosophical essay of earth . . . To which is annexed Pomona . . . Also Acetaria: or, a discourse of sallets. With Kalendarium hortense . . . All which several treatises are in this fourth edition much inlarg'd and improv'd, etc. London, for Robert Scott, Richard Chiswell, George Sawbridge, etc. 1706. 32×20 cm. fol. pp. [xxxvi], 384 [i.e. 392], [iv], 275, [5]: frontis. (port. of author), illust.

The four appended treatises, 'Terra', 'Pomona', 'Acetaria' and 'Kalendarium hortense', have separate title-pages, dated 1706, and are of the 'third', 'fourth', 'second' and 'tenth' editions respectively.

Copies: LBM; LBMNH; LRHS; KRBG; OWaC.

136. — Ed. 5. London, for J. Walthoe, J. Knapton, D. Midwinter, etc. 1729. 32×20 cm. fol. pp. [ii], xxviii, 329 [i.e. 335], [1], vi, [iv], 235, [5]: illust.

'Terra', 'Pomona', 'Acetaria' and 'Kalendarium hortense' have each a separate title-page but these are undated and have no imprint.

Copies: LBM; HRES.

137. — Silva: or, a discourse of forest-trees, and the propagation of timber in His Majesty's Dominions . . . Together with an historical account of the sacredness and use of standing groves . . . With notes by A. Hunter, etc. York, printed by A. Ward for J. Dodsley . . . T. Cadell . . . J. Robson . . . and T. Durham . . . London, W. Creech and J. Balfour, Edinburgh. 1776. 29×22 cm. 4°. pp. [lvi], 649, [11]: frontis. (port. of author), 40 pls., 1 folding table.

Leaf *c1 (i.e. pp. [xvii–xviii]) is blank.

Copies: LBM; LBMNH; LRHS; HRES; OBL.

Copy with plates coloured by hand: PBN (Rés. S. 822).

138. — Silva . . . With notes by A. Hunter . . . A new edition. To which is added the Terra: a philosophical discourse of earth, etc. 2 vols. York, printed by A. Ward for J. Dodsley . . . T. Cadell . . . J. Robson . . . and R. Baldwin . . . London; J. Todd, York. 1786. 30×23 cm. 4°.

1. pp. [xlvi], 311, [11]: frontis. (port. of author), 28 pls., 1 folding table.

2. pp. [ii], 343, [11]; [viii], 74, [4]: 14 pls., 2 folding tables.

'Terra' has a separate title-page.

Copies: LBM; LBMNH; LRHS; KRBG; HRES.

Copies with plates coloured by hand: LBM (G.2467–68); LRHS.

139. — Ed. 3, revised, corrected, and . . .

enlarged, etc. 2 vols. York, printed by T. Wilson and R. Spence . . . Sold by J. Mawman . . . Cadell, jun. and Davies . . . London. Wilson and Spence . . . York. 1801. 29×22 cm. 4°.

1. pp. 50, [2], 330: frontis. (port. of author), 28 pls.

2. pp. 393 [i.e. 395], [1]; [viii], 88, [2]: 17 pls.

In the above edition of 1801, and in subsequent editions, 'Terra' has a separate title-page, but with no imprint or date.

Copies: LBMNH; LRHS; KRBG.

140. — Ed. 4, with the editor's last corrections, and a short memoir of him, etc. 2 vols. York, printed by Thomas Wilson and Son . . . for Longman, Hurst, Rees, [etc.] . . . London; and for Wilson and Son, York. 1812. 29×24 cm. 4°.

1. pp. 50, [2], 330: frontis. (port. of author), 28 pls.

2. pp. 393 [i.e. 395], [1]; [viii], 88, [2]: 17 pls.

Copies: LBM; LBMNH; KRBG.

141. — Ed. 5, with the editor's last corrections, etc. 2 vols. London, Henry Colburn. 1825. 29×23 cm. 4°.

1. pp. 50, [2], 330: frontis. (port. of author), 28 pls.

2. pp. 393 [i.e. 395], [1]; [viii], 88, [2]: 17 pls.

Copy: Q.

EVELYN (JOHN) *the Younger* [1655–1699]

Of gardens. Four books first written in Latine verse . . . now made English by J. E. [i.e. J. Evelyn the Younger, who also supplied the dedication.] See RAPIN (R.) 1672. 8°.

— [Another issue.] 1673. 8°.

EXPERT GARDENER.

See COUNTRY-MANS RECREATION. The countrymans recreation . . . Whereunto is added, The expert gardener, etc. 1640, etc. 4°.

F., N.

142. The fruiterers secrets: containing directions, for the due time, and manner, of gathering all kindes of fruite . . . how they are . . . to be ordered in packing, carrying and conueighing. etc. [With a dedication and preface by N. F.] London, R. B. solde by Roger Iackson. 1604. 18×13 cm. 4°. pp. [iv], 28. 𝕭.𝕷.

Copies: LRHS; OBL.

143. — [Another issue.] The husbandmans fruitfull orchard. Shewing diuers care [*sic*] new secrets for the true ordering of all sortes of fruite in their due seasons, etc. [With a preface by N. F.] London, for Roger Iackson. 1608. 18×14 cm. 4°. pp. [iv], 28. 𝕭.𝕷.

The above issue is the work of 1604 with a cancel title-page.

Copy: LBM.

144. — [Another issue.] London, for Roger Iackson. 1609. 17×13 cm. 4°. pp. [iv], 28. 𝕭.𝕷.

The above issue is the work of 1608 with the date on the title-page altered to 1609.

Copy: LBM.

FORSTER (JOHN)

145. Englands happiness increased, or a sure and easie remedy against all succeeding dear years; by a plantation of the roots called potatoes, etc. London, for A. Seile. 1664. 18×13 cm. 4°. pp. [viii], 30.

Copies: LBM; LUL; HRES.

FRENCH GARDINER.

146. The French gardiner: instructing how to cultivate all sorts of fruit-trees, and herbs for the garden: together with directions to dry and conserve them in their natural . . . written originally in French [by Nicolas de Bonnefons], and now transplanted into English, by John Evelyn . . . Whereunto is annexed, The English vineyard vindicated by John Rose . . . with a tract of the making and ordering of wines in France. London, J. M. for John Crooke. 1669. 15×9 cm. 8°. pp. [viii], 294; 48, [16]: frontis., 4 pls.

In the above edition (1669) of *The French gardiner*, and in the editions below of 1672 and 1675, pages 48, [16] (signed A–D⁸) consist of 'The English vineyard' (pp. 48), and tables (one of which is alphabetical) of 'the principal matters' contained in *The French gardiner* (pp. [1–15]), followed by a table of the contents of 'The English vineyard' (p. [16]). In each edition 'The English vineyard' has its own title-page.

Copies: LBM; HRES; OBL.

147. — Ed. 3. London, S. S. for Benj. Tooke. 1672. 15×9 cm. 8°. pp. [viii], 294; 48, [16]: frontis., 4 pls.

Copies: LBM; LRHS; HRES; CUBG.

148. — Ed. 3. London, T. R. & N. T. for B. Tooke. 1675. 15×9 cm. 8°. pp. [viii], 294; 48, [16]: frontis., 4 pls.

In the above 'Ed. 3' (1675) the type has been entirely reset. *See* Keynes (G.), *John Evelyn a study in bibliophily*, etc. 54 (1937).

Copies: LRHS; KRBG; HRES; OBL; CUL.

149. — Ed. 4. London, T. B. for B. Took. 1691. 15×8 cm. 12°. pp. [vi], 215, [1]; [viii], 24 [i.e. 26], [8]: frontis., 4 pls.

In the above edition (1691) 'The English vineyard' pp. 24 [i.e. 26], [8]: 1 pl., has a separate title-page with imprint and date. The signatures, however, are continuous with those of *The French gardiner*.

Copies: LBM; HRES; OBL.

For an earlier edition of *The French gardiner*, **see** N., R. D. C. D. W. B. D. 1658. 12°.

G., S.

The compleat English gardner . . . The tenth edition . . . Begun by Leonard Meager . . . and now enlarged by way of Supplement [by 'S. G.'], etc. **See** Meager (L.) 1704. 4°.

— Ed. 11. [1710?] 4°.

GARDINER (Richard)

150. Profitable instructions for the manuring, sowing, and planting of kitchin gardens. Very profitable for the commonwealth and greatly for the helpe and comfort of poore people, etc. London, Edward Allde for Edward White. 1599. 18×13 cm. 4°. Signn. A–D⁴. 𝔅.𝔏.

The compiler is indebted to the Curator of rare books, University of Wisconsin, for the title and collation of the above work of 1599.

Copy: [WUL].

151. — [Another edition.] London, Edward Allde for Edward White. 1603. 19×15 cm. 4°. Signn. A–D⁴. 𝔅.𝔏.

Copies: LBM; CUL.

GERARD (John) [1545–1612]

152. Catalogus arborum, fruticum ac plantarum tam indigenarum, quam exoticarum, in horto Iohannis Gerardi . . . nascentium. Londini, ex officina Roberti Robinson. 1596. 17×12 cm. 4°. pp. [vi], 18.

Copy: LBM.

153. — [Another edition.] Londini, ex officina Arnoldi Hatfield, impensis Ioannis Norton. 1599. 33×23 cm. fol. pp. [iv], 22.

The above edition (1599) is sometimes found bound at the end of the first edition of Gerard's *Herball*.

Copies: LBMNH; LRHS; KRBG; OBS.

154. The herball or generall historie of plantes, etc. London, imprinted by Iohn Norton. 1597. 32×22 cm. fol. pp. [xviii], 1392, [72]: engr. tp., illust.

Colophon: Imprinted at London by Edm. Bollifant, for Bonham and Iohn Norton. M.D.XCVII.

Gerard's *Herball* was entered in the Stationers' Register on 6 June 1597. The title-page and colophon are dated 1597. Two of the commendatory letters and Gerard's epistle to the reader are dated 1 December 1597. The engraved portrait of Gerard on the verso of the last leaf of the preliminaries is inscribed: 'anno ætatis suæ, 53. 1598'.

Copies: LBM; LBMNH; LRHS; LRCS; KRBG; OBL; ORSL; OBS; CUL; CBS.

155. — [Another edition.] The herball or generall historie of plantes . . . very much enlarged and amended by Thomas Iohnson, etc. London, Adam Islip, Ioice Norton and Richard Whitakers. 1633. 34×23 cm. fol. pp. [xxxvi], 1630 [i.e. 1634], [48]: engr. tp., illust.

Copies: LBM; LBMNH; LRHS; LCPG; LRCS; LWML; KRBG; HRES; CBS.

156. — (Second edition, revised.) London, Adam Islip, Ioice Norton and Richard Whitakers. 1636. 35×23 cm. fol. pp. [xxxvi], 1630 [i.e. 1634], [48]: engr. tp., illust.

Copies: LBM; LWML; LRHS; KRBG; HRES.

GILBERT (Samuel)

157. The florists vade-mecum. Being a choice compendium . . . for the propagation, raising, planting, encreasing and preserving the rarest flowers and plants that our climate and skill . . . will perswade to live with us. With several new experiments for raising new varieties . . . together with The gardiners almanack . . . directing him what to do . . . in both orchard and flower-garden, etc. London, for Thomas Simmons. 1682. 14×8 cm. 12°. pp. [xxii], 252 [i.e. 242], [22], [36]: frontis. (port. of author), illust.

The almanack (pp. [36]) has a separate title-page reading: 'The gardeners almanack . . . With monthly directions what ought to be done in either kitchin or flower-garden.'

Copies: LRHS; KRBG.

158. — Ed. 2. London, for Thomas Simmons. 1683. 14×8 cm. 12°. pp. [xxii], 252 [i.e. 242], [22], [36]: frontis. (port. of author), illust.

'The gardeners almanack' has a separate title-page dated 1682.

This so-called 'second edition' is the same as the work of 1682 except for a new title-page.

Copy: LBM.

159. — Ed. 2. London, for T. S. and B. Cox. 1690. 15×8 cm. 12°. pp. [xii], 137, [31]: illust.

In the above edition of *The florists vade-mecum* (1690), and in subsequent editions, 'The gardeners almanack' is omitted and only the 'Monthly directions' are included.

Copy: LBM.

160. — Ed. 2, corrected. London, for J. Taylor, and J. Wyat. 1693. 15×8 cm. 12°. pp. [xii], 137, [31]: illust.

This so-called 'second edition' is the same as the work of 1690 except for a new title-page.

Copies: LRHS; KRBG.

161. — Ed. 3, enlarged. London, for J. Taylor; G. Coniers, and T. Ballard. 1702. 15×8 cm. 12°. pp. 149, [19]: illust.

Copies: LBM; LRHS.

GREAT HERBALL.

See HERBAL.

GRETE HERBALL.

See HERBAL.

GREW (NEHEMIAH) [1641–1712]

162. The anatomy of plants. With an idea of a philosophical history of plants. And several other lectures, read before the Royal society. [London], W. Rawlins, for the author. 1682. 31×20 cm. (36×23 cm. large paper.) fol. pp. [xxii], 24, [x], 212, [iv], 221–304, [20]: 83 pls.

The above work comprises the following lectures each with its own title-page:

An idea of a philosophical history of plants . . . The second edition.
The anatomy of plants, begun . . . The second edition.
The anatomy of roots . . . The second edition.
The anatomy of trunks . . . The second edition.
The anatomy of leaves, flowers, fruits and seeds.
Several lectures read before the Royal society.

Copies: LBM; LBMNH; LRHS; LCPG; LRCS; LPS; KRBG; CBS.

163. The anatomy of vegetables begun. With a general account of vegetation founded thereon, etc. London, for Spencer Hickman. 1672. 16×10 cm. 8°. pp. [xxxii], 198 [i.e. 186], [20]: 3 pls.

Leaf N6 (i.e. pp. [1–2]) is blank.

Copies: LBM; LBMNH; LRHS; LLS; LRCS; KRBG; HRES.

164. The comparative anatomy of trunks, together with an account of their vegetation grounded thereupon, etc. London, J. M. for Walter Kettilby. 1675. 18×11 cm. 8°. pp. [xxvi], 81, [23]: 19 pls.

Copies: LBM; LLS; LCPG; LRCS; KRBG.

165. An idea of a phytological history propounded. Together with a continuation of the anatomy of vegetables, particularly prosecuted upon roots. And an account of the vegetation of roots grounded chiefly thereupon, etc. London, J. M. for Richard Chiswell. 1673. 18×12 cm. 8°. pp. [xxii], 144, [32]: 7 pls.

Copies: LBM; LLS; LCPG; LPS; KRBG; OBL; CBS.

H., W.

166. The flower-garden. Shewing how all flowers are to be ordered, the time of flowering, the taking up of the plants, and the increasing of them . . . By W. H. [i.e. William Hughes.] To which may be added The compleat vineyard . . . by the same author. London, H. B. for William Crook. 1671. 16×10 cm. 8°. pp. [vi], 30 [i.e. 39], [7].

The only copy of the above edition of 1671, seen by the compiler, is in the Brit. Mus. (Bloomsbury) (967.c.30). It does not contain 'The compleat vineyard'. The copy of *The flower-garden* (1671) in the Yale University Library is followed by the 1670 edition of 'The compleat vineyard'.

Copies: LBM; [YUL].

For later editions of 'The *flower-garden* see HUGHES (W.) 1672, etc.' 12°.

HAMILTON (THOMAS) 6th *Earl of Haddington* [1680–1735]

See REID (J.) The Scots gardiner . . . Together with . . . the Earl of Haddington's Treatise on forest-trees, etc. 1756, etc. 12°.

HARTLIB (SAMUEL) [–1670?]

167. A designe for plentie, by an vniversall planting of fruit-trees: tendred by some welwishers to the publick, etc. [Edited, with a preface, by Samuel Hartlib.] London, for Richard Wodenothe. [1653.] 19×14 cm. 4°. pp. [viii], 24.

The British Museum's copy in the Thomason collection (E.686(5)) bears the date Feb. 1652 [i.e. 1653] in Thomason's hand on the title-page.

Copy: LBM.

HARWARD (SIMON)

See LAWSON (W.) A new orchard and garden . . . Whereunto is newly added the art of propagating plants (by Simon Harward), etc. 1623, 1626. 4°.

HERBAL.

168. The grete herball whiche geueth parfyt knowlege and vnderstandyng of all maner of herbes ꝛ there gracyous vertues . . . Also it geueth full parfyte vnderstandynge of the booke lately prentyd by me (Peter Treueris) named the noble experiens of the vertuous hand warke of surgery. ([End] Thus endeth The grete herball . . . which is translated out yᵉ Frensshe [i.e. from 'Le grant herbier', a French translation of the Latin work 'Circa instans'], etc.) 26×18 cm. fol. Signn. ✠⁶A–Z⁶ Aa–Ee⁶: woodcut on tp., illust., B.L.

Colophon: Impretyd at London in Southwarke by me Peter Treueris . . . In the yere . . . M.D.xxvi. The xxvii. day of July.

Copies: LBM; LRHS; ORSL; OMaC; CUL.

169. — [Another edition.] The grete herball, etc. 26×18 cm. fol. Signn. ✠⁶A–Z⁶ Aa–Ee⁶, woodcut on tp., illust., B.L.

Colophon: Impryntyd at London in Southwarke by me Peter Treueris. In the yere . . . M.D.xxix. the xvii. day of Marce.

In the above edition of 1529 leaf ✠6 is blank.

Copies: LBM; CBS; OBL.

170. — [Another edition.] The great herball newly corrected, etc. Londini in edibus Thome Gybson anno M.D.XXXIX. 26×18 cm. fol. Signn.⟨-⟩⁴ A–Z⁴ Aa–Bb⁴ Cc⁶: title within a woodcut compartment. B.L.

Copies: LBM; OMaC.

171. — [Another edition.] The greate herball, which geueth parfyte knowledge ꝛ vnderstandinge of al maner of herbes, and theyr gracious vertues . . . Newlye corrected and diligently ouersene. In the yeare . . . M.CCCCC.LXI. 27×19 cm. fol. Signn. ✠⁶ A–X⁶ Y⁸ Aa⁶ Bb²: woodcut on tp., illust., B.L.

Colophon: Imprynted at London . . . at the signe of the Swane, by Ihon Kynge. In the yeare . . . M.D.LXI.

Copies: LBM; LRCP; LRCS.

172. Here bygynnyth a newe mater, the whiche sheweth and treateth of yᵉ vertues ꝛ proprytes of herbes, the whiche is called an herball, etc. 19×14 cm. 4°. Signn. A–I⁴: woodcut on tp., B.L.

Colophon: Imprynted by me Rycharde Banckes, dwellynge in Lōdō . . . in yᵉ Pultry, yᵉ. xxv. day of Marche . . . M.CCCCC. ꝛ. xxv.

Copy: LBM (C.71.d.22).

For convenience, the various editions of the 'Herball' first printed by R. Banckes in 1525 have been placed under the heading Herbal, including the three editions entitled respectively: *Hereafter foloweth the knowledge, properties, and the vertues of herbes, A newe herball of Macer*, and *Macers herbal*. For undated editions the compiler received the assistance of the late Dr. F. S. Ferguson. This authority gave her, in some instances, the dates which he considered to be most nearly correct, selecting them from those given by the library catalogue concerned, from the *Short-title catalogue* or from Barlow (H. M.), Old English herbals, 1525–1640. *Proc. Roy. Soc. Med.* 6: 108–123 (1913). For some editions Dr. Ferguson himself suggested a date.

173. — [Another edition.] Here begynneth a newe marer [*sic*], yᵉ whiche sheweth and treateth of the vertues ꝛ propertes of herbes, the whiche is callyd an herball, etc. 19×13 cm. 4°. Signn. A–I⁴: woodcut on tp., B.L.

Colophon: Imprynted by me Rycharde Banckes, dwellynge in Lōdō . . . in yᵉ Pultry, yᵉ. xxv. daye of June . . . M.CCCCC. ꝛ. xxvi.

Copy: CUL (Sel.5.1751).

174. — [Another edition.] A newe herball of Macer, translated out of Laten in to Englysshe. [1535?] 13×9 cm. 8°. Signn. A–P⁴: woodcut on tp., B.L.

Colophon: Imprynted by me Robert Wyer . . . at the sygne of Saynt Iohn̄ Euangelyst, besyde Charynge Crosse.

Copy: LBM (C.58.cc.32).

175. — [Another edition.] A boke of the propertyes of herbes the which is called an herbal. [*c.* 1537.] 13×8 cm. 8°. Signn. A–I⁸ K⁴: B.L.

Colophon: Imprynted at London by my Iohan Skot dwellynge in Fausterlane.

Copy: ORSL (RR.z.241).

176. — [Another edition.] A boke of the propertyes of herbes the whiche is called an herbal. [1539?] 14 × 9 cm. 8°. Signn. A–I⁸ K⁴: woodcut on tp., 𝕭.𝕷.

Colophon: Imprynted at London in Fletestrete . . . by me Robert Redman.

Copy: LBM (546.b.31).

177. — [Another edition.] Hereafter foloweth the knowledge, properties, and the vertues of herbes. [1540?] 13 × 9 cm. 8°. Signn. A–P⁴: woodcut on tp., 𝕭.𝕷.

Colophon: Imprynted by me Robert Wyer . . . at the syne of Saynt Iohñ Euangelyst, besyde Charynge Crosse.

Copy: LBM (C.31.a.39).

178. — [Another edition.] A boke of the propertyes of herbes the whiche is called an herbal. [1541?] 13 × 9 cm. 8°. Signn. A–I⁸ K⁴: woodcut on tp., 𝕭.𝕷.

Colophon: Imprynted at London in Fletestrete by me Elizabeth late wyfe to Robert Redman, etc.

The compiler is indebted to the Bibliographer of the Henry E. Huntington Library, California, for the title and collation of the above work of [1541?]. In this country the only known copy is in the Wellcome Historical Medical Library. This copy is imperfect, wanting signature A.

Copies: LWML; [HEHL].

179. — [Another edition.] A boke of the propertyes of herbes the whiche is called an harbal, M.D.XLj. 14 × 9 cm. 8°. Signn. A–I⁸ K⁴: 𝕭.𝕷.

Colophon: Imprynted at London . . . by Thomas Petyt. M.D.xlj.

Copy: OBL (Crynes 873(4)).

180. — [Another edition] Macers herbal. Practysyd by Doctor Lynacro. Translated out of Laten, in to Englysshe, whiche shewynge theyr operacyons ƶ vertues, set in the margent of this boke, to the entent you myght knowe theyr vertues. [1542?] 13 × 9 cm. 8°. Signn. A–W⁴: 𝕭.𝕷.

Colophon: Imprynted by me Robert Wyer . . . at the sygne of Seynt Iohñ Euangelyst, besyde Charynge Crosse.

Copy: LBM (C.58.cc.33).

181. — [Another edition.] A boke of the propertyes of herbes the whiche is called an herbal. 14 × 9 cm. 8°. Signn. A–I⁸ K⁴: 𝕭.𝕷.

Colophon: Imprinted at London . . . by me Wyllyam Myddylton. In the yere . . . M.CCCCC.xlvi. The thyrde day of July.

Copy: OBL (8°. L.544(1)BS).

182. — [Another edition.] A boke of the propertyes of herbes the whiche is called an herball. [1547?] 13 × 8 cm. 8°. Signn. A–I⁸ K⁴: 𝕭.𝕷.

Colophon: Imprinted at London in Fletstrete at the syne of the Rose garland by me Robart Copland.

Copy: OBL (Antiq.f.E.93(1)).

183. — [Another edition.] A boke of the propertes of herbes the which is called an herball. [1548?] 13 × 8 cm. 8°. Signn. A–I⁸ K⁴: woodcut on tp., 𝕭.𝕷.

Colophon: Imprynted at London by Iohan Waley, dwellynge in Foster lane.

Regarding the date of publication *see* Barlow (H. M.), Old English herbals, 1525–1640. *Proc. Roy. Soc. Med.* **6**: 114–115 (1913) (Section of the history of medicine).

Copy: MUML.

184. — [Another edition.] A lytel herball of the properties of herbes newely amended . . . with certayne addicions at the ende of the boke, declaryng what herbes hath influence of certaine sterres and constellations, wherby may be chosen the beast . . . tymes ƶ dayes of their ministracion, accordynge to the moone being in the signes of heauen, the which is dayly appoynted in the almanacke, made and gathered in . . . M.D.L. the xii. day of February by Anthonye Askham phisycyon. 13 × 8 cm. 8°. Signn. A–K⁸: 𝕭.𝕷.

Colophon: Imprynted at London, in Fletestrete at the signe of the George . . . by Wyllyam Powell. In . . . M.D.L. the twelfe day of Marche.

Leaf K8 is blank.

Copies: LRCS; LWML (in this copy the title-page is wanting).

185. — [Another edition.] A booke of the properties of herbes, called an herball. Whereunto is added the tyme that herbes, floures and seedes should bee gathered to bee kept the whole yeare, wyth the vertue of the herbes when they are stylled. Also a generall rule of all maner of herbes, drawen out of an auncient booke of physycke by VV. C. [c. 1550.] 13 × 9 cm. 8°. Signn. ¶⁴ A–I⁸ K⁴: 𝕭.𝕷.

Colophon: Imprinted at London for Autony Kytson.

The compiler is indebted to the Curator of rare books, University of Wisconsin, for the title and collation of the above work of [c. 1550].

Copy: [WUL].

186. — [Another edition.] A boke of the propreties of herbes called an herball, wherunto is added the time of ye herbes, floures and sedes shold be gathered to be kept the whole yere, wyth the vertue of ye herbes when they are stilled. Also a generall rule of all manner of herbes drawen out of an auncyent booke of phisyck by W. C. [1552?] 14×8 cm. 8°. Signn. A–K^8: woodcut on tp., 𝕭.𝕷.

Colophon: Imprynted at London in the Fletestrete at the sygne of the Rose garland by me Wyllyam Copland. for Iohn Wyght.

Copy: LBM (449. a. 9).

187. — [Another edition.] A boke of the propreties of herbes called an herball, wherunto is added the tyme ye herbes, floures and sedes shoulde be gathered to be kept the whole yere, with the vertue of ye herbes whē they are stylled. Also a generall rule of al manner of herbes drawen out of auncient boke of physycke by W. C. [1560?] 14×9 cm. 8°. Signn. ❡✳^{4} A–I^8 K^4: 𝕭.𝕷.

Colophon: Imprinted at London by Wyllyam Copland.

Copies: OBL (Tanner 35); CUL (SSS.46.34).

188. — [Another issue.] A boke of the propreties of herbes called an herball, wherunto is added the tyme ye herbes, floures and sedes shoulde be gathered to be kept the whole yere, with the vertue of ye herbes whē they are stylled. Also a generall rule of al manner of herbes drawen out of an auncient boke of physycke by W.C. [1560?] 14×9 cm. 8°. Signn. ❡✳ ^{4}A–I^8 K^4: 𝕭.𝕷.

Colophon: Imprinted at London by Wyllyam Copland.

Identical with the previous work of [1560?], except for the addition of the word 'an' before 'auncient boke' on the title-page.

Copies: LBM (546.b.30); KRBG.

189. — [Another edition.] A boke of the propreties of herbes called an herball, wherunto is added the time ye herbes, floures and sedes shold be gathered to be kept the whole yere,

with the vertue of ye herbes when they are stilled. Also a general rule of al maner of herbes drawen out of an auncient boke of phisyck by W. C. [1560?] 13×9 cm. 8°. Signn. A–K^8: woodcut on tp., 𝕭.𝕷.

Colophon: Imprinted at London by Ihon Kynge, for Ihon Waley.

Copies: LBM (1405.a.24); LRCS.

190. — [Another issue.] A boke of the propreties of herbes called an herball, wherunto is added the time ye herbes, floures and sedes shold be gathered to be kept the whole yere, with the vertue of ye herbes when they are stilled. Also a general rule of al maner of herbes drawen out of an auncient boke of phisyck by W. C. [1560?] 13×9 cm. 8°. Signn. A–K^8: woodcut on tp., 𝕭.𝕷.

Colophon: Imprinted at London by Ihon Kynge, for Abraham Vele.

The compiler is indebted to the Curator of rare books, in the Henry E. Huntington Library, for the title and collation of the above work of [1560?].

Copy: [HEHL].

191. — [Another issue.] A boke of the propreties of herbes called an herball, wherunto is added the time ye herbes, floures and sedes shold be gathered to be kept the whole yere, with the vertue of ye herbes when they are stilled. Also a general rule of al maner of herbes drawen out of an auncient boke of phisyck by W. C. [1560?] 13×8 cm. 8°. Signn. A–K^8: woodcut on tp., 𝕭.𝕷.

Colophon: Imprinted at London by Ihon Kynge, for Abraham Vely.

Copy: LRCP.

The above three issues of [1560?] contain respectively the names Ihon Waley, Abraham Vele, and Abraham Vely in the last line of the colophon. Apart from this line the three issues are identical.

192. — [Another edition.] A litle herball of the properties of herbes, newly amended . . . wyth certayn additions at the ende of the boke, declaring what herbes hath influence of certain sterres and constellations, wherby maye be chosen the best . . . tymes and dayes of their ministracion, according to the moone beyng in the signes of heauē the which is daily appoīted in the Almanacke, made and gathered in . . . M.D.L. the xii. daye of February, by Anthony Askhā, physycyon. [1561?] 14×9 cm. 8°. Signn. A–K^8: 𝕭.𝕷.

Colophon: Imprynted at London, in Paules churcheyearde, at the signe of the Swanne, by Ihon Kynge.

Leaf K8 is blank.

Copy: LBM (C. 31.b.21).

HEREAFTER FOLOWETH THE KNOWLEDGE.

Hereafter foloweth the knowledge, properties, and the vertues of herbes. **See** HERBAL. Here begynnyth a newe mater, etc. [Another edition.] Hereafter foloweth, etc. [1540?] 8°.

HILL (*Sir* JOHN) [1716?–1775]

See CULPEPER (N.) Culpeper's English family physician; or, medical herbal enlarged, with several hundred additional plants, principally from Sir John Hill, etc. 2 vols. 1792. 8°.

HILL (THOMAS) **see** MOUNTAIN (DIDYMUS) pseud.

HILL (THOMAS)

193. A most briefe and pleasaunte treatise, teachyng how to dresse, sowe, and set a garden: and what remedies also may be had and vsed agaynst suche beastes, wormes, flies, and suche like, that noye gardens, gathered oute of the principallest aucthors which haue writtē of gardening, as Palladius, Columella, Varro, Ruellius, Dyophanes, learned Cato, and others manye moe. And nowe englished by Thomas Hyll Londiner. [1558?] 13×8 cm. 8°. Signn. A–E⁸: woodcut on tp., illust., 𝔅.𝔏.

Colophon: Imprinted at London by Ihon Day for Thomas Hyll.

According to Henrey (B.), The earliest English gardening book. *J. Soc. Bibl. nat. Hist.* **2**: 386 (1952) the above treatise was published about 1558.

Copy: GUL.

194. — [Another edition.] A most briefe and pleasaunt treatyse, teachynge howe to dress, sowe, and set a garden . . . gathered out of the principallest authors in this art by Thomas Hyll Londyner. 13×8 cm. 8°. Signn. A–H⁸ I⁴: woodcut on tp., illust., 𝔅.𝔏.

'The conclusion' is dated 'Anno. 1563. Mense Martii'. The colophon reads: 'Imprynted at London . . . by Thomas Marshe'.

Copy: LBM.

195. — [Another edition.] The proffitable arte of gardening, now the third tyme set fourth . . .

To this annexed, two propre [*sic*] treatises, the one entituled The marueilous gouernment, propertie, and benefite of the bees . . . And the other, The yerely coniectures, meete for husbandmē to knowe: englished by Thomas Hill, etc. London, Thomas Marshe. 1568. 14×9 cm. 8°. pp. [xxxii], ff. 192, pp. [16]; [xii], ff. 83: 1 pl. illust., 𝔅.𝔏.

Leaf dd8 (i.e. pp. [15–16]) is blank.

In the above edition of 1568, and in subsequent editions the 'two . . . treatises' have a separate title-page.

Copies: LBM; LBMNH.

196. — [Another edition.] Wherunto is newly added a treatise, of the arte of graffing and planting of trees. London, Thomas Marshe. 1572. 14×9 cm. 8°. pp. [xxxii], ff. 198 [i.e. 199]: 1 pl., illust., 𝔅.𝔏.

The collation of the above edition of 1572 has been made from the copy of the work in the Brit. Mus. (Bloomsbury). A collation by signatures reads: A–Z⁸ Aa–Dd⁸ (Dd8 is blank). This is the only copy so far known to the compiler in this country. According to the title-page the two treatises 'annexed' to the edition of 1568 are also appended to this edition, but in the Museum copy they are both wanting, and so is the 'newly added' treatise on 'the arte of graffing'. A complete copy of the work is in the Henry E. Huntington Library, California. A collation by signatures reads: A–Z⁸ Aa–Dd⁸ (Dd8 is blank); 6 unsigned leaves, Aa–Mm⁸: 1 pl. (Collation supplied by the Bibliographer of the Huntington Library, in epist. 10.viii.49.)

Copies: BM; [HEHL].

197. — [Another edition.] London, Henrie Bynneman. 1574. 19×14 cm. 4°. pp. [xii], 134, [2]; [viii], 87, [1]: illust., 𝔅.𝔏.

Copies: LBM; OBL; HRES.

198. — [Another edition.] London, Henry Bynneman. 1579. 18×14 cm. 4°. pp. [viii], 152; viii, 92 [i.e. 100]: illust., 𝔅.𝔏.

Copies: LBM; LRHS; OBL; OCCC.

199. — [Another edition.] London, Robert Walde-graue, 1586. 17×13 cm. 4°. pp. [viii], 152; [viii], 92 [i.e. 100]: illust., 𝔅.𝔏.

Copy: LBM.

200. — [Another edition.] London, Edward Allde. 1593. 19×14 cm. 4°. pp. [viii], 164; [viii], 92: illust., 𝔅.𝔏.

Copies: LBM; OBL.

201. — [Another edition.] The arte of garden-

ing, etc. London, Edward Allde. 1608. 19×14 cm. 4°. pp. [viii], 164; [viii], 92: illust., 𝕭.𝕷.

Copies: LBM; LWML; OBL; CUL.

HISTORIÆ NATURALIS SCIAGRAPHIA.

202. Historiæ naturalis sciagraphia [by Jacob Bobart the Younger]. Oxon. 1720. 16×10 cm. 8°. pp. [ii], 12.

According to Vines (S. H.) in *Makers of British botany . . . Edited by F. W. Oliver*: 23 (1913) Cambridge, the above tract: 'is anonymous, but the matter that it contains is Bobart's work, whether it was written by himself or by some one who had access to his papers'.

Copy: OBL.

HOW (WILLIAM) [1620–1656]

Phytologia britannica, etc. [By W. How.] **See** PHYTOLOGIA. 1650. 8°.

Matthiæ de l'Obel . . . stirpium illustrationes . . . Accurante Guil: How, Anglo. **See** L'OBEL (M. DE) 1655. 4°.

HUGHES (WILLIAM)

203. The American physitian; or, a treatise of the roots, plants, trees, shrubs, fruit, herbs, &c. growing in the English plantations in America . . . whereunto is added a discourse of the cacao-nut-tree, and the use of its fruit; with all the ways of making of chocolate, etc. London, J. C. for William Crook. 1672. 14×8 cm. 12°. pp. [xxii], 159, [7].

Copies: LBM; KRBG; CBS.

204. The compleat vineyard: or a most excellent way for the planting of vines: not onely according to the German and French way, but also long experimented in England . . . with the manner of bruising and pressing; and also how to advance our English wines, etc. London, G. M. for W. Crooke, and John Playfere. 1665. 17×13 cm. 4°. pp. [viii], 27, [1]: illust.

Copies: LBM; CBS.

205. — [Another edition.] Enlarged above half by the author, etc. London, J. C. for Will. Crook. 1670. 16×10 cm. 8°. pp. [xxxii], 92, [4]: 1 pl.

Copies: LBM; LRHS; KRBG; HRES.

In Yale University Library is preserved a copy of the 'third edition' of *The compleat vineyard*, with the imprint and date 'London . . . for Will. Crook . . . 1683'. The pagination is [xxiv], 103, [5] and a collation by signatures reads: A–E¹² F⁶. There is no plate (information supplied by the Librarian of the Reference Department, Yale University Library, in epist. 26.ix.68 and 11.xi.68).

'The third edition' (1683) was also published appended to the third edition (1683) of *The flower garden* by W. Hughes.

The flower-garden . . . By W. H. [i.e. William Hughes], etc. **See** H., W. 1671. 8°.

206. — [Another edition.] The flower garden. Shewing . . . how most flowers are to be ordered, the time of flowering, taking of them up, and of planting them again. And how they are increased . . . VVhereunto is now added. The gardiners or planters dialling, (viz.) how to draw a horizontal diall, as a knot in a garden, on a grass-plot, or elsewhere, etc. London, for William Crook. 1672. 14×8 cm. 12°. pp. [xii], 100 [i.e. 102], [6]: 4 pls., illust.

Copies: LBM; KRBG; OBL.

207. — [Another issue.] The flower garden enlarged. Shewing how to order and increase all sorts of flowers . . . Also how to draw a horizontal dial as a knot in a garden. To which is now added a treatise of all the roots, plants, trees, shrubs, fruits, herbs, &c. growing in His Majesties plantations, etc. London, for C. Wall. [1675?] 13×7 cm. 12°. pp. [xii], 100 [i.e. 102], [6]: 4 pls., illust.

The only copy of the above issue seen, so far, by the compiler is in the Brit. Mus. (Bloomsbury) (969.a.2). It has been cropped and no date of publication is visible. The Museum *Catalogue of printed books* records the date as [1675?]. Except for a new title-page this issue is identical with the work of 1672.

Copy: LBM.

208. — The flower garden and Compleat vineyard. In two parts . . . The third edition, improved. London, for William Crook. 1683. 13×8 cm. 12°. pp. [xii], 47, [1]; [xxiv], 103, [5]: 1 pl.

'The compleat vineyard' has a separate title-page and is of the third edition (1683).

Copies: LBM; LRHS; LWML.

HUNTER (ALEXANDER) [1729–1809]

Silva: or, a discourse of forest-trees . . . With notes by A. Hunter, etc. **See** EVELYN (J.) 1776. 4°.

— A new edition. 2 vols. 1786. 4°.

— Ed. 3. 1801. 2 vols. 4°.

— Ed. 4. 1812. 2 vols. 4°.

— Ed. 5. 1825. 2 vols. 4°.

INSTRUCTIONS.

209. Instructions for the increasing of mulberrie trees, and the breeding of silke-wormes for the making of silke in this kingdome. Whereunto is annexed His Maiesties letters to the Lords Lieftenants . . . tending to that purpose. [By William Stallenge.] [London.] 1609. 19×14 cm. 4°. Signn. A–C⁴, illust.

Leaf A1 is signed 'A', otherwise it is blank.

Copy: LBM.

For another edition see S., W. 1609. 4°.

JOHNSON (THOMAS) [1595/1597–1644]

210. Descriptio itineris plantarum investigationis ergô suscepti, in agrum cantianum anno Dom. 1632. Et enumeratio plantarum in Ericeto hampstediano locisǥ vicinis crescentium, etc. [The address to the reader is by Thomas Iohnson.] [London], excudebat, Tho. Cotes. 1632. 14×8 cm. 12°. pp. 7, [1], 39, [1]: 2 pls.

Copies: LBM; OMaC; CBS.

211. — [Another edition.] Nup. edit. T. S. Ralph. Londini, sumptibus Guliel. Pamplin. 1849. 21×17 cm. 4°. pp. [ii], 48: 1 pl.

Copy: LBMNH.

The herball or generall historie of plantes . . . very much enlarged and amended by Thomas Iohnson, etc. See GERARD (J.) 1633. fol.

— (Second edition, revised). 1636. fol.

212. Iter plantarum investigationis ergo susceptum a decem socijs, in agrum cantianum. Anno Dom. 1629 . . . Ericetum hamstedianum sive plantarum ibi crescentium observatio habita, anno eodem, etc. [London.1629.] 19×15 cm. 4°. Signn. A–B⁴.

The Catalogue of printed books, in the Brit. Mus. (Bloomsbury) gives the imprint and date of publication as '[London, 1629.]'.

Copies: LBM; OMaC.

213. Mercurius botanicus; sive plantarum gratiâ suscepti itineris, anno M.DC.XXXIV. descriptio. Cum earum nominibus Latinis, & Anglicis, &c. Huic accessit de Thermis Bathonicis tractatus. [With a dedication by Thomas Johnson and his associates.] Londini, excudebat Thom. Cotes. 1634. 16×10 cm. 8°. pp. [vi], 78; [iv], 19, [1]: 1 map, illust.

The first and last leaf (i.e. A1 and H4) are blank, and are not included in the above collation.

The tract on Bath has a separate title-page reading: 'Thermæ Bathonicæ, sive earum descriptio, vires, utendi tempus, modus', etc.

Copies: LBM; LBMNH; LCPG; KRBG; CBS.

214. — Mercurii botanici pars altera, sive plantarum gratia suscepti itineris in Cambriam . . . descriptio exhibens reliquarum stirpium nostratium (quæ in priore parte non enumerabantur) catalogum. [With a dedication by Thomas Johnson.] Londini, excudebat T. & R. Cotes. 1641. 16×10 cm. 8°. pp. [viii], 37, [1].

The signatures in the 'pars altera' are continuous with those of the work of 1634. The last leaf (i.e. M4) is blank, and is not included in the above collation.

Copies: LBM; LBMNH; CBS.

LANGFORD (T.)

215. Plain and full instructions to raise all sorts of fruit-trees that prosper in England . . . And . . . the best directions . . . for making liquors of the several sorts of fruit, etc. London, J. M. for Rich. Chiswel. 1681. 18×11 cm. 8°. pp. [xx], 148, [8]: 2 pls.

Facing plate 1 is an unnumbered leaf with descriptive letterpress.

Copy: LBM.

216. — Ed. 2, revised and enlarged . . . together with an addition of two intire chapters of greens and green-houses, etc. London, for Richard Chiswell. 1696. 18×11 cm. 8°. pp. [xxx], 220, [6]: 2 pls.

Facing plate 1 is an unnumbered leaf with descriptive letterpress.

Copies: LBM; LRHS; LRCS; KRBG; HRES.

217. — Ed. 2, revised and enlarged . . . together with an addition of two intire chapters of greens and green-houses, etc. London, for R. Chiswell, sold by D. Midwinter and T. Leigh. 1699. 18×11 cm. 8°. pp. [xxx], 220, [6]: 2 pls.

Facing plate 1 is an unnumbered leaf with descriptive letterpress. 'Ed.2' (1699) is identical with 'Ed.2' (1696) except for a cancel title-page.

Copy: LBM.

LA QUINTINIE (Jean de) [1626-1688]

218. The compleat gard'ner; or, directions for cultivating and right ordering of fruit-gardens and kitchen-gardens; with divers reflections on several parts of husbandry . . . [from 'Instruction pour les jardins fruitiers et potagers', etc.] By . . . Monsᵉʳ de La Quintinye . . . To which is added his treatise of orange-trees, with the raising of melons, omitted in the French editions. Made English by John Evelyn, etc. [2 vols. in 1.] London, for Matthew Gillyflower, and James Partridge. 1693. 32 × 20 cm. fol. pp. [xliv], 184 [i.e. 192], [4]; 204 [i.e. 184], [4], 4, 80: engr. frontis. (port. of author), 11 pls., illust.

Copies: LBM; LBMNH; LRHS; KRBG; HRES; CUBG.

219. The compleat gard'ner: or, directions for cultivating and right ordering of fruit-gardens, and kitchen-gardens. By Monsieur de La Quintinye. Now compendiously abridg'd, and made of more use, with very considerable improvements. By George London, and Henry Wise. London, for M. Gillyflower. 1699. 19 × 12 cm. 8°. pp. [ii], xxxv, [i], 309 [i.e. 325], [7]: frontis., 10 pls., illust.

Copies: LBM; KRBG; HRES; CUBG.

Four unnumbered pages entitled: 'An advertisement of J. Evelyn, Esq; to the folio edition of Monsieur La Quintinye' are inserted between pages xiv and xv of some copies of the first edition of The compleat gard'ner, and in all copies of the second (1699), third (1701), and fourth (1704) editions of the work. In the fifth edition (1710), and in subsequent editions, this 'Advertisement' is included in the pagination i–xxxvi occupying pages xiv–xvi.

220. — Ed. 2, corrected. London, for M. Gillyflower, sold by Andrew Bell. 1699. 19 × 12 cm. 8°. pp. [ii], xxxv [i.e. xxxix], [i], 309 [i.e. 325], [7]: frontis., 10 pls., illust.

Copies: LBM; LRHS.

221. — Ed. 3, corrected. London, for Andrew Bell. 1701. 19 × 11 cm. 8°. pp. [ii], xxxv [i.e. xxxix], [i], 309 [i.e. 325], [7]: frontis., 10 pls., illust.

Copies: LBM; LRHS; OBL.

222. — Ed. 4, corrected, London, for Andrew Bell. 1704. 19 × 12 cm. 8°. pp. [ii], xxxv [i.e. xxxix], [i], 309 [i.e. 325], [7]: frontis., 10 pls., illust.

Copies: LBM; LRHS.

223. — Ed. 5, corrected. London, for Andrew Bell. 1710. 19 × 11 cm. 8°. pp. [ii], xxxvi, 325, [7]: frontis., 10 pls., illust.

Copies: LBM; LRHS; HRES.

224. — Ed. 6, corrected. London, A. and W. Bell. 1717. 19 × 11 cm. 8°. pp. [ii], xxxvi, 325, [7]: frontis., 10 pls., illust.

Copies: LWML; LCPG; CUBG.

The compiler has been unable, so far, to find any further edition of The compleat gard'ner. Keynes (G.), John Evelyn a study in bibliophily, etc. 223 (1937), records a 'seventh edition, A. and W. Bell (1719)'.

LAWRENCE (Anthony)

225. Nurseries, orchards, profitable gardens, and vineyards encouraged . . . In several letters . . . to Henry Oldenburg . . . The first letter from Anthony Lawrence; all the rest from John Beale, etc. London, for Henry Brome. 1677. 18 × 13 cm. 4°. pp. [ii], 28.

Copies: LBM; LRHS; KRBG; HRES.

LAWSON (William)

226. A new orchard and garden. Or the best way for planting, grafting, and to make any ground good, for a rich orchard: particularly in the north parts of England: generally for the whole kingdome . . . With The country housewifes garden for hearbes of common vse . . . As also, the husbandry of bees, etc. London, Bar: Alsop for Roger Iackson. 1618. 18 × 13 cm. 4°. pp. [viii], 59, [i]; [ii], 25, [i]: woodcut on tp., illust., 𝕭.𝕷.

'The country housewifes garden' in the above edition of A new orchard and garden, and in the editions of 1623 and 1626 of that work, has its own title-page and pagination and includes 'the husbandry of bees'. In the edition of 1618 'The country housewifes garden' is dated 1617.

Copies: LBM; HRES.

227. A new orchard and garden . . . With The country housewifes garden . . . As also the husbandry of bees . . . now the second time corrected and much enlarged, by William Lawson. Whereunto is newly added the art of propagating plants (by Simon Harward), with the true ordering of all manner of fruits, in their gathering, carrying home, and preseruation. London, I. H. for Roger Iackson. 1623. 19 × 14 cm. 4°. pp. [viii], 57, [i]; [ii], 24; 10; 7, [i]: woodcut on tp., illust., 𝕭.𝕷.

In this edition and in the 1626 edition the sections

on the propagation of plants and the ordering of fruits have separate pagination.

Copy: OBL.

228. A new orchard and garden . . . With The country housewifes garden . . . As also the husbandry of bees . . . now the third time corrected and much enlarged, by William Lawson. Whereunto is newly added the art of propagating plants, etc. London, I. H. for Francis Williams. 1626. 18×14 cm. 4°. pp. [viii], 57, [1]; [ii], 24; 10; 7, [1]: woodcut on tp., illust., **B.L.**

Copy: LBM.

Editions of Lawson's *New orchard and garden* were included together with several works by Gervase Markham in a volume entitled *A way to get wealth*, published many times during the years 1623 until 1695 inclusive. *See* Poynter (F. N. L.), A bibliography of Gervase Markham 1568?–1637, pp. 152–178 (1962), *Publ. Oxford bibl. Soc.* New series. Vol. XI.

LE GENDRE (Antoine) [1590–1665]

229. The manner of ordering fruit-trees. By the Sieur Le Gendre, Curate of Henonville. Wherein is treated of nurseries, wall-fruits, hedges of fruit-trees, dwarf-trees, high-standers, &c. Written originally in French [under the title of 'La maniere de cultiver les arbres fruitiers', etc.], and translated faithfully into English [by John Evelyn?], etc. London, Humphrey Moseley. 1660. 14×8 cm. 12°. pp. [xxxvi], 154: frontis.

A translation attributed to J. Evelyn. *See* Budd (F. E.), *Review of English studies*, **14**: 285–297 (1938), and Keynes (G.), *John Evelyn a study in bibliophily* 83 (1968).

Copies: LBM; LRHS; HRES.

LEMNIUS (Levinus) [1505–1568]

230. An herbal for the Bible. Containing a plaine . . . exposition of such similitudes, parables, and metaphors, both in the olde Testament and the newe, as are borrowed and taken from herbs, plants, trees, fruits and simples . . . Drawn into English by Thomas Newton. London, Edmund Bollifant. 1587. 16×10 cm. 8°. pp. [viii], 287, [9].

The first leaf (i.e. pp. [i–ii]) is blank, except for the signature 'A' on the recto.

Copies: LBM; LWML; LPS; KRBG; CUL.

L'OBEL (Matthias de) [1538–1616]

231. Balsami, opobalsami, carpobalsami, & xylobalsami, cum suo cortice explanatio, etc.

Londini, excudebat Arnoldus Hatfield, impensis Ioannis Norton. 1598. 20×14 cm. 4°. pp. [vi], 40, [2]: illust.

Copies: LBM; CUL.

232. Matthiæ de l'Obel . . . in G. Rondelletii . . . methodicam pharmaceuticam officinam animaduersiones . . . Accesserunt auctaria . . . Aduersariorumque volumen, eorumcᵹ pars altera, etc. Londini, excudebat prælum Thomæ Purfootij. 1605. 28×19 cm. fol. pp. [viii], 156; [xvi], 455, [1], 456–549: woodcut arms on tp., illust.

The 'Aduersariorumque volumen' is entitled 'Dilucidæ simplicium medicamenorum [*sic*] explicationes, & stirpium aduersaria', etc. There are three printed slips inserted facing pages 11, 33, and 150, and two pasted-in slips on pages 252 and 400 respectively. The 'pars altera' is composed of the 'Rariorum aliquot stirpium appendix', followed by 'Matthiæ de l'Obel Balsami, opobalsami, carpobalsami, & xylobalsami cum suo cortice explanationes & collectanea' and two tracts by G. Rondeletius.

Copies: LBM; LBMNH; LRHS; LWML; KRBG; CUL.

See also Pena (P.) and L'Obel (M. de) 1570(–71) fol.

233. Matthiæ de l'Obel . . . stirpium illustrationes. Plurimas elaborantes inauditas plantas, subreptitiis Joh: Parkinsoni rapsodiis (ex codice MS. insalutato) sparsim gravatæ. Ejusdem adjecta sunt ad calcem Theatri botanici ἁμαρτήματα. Accurante Guil: How, Anglo. Londini, typis Tho: Warren, impensis Jos: Kirton. 1655. 18×14 cm. (23×17 cm. large paper.) 4°. pp. [xxxviii], 170, [6].

Copies: LBM; LBMNH; LCPG; KRBG; OMaC; CBS.

L'OBEL (Matthias de) and PENA (P.)

Stirpium aduersaria noua, etc. **See** Pena (P.) and L'Obel (M. de) 1570(–71). fol.

LONDON (George) [–1714] and WISE (H.)

The compleat gard'ner . . . By Monsieur de La Quintinye . . . abridg'd . . . By George London, and Henry Wise.

See La Quintinie (J. de) 1699. 8°.

— Ed. 2. 1699. 8°.
— Ed. 3. 1701. 8°.
— Ed. 4. 1704. 8°.
— Ed. 5. 1710. 8°.
— Ed. 6. 1717 87.°.

LOVELL (ROBERT) [1630?-1690]

234. Παμβοτανολογια. Sive enchiridion botanicum. Or a compleat herball containing the summe of what hath hitherto been published . . . touching trees, shrubs . . . flowers, &c. . . . with an . . . universall index of plants: shewing what grow wild in England, etc. Oxford, William Hall, for Ric. Davis. 1659. 14×8 cm. 12°. pp. [lxxxiv], 671, [1].

Copies: LBM; LBMNH; LWML; LCPG; KRBG; OBL; ORSL; CBS.

235. — Παμβοτανολογια. Sive, enchiridion botanicum. Or, a compleat herball, containing the summe of ancient and moderne authors . . . touching trees, shrubs . . . flowers, &c. . . . with an . . . universal index of plants: shewing what grow wild in England. The second edition, with many additions, etc. Oxford, W. H. for Ric. Davis. 1665. 15×9 cm. 12°. pp. 84, 675 [i.e. 673], [7].

The copies of the above 'second edition' (1665) seen, so far, by the compiler have a cancel title-page this being indicated in some copies by a stub belonging to a leaf conjugate with A12 (i.e. pp. 23-24). A copy in the Bodleian Library, Oxford (8°. D. 62. Med.) originally contained the cancelland title, but this has been torn leaving only a narrow strip with a few words and parts of words visible. In the cancel title the line containing the word 'herball' is followed by two lines starting 'containing' and 'moderne' respectively. In the cancelland title the word 'her [ball]' is followed by a line beginning 'containin[g]', and 'moder[ne]' is the first word in the next line but one. (In the title of 1659 'herball' is followed by a line beginning 'containing' while 'moderne' is in the next line but one, but it is not the first word.)

In copies of the work of 1665 in the Bodleian Library, Oxford (8°. A. 41. Med. BS.—Sherard 197) and in the Wellcome Medical Historical Library there is an additional leaf conjugate with the cancel title-page. This contains a longitudinal half-title on the recto reading 'Lovel's herball'. The verso is blank.

Copies: LBM; LBMNH; LRHS; LRCS; LPS; KRBG; OBL; ORSL; OMaC; CUL.

LYTE (HENRY) [c. 1529-1607]

A nievve herball, or historie of plantes . . . First set foorth in the Doutche or Almaigne tongue, by Rembert Dodoens . . . nowe first translated out of French into English, by Henry Lyte, etc. See DODOENS (R.) 1578. fol.

— [Another edition.] 1586. 4°.

— [Another edition.] 1595. 4°.

— [Another edition.] 1619. fol.

Rams little Dodeon. A briefe epitome of the new Herbal, or history of plants . . . first set forth in the Dutch or Almayne tongue, by . . . Reinbert Dodeon . . . translated into English by Henry Lyte . . . and now collected and abbridged by William Ram, etc. See DODOENS (R.) 1606. 4°.

M., D.

236. The gardeners labyrinth, or, a new art of gardning: wherein is laid down new and rare inventions and secrets of gardning . . . For sowing, planting, and setting all manner of roots, herbs, and flowers, both for the use of the kitchin garden, and a garden of pleasure . . . Likewise here is set forth divers knots . . . Lastly, here is set down the physical benefit of each herbe, with the commodities of the waters distilled out of them . . . Collected from the best approved authors . . . by D. M. [i.e. Didymus Mountain.] And now newly corrected and inlarged. 2 Pts. London, Jane Bell. 1652 [1651]. 18×14 cm. 4°. pp. [vi], 90; 173, illust.

The British Museum's copy of the above edition of The gardeners labyrinth in the Thomason collection (E.650(13)) is dated 15 December 1651 in Thomason's hand on the title-page.

The second part of the work has a separate title-page, dated 1651.

Copies: LBM; HRES.

237. — [Another edition.] 2 Pts. London, J. Bell. 1656. 17×13 cm. 4°. pp. [vi], 60 [i.e. 90]; 173, [13]: illust.

Part 2 has a separate title-page.

Copy: LBM.

238. — [Another edition.] 2 Pts. London, H. Bell for Edward Brewster. 1660. 17×13 cm. 4°. pp. [vi], 60 [i.e. 90]; 173, [13]: illust.

Part 2 has a separate title-page dated 1656.

Copy: KRBG.

For earlier editions see MOUNTAIN (DIDYMUS) pseud. [i.e. T. HILL.] 1577, etc. 4°.

MACER (ÆMILIUS) pseud. [i.e. ODO, a. physician.]

A newe herball of Macer, translated out of Laten in to Englysshe. See HERBAL. Here begynnyth a newe mater, etc. [Another edition.] A newe herball of Macer, etc. [1535?] 8°.

— [Another edition.] Macers herbal. Practysyd by Doctor Lynacro. [1542?] 8°.

MALPIGHI (Marcello) [1628–1694]

239. Marcelli Malpighii . . . anatome plantarum. Cui subjungitur appendix, iteratas & auctas ejusdem authoris de ovo incubato observationes continens, etc. 2 Pts. Londini, impensis Johannis Martyn. 1675–79. 36×23 cm. fol.

Pt. 1. 1675. pp. [ii], 15, [5], 82; [ii], 20: engr. half-title, pls. 1–54 and pls. 1–7.

The 'Appendix de ovo incubato' has its own title-page and pagination, and its plates are numbered separately.

Pt. 2. 1679. pp. [vi], 93, [3]: engr. half-title (same as Pt. 1), pls. 1–39.

Copies: LBM; LRS; KRBG; OMaC.

MASCALL (Leonard) [–1589]

A booke of the art and maner, howe to plante and graffe all sortes of trees . . . by one of the abbey of S. Vincent in Fraunce [i.e. D. Brossard] . . . englished, by Leonarde Mascal. See Book. [1569.] 4°.

— [Another edition.] [1572.] 4°.

— [Another edition.] 1575. 4°.

— [Another edition.] 1582. 4°.

— [Another edition.] 1590. 4°.

— [Another edition.] 1592. 4°.

— [Another edition.] 1596. 4°.

— [Another edition.] 1599. 4°.

— [Another edition.] The country-mans recreation . . . in three bookes. The first [by D. Brossard, translated by L. Mascall], etc. See Country-Mans Recreation. 1640. 4°.

— [Another edition.] 1654. 4°.

— [Another edition.] The country-mans new art of planting and graffing, etc. [By D. Brossard, translated by L. Mascall.] See Country-Mans New Art. 1651. 4°.

— [Another edition.] 1651. 4°.

— [Another edition.] 1652. 4°.

— [Another edition.] 1656. 4°.

MAXWELL (Robert) [1695–1765]
See Reid (J.) The Scots gardiner . . . Together with . . . The practical bee-master (by Robert Maxwell), etc. 1756, etc. 12°.

MEAGER (Leonard)

240. The English gardener: or, a sure guide to young planters and gardeners . . . shewing the way . . . of planting and raising all sorts of stocks, fruit-trees, and shrubs . . . how to order the kitchin-garden . . . the ordering of the garden of pleasure, etc. London, for P. Parker. 1670. 20×15 cm. 4°. pp. [viii], 252 [i.e. 168]: 24 pls.

Copies: LBM; HRES; OBL.

241. — [Another edition.] London, for J. Wright. 1683. 19×15 cm. 4°. pp. [viii], 144: 24 pls.

Copies: LBM; HRES.

242. — [Another edition.] London, J. Rawlins, for M. Wotton, and G. Conyers. 1688. 20×16 cm. 4°. pp. [viii], 144: 24 pls.

Copies: LBM; LRHS; KRBG; HRES; CUBG.

243. — Ed. 9, with large additions. London, J. Dawks, for M. Wotton, and G. Conyers. 1699. 20×16 cm. 4°. pp. [viii], 144: 24 pls.

Copies: LBM; LRHS; OBL.

244. — The compleat English gardner: or, a sure guide to young planters and gardners . . . The tenth edition . . . Begun by Leonard Meager . . . and now enlarged by way of Supplement [by 'S. G.'] (An appendix), etc. London, for M. Wotton; and G. Conyers. 1704. 21×16 cm. 4°. pp. [viii], 150: 24 pls.

'A supplement to the English gardner', pp. 117–144.

'An appendix', pp. 145–150.

It seems possible that the initials 'S. G.' stand for Samuel Gilbert, the floriculturist and author of *The florists vade-mecum*. 1682, etc.

Copy: BM.

245. — Ed. 11, etc. London, M. Wotton; and G. Conyers. [1710?] 20×16 cm. 4°. pp. [iv], 156: 24 pls.

In the above undated edition the 'Appendix' forms part of the Supplement which occupies pp. 117–156.

In the *Catalogue of printed books in the Brit. Mus.* (*Bloomsbury*) the date of the work is given as [1710?].

Copies: LBM; LRHS; KRBG; CUL.

246. The mystery of husbandry: or, arable, pasture, and wood-land improved . . . To which is added, the countryman's almanack, etc. London, printed by W. Onley, for Henry Nelme. 1697. 16×9 cm. 12°. pp. [xii], 161, [7]: 1 pl.

Copies: LBM; LRHS; HRES.

247. — [Another issue.] London, printed by W. Onley, and are to be sold by Will. Majore, bookseller, in Newport, Cornwall. 1697. 15×9 cm. 12°. pp. [xii], 161, [7]: 1 pl.

Except for the imprint, the above issue is identical with the preceding work of 1697.

Copy: ORSL.

248. The new art of gardening, with the gardener's almanack: containing the true art of gardening in all its particulars, etc. London, for Henry Nelme. 1697. 16×9 cm. 12°. pp. [iv], 164, [12]: folding frontis.

Copy: LBM.

249. — [Another edition.] London, for Peter Parker. 1699. 15×9 cm. 12°. pp. [iv], 160, [4]: folding frontis.

Copy: OBL.

250. — [Another edition.] London, for Peter Parker. 1713. 15×9 cm. 12°. pp. [viii], 160: folding frontis.

Copy: KRBG.

251. — [Another edition.] London, for Peter Parker. 1718. 15×9 cm. 12°. pp. [viii], 160: folding frontis.

Copy: ORSL.

252. — [Another edition.] London, for R. Ware, sold by T. Norris, S. Bates, A. Bettesworth. [1720?] 14×8 cm. 12°. pp. [viii], 160: folding frontis.

Copy: LBM.

253. — [Another edition.] London, for R. Ware. 1732. 14×8 cm. 12°. pp. [viii], 159, [1]: folding frontis.

On the title-page of the above work of 1732 is the statement: 'The second edition corrected.'

Copy: LBM.

MERRET (CHRISTOPHER) [1614–1695]

254. Pinax rerum naturalium britannicarum, continens vegetabilia, animalia et fossilia, in hac insulâ repperta [*sic*] inchoatus, etc. Londini, impensis Cave Pulleyn, typis F. & T. Warren. 1666. 16×10 cm. 8°. pp. [xxxii], 221 [i.e. 223], [1].

Leaf A8 (i.e. pp. [xxxi–xxxii]) is blank.

Copies: LBM; LBMNH; LRHS; OBL.

255. — [Another edition.] Londini, typis T. Roycroft, impensis Cave Pulleyn. 1667. 15×10 cm. 8°. pp. [xxxii], 223, [1].

Copies: LBM; LBMNH; LCPG; KRBG; OBL.

256. — Editio secunda, etc. Londini, typis T. Roycroft, impensis Cave Pulleyn, prostat apud Sam. Thomson. 1667. 16×9 cm. 8°. pp. [xxxii], 223, [1].

The above 'Editio secunda' (1667) is the same as the previous edition of 1667 except for a cancel title-page. In an 'Advertisement' in *Phil. Trans.* 2: 448 (April 1667) Merret 'wholly disclaims the second edition . . . as being printed and published without his knowledge'.

Copies: LBMNH; OBL; CUL.

MOLLET (ANDRÉ) [–1665?]

257. The garden of pleasure, containing several draughts of gardens both in embroyder'd-ground-works, knot-works of grass, as likewise in wildernesses, and others, etc. In the Savoy. Printed by T. N. for John Martyn, and Henry Herringman. 1670. 43×27 cm. fol. pp. [viii], 15, [1]: 37 designs on 39 pls. (1, 9, and 25 each printed from 2 pls., and 19, 18, on one plate), designs numbered 1–17, 19, 18, 19–30, 25–30.

The compiler has seen two copies of *The garden of pleasure*, the copy in the Lindley Library, R.H.S., from which the above collation has been made, and the copy in the University Library, Cambridge (Bb*.8.31¹) which contains no plates.

Copies: LRHS; CUL.

MORISON (ROBERT) [1620–1683]

258. Hortus regius blesensis auctus, cum notulis durationis & charactismis plantarum tam additarum, quam non scriptarum; item plantarum in eodem Horto . . . contentarum, nemini hucusque scriptarum . . . delineatio

. . . Præludiorum botanicorum pars prior. (Hallucinationes Caspari Bauhini in Pinace . . . item animadversiones, in tres tomos, universalis historiæ, plantarum; Johannis Bauhini. Quibus accessit dialogus inter socium Collegii regii londinensis, Gresham dicti, & botanographum regium. Præludiorum botanicorum pars altera.) Londini, typis Tho. Roycroft, impensis Jacobi Allestry. 1669. 15×10 cm. 8°. pp. [xxiv], 347, [1]; [x], 351–499, [5].

The half-title of the above work reads 'Præludia botanica Roberti Morison', etc.

'Hallucinationes Caspari Bauhini' has a separate title-page, it has no imprint.

Copies: LBM; LBMNH; LRHS; LLS; LCPG; KRBG; CBS.

Icones & descriptiones rariorum plantarum Siciliæ, Melitæ, Galliæ, & Italiæ, etc. [Edited, and with a dedication by R. Morison.] **See** BOCCONE (P.) 1674. 4°.

259. Plantarum historiæ universalis oxoniensis pars secunda (—pars tertia) seu herbarum distributio nova, per tabulas cognationis & affinitatis ex libro naturæ observata & detecta (Partem hanc tertiam, post auctoris mortem . . . absolvit Jacobus Bobartius), etc. 2 Pts. [in 2 vols.] Oxonii, e Theatro Sheldoniano. 1680–99. 44×28 cm. fol.

Pt. 1. Never published.

Pt. 2. 1680. pp. [vi], 617 [i.e. 619], [5]: engr. on tp., 126 engr. pls. on 65 leaves.

Pt. 3. 1699. pp. [xxiv], 657, [11]: engr. on tp., frontis. (port. of author), 166 engr. pls. on 87 leaves.

The twenty-four preliminary pages of the Pars tertia are made up as follows: a half-title, title-page, dedication, 'Vita Roberti Morisoni M.D.', 'Ad lectorem candidum præfatio', 'Botanologiæ summarium', 'Errata' and 'Errata in tabulis æneis'. Not all copies of the Pars tertia, however, contain all these items.

In the Brit. Mus. (Nat. Hist.) is a volume, formerly in the library of Sir Hans Sloane, containing an unpublished and cancelled fragment of the second part of the *Plantarum historia*. The text includes notes ('annotationes') by Dr. Thomas Hyde, D.D. (1636–1703), Chief Keeper of the Bodleian Library Oxford, on the oriental names of plants. Bobart extended the text and made it the beginning of Part 3 of the *Plantarum historia* but omitted the oriental names.

Copies: LBM; LBMNH; LLS; LCPG; OBL.

260. — [Another edition] Plantarum historiæ

universalis oxoniensis . . . Tomus primus (—secundus—tertius). 3 vols. Oxonii, e Theatro Sheldoniano. 1715. 42×28 cm. fol.

1. pp. [x], 91, [1]: engr. on tp., frontis. (port. of author), 8 pls. (tables) with letterpress explanations on the back of 7 pls. 12 pls. (of plants) with descriptive text.

2. pp. [vi], 617 [i.e. 619], [5]: engr. on tp., 126 engr. pls. on 65 leaves.

3. pp. [xxii], 657, [11]: engr. on tp., 166 engr. pls. on 87 leaves.

Except for new title-pages, this is a reissue of the same setting as the preceding, with the author's 'Plantarum Umbelliferarum distributio', without its title-page, forming the first volume.

Copies: LBMNH; LRHS; OBL.

261. — [Another edition.] Plantarum historiæ universalis oxoniensis . . . Tomus primus (—secundus). 2 vols. Oxonii, e Theatro Sheldoniano. 1738. 41×27 cm. fol.

1. pp. [vi], 617 [i.e. 619], [5]: engr. on tp., frontis. (port. of author), 126 engr. pls. on 65 leaves.

2. pp. [xxii], 657, [11]: engr. on tp., 166 engr. pls. on 87 leaves.

This is another reissue of the original setting, with new title-pages. 'Plantarum Umbelliferarum distributio' is not included in this edition.

Copy: LBMNH.

262. Plantarum Umbelliferarum distributio nova, per tabulas cognationis et affinitatis ex libro naturæ observata & detecta, etc. Oxonii, e Theatro Sheldoniano. 1672. 41×26 cm. fol. pp. [x], 91, [1]: 8 engr. pls. (tables) with letterpress explanations on the back of 7 pls. 12 engr. pls. (of plants) with descriptive text.

The above work also forms volume **1** of the 1715 edition of Morison's *Plantarum historia universalis oxoniensis*.

Copies: LBM; LBMNH; LCPG; KRBG.

MOUNTAIN (DIDYMUS) pseud. [i.e. THOMAS HILL.]

263. The gardeners labyrinth: containing a discourse of the gardeners life, in the yearly trauels to be bestovved on his plot of earth, for the vse of a garden: with instructions for the choise of seedes, apte times for sowing, setting, planting, ʒ watering, and the vessels and instruments seruing to that vse and purpose: wherein are set forth diuers herbers, knottes and mazes

. . . Also the physike benefit of eche herbe, plant, and floure, with the vertues of the distilled waters of euery of them, as by the sequele may further appeare. Gathered out of the best approued writers of gardening, husbandrie, and physicke: by Dydymus Mountaine. [Completed by Henry Dethick.] 2 Pts. London, Henry Bynneman. 1577. 18×14 cm. 4°. pp. [viii], 80; 180, [12]: woodcut on tp., 4 pls., illust., 𝕭.𝕷.

In the above edition, and in subsequent editions, the second part of *The gardener's labyrinth* has a separate title-page, but with neither imprint nor date.

The real name of the author appears in Southerne (E.), *A treatise concerning the right vse and ordering of bees*, B4ᵃ (1593), where reference is made to a statement by 'one M. Hill of London in his booke intituled, The gardners labyrinth'.

Copies: LBM; OBL.

264. — [Another issue.] 2 Pts. London, Henry Bynneman. 1578. 19×14 cm. 4°. pp. [viii], 80; 180, [12]: woodcut on tp., 4 pls., illust., 𝕭.𝕷.

Except for the date on the title-page the above issue is identical with the work of 1577.

Copy: OBL.

265. — [Another edition.] 2 Pts. London, Iohn VVolfe. 1586. 18×14 cm. 4°. pp. [viii], 80; 180, [12]: woodcut on tp., 4 pls., illust., 𝕭.𝕷.

Copies: HRES; OBL.

266. — [Another edition.] 2 Pts. London, Adam Islip. 1594. 19×14 cm. 4°. pp. [viii]; 80; 180, [12]: woodcut on tp., 4 pls., illust., 𝕭.𝕷.

Copies: LBM; LPS; OBL; CTH; CUBG.

267. — [Another edition.] 2 Pts. London, Henry Ballard. 1608. 18×14 cm. 4°. pp. [viii]; 80; 180, [12]: woodcut on tp., 4 pls., illust., 𝕭.𝕷.

Copies: LBM; LWML; HRES; OBL; CUL.

— [Another edition.] The gardeners labyrinth . . . By D. M. [i.e. Didymus Mountain], etc. See M., D. 2 Pts. 1652[1651]. 4°.

— [Another edition.] 2 Pts. 1656. 4°.

— [Another edition.] 2 Pts. 1660. 4°.

MOUNTAINE (Dydymus)
See Mountain (Didymus)

N., G. V.
The Belgick, or Netherlandish Hesperides.

That is. The management . . . of the limon and orange trees . . . Made English by G. V. N. See Commelin (J.) 1683. 8°.

N., R. D. C. D. W. B. D.

268. The French gardiner: instructing how to cultivate all sorts of fruit-trees, and herbs for the garden: together with directions to dry and conserve them in their natural; six times printed in France, and once in Holland . . . first written [under the title of 'Le jardinier françois', etc.] by R. D. C. D. W. B. D. N. [i.e. Nicolas de Bonnefons] and now transplanted into English by Philocepos [i.e. John Evelyn, who signs the dedication J. E.], etc. London, J. C. for John Crooke. 1658. 14×8 cm. 12°. pp. [x], 294, [14]: frontis., 3 pls.

An errata leaf is inserted at the end of the work.

Copy: CUBG.

269. — [Another issue.] London, J. C. for John Crooke. 1658. 14×9 cm. 12°. pp. [x], 294, [16]: frontis., 3 pls.

The only copy of the above issue known to the present writer is in the Henry E. Huntington Library. This copy has a statement on the title-page reading 'three times printed in France' instead of 'six times printed' as in the previous issue. There is no errata leaf and the last five pages contain 'Books printed for John Crooke'. *See* Keynes (G.), *John Evelyn a study in bibliophily*, etc. 48–51 (1937).

Copy: [HEHL].

270. — [Another issue.] London, for John Crooke. 1658. 14×9 cm. 12°. pp. [xii], 294, [16]: frontis., 3 pls.

The above issue has a cancel title-page, with the words 'six times printed' instead of 'three times printed', followed by a leaf with errata.

Copies: LBM; CUL.

For later editions of *The French gardiner* see French Gardiner. 1669, etc. 8°.

NATURAL HISTORY.

271. The natural history of coffee, thee, chocolate, tobacco . . . with a tract of elder and juniper-berries . . . and also the way of making mum, etc. London, for Christopher Wilkinson. 1682. 18×14 cm. 4°. pp. 36, [4].

Copies: LBM; LBMNH.

NEW DIRECTIONS.

272. New directions of experience by the authour for the planting of timber and fire-wood. With a neere estimation what millions

of acres the kingdome doth containe, etc. [By Arthur Standish.] [London?] 1613. 17×14 cm. 4°. pp. [ii], 22.

Copy: O.B.L. (Ashm. 1672 (1)).

For later editions **see** STANDISH (A.) New directions of experience, etc. [Another edition.] 1613, etc. 4°.

NEWTON (THOMAS) [1542?-1607]

An herbal for the Bible... Drawen into English by Thomas Newton. **See** LEMNIUS (L.) 1587. 8°.

OLDENBURG (HENRY) [1615?-1677]

Nurseries, orchards, profitable gardens, and vineyards encouraged . . . In several letters . . . directed to Henry Oldenburg, etc. **See** LAWRENCE (A.) 1677. 4°.

ORCHARD.

273. The orchard, and the garden: containing certaine necessarie, secret, and ordinarie knowledges in grafting and gardening. Wherein are described sundrie waies to graffe, and diuerse proper new plots for the garden. Gathered from the Dutch and French. Also to know the time and season, when it is good to sow and replant all manner of seedes. London, Adam Islip. 1594. 18×13 cm. 4°. pp. [ii], 61, [1]: woodcut on tp., illust., 𝕭.𝕷.

Copies: LBM; OCCC.

274. — [Another edition.] London, Adam Islip. 1596. 18×13 cm. 4°. pp. [ii], 61, [1]: woodcut on tp., illust., 𝕭.𝕷.

The only copy of the above edition of 1596 seen, so far, by the compiler is in Corpus Christi College, Oxford. This copy is imperfect wanting pp. 49–52.

Copy: OCCC.

275. — [Another edition.] London, Adam Islip. 1597. 18×13 cm. 4°. pp. [ii], 61, [1]: woodcut on tp., illust., 𝕭.𝕷.

Although the date on the title-page of the copy of the above work in the Lindley Library, R.H.S. has been cropped by the binder enough is left to show that it can only be read as 1597. An imperfect copy of this edition is in the library, Rothamsted Experimental Station.

Copies: LRHS; HRES.

276. — [Another edition.] London, Adam Islip. 1602. 18×13 cm. 4°. pp. [ii], 61, [1]: woodcut on tp., illust., 𝕭.𝕷.

Copies: LRHS; CUL.

The orchard, and the garden was also published in *The country-mans recreation,* where it appeared under the title of 'The expert gardener'. **See** COUNTRY-MANS RECREATION. 1640, etc. 4°.

'The expert gardener' may also have been sold separately but the present writer has seen no copy bound in the original binding.

OVINGTON (JOHN)

277. An essay upon the nature and qualities of tea. Wherein are shown, I. The soil and climate where it grows. II. The various kinds of it. III. The rules for chusing what is best. IV. The means of preserving it. V. The several virtues for which it is fam'd, etc. London, printed by and for R. Roberts. 1699. 15×10 cm. 8°. pp. [vi], 39, [1]: 1 pl.

Copies: LBM; CUL.

278. — Ed. 2, with additions. London, for John Chantry, sold by Ben. Bragg. 1705. 15×10 cm. 8°. pp. [vi], 40: 1 pl.

Copy: LBM.

OXFORD.—UNIVERSITY.—*Botanic garden.*

[Founded 1621.]

279. Catologus [*sic*] plantarum Horti medici oxoniensis sc. latino anglicus, & anglico latinus, etc. [By J. Bobart.] [Oxford], excudebat Henricus Hall. 1648. 14×9 cm. 8°. pp. [iv], 54, [2]; 51, [1].

The catalogue in English–Latin has a separate title-page and pagination.

Leaf E4 (i.e. pp. [1–2]) is blank.

According to Vines (S. H.) and Druce (G. C.), *An account of the Morisonian herbarium,* p. xxi (1914) the catalogue 'is attributed to Bobart, mainly on the authority of Dillenius, who presented a copy to Haller (*see* Haller, *Bibl. bot.,* 1771, t. i, p. 474)'.

Copies: LBM (C. 110. a. 13 (6)); OBL (Sherard 23.—Sherard 24 (1).—Sherard 164 (2)); ORSL (RR. z. 270).

Some copies of the above work (LBMNH; LRCS; OBL (Ashm. 1361)) have A2ᵃ (i.e. p. [iii] headed 'Ad lectorem') reset, e.g. instead of the fifth and sixteenth lines ending with the words 'summâ' and 'ejusdem muni-' respectively they end with the words 'ut' and 'ejusdem'.

280. — [Another issue.] [Oxford], excudebat Henricus Hall. 1648. 14×9 cm. 8°. pp. [iv], 54, [2]; 51, [1].

In this issue the title-page has been reset, 'Catalogus' in the title being now correctly spelt and a hyphen added between the two words in the title 'latino anglicus', and 'anglico latinus', respectively. A2ᵇ (i.e.

p. [iv]), the second page of the 'Ad lectorem', is also reset. A2ᵃ (i.e. p. [iii]) is the setting of the previous issue, with the fifth and sixteenth lines ending with the words 'ut' and 'ejusdem'.

Copies: LBM (449. a. 15.—449. a. 49); LBMNH; LCPG; OBL (8° R. 16 (3). Art. BS); ORSL; CBS.

281. — [Another edition.] Catalogus Horti botanici oxoniensis . . . Cui accessere plantæ minimùm sexaginta suis nominibus insignitæ, quæ nullibi nisi in hoc opusculo memorantur. Curâ & operâ sociâ Philippi Stephani . . . et Gulielmi Brounei . . . Adhibitis etiam in consilium D. Boberto patre . . . ejusque filio, etc. Oxonii, typis Gulielmi Hall. 1658. 14×9 cm. 8°. pp. [xvi], 187, [1]; [vi], 193–214.

Pages [vi], 193–214 consist of a title-page reading: 'The second part of the Catalogue of the trees and plants of the physick garden in the University of Oxford' followed by an English translation of the preface to the first part and a short catalogue of names in English and Latin.

Copies: LBM; LBMNH; LRHS; LCPG; OBL; ORSL.

PARKINSON (JOHN) [1567–1650]

282. Paradisi in sole paradisus terrestris. Or a garden of all sorts of pleasant flowers . . . with a kitchen garden . . . and an orchard . . . together with the right orderinge planting & preseruing of them and their vses & vertues, etc. ([Colophon:] London, Humfrey Lownes and Robert Young.) 1629. 34×21 cm. fol. pp. [xii], 612, [16]: illust.

The title-page is a woodcut.

Copies: LBM; LBMNH; LRHS; LLS; LRSM; LWML; LPS; LPO (BM); KRBG; OBL; OMaC; CUL; CFM.

283. — [Another edition.] ([Colophon:] London, Humfrey Lownes and Robert Young.) 1629. 33×22 cm. fol. pp. [xii], 612, [16]: illust.

The title-page is a woodcut.

The above work is made up of the sheets of the previous edition of 1629, except for pages 1–12 inclusive (i.e. signature A); these are entirely reset. Differences in the new setting include a new ornamental headpiece to page 1, and the modern usage of the letters v and u (e.g. the words 'severall' and 'unremoveable' in the first two lines of text on page 1, were previously spelt 'seuerall' and 'vnremoueable'). The new practice regarding this pair of letters, which did not become the general rule until about 1630, is consistently used throughout the above new setting of pages 1–12, but nowhere else in the work. The headpiece to page 1 is also found on page 149 of Parkinson's *Theatrum botanicum* of 1640, printed by Thomas Cotes. Both these facts indicate that copies

of the *Paradisus* with the new setting were issued after 1629.

Copies: HRES; BH.

284. — [Another issue of the original edition of 1629.] London, Tho. Cotes, sold by Richard Royston. 1635. 34×21 cm. fol. pp. [xiv], 612, [16]: illust.

The above issue is made up of the sheets of the 1629 edition, with a letterpress title-page dated 1635 additional to the woodcut title-page.

Copy: LBM (in this copy the letterpress title-page is a facsimile); Q.

285. — The second impression much corrected and enlarged. London, R. N. sold by Richard Thrale. 1656. 36×23 cm. fol. pp. [xii], 612, [16]: illust.

The above edition has both woodcut and letterpress title-pages.

Copies: LBM; LLS; LRCP; KRBG; HRES; OBL; CUL.

286. Theatrum botanicum: the theater of plants. Or, an herball of a large extent, etc. London, Tho. Cotes. 1640. 35×23 cm. fol. pp. [xviii], 1755 [i.e. 1745], [3]: illust.

There is an additional title-page, engraved.

Copies: LBM; LBMNH; LRHS; LCPG; LWML; LRCS; KRBG; CBS.

PECHEY (JOHN) [1654–1717]

287. The compleat herbal of physical plants. Containing all such English and foreign herbs, shrubs and trees, as are used in physick and surgery, etc. London, for Henry Bonwicke. 1694. 16×10 cm. 8°. pp. [viii], 349, [33].

Copies: LBM; LBMNH; LRHS; OMaC.

288. — Ed. 2, with the addition of many physical herbs, and their vertues, etc. London, for R. and J. Bonwicke. 1707. 16×10 cm. 8°. pp. [viii], 349 [i.e. 411], [29].

Copies: LBM; LBMNH; LWML; LPS; KRBG.

PENA (PIERRE) and L'OBEL (M. DE)

289. Stirpium aduersaria noua, perfacilis vestigatio, luculentaque accessio ad priscorum, præsertim Dioscoridis & recentiorum, materiam medicam, etc. Londini. 1570(-71). 30×20 cm. fol. pp. [xviii], 455, [3]: engr. tp., illust.

Colophon: Londini. 1571. Calendis Ianuarijs, excudebat prelum Thomæ Purfoetij, etc.

There are three printed slips inserted facing pages 11,

33 and 150, and two pasted-in slips on pages 252 and 400 respectively. The late Dr. Ferguson told the compiler that he had seen copies of the *Stirpium aduersaria noua* with a pasted-in slip containing an uninscribed cut of a cactus on the verso of leaf Pp5 (i.e. p. 454) but in most copies of the work this cut is correctly printed with the text. A certain number of copies of this work were apparently circulated in France and for these, with a view to retaining his copyright, de l'Obel obtained a 'Privilege' for ten years from Charles IX of France. This 'Privilege', dated 12 December 1570, is either found on the verso of the last leaf of the index (i.e. p. [xviii]) or printed on a separate leaf.

Following leaf Pp6 (i.e. p. 455 and one unnumbered page) is an unsigned leaf containing the end of the text and the colophon. In the copy of *Stirpium aduersaria noua* in the library of the Royal Botanic Gardens, Kew, this leaf is omitted. Instead there is a leaf printed on one side only containing a woodcut headed 'Arbor Chisti Ledj folio, superius. Pag 452'. A passage headed 'Erudito lectorj' and two columns of 'Errata'.

Copies: LBM; LBMNH; LRHS; LWML; KRBG; ORSL; OBS.

See also L'OBEL (M. DE) 1605. fol.

PHYTOLOGIA.

290. Phytologia britannica, natales exhibens indigenarum stirpium sponte emergentium, etc. [By William How.] Londini, typis Ric. Cotes, impensis Octaviani Pulleyn. 1650. 14×9 cm. (17×10 cm. large paper.) 8°. pp. [xvi], 133, [1].

The first leaf is signed 'A' on the recto, otherwise it is blank.

'Phytologia britannica à D. How edita, Londini 1650'. (*See* [Ray (J.)] *Catalogus plantarum circa Cantabrigiam nascentium*, etc. ＊＊7ᵇ (i.e. p. [xxviii] (1660)).

'Dr. How, Phytologiam britannicam anno 1650 edidit, auctioremque [*sic*] reddidit', etc. (*See* Merrett (C.), *Pinax*, etc.: A2ᵃ (i.e. p. [xix] (1666)).

Copies: LBM; LBMNH; LCPG; KRBG; OWaC; CBS.

PLATT (*Sir* HUGH) [1552–1608]

291. Floræs Paradise, beautified and adorned with sundry sorts of delicate fruites and flovvers, by the industrious labour of H. P. *Knight*: with an offer of an English antidote, (beeing a . . . remedy in . . . feavers, and intermitting agues) as also of some other rare inventions. etc. [With a preface by H. Platt, *Miles*.] London, H. L. for William Leake. 1608. 14×9 cm. 8°. pp. [xvi], 175, [41].

The first leaf (i.e. pp. [i–ii]) is signed 'A' on the recto, and has a border of rules both on the recto and verso.

Copies: LBM; OMaC.

292. — [Another issue.] The garden of Eden. Or, an accurate description of all flowers and fruits now growing in England, with particular rules how to advance their nature and growth . . . By . . . Sir Hugh Plat, *Knight*. London, for H. R. 1653. 14×9 cm. 8°. pp. [xvi], 175, [41].

The above issue differs from the preceding only in the title-page. The work was subsequently edited by Charles Bellingham.

Copy: Q.

293. — [Another edition.] London, for William Leake. 1653 [1652]. 14×9 cm. 8°. pp. 175, [1].

The British Museum's copy in the Thomason collection (E.1294) is dated 4 December 1652 in Thomason's hand on the title-page.

Copies: LBM; LBMNH.

294. — Ed. 4. London, for William Leake. 1654. 14×9 cm. 8°. pp. 175, [1].

Copies: LBM; CUL.

295. — Ed. 4. London, for William Leake. 1655. 14×9 cm. 8°. pp. 175, [1].

Copies of the fourth edition of *The garden of Eden* (1655) appear to be identical with the previous fourth edition (1654), except for the date on the title-page.

Copies: LRHS; HRES.

296. — Ed. 5. London, for William Leake. 1659. 13×8 cm. 8°. pp. 175, [1].

Copies: LBM; KRBG.

297. — The second part of the garden of Eden. Or an accurate description of all flowers and fruits growing in England; with partuicular [*sic*] rules how to advance their nature and growth, etc. London, for William Leak. 1660 [1659]. 14×8 cm. 8°. pp. [xvi], 159, [1].

The British Museum's copy of *The second part of The garden of Eden* in the Thomason collection E. 1804 (2)) is dated November 1659 in Thomason's hand on the title-page.

Copies: LBM; LBMNH; KRBG.

298. — The garden of Eden . . . The fifth edition. (The second part of The garden of Eden, etc.) 2 Pts. London, for William Leake. 1660. 13×8 cm. 8°. pp. 175, [1]; [xvi], 159, [1].

The fifth edition (1660) of *The garden of Eden* is a different edition from the fifth edition (1659). 'The second part' has a separate title-page and pagination and is the work of 1660 [1659].

Copies: LBM; CUL.

299. — The garden of Eden . . . In two parts
. . . The sixth edition. London, for William and
John Leake. 1675. 14×9 cm. 8°. pp. [xxviii],
148; [xvi], 159, [1].

'The second part of The garden of Eden' has a
separate title-page and pagination.

Copies: LBM; LRHS; LWML; LRCP; HRES.

300. The nevv and admirable arte of setting of
corne: with all the necessarie tooles and other
circumstances belonging to the same: the particular titles whereof, are set downe in page the
following. [Signed at end of text: 'H. Plat
Esquire'.] London, Peter Short. 1600. 18×13
cm. 4°. Signn. A–D⁴: woodcut on tp.

Copy: LPO (BM).

301. — [Another issue.] London, Peter Short.
1600. 17×13 cm. 4°. Signn. A–D⁴: woodcut
on tp.

The above issue differs only in the wording on the
title-page, 'in page the following' being altered to 'in
the page following'.

Copy: HRES.

302. — [Another edition.] London, Peter Short.
1600. 17×13 cm. 4°. Signn. A–D⁴: woodcut
on tp.

In the above edition leaf C1ᵃ line 11 of the text reads:
'foules of the ayre, by moles, wormes and other
cree-'; in the previous edition of 1600 it is 'the foules
of the aire, by moles, wormes and other'.

Copy: LBM.

A copy of another issue [1600?] of Platt's work on corn,
wanting the title-page, is preserved in the Brit. Mus.
(Bloomsbury). Quires C and D are reset. A collation
by signatures reads A2–4 B–D⁴. Leaf C1ᵃ line 11 of
the text reads: 'foules of the ayre, by moles, wourmes
and other cree-'.

303. — [Another issue.] London, Peter Short.
1601. 17×13 cm. 4°. Signn. A–D⁴: woodcut
on tp.

In the 1601 Issue quires A and C are reset. Leaf C1ᵃ
line 11 reads: 'foules of the ayre, by moles, woormes
and other cree-'.

Copies: LBM; LPO (BM); HRES.

PLATTES (Gabriel)

See Cook (M.) The manner of raising, ordering; and improving forest and fruit-trees . . .
Whereunto is now added, that ingenious treatise
of Mr. Gabriel Plattes, viz. A discovery of
subterranean treasure. 1679. 4°.

PLUKENET (Leonard) [1642–1706]

304. Leonardi Plukenetij Phytographia, sive
stirpium illustriorum, & minus cognitarum
icones . . . Pars prior (—quarta), etc. 4 Pts. Londini, sumptibus autoris. 1691–96. 28×21 cm.
4°.

Pt. 1. 1691. Frontis. (port. of author), engr. tp.,
engr. ded., engr. preface, pls. 1–17, 18–19 (on
1 leaf), 20–72.

Copies: LBM; LBMNH; LCPG; KRBG.

Pt. 2. 1691. Engr. tp., engr. ded., pls. 73–114,
engr. title reading 'Appendix ad rariorum
plantarum icones', pls. 115–117, engr. title
reading 'Altera appendix', etc., pls. 118–120.

Copies: LBM; LBMNH; LCPG; KRBG.

Pt. 3. 1692. Engr. tp., engr. ded. (on 2 leaves),
engr. preface, pls. 121–239, engr. title reading
'Appendix ad tertiam partem', etc., pls. 240–250,
pp. 4.

Copies: LBM; LBMNH; LCPG; KRBG.

Pt. 4. 1696. pp. [ii], engr. on tp., pls. 251–328.

It is usual to find the fourth part of the *Phytographia*
bound at the end of the author's *Almagestum botanicum*. According to Pulteney (R.), *Historical and
biographical sketches of the progress of botany in
England*, etc. 2: 24 (1790): 'In the same year with
the fourth part of the "Phytographia", came out,
"Almagestum botanicum".'

Pulteney (R.), op. cit. 2: 28 (1790) also states that
a few plates were wanting in some copies of the fourth
part of the *Phytographia*.

Copies with plates complete: LBM (441. g. 6 (2).—
441. g. 9 (2)); LCPG; KRBG; Copies with a few
plates wanting: LBM (441. g. 3 (2)); LBMNH.

Almagestum botanicum sive Phytographiæ
Pluc'netianæ onomasticon methodo syntheticâ
digestum exhibens stirpium exoticarum, rariorum, novarumque nomina . . . Adjiciuntur &
aliquot novarum plantarum icones, etc. Londini, sumptibus autoris. 1696. 28×21 cm. 4°.
pp. [iv], 402, [2]: engr. on tp.

Copies: LBM; LBMNH; LCPG; KRBG.

Almagesti botanici mantissa plantarum novis-
simè detectarum ultrà millenarium numerum
complectens . . . Cum indice totius operis ad
calcem adjecto, etc. Londini, sumptibus autoris.
1700. 28×21 cm. 4°. pp. [xii], 191, [29]:
engr. on tp., pls. 329–350.

Facing plate 329 is a leaf which is blank except for
a small engraving on the recto. In the above collation

of the *Mantissa* the twelve unnumbered preliminaries include: the title-page (2 pp.), prefatory letter (2 pp.), letter signed 'Ludovicus Peuzæus' (3 pp.), and verses by the author's son (5 pp.). The last eight preliminary pages containing the letter and verses, however, are not found in all copies of the work.

Copies: LBM; LBMNH; LCPG; KRBG.

Leonardi Plukenetii amaltheum botanicum. (i.e.) Stirpium indicarum alterum copiæ cornu millenas ad minimum & bis centum diversas species novas & indictas nominatim comprehendens, etc. Londini. 1705. 28×21 cm. 4°. pp. [vi], 214, [10]: engr. on tp., pls. 351–454.

Some copies do not have a leaf (i.e. pp. [iii–iv]) with a list of subscribers.

Facing plate 351 is a leaf which is blank, except for a small engraving on the recto.

Copies: LBM; LBMNH; LCPG; KRBG.

305. Leonardi Plukenetii, M.D. opera omnia botanica, in sex tomos divisa; viz. I, II, III. Phytographia, IV. Almagestum botanicum, V. Almagesti botanici mantissa, VI. Amaltheum botanicum, etc. 6 vols. Londini, apud Guil. & Joan. Innys. 1720. 28×21 cm. 4°.

This edition consists of copies of the original works, just as published, brought together under the above collective title to Volume **1**. There is also a half-title to Volume **1** reading: 'Leonardi Plukenetii, M.D. Opera omnia botanica, in sex tomos divisa.' In this edition pls. 18–19 in the *Phytographia* are sometimes found printed on two separate leaves, instead of on one leaf, as previously.

Copies: LBM; LBMNH.

306. — [Another edition.] Plukenetii opera: voluminibus quatuor. 4 vols. ([London.] Secundo excusum, ediderunt T. Davies, T. Payne, L. Davis, etc. 1769). 27×21 cm. 4°.

1. Phytographia. Pt. 1. pp. [viii]: frontis. (port. of author), engr. tp., engr. ded., engr. preface, pls. 1–72.—Pt. 2. Engr. tp., engr. ded., pls. 73–113, engr. title reading 'Appendix ad rariorum plantarum icones', pls. 114–120.—Pt. 3. Engr. tp., engr. ded. (on 2 leaves), engr. preface, pls. 121–250.—Pt. 4. pp. [ii]: engr. on tp., pls. 251–328, pp. [6].

2. Almagestum botanicum. pp. [viii], 402, [2]: engr. on tp.

3. Almagesti botanici mantissa. pp. [viii], 191, [29]: engr. on tp., pls. 329–350.

4. Amaltheum botanicum. pp. [viii], 216, [12]: engr. on tp., pls. 351–454.

The above collective title: *Plukenetii opera: voluminibus quatuor* appears as the half-title of Volume **1**. The letter signed 'Ludovicus Peuzæus' and the verses by the author's son, previously included in the *Almagesti botanici*, are now omitted, and in the *Amaltheum* references to the plates have been added to the text.

Copies: LBM; LBMNH; KRBG.

RALPH (THOMAS SHEARMAN) [1813–1891]
Thomæ Johnsoni descriptio itineris plantarum ... Nup. edit. T. S. Ralph. **See** JOHNSON (T.) 1849. 4°.

RAM (WILLIAM)
Rams little Dodeon. A briefe epitome of the new Herbal, or history of plants . . . first set forth in the Dutch or Almayne tongue, by . . . Reinbert Dodeon . . . translated into English by Henry Lyte . . . and now collected and abbridged by William Ram, etc. **See** DODOENS (R.) 1606. 4°.

RAPIN (RENÉ) [1621–1687]
307. Of gardens. Four books first written in Latine verse by Renatus Rapinus, and now made English by J. E. [i.e. J. Evelyn the Younger, who also supplied the dedication.] London, T. R. & N. T. for Thomas Collins and John Ford, and Benjamin Tooks. 1672. 16×10 cm. 8°. pp. [xxiv], 237, [1]: engr. on tp.

Some copies of the above work contain an extra gathering of sixteen unnumbered pages headed 'The table'.

Copy: CUL.

308. — [Another issue.] London, T. R. & N. T. for Thomas Collins and John Ford, and Benjamin Tooks. 1673. 16×10 cm. 8°. pp. [xxiv], 237, [1]: engr. on tp.

Some copies of the above work of 1673 contain 'The table', and a leaf of errata.

Copies: LBM; LRHS; OWaC; CUL.

RAPINUS (RENATUS)
See RAPIN (RENÉ)

RAY (JOHN) [1627–1705]
309. Catalogus plantarum Angliæ, et insularum adjacentium . . . unà cum observationibus & experimentis novis medicis & physicis, etc. Londini, typis E. C. & A. C., impensis J. Martyn. 1670. 16×10 cm. 8°. pp. [xxii], 358, [2].

Copies: LBM; LBMNH; LCPG; LWML; KRBG; CBS.

310. — Editio secunda, plantis circiter quadraginta sex, & observationibus aliquammultis [*sic*] auctior, etc. Londini, typis Andr. Clark, impensis Joh. Martyn. 1677. 15×10 cm. 8°. pp. [xxviii], 311, [17]: 2 pls.

Copies: LBM; LBMNH; LRHS; LWML; KRBG; CBS.

The 'Emendanda' to the *Catalogus plantarum Angliæ* were published in the first and second editions of the author's *Synopsis methodica stirpium britannicarum*.

Catalogus plantarum circa Cantabrigiam nascentium, etc. [By J. Ray.] **See** CAMBRIDGE. 1660. 8°.

— [Another issue.] 1660. 8°.

— Appendix, etc. [By J. Ray.] 1663. 8°.

311. Joannis Raii de variis plantarum methodis dissertatio brevis. In qua agitur I. De methodi origine & progressu. II. De notis generum characteristicis. III. De methodo sua in specie. IV. De notis quas reprobat . . . D. Tournefort. V. De methodo Tournefortiana. Londini, impensis S. Smith & B. Walford. 1696. 19×11 cm. 8°. pp. [xiv], 48.

De variis plantarum methodis dissertatio brevis is also found bound up with Ray's *Synopsis . . . Editio secunda.*

Copies: LBM; LBMNH; LCPG; KRBG; OWaC.

312. Fasciculus stirpium britannicarum, post editum plantarum Angliæ catalogum observatarum, etc. Londini, apud Henricum Faithorne. 1688. 16×9 cm. 8°. pp. [iv], 27, [1].

Copies: LBM; LBMNH; LCPG; CBS.

313. Historia plantarum species hactenus editas aliasque insuper multas noviter inventas & descriptas complectens, etc. (Accessit Historia stirpium ins. Luzonis & reliquarum Philippinarum a . . . Geo. Jos. Camello . . . conscripta. Item . . . Jos. Pitton Tournefort . . . Corollarium institutionum rei herbariæ.) 3 vols. 1686–1704. 36×23 cm. (44×28 cm. large paper.) fol.

1. Londini, typis Mariæ Clark: prostant apud Henricum Faithorne & Joannem Kersey. 1686. pp. [xxiv], 983 [i.e. 987], [1]:1 illust. (p. 27).

2. Londini, typis Mariæ Clark: prostant apud

Henricum Faithorne. 1688. pp. [viii], 985–1350, [2], 1351–1944, [36].

3. Londini, apud Sam. Smith & Benj. Walford. 1704. pp. [ii], ix, [i], 666 [i.e. 664], 135, [1], 112, 225–255, [9].

In some copies of Vol. 2, page 1944 is found misprinted 1940. A second state of Vol. 1 (1686), which is the more usual, has a cancel title-page and an *imprimatur* leaf: the first state has no *imprimatur* leaf. The imprint on the cancel title reads: 'Londini: typis Mariæ Clark: prostant apud Henricum Faithorne'.

In Vol. 3, Books XVIII–XXIII are marked in the running headline as XVII–XXII. Books XXIV–XXXI have separate pagination (pp. 1–135) and the first word on page 1 is 'Historiæ' although the catchword on the previous page (p. 666) is 'Den-'. Some copies of Vol. 3 have an emendatory slip pasted in at the end of Book XXIII (i.e. on p. 666). It reads as follows: 'Botanologiæ finis. Inter Botanologiam & Dendrologiam integri Libri defectus esse videtur', etc. The error in numeration is explained and the catchword altered from 'Den-' to 'Histo-'. The pagination of the 'Appendix. Herbarum . . . in . . . Luzone' in Vol. 3 runs up to 112, and according to the *Catalogue of the library of the Brit. Mus. (Nat. Hist.)* 4: 1653 (1913) these pages, in some copies of the work, are printed on one side of the paper only, this apparently being the original form of issue. The numeration is resumed with page 225 when various short treatises, not named on the title-page, begin. For a list of these treatises *see ibid.* 4: 1653.

Copies: LBM; LBMNH; LRHS; LCPG; LRCS; KRBG; OWaC; CBS.

314. — [Another issue.] Joannis Raii . . . Historia plantarum generalis. Species hactenus editas aliasque insuper multas noviter inventas & descriptas complectens, etc. 3 vols. 1693–1704. 36×23 cm. fol.

1. Londini, impensis Samuelis Smith & Benjamini Walford. 1693. pp. [xxiv], 983 [i.e. 987], [1]: frontis. (port. of Ray), 1 illust. (p. 27).

2. Londini, impensis Samuelis Smith & Benjamini Walford. 1693. pp. [viii], 985–1350, [2], 1351–1940 [i.e. 1944], [36]: frontis. (port. of Ray).

3. Londini, apud Sam. Smith & Benj. Walford. 1704. pp. [ii], ix, [i], 666 [i.e. 664], 135, [1], 112, 225–255, [9].

The above collation of the issue of 1693–1704 has been made from the copy of the work in the Brit. Mus. (Bloomsbury). It is the same as the original work of 1686–1704 except that the title-pages of Vols. 1 and 2 are cancels. Vol. 1 has no *imprimatur* leaf. In the copy of this issue in the Pharmaceutical Society of Great Britain the misprinted page number 1940 for 1944, in Vol. **2**, is corrected and the portrait of Ray is in Vol. **1** only. The same portrait (a line engraving by W. Elder after a drawing by W. Faithorne) was also used as the frontispiece of Ray's *Synopsis methodica animalium* (1693) and *Stirpium europæarum . . . sylloge* (1694).

Copies: LBM; LPS.

For further bibliographical details concerning Ray's *Historia see* Barr (C. B. L.) and Pollard (M.), The Historia plantarum of John Ray, *Trans. Cambridge bibl. Soc.* **3**: 335–338 (1962).

315. Methodus plantarum nova . . . synoptice in tabulis exhibita; cum notis generum . . . characteristicis, observationibus nonnullis de seminibus plantarum, etc. Londini, impensis Henrici Faithorne, & Joannis Kersey. 1682. 16×10 cm. 8°. pp. [xxii], 166, [34]: engr. half-title, 1 pl.

Copies: LBM; LBMNH; LCPG; LWML; KRBG; OWaC; CBS.

316. — [Another issue.] Amstelædami, prostant apud Janssonio-Waesbergios. 1682. 15×10 cm. 8°. pp. [xxii], 166, [34]: engr. half-title, 1 pl.

Keynes (G.), *John Ray, a bibliography*, 62 (1951) records a copy of the above issue of 1682 with 'five additional plates'.

Copy: OMaC.

317. — [Another edition.] Joannis Raji . . . Methodus plantarum emendata et aucta . . . Accedit methodus Graminum, Juncorum et Cyperorum specialis. Eodem auctore. Londini, impensis Samuelis Smith & Benjamini Walford . . . MDCCIII. Et veneunt Amstelædami apud Janssonio-Waasbergios. 19×11 cm. (21×12 cm. large paper.) 8°. pp. [xxxiv], 202, [26]: frontis. port. of author), 2 tables.

This edition (1703) was finished in 1698 but was refused by the London publishers. However, Ray's friend, Dr. Hotton, Professor of Botany at Leyden, 'got the Waasbergs of Amsterdam to undertake it, who printed 1100 copies at Leyden (where Dr. Hotton lived) that he might supervise the press. The printers finished their task in 1703; and the Waasbergs (thinking it for their interest) had it said in the title-page, that it was printed at London, for Smith and Walford, (who used to print Mr. Ray's things) and desired Mr. Ray's leave to say so; but he refused his consent, it being a manifest falshood. However, they did it without his leave, pleading it to be their right', etc. (*see* Derham (W.), *Select remains of . . . John Ray . . . with his life*, 76–77 (1760).)

Copies: LMB; LBMNH; LRHS; LCPG; LRCS; KRBG; OWaC.

318. — [Another issue.] Prostant Amstelædami, apud Rud. & Gerh. Wetstenios HFF. 1710. 19×11 cm. 8°. pp. [xxxiv], 202, [26]: frontis. (port. of author), 2 tables.

Copies: CUL; GUL.

The above issue of 1710 is the same as the work of 1703 except for a cancel title-page. Keynes (G.), *John Ray, a bibliography*, 64 (1951) records a further issue of the 1703 edition with a cancel title-page, and imprint and date as follows: 'Prostant Amstelædami, apud Janssonio Waesbergios. MDCCXI.'

319. — [Another edition.] Londini, apud Christianum Andream Myntsing. 1733. 18×10 cm. 8°. pp. [xxxii], 196, [28]: 2 tables.

Leaf **8 (i.e. pp. [xxxi–xxxii]) is blank.

Séguier (J. F.), *Bibliotheca botanica*, 153 (1740) gives 'Tubingæ' as the correct imprint for this edition, and adds 'falso Londini nomine'.

Copies: LBM; LBMNH; KRBG.

320. Stirpium europæarum extra Britannias nascentium sylloge . . . Adjiciuntur catalogi rariorum alpinarum & pyrenaicarum, baldensium, hispanicarum Grisleii, græcarum & orientalium, creticarum, ægyptiacarum aliique: ab eodem, etc. Londini, prostant apud Sam. Smith & Benj. Walford. 1694. 19×11 cm. 8°. pp. [xxviii], 45–220, 225–400, 45, [3]: frontis. (port. of author).

In some copies of the above work the last three unnumbered pages are blank, in other copies these pages contain a publisher's book list, headed 'Catalogus librorum, qui prostant venales apud Sam. Smith & Benj. Walford', etc. The *Sylloge* is a revision of 'Catalogus stirpium in exteris regionibus a nobis observatarum' which is appended to Ray's *Observations . . . made in a journey through part of the Low-Countries*. London. 1673. 8°.

Copies: LBM; LBMNH; LRHS; LCPG; KRBG; OWaC.

321. Synopsis methodica stirpium britannicarum, in qua tum notæ generum characteristicæ traduntur, tum species singulæ breviter describuntur, etc. Londini, prostant apud Sam. Smith. 1690. 18×11 cm. 8°. pp. [xxiv], 317, [3]: 2 pls.

Copies: LBM; LBMNH; LRCS; KRBG; OMaC.

322. — Joannis Raii Synopsis methodica stirpium britannicarum . . . Editio secunda . . . Accessit . . . Aug. Rivini epistola ad Joan. Raium de methodo: cum ejusdem responsoria, in qua D. Tournefort elementa botanica tanguntur. Londini, impensis S. Smith & B.

Walford. 1696. 19×11 cm. 8°. pp. [xl], 346, [22]; 55, [1].

'Rivini epistola', etc. has a separate title-page and pagination. With some copies of Ray's *Synopsis . . . Editio secunda*, 1696, is bound the author's *De variis plantarum methodis dissertatio brevis*, 1696.

Copies: LBM; LBMNH; LCPG; KRBG; OMaC; OWaC.

323. — Editio tertia multis locis emendata, & quadringentis quinquaginta circiter speciebus noviter detectis aucta, etc. [Edited by J. J. Dillenius.] Londini, impensis Gulielmi & Joannis Innys. 1724. 19×12 cm. 8°. pp. [xvi], 288, *281-*288, 289-482, [30]: 24 pls.

Copies: LBM; LBMNH; LPS; OWaC.

324. —[Another issue.] 2 vols. Londini, impensis Gulielmi & Joannis Innys, & S. Tooke & B. Motte. 1724. 19×12 cm. 8°.

1. pp. [xvi], 288, *281-*288: pls. 1-11.

2. pp. [ii], 289-482, [30]: pls. 12-24.

The above issue of 1724 differs from the preceding only in being in two volumes, each with its title-page.

Copies: LWML; KRBG; CUBG.

REA (JOHN) [-1681]

325. Flora: seu, de florum cultura. Or, a complete florilege, furnished with all requisites belonging to a florist. In III. books (Flora.—Ceres.—Pomona), etc. London, J. G. for Richard Marriott. 1665. 31×20 cm. fol. pp. [xxiv], 239, [5]: 8 pls.

An additional title-page, engraved, reads: 'Flora Ceres & Pomona'. 'Pomona' has a separate title-page.

Copies: LBM; LRHS; KRBG; HRES; CUBG.

A copy of this work of 1665 in the library of Magdalen College, Oxford, has the title-page mounted on a stub and an imprint reading: 'London, printed by J. G. for Thomas Clarke', etc. This copy lacks the engraved title.

326. — The second impression corrected, with many additions, etc. London, T. N. for George Marriott. 1676. 32×20 cm. fol. pp. [xxiv], 231, [9]: engr. headpiece to each book, 8 pls.

An additional title-page, engraved, reads: 'Flora Ceres & Pomona', etc.

Copies: LBMNH; LRHS; LCPG; KRBG.

327. — The third impression, corrected. With many additions, etc. London, for G. M., sold

by Peter Buck. 1702. 31×20 cm. fol. pp. [xxii], 231, [9]: engr. headpiece to each book, 8 pls.

The above 'third impression' of Rea's work has no engraved title-page and therefore no leaf with the verses headed 'The mind of the front'.

Copy: LBM.

REID (JOHN)

328. The Scots gard'ner in two parts, the first of contriving and planting gardens, orchards, avenues, groves . . . The second of the propagation & improvement of forrest, and fruit-trees, kitchen-hearbes, roots and fruits . . . Appendix shewing how to use the fruits of the garden: whereunto is annexed The gard'ners kalendar. Published for the climate of Scotland, etc. Edinburgh, David Lindsay, and his partners. 1683. 19×14 cm. 4°. pp. [xii], 125, [1]; 14: 4 pls.

The unsigned leaf (recto numbered p. 125) is not found in all copies of *The Scots gard'ner* (1683). This leaf contains: 'The conclusion proposing Scotlands improvement' and a list of errata. The verso is blank. 'The gard'ners kalendar' has a separate title-page and pagination (pp. 14).

Copies: LBM; LRHS; HRES.

329. — Ed. 2, corrected, with additions. Edinburgh, John Moncur. 1721. 18×11 cm. 8°. pp. [x], 124 [i.e. 214]; [ii], 54; 24: frontis., 4 pls.

'The gard'ners kalendar' has a separate title-page and pagination (pp. [ii], 54). To this edition of *The Scots gard'ner* is added 'The florists vade-mecum' (pp. 24).

Copies: LBM; LRHS; KRBG; HRES.

330. — [Another edition.] The Scots gardiner for the climate of Scotland . . . Together with The gardiner's kalendar, The florist's vade-mecum, The practical bee-master (By Robert Maxwell), Observations on the weather (By John Claridge), and the Earl of Haddington's Treatise on forest-trees. Written originally by John Reid . . . and now carefully corrected, with alterations and additions, by an eminent hand. Edinburgh, for James Reid. 1756. 16×10 cm. 12°. pp. xii [i.e. viii], 208; viii, 40; viii, 138; 48: 4 pls.

The above collation has been made from the copy of *The Scots gardiner* (1756) in the Bodleian Library, Oxford (Gough. Scotland 160). The three works on bees, the weather, and on forest-trees, respectively, have their own title-pages and pagination; they appear in the following order and are entitled: 'The shepherd of Banbury's rules to judge of the changes of the weather', etc. (1755) (pp. viii,

40); 'The practical bee-master ... The second edition' (1750) (pp. viii, 138); and 'A short treatise on forest-trees, aquaticks, ever-greens, fences and grass-seeds', etc. (1756) (pp. 48).

In the Bodleian copy following the title-leaf (pp. [i–ii]) of 'The practical bee-master' and preceding the dedication (pp. iii–viii) of this treatise, is a leaf conjugate with the title having on the recto page '7' of 'The preface', and on the verso a list of books sold by James Reid. This leaf was presumably intended to cancel the leaf consisting of pages 7–8 (i.e. Sign. A4) of 'The preface' which is also present in this copy.

Copy: OBL.

331. — [Another edition.] Edinburgh, for James Reid. 1766. 16×10 cm. 12°. pp. viii, 208; 48; viii, 40; viii, 138: 4 pls.

The above collation has been made from the copy of *The Scots gardener* (1766) in the library of Rothamsted Experimental Station, Harpenden. The three works on bees, the weather, and on forest-trees, respectively, have their own title-pages and pagination; they appear in the following order and are entitled: 'A short treatise on forest-trees', etc. (1765) (pp. 48); 'The shepherd of Banbury's rules to judge of the changes of the weather', etc. (1765) (pp. viii, 40); 'The practical bee-master ... The second edition' (1750) (pp. viii, 138).

The Rothamsted copy has the conjugate leaf mentioned under the 1756 edition, but the cancelled leaf, A4 (pp. 7–8), is not present in this copy.

Copies: LBM; LRHS; HRES.

'A short treatise on forest-trees' (1765) was also published as a separate publication. See HAMILTON (T.) *6th Earl of Haddington* 1765. 12°.

RICHARDSON (RICHARD) [–1706?]

332. Ric. Ricardsoni ... de cultu hortorum ... carmen, etc. Londini, apud Joannem Nutt. 1699. 21×15 cm. 4°. pp. [ii], 24.

Copy: LBM.

ROSE (JOHN) [1622?–1677]

333. The English vineyard vindicated ... With an address, where the best plants may be had at easie rates. [Edited, with a preface, by Philocepos, pseud., i.e. John Evelyn.] London, J. Grismond for John Crook. 1666. 14×9 cm. 8°. pp. [xvi], 41, [3]: 1 pl.

Copy: LBM.

The English vineyard was not reprinted separately but it was appended to *The French gardiner* (see above, FRENCH GARDINER 1669, etc. 8°). In the 1669, 1672 and 1675 editions of this work *The English vineyard* has a separate title-page with imprint and date and a collation which reads pp. 48, [16] (signed A–D8). Although the last page (i.e. p. [16]) is a table of the contents of *The English vineyard*, pp. [1—15]

consist of tables of the contents of *The French gardiner*. In spite of this, these three appended editions of *The English vineyard* are sometimes found bound as separate works and listed accordingly in library catalogues.

S., W.

334. Instructions for the increasing of mulberie trees, and the breeding of silke-wormes, for the making of silke in this kingdome. Whereunto is annexed His Maiesties letters to the Lords Liefetenants ... tending to that purpose [with a preface by W. S. i.e. William Stallenge]. London, E. A. for Eleazar Edgar. 1609. 19×14 cm. 4°. Signn. A–C4: illust.

Copies: LBM; OMaC.

For another edition see INSTRUCTIONS. 1609. 4°.

SAINFOIN.

335. St. foine improved, a discourse shewing the utility and benefit which England hath and may receive by the grasse called St. foine, and answering the objections urged against it ... Written by a person of honour lately deceased. London, S. G. and B. G. for Nath. Brooke. 1671. 18×13 cm. 4°. pp. [ii], 20.

Copy: HRES.

336. [Another edition.] London, S. G. and B. G. for Nath. Brooke. 1674. 18×11 cm. 4°. pp. [ii], 20.

Copies: LBM; LUL; HRES.

SCOT (REGINALD) [1538?–1599]

337. A perfite platforme of a hoppe garden, and necessarie instructions for the making and mayntenaunce thereof, with notes and rules for reformation of all abuses, commonly practised therein, etc. London, Henrie Denham. 1574. 17×13 cm. 4°. pp. [xvi], 56: illust., 𝕭.𝕷.

Copies: LBM; OBL.

In the above edition, and in the editions of 1576 and 1578, the first leaf (i.e. pp. [i–ii]) is blank, except for the signature 'A.j.' below a type ornament on the recto.

338. — [Another edition.] Nowe newly corrected and augmented, etc. London, Henrie Denham. 1576. 18×14 cm. 4°. pp. [xiv], 63, [1]: illust., 𝕭.𝕷.

Copies: LBM; HRES; OBL; ORSL.

339. — [Another edition.] Now newly corrected and augmented, etc. London, Henrie Denham.

1578. 17×13 cm. 4°. pp. [xiv], 93 [i.e. 63], [1]: illust., 𝔅.𝔏.

Copies: LBM; HRES; OBL.

— See COUNTRY-MANS RECREATION. The country-mans recreation . . . in three bookes . . . The second [R. Scot's 'A perfect platforme of a hoppe-garden'] treateth of the hop-garden, etc. 1640, etc. 4°.

SHARROCK (ROBERT) [1630–1684]

340. The history of the propagation & improvement of vegetables by the concurrence of art and nature: shewing the several ways for the propagation of plants usually cultivated in England, etc. Oxford, A. Lichfield, for Tho. Robinson. 1660[1659]. 16×11 cm. 8°. pp. [xviii], 150, [2]: 1 pl. with descriptive letterpress (pp. [2]).

The British Museum's copy in the Thomason collection (E.1731 (2)) is dated December 1659 in Thomason's hand on the title-page.

Some copies of this edition have a different typesetting of pp. 1–2 (i.e. leaf B1). The two versions are identical in content except for the heading above the text on page 1. In the version most commonly found this reads: 'Cap. I. Of Propagation by Seed. Num. I. Of Propagation of Vegetables in general, with a Preface to the Discourse.' The same wording is found in the list of 'Contents'. In the less usual version the heading on page 1 reads: 'N. 1. Of propagation of Vegetables in general.' In the most commonly found version the first line of the text on page 1 ends: 'Renowned Lord Bacon' instead of 'renowned Lord Ba-' and the first line on page 2 ends: 'complains of the want of an In-', instead of 'an Inventory of what in'.

When the omission of the chapter heading (i.e. 'Cap. I. Of Propagation by Seed') was noticed a new version of B1 was presumably set up and the earlier version of B1 cancelled. A copy of the work known to the compiler in private hands contains both versions of B1, the binder having apparently neglected to cancel the second leaf, this being the one without the chapter heading. To assist with identification the quotations in this footnote have been transcribed with capitals exactly as found in the original work.

Copy of the first edition (first issue) HRES.

Copies of the first edition (second issue) LBM; LBMNH; LRHS; KRBG.

341. — Ed. 2, much enlarged, etc. Oxford, W. Hall, for Ric. Davis. 1672. 15×10 cm. 8°. pp. [xvi], 255, [1]: 1 pl. with descriptive letterpress (pp. [2]).

Some copies of the above edition of 1672 contain a leaf of errata.

Copies: LBM; LBMNH; LRHS; LRCS; HRES; CUL; CBS.

342. — An improvement to the art of gardening: or, an exact history of plants. Shewing the several ways for the propagation of plants, usually growing in England . . . The third edition with additions, etc. London, Nathanael Sackett. 1694. 15×10 cm. 8°. pp. [xvi], 255, [1]: 1 pl. with descriptive letterpress (pp. [2]).

Some copies of the above edition of 1694 contain a leaf of errata.

Copies: LBM; LRHS; KRBG.

SHORT INSTRUCTION.

343. A short instruction veric [sic] profitable and necessarie for all those that delight in gardening, to know the time and season when it is good to sow and replant all maner of seedes. Whereunto is annexed diuers plots both for planting and grafting for the better ease of the gardner. Translated out of French into English. London, Iohn Wolfe. 1591. 18×13 cm. 4°. pp. 8, [24]: woodcut on tp., illust., 𝔅.𝔏.

Pages [22–23], consisting of a woodcut, are printed on two conjugate leaves. The only copy of the above edition of 1591, known to the compiler, is in the library of Mr. A. E. Lownes, of Providence, R.I., U.S.A.

Copy: [AEL.]

344. — [Another edition.] London, Iohn Wolfe. 1592. 18×14 cm. 4°. pp. 8, [24]: woodcut on tp., illust., 𝔅.𝔏.

Pages [22–23], consisting of a woodcut, are printed on two conjugate leaves.

Copy: LBM.

SIBLY (EBENEZER) [1751–c. 1800]

Culpeper's English physician; and complete herbal . . . Illustrated with notes and observations . . . By E. Sibly. See CULPEPER (N.) 2 vols. [in 1.] [1789], etc. 4°.

SLOANE (Sir HANS) Bart. [1660–1753]

345. Catalogus plantarum quæ in insula Jamaica sponte proveniunt, vel vulgò coluntur, cum earundem synonymis & locis natalibus; adjectis aliis quibusdam quæ in insulis Maderæ, Barbados, Nieves, & Sancti Christophori nascuntur. Seu Prodromi historiæ naturalis Jamaicæ pars prima.† etc. Londini, impensis D. Brown. 1696. 17×11 cm. 8°. pp. [xii], 232, [44].

The first leaf contains a half-title (recto), and the imprimaturs of the Royal Society, and of the College of Physicians (verso). The third leaf contains a dedication addressed by the author to the Royal Society and the College of Physicians.

Copies: LBM (450.c.15); LRCS; CBS.

Copies that are imperfect (For reason *see above*, *History*, p. 150): LRS; LCPG; LRCP.

346. — [Another issue.] Londini, impensis D. Brown. 1696. 17×11 cm. 8°. pp. [viii], 232, [44].

This issue is identical with the preceding work of the same date, except that it does not contain the two leaves with the *imprimaturs* and the dedication.

Copies: LBM; LBMNH; LRHS; LLS; KRBG; OBL; OWaC; CUL; CBS.

SMITH (JOHN)

347. England's improvement reviv'd: digested into six books, etc. In the Savoy, Tho. Newcomb for the author. 1670. 21×16 cm. 4°. pp. [xii], 270.

Copies: LBM; LRHS; HRES.

348. — [Another issue.] England's improvement reviv'd: in a treatise of all manner of husbandry & trade by land and sea . . . digested into six books, etc. London, Tho. Newcomb, for Benjamin Southwood; and Israel Harrison. 1673. 21×16 cm. 4°. pp. [xiv], 270.

The above issue is identical with the preceding except for a cancel half-sheet containing on the verso of the first leaf a note from 'The bookseller, to the reader'. The other leaf is a cancel title-page.

Copies: LBM; KRBG; HRES.

SPEED (ADOLPHUS)

349. Adam out of Eden, or, an abstract of divers excellent experiments touching the advancement of husbandry, etc. London, for Henry Brome. 1659[1658]. 14×8. cm. 8°. pp. [viii], 163 [i.e. 177], [7].

The British Museum's copy in the Thomason collection (E.2135 (1)) is dated October 1658 in Thomason's hand on the title-page.

The seven unnumbered pages at the end of the treatise are composed of three pages of 'Books printed for Henry Brome', a blank leaf, a blank page, and the last page with a longitudinal half-title, reading: 'Speeds husbandry'.

Copies: LBM; HRES.

SPRAT (THOMAS) *Bishop of Rochester* [1635-1713]

Abrahami Couleij Angli, poemata latina, etc. [Edited, with an introduction, by T. Sprat, Bishop of Rochester.] See COWLEY (A.) 1668. 8°.

— [Another edition.] 1678. 12°.

STALLENGE (WILLIAM)

Instructions for the increasing of mulberie trees, and the breeding of silke-wormes, etc. [With a preface by W. S., i.e. William Stallenge.] See S., W. 1609. 4°.

— [Another edition.] Instructions for the increasing of mulberrie trees, and the breeding of silke-wormes, etc. [By W. Stallenge.] See INSTRUCTIONS. 1609. 4°.

STANDISH (ARTHUR)

350. The commons complaint. Wherein is contained two speciall grieuances. The first is, the generall destruction and waste of woods in this kingdome, with a remedie for the same . . . The second grieuance is, the extreame dearth of victuals. Foure remedies for the same, etc. [With a dedication by Arthur Standish.] London, William Stansby. 1611. 20×15 cm. 4°. pp. [x], 33, [1]: 1 folding leaf.

The above collation has been made from the copy of *The commons complaint* (1611) in the Bodleian Library, Oxford (Tanner 820 (1)). The copy of this edition in the Brit. Mus. (Bloomsbury) (809.d.3 (1)) has an extra leaf at the end, printed on one side only, with commendatory verses by Henry Peacham. It has also numerous corrections made either in MS. in ink, or with printed slips pasted over the errors. This was probably the presentation copy to the King, to whom the work is dedicated. The folding leaf bears a woodcut of a fowl-house, with accompanying text.

Copies: LBM; LUL; OBL.

351. — [Another edition.] London, William Stansby. 1611. 18×13 cm. 4°. pp. [x], 34: 2 folding leaves.

The above collation has been made from the copy in the Bodleian Library, Oxford (Pamph. 9 (3)). The two folding leaves consist respectively of (1) the King's approval of the book, given on August 1611, granting Standish sole rights in the publication of the work; (2) the woodcut of a fowl-house; as in the earlier edition.

352. — [Another edition.] London, William Stansby. 1611. 17×12 cm. 4°. pp. [xvi], 50 [i.e. 40]: 1 folding leaf.

Copies: L.B.M. (1028.i.1 (1).); C.U.L. (Syn. 7. 61. 218); O.B.L. (4°. A. 9 (6) Art. BS.). The Oxford copy has no folding leaf of the fowl-house. The library of Rothamsted Experimental Station, Harpenden, has two copies, one of which has no folding leaf. In this edition, and in the edition of 1612 below, the King's approval of 1 August 1611 is printed on pages iii–v.

353. — [Another edition.] Newly corrected and augmented. London, William Stansby. 1612. 17×13 cm. 4°. pp. [xiv], 46: 1 folding plate.
Copies: LBM; LUL.

New directions of experience . . . for the planting of timber and firewood, etc. [By A. Standish.] **See** NEW DIRECTIONS. 1613. 4°.

354. — [Another edition.] New directions of experience to the commons complaint by the incouragement of the Kings most excellent Maiesty, as may appeare, for the planting of timber and fire-wood. With a neere estimation what millions of acres the kingdome doth containe, etc. [London?] 1613. 17×12 cm. 4°. pp. [iv], 23, [1].
This edition, and subsequent editions, contain the King's approval of the book, given on 1 August 1611, that had appeared in the author's *Commons complaint* (*see above*).
Copies: LRHS; LUL; LWML.

355. — [Another edition.] [London, N. Okes.] 1613. 19×14 cm. 4°. pp. [iv], 34.
This work appears to be the same as the previous edition of 1613 in the Lindley Library, R.H.S., etc., except for the addition of pages 25–34 with the heading 'A second direction, for the . . . increasing of fire-wood, agreeable to the nature of this age, 1613. February 1'. The first sentence on page 25 opens with the words: 'Hearing daily that this more then necessary business is much desired to be effected.'
Copy: LBM (966.c.26 (2)).

356. — [Another edition.] [London?] 1613. 18×11 cm. 4°. pp. [iv], 36.
Pages 25–36 headed: 'A second direction, for the . . . encreasing of fire-wood, agreeable to the nature of this age, 1613. February 1.'
Copy: HRES.

357. — [Another edition.] New directions of experience authorized by the Kings most excellent Maiesty, as may appeare, for the planting of timber and fire-wood, etc. [London?] 1614. 19×14 cm. 4°. pp. [viii], 5, [1], [2], 7, [1], 28: 1 folding plan col.
The above work of 1614 contains an epistle 'To the reader' (pp. 5) followed by two commendatory verses (pp. [2]) and another epistle 'To the reader' (pp. 7).
Although this edition of 1614 and the two editions below of 1615 and 1616 do not have the section entitled 'A second direction' all three works contain much of the material previously published in the two editions of 1613 containing this heading.
Copy: ENLS.

358. — [Another edition.] [London?] 1615. 19×14 cm. 4°. pp. [xx], 28: 1 folding plan col.
This edition consists of the work of 1614, with much of the type reset, and without the first epistle 'To the reader' and the two commendatory verses.
Copies: LBM (1146.d.32); OBL (Crynes 827(2)); CUL (Syn.8.61.1). The two last copies have no folding plan.

359. — [Another edition.] [London?] 1616. 17×12 cm. 4°. pp. [xx], 28.
This edition consists of the work of 1615 with minor additions and omissions and the type reset.
Copy: CUL.

In the library of Harvard University a copy of *New directions* (1613), pp. 22, is bound together in one volume with two other items. The first consists of eight numbered pages headed 'A second direction, for the increasing of wood, and the destroying of vermine, this present yeare, 1613. Febr. 1'. It is signed 'Arthur Standish'. The text, which is different from that in the 'Second direction' published in the thirty-four and thirty-six page editions of *New directions* (1613), opens on page 1 with the words: 'Acknowledging my selfe to bee animated by God.' The second item which is apparently by the same author is unsigned. It consists of six numbered pages headed 'A third edition by the authority of the King, Iune the nine and twentie day, anno Dom. 1614'.
Copy: [Harv CL].

(Information supplied to the present writer by Miss K. F. Pantzer of the Houghton Library, Harvard University, in epist. 21.ix.66.)

STEPHENS (PHILIP) [1620?–1679] and BROWNE (W.)

Catalogus Horti botanici oxoniensis . . . Curâ & operâ sociâ Philippi Stephani . . . et Gulielmi Brounei . . . Adhibitis etiam in consilium D. Boberto patre . . . ejusque filio, etc. **See** OXFORD.—UNIVERSITY.—*Botanic garden*. Catologus [*sic*] plantarum Horti medici oxoniensis, etc. [Another edition.] 1658. 8°.

SUTHERLAND (JAMES) [1639?–1719]
360. Hortus medicus edinburgensis: or, a catalogue of the plants in the physical garden at Edinburgh; containing their . . . Latin and English names; with an English alphabetical index, etc. Edinburgh, printed by the heir of Andrew Anderson, sold by Mr. Henry Ferguson, and by the author. 1683. 17×11 cm. 8°. pp. [xvi], 367, [63].
Some copies of the above catalogue have the list of errata at the end of the work (i.e. on p. [63]) pasted over with a new list running to thirty-one lines of print. Pritzel (G. A.), *Thesaurus literaturae botanicae*,

309 (1872) records that Sutherland's catalogue was also published in 1692. The compiler has been unable to find this edition.

Copies: LBM; LBMNH; LRHS; LCPG; LRCS; LPS; KRBG; CUBG.

TAYLOR (SILVANUS)

361. Common-good: or, the improvement of commons, forrests, and chases, by inclosure ... By S. T. [With a dedication by Silvanus Taylor.] (An appendix, shewing the chiefe cause of wandring poor in England, etc.] London, for Francis Tyton. 1652. 18 × 14 cm. 4°. pp. 60.

Copy: LBM.

TURNER (ROBERT) [1626–   ]

362. Βοτανολογια. The Brittish physician: or, the nature and vertues of English plants. Exactly describing such plants as grow naturally in our land, with their several names ... places where they grow, times when they flourish, and are most proper to be gathered, etc. London, R. Wood for Nath. Brook. 1664. 17 × 11 cm. 8°. pp. [xiv], 363, [21]: frontis.

The frontispiece shows the portrait of a man, probably the author. Entitled above: 'The Brittish or English physitian'. In margin below: 'Sold by Nathaniel Brooke at the Angel in Cornhill. 1664'.

Copies: LBM; LBMNH; OBL; CUL.

363. — [Another edition.] London, for Obadiah Blagrave. 1687. 17 × 11 cm. 8°. pp. [viii], 363, [29]: frontis.

In this edition the imprint and date on the frontispiece have been erased.

Copies: LBM; KRBG.

TURNER (WILLIAM) [c. 1508–1568]

364. Libellus de re herbaria, nouus, in quo herbarum aliquot nomina greca, latina, & anglica habes, vna cum nominibus officinarum, etc. [The address to the reader is headed 'Guilielmus Turnerus candido lectori SPD.] 18 × 13 cm. 4°. Signn. A–B⁴ C².

Colophon: Londini apud Ioannem Byddellum ... 1538.

Copies: LBM; OMHS (in the Gunther loan collection).

365. The names of herbes in Greke, Latin, Englishe Duche ɀ Frenche wyth the commune names that herbaries and apotecaries vse. Gathered by William Turner. 14 × 9 cm. 8°.

Signn. A–H⁸: title within a woodcut compartment, 𝕭.𝕷.

Colophon: Imprinted at London by Iohn Day and Wyllyam Seres, etc.

The dedication is dated 'anno Dom. M.CCCC xlviij. Martii.xv'. Leaf H8 is blank.

Copies: LBM; KRBG.

366. A new herball, wherin are conteyned the names of herbes in Greke, Latin, Englysh, Duch Frenche, and in the potecaries and herbaries Latin, with the properties degrees and naturall places of the same, gathered and made by Wylliam Turner, etc. London, Steuen Mierdman (soolde ... by Iohn Gybken) 1551. 30 × 19 cm. fol. Signn. A⁶ B⁸ C–O⁶ P⁸: title within a woodcut compartment, illust., 𝕭.𝕷.

Copies: LBM; LBMNH; KRBG; OBL; CBS.

367. — The seconde parte of Vuilliam Turners herball, wherein are conteyned the names of herbes in Greke, Latin, Duche, Frenche, and in the apothecaries Latin, and somtyme in Italiane, wyth the vertues of the same herbes wyth diuerse confutationes of no small errours, that men of no small learning haue committed in the intreatinge of herbes of late yeares. Here vnto is ioyned also a booke of the bath of Baeth in Englande, and of the vertues of the same wyth diuerse other bathes moste holsum and effectuall, both in Almany and Englande, set furth by William Turner Doctor of Physik. Collen, Arnold Birckman. 1562. 31 × 20 cm. fol. Signn. A⁴ A–Ee⁶ Ff⁴ Gg²; A⁴ B–D⁶: illust., 𝕭.𝕷.

The title-page of the treatise on baths reads: 'A booke of the natures and properties, as well of the bathes in England as of other bathes in Germany and Italy', etc.

In the above work of 1562 one or more of the following leaves are sometimes found missing:

Herbal (Pt. 2). First A4 (blank), Ff4 (blank), Gg1–2 ('The fautes and errores conteined in thys [second] booke'). On Gg2 is sometimes pasted a slip, containing 'Errours in figures').

Treatise on baths. D6 (blank).

Copies: LBM; KRBG.

368. — The first and seconde partes of the herbal of William Turner Doctor in Phisick, lately ouersene, corrected and enlarged with the thirde parte, lately gathered, and nowe set oute with the names of the herbes, in Greke Latin, English, Duche, Frenche, and in the

apothecaries and herbaries Latin, with the properties, degrees, and naturall places of the
same. Here vnto is ioyned also a booke of the
bath of Baeth in England, etc. Collen, Arnold
Birckman. 1568. 31×20 cm. fol. Signn.
⁴ A–B⁶ C⁸ D–T⁶ A²; ⟨⟩² A–Ee⁶ Ff⁴ Gg²;
*⁴ Aaa–Ggg ⁶*¹; *⁴ B–D⁶: woodcut arms on tp.,
illust., 𝕭.𝕷.

It is rare to find copies of the above work of 1568
complete as some of the following leaves are generally
found missing.

Herbal (Pt. 1). T5–6 (blank), second A1–2 ('Peter
Turner to the reader' and 'Faultes to be corrected in
the first part').

Herbal (Pt. 2). Ff4 (blank), Gg1–2 ('The fautes and
errores conteined in thys [second] booke'. On Gg2
is sometimes pasted a slip containing 'Errours in
figures').

Herbal (Pt. 3). Ggg6 (blank), *1 following Ggg6
('Faultes to be amended in the thirde part').

Treatise on baths, D6 (blank).

Instead of the three leaves A1–2 ('Peter Turner to the
reader' and 'Faultes . . . in the first part') and *1
('Faultes . . . in the thirde part') there are sometimes
found two leaves, the first of which is signed ℭ,
following Gg2. These leaves contain 'Errata. Faultes
escaped in the printing. In the preface . . . In the
first part . . . The thirde parte . . . Faultes committed
by the wryter of the authors copye. The firste parte
. . . The thirde parte'. The two leaves ℭ were probably superseded by the three leaves A1–2 and *1.

A translation of Hieronymus Braunschweig's 'Thesaurus pauperum', entitled *A most excellent . . .
homish apothecarye* (1561) is often found bound up
with Turner's herbal (1562) and (1568).

Copies: LBM; LBMNH; LRHS; LCPG; LRCS;
KRBG.

VENETTE (Nicolas) [1633–1698]

The art of pruning fruit-trees . . . Translated
from the French original [i.e. from 'L'Art de
tailler les arbres fruitiers', by Nicolas Venette],
etc. See Art. 1685. 8°.

— See Compleat Planter and Cyderist.
The compleat planter & cyderist. Together
with The art of pruning fruit-trees, etc. 1690. 8°.

W., J.

369. Systema horti-culturæ: or, the art of
gardening . . . By J. W. *Gent.* [i.e. John Worlidge.] London, for Tho. Burrel, and Will.
Hensman. 1677. 18×11 cm. 8°. pp. [xxiv],
285, [19]: 3 pls.

With an additional title-page, engraved.
Copies: LBM; LRHS.

370. — Ed. 2, with large additions. London, for
Tho. Dring. 1683. 17×11 cm. 8°. pp. [xxiv],
298, [22]: 3 pls.

With an additional title-page, engraved and dated
1682. Pages 276–298 are headed 'The gardeners
monthly directions'.
Copies: LBM; KRBG.

371. — [Another issue.] London, for Tho.
Dring. 1683. 17×11 cm. 8°. pp. [xxiv], 298,
[22]: 3 pls.

With an additional title-page, engraved and dated
1682. Pages 276–298 are headed 'The gardeners
monthly directions'.
Copy: HRES.

For later editions **see** Worlidge (J.) 1688, etc. 8°.

WESTMACOTT (William)

372. Θεολοβοτογολογια sive historia vegetabilium
sacra: or, a scripture herbal; wherein all the
trees, shrubs . . . flowers, fruits, &c. . . . mentioned in the Holy Bible . . . are . . . discoursed
of, etc. London, for T. Salusbury. 1694.
15×9 cm. 12°. pp. [xxiv], 232, [8].

The spelling of the Greek title is as it appears on the
title-page. The first leaf (i.e. pp. [i–ii]) consists of
a list of books 'printed for T. Salusbury'.
Copies: LBM; LRHS; OBL; OMaC.

373. — [Another issue.] Historia vegetabilium
sacra: or, a scripture herbal, etc. London, for
John Salusbury. 1695. 15×8 cm. 12°. pp. [xxii],
232, [8].

Except for a new title-page, and the omission of the
leaf giving a list of books 'printed by T. Salusbury',
the above issue appears to be identical with that of
1694.
Copy: OBL.

WISE (Henry) [1653–1738] and LONDON (G.)

The compleat gard'ner . . . By Monsieur de La
Quintinye . . . abridg'd . . . By George London,
and Henry Wise. See La Quintinie (J. de)
1699. 8°.

— Ed. 2. 1699. 8°.

— Ed. 3. 1701. 8°.

— Ed. 4. 1704. 8°.

— Ed. 5. 1710. 8°.

— Ed. 6. 1717. 8°.

WORLIDGE (John)

Systema horti-culturæ: or, the art of gardening . . . By J. W. *Gent.* [i.e. John Worlidge] **See** W., J. 1677. 8°.

— Ed. 2. 1683. 8°.

— [Another issue.] 1683. 8°.

374. — Systema horti-culturæ: or, the art of gardening . . . The third edition, with large additions. London, for Tho. Dring. 1688. 16×10 cm. 8°. pp. [ii], x, [iv], 278, [18]: 3 pls.

With an additional title-page, engraved. Pages 243–267 consist of a section entitled 'The gardeners monthly directions' with a separate title-page.

Copies: LBM; LRHS; LCPG; HRES; CUBG.

375. — Ed. 4. To which is added The gardener's monthly directions, etc. London, for Will. Freeman. 1700. 17×11 cm. 8°. pp. [ii], viii, [iv], 278, [16]: 3 pls.

With an additional title-page, engraved. 'The gardener's monthly directions' has a separate title-page.

Copy: HRES.

376. — Ed. 4. To which is added The gardiner's monthly directions, etc. London, for W. Mears. 1719. 17×11 cm. 8°. pp. [ii], viii, [iv], 278, [16]: 3 pls.

The title-page of the above 'Ed. 4' of 1719 is a cancel. There is an additional title-page, engraved. 'The gardiner's monthly directions' has a separate title-page dated 1700.

Copy: LRHS.

WRAY (John)

See Ray

ADDENDUM

TRADESCANT (John) [–1638]

Plantarum in horto Iohannem [*sic*] Tradescanti nascentium catalogus. Nomina solummodo solis vulgata exhibens. Anno 1634. [London? 1634.] 14×9 cm. 8°. pp. 30.

Copy: OMaC.

INDEX

This index covers only the *History* section. Books are indexed under both author and title. Plants are indexed under Latin or English names, with cross-references when necessary. Artists, engravers, booksellers, printers, and gardens are indexed individually and in grouped subject entries. Page numbers in italics refer to illustrations, or their captions.

Beale, John 103 n., 106, 172, 173, 174, 191
  Herefordshire orchards 160, 172–3
  *Nurseries, orchards, profitable gardens, and
    vineyards encouraged* 172, 173, 178
Beauchamp, Lord *see* Seymour, Henry
Bedford, 5th Earl of *see* Russell, William
bee-keeping 160
Behn, Aphra 208 n.
Belasyse, Thomas, 2nd Viscount Fauconberg
  182
Belgic, or Netherlandish Hesperides, The (1683)
  182
Bellasis (or Belasyse), Sir Henry 158, 160
Bellingham, Charles 156
Bennet, Henry, 1st Earl of Arlington 209
Bentinck, Hans Willem, 1st Earl of Portland
  111, 144
Bentley, William 87
Bertier, Antoine 179
Bill, John 48
Birckman, Arnold 26
Blagrave, Joseph 90, 92
  Supplement . . . to Culpeppers English physitian
    91, 92
Blake, Stephen
  Compleat gardener's practice, The 193, *194*
Blith, Walter 192
  English improver improved, The 169
Blois, Abraham de *130*, 131
Blois:
  Duc d'Orléans' garden 119, 120
Blooteling, Abraham 123
Blount, Charles, Earl of Devonshire and 8th
  Lord Mountjoy 157
Bobart, Jacob 96, 184
Bobart, Jacob, the Younger 96, 124, 126, 198
Boccone, Paul 121
  *Icones & descriptiones rariorum plantarum
    Siciliæ* 120–2
  Recherches et observations naturelles 122
Bock, Jerome 8, 9, 22
  New Kreütter Bůch 8
Bodley, Sir Thomas, frontispiece, 43
Boke of husbandry, The (1523) 73
Boke of the propreties of herbes, A (1552) 15
Bollifant, Edmund 40
Bonnefons, Nicolas de 183, 187
  French gardiner, The 173, 178, 183, 186–7,
    188, 213
  Jardinier françois, Le 186
*Booke of the art and maner, howe to plante and
  graffe all sorts of trees, A* (1569) 63–4, 167
books:
  size of 214; spread of 19, 21, 71, 77; trade
    167, 213
booksellers:
  Allestry, James 102, 187; Bateman, Christo-
    pher 99; Bertier, Antoine 179; Bowman,
    Thomas 170; Brooke, Nathaniel 90; Chiswel,

Richard 179; Crook, John 177–8; Dewes,
  Garrat 32; Edgar, Eleazar 157; Faithorne,
  Henry 129, 131; Gillyflower, Matthew 189,
  190; Herringman, Henry 201, 203; Jansson-
  Waesberg 129; Kersey, John 129; Marriott,
  John 160–1; Martyn, John 102, 128, 129,
  187, 201, 203; Moseley, Humphrey 173;
  Norton, John, frontispiece, 31, 40, 41, 43, 44,
  48, 80; Partridge, James 189; Pulleyn, Octavian
  97, 99; Robinson, Thomas 170; Smith,
  Samuel, 129, 130, 132, 133; Walford, Ben-
  jamin 129; White, Edward 68; Wight, John 63
Borcht, Pierre van der 9, 10, 32
Botanologia (1664) 90, *91*
botany 21, 53, 80, 82, 101, 119, 213
Boutcher, William 108
  Treatise on forest-trees, A 108
Bowle (or Bowles), George 97
Bowman, Thomas 170
Boyle, Robert 140, 169, 170, 172, 173, 193, 195
Bradley, Richard 108, 158
  New improvements of planting and gardening
    173
Braunschweig, Hieronymus 18
  Liber de arte distillandi de simplicibus 18
Bredwell, Stephen 40, 44, 45, 46
*Brief and most pleasaũt epitomye of . . .
  phisiognomie, A* (1556) 57
British Museum 146, 151
Brittish or English physitian, The see *Botano-
  logia* (1664)
Brompton Park (London) 180–1, 190
Brooke, Nathaniel 90
Brossard, Davy 63–4
  L'Art & maniere de semer 63, 167
Brouncker, William, 2nd Viscount 103, 115–16,
  136
Browne, Lancelot 40
Browne, Sir Richard 105, 184
Browne, William 96, 97, 178
Brunfels, Otto 6–7, 21
  Herbarum vivæ eicones, 6, 7, 8, 21
Brunyer, Abel 119, 120
Burgh, William 111, *113*
Burghers, Michael 123, 126
Burghley, 1st Baron *see* Cecil, William
Butler, James, 1st Duke of Ormonde 122
Byddell, John 22
Bynneman, Henry 60, *61*, 63

C., R. *see* Church, Rocke
C., W. *see* Copland, William
Callitriche see chickweed, creeping water
Cambridge:
  Trinity College 207
Capel, Arthur, 1st Earl of Essex 116, 177, 181
Capel, Henry, 1st Baron 177, 189–90
Carlisle, Nicholas
  Topographical dictionary of Scotland, A 206